The Hardball Tim‌‌‌‌‌ ‌‌‌nual
2C

Featuring contributions by FanGraphs & THT staff writers:

Peter Bonney • Dave Cameron • Carson Cistulli
Bryan Cole • Joe Distelheim • Adam Dorhauer
August Fagerstrom • Tim Healey • Frank Jackson
Brad Johnson • David Kagan • Kiley McDaniel
Chris Mitchell • Jack Moore • Dustin Nosler
John Paschal • Jonah Pemstein • Alex Remington
Eno Sarris • Greg Simons • Alex Skillin
Scott Spratt • Jeff Sullivan • Shane Tourtellotte
Steve Treder • Owen Watson • Neil Weinberg
Miles Wray • Jeff Zimmerman

With additional contributions by guest writers:
Phil Birnbaum • Dan Kopitzke • Mitchel Lichtman
Erik Malinowski • Joe Rosales

Produced by Paul Swydan
Edited by Joe Distelheim, Jason Linden & Greg Simons
Graphics edited by Sean Dolinar

The Hardball Times Baseball Annual 2016

A FanGraphs production

New content daily at hardballtimes.com and fangraphs.com

Edited by Joe Distelheim, Jason Linden, Greg Simons and Paul Swydan
Graphics edited by Sean Dolinar
Stats developed by FanGraphs
Cover design by Travis Howell
Typesetting by Paul Swydan

Published by FanGraphs and The Hardball Times

ISBN-13: 978-1519402684
ISBN-10: 1519402686
Printed by CreateSpace

What's Inside

History

Analysis

Et Cetera

Welcome to Our Book

Hi everybody! Thank you so much for buying our book. Or, if you borrowed it, or stole it somehow, thanks for reading. We're pretty excited about this, our 12th annual edition of *The Hardball Times Baseball Annual.*

As you may have surmised from the "What's Inside" section you just flipped past, this book is divided into four sections. The first covers the 2015 season that just concluded. We've tweaked this section a little bit. Last year, we went deep on 10 things from the season that we wanted you to remember. While valuable, this approach got a little unwieldly, so we dialed back the "10 things" to sidebar status.

In its place, we dug into the spreadsheets to pick out the three games or series per division that swung the balance of the Division Odds—per our sister site, FanGraphs—more than the rest. The interesting thing about this approach is that not all these games or series took place in September. We think it's a unique way to look back on the season. In so doing, we added a graph to each division's view. The "games above .500" graph remains, but we've added the season's Division Odds graph as well. More graphs equals more fun. We cap the section with Brad Johnson's annual ChampAdded look at the postseason. Still more fun!

From there, we move into Commentary, and here we continue two *Annual* traditions—the Year in Frivolity, and the GM in a Box. John Paschal picks up the former right where he left it last season, while Alex Skillin picks up the ball for the latter to dissect long-time executive Dan Duquette. It's not often that we box a GM who's held the mantle with three different teams.

Elsewhere in Commentary, we have our usual strong contributions from Dave Cameron, Jeff Sullivan and Jack Moore. I'm thrilled also to have outside contributors Phil Birnbaum and Erik Malinowski in the book this year. While they bring very different perspectives, they're both invaluable. One of the book's highlights comes from Kiley McDaniel, who explored whether a prospective international draft should be separate from or combined with the domestic draft. Kiley actually hadn't finished his piece by the time he accepted his new job with the Atlanta Braves, but he graciously finished it anyway. We'll miss Kiley.

The History section is filled with moments we miss these days. Mainstays Steve Treder, Frank Jackson and editor extraordinaire Joe Distelheim are joined by the always solid Adam Dorhauer, whose exhaustively researched piece on the crucial 1904 World Series cancellation is a must-read. The vivacious Carson Cistulli also pops into the History section to take a historical look at his NERD scores, and to hurl some invective at me. (For some reason, I didn't edit it out.)

Finally, we have Analysis. I'd have to go back and check all the *Annuals*, but in my time working on the book (this is my fourth year), we haven't had a larger Analysis section. This year we clock in with nearly 150 pages of delicious nerdery. And it's all gold, Jerry. Seriously, we have so much good stuff in this section, I'm blown away.

We kick it off with Eno Sarris' great look at pitcher command, and wrap it with Peter Bonney's new metric for evaluating umpire strike zones. In between, Jeff Zimmerman develops a way to value prospects who get traded, Neil Weinberg gets his hand on some unreleased Statcast data on catcher pop times and the great Mitchel Lichtman studies the always divisive "hot hand." Honestly, there's too much good stuff to name check it all. Just read it, you won't be sorry.

Of course, nerdy analysis might not be your thing. And if so, that's fine. But no matter your tastes as a baseball fan, I'm confident this book has something for you. That is, in fact, our aim—to create a book that appeals to as many serious baseball fans as possible. There is no one *correct* way to enjoy the game, and we strive to present as many different viewpoints and tackle as many different angles as possible.

I am writing this intro, but obviously I didn't pull this book together alone. My three editing amigos—Joe Distelheim, Jason Linden and Greg Simons—simply put, I couldn't do this without them. They all have been with the book and the site longer than I have, and each brings a unique perspective that is so valuable. Especially Joe. If I ever grow up, I want to be like Joe. He's never wrong.

This year, we added Sean Dolinar to the process, to help with editing of the graphics. The graphics look a lot more consistent this year, and that is thanks exclusively to Sean. He has been a great resource for us behind the scenes at FanGraphs and THT for awhile now, and I'm glad he was able to contribute to the book. Speaking of being valuable behind the scenes, Dustin Nosler deserves mention as well. He didn't directly help with the *Annual* (besides his NL West chapter, that is), but he kept the website in shape while the rest of us were working on the book, and that is much appreciated.

You may also have noticed there is a new cover design. That is thanks to my dear friend, and excellent graphic designer, Travis Howell. We wanted a new design this year, and Travis was patient through all of our questions, suggestions and changes.

None of this happens without three entities. The first two are the Daves—Dave Studenmund and David Appelman—and the faith they have put in me to take up the torch. I think we did them proud this year. And finally, you, dear and faithful reader. We do this for and because of you. So, thank you once again for your support. It means the world.

May your manager never force feed you nerve tonic. May the pitcher hang you a slider. May the dogpile rise up to meet you. May your flags fly forever.

Happy Baseball,
Paul Swydan

The 2015 Season

The American League East View

by Tim Healey

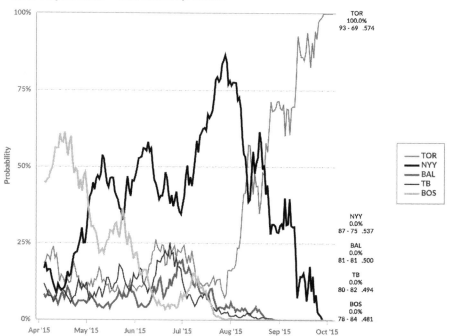

2015 Playoff Odds -- Win Division, AL East

TOR 100.0% 93 - 69 .574

NYY 0.0% 87 - 75 .537

BAL 0.0% 81 - 81 .500

TB 0.0% 80 - 82 .494

BOS 0.0% 78 - 84 .481

Legend: TOR, NYY, BAL, TB, BOS

I n the major leagues, a six-month regular season can seem like an eternity.

At the end of spring training, the story of the 2015 American League East seemed like it would be relatively straightforward: The defending champion Orioles would probably see some degree of dropoff. The Yankees had a ton of question marks, mostly health-related, and pr   obably wouldn't be a threat. The Blue Jays had a busy offseason, this time adding Josh Donaldson and Russell Martin, but they'd already won the last several winters and had nothing to show for it. The Andrew Friedman/Joe Maddon-less Rays were seemingly in need of a new identity. And the Red Sox, terrible in 2014, were a good bet to bounce back.

It all added up to not a lot of respect from outsiders. The AL East isn't what it used to be, they said. It's the division nobody wants to win, they said.

So much for that. The AL East wound up far more compelling and competitive than most anticipated. Heading into the final weekend of the regular season, there was a chance all five teams would finish with a .500 record or better—the only division in baseball that could lay claim to that feat.

As for the teams, the on-paper prognostications hardly matched up with the on-field results. The Blue Jays, after adding Troy Tulowitzki and David Price around the trade deadline, ran away with the title. The Yankees stayed healthy enough to secure a Wild Card berth. The Orioles and Rays hovered for a while, but were largely non-competitive in the second half. And the Red Sox very much did not bounce back.

That's why, as they say, you play the games. With the benefit of hindsight, here are three games that loomed especially large.

Friday, May 1: Red Sox Lose Game to Yankees, Hanigan to Injury

What's the value of a backup catcher? The Red Sox found out in the weeks and months after May 1.

At first glance, this game looks routine, just one of 162. Red Sox-Yankees on a Friday night at Fenway Park, so that's fun, but it was seasonably chilly out and the pitching matchup—CC Sabathia vs. Justin Masterson, two tall hurlers who ended up with less-than-spectacular years—wasn't very exciting. The environment didn't exactly lend itself to the dramatic.

Then journeyman reliever Tommy Layne unfurled a pitch that proved to be a turning point in Boston's season. On an 0-2 count to Mark Teixeira in the top of the seventh, a 90-mph four-seam fastball came too far inside and clipped Teixeira's right wrist—his back wrist—then caught Red Sox catcher Ryan Hanigan's naked right hand. Teixeira took his base. Hanigan took an X-ray. The result? A displaced fracture of the fifth metacarpal on his little finger. In other words, a broken pinky. Hanigan didn't play again for two months.

The Red Sox, a sexy preseason pick to win the division despite a last-place finish in 2014, spiraled in his absence. It began that night with a 3-2 loss to New York, dropping their chances of winning the AL East, per FanGraphs' division odds, down from 47.8 percent—a coin flip—to 43.2, a considerable drop for what was just the fourth week of the season. The Yankees' chances of winning the division bumped up from 24.7 to 29.6. By the end of the weekend, which yielded a Yankees sweep, Boston stood at 33.7 percent, New York at 40.2. That was the first time the Yankees were the purported favorites over the Red Sox.

By the time the sun rose on June 1, one month later, the Red Sox's odds had been cut more than half from the time of Hanigan's injury, down to 19.7 percent. They went 10-19 in May, that .345 winning percentage the only time they finished a given month under .400.

Can Hanigan and his pinky alone be credited/blamed for that drop? Of course not. The Red Sox offense all but disappeared in May in particular, going from 5.1

runs per game in April to 2.8 the next month, and they still didn't have a true No. 1 pitcher. But you can be sure the backstop's absence was felt.

Red Sox senior baseball analyst Tom Tippett, speaking at the Saber Seminar in Boston in August, pointed to this game and Hanigan's ensuing two-month layoff as an early turning point—*the* early turning point. The Red Sox opened that Yankees series at 12-10—a seemingly pedestrian record, but one that equates to about 88 wins over the course of a full season. The eventual AL Wild Card teams finished with 87 (Yankees) and 86 (Astros) wins. The Blue Jays, who went on a tear in the second half to claim the division crown, totaled 93. The Red Sox would have been thoroughly in that conversation if they maintained their so-so April pace.

Also, consider that Hanigan's injury was the second significant hit to the organization's catching depth. The Red Sox lost their No. 1 catcher, the rocket-armed Christian Vazquez, to Tommy John surgery in early April. So just a month into the season, the Red Sox were left with a duo of 21-year-old Blake Swihart (who had all of 36 games of Triple-A experience and in a best-case scenario would not have been called upon until late 2015) and the offensively hapless Sandy Leon (whom the team acquired when Vazquez went down).

2015 Games Above or Below .500, AL East

To be sure, the reps Swihart received as a result could pay dividends in the future. He's still highly thought of at the plate and behind it, and the potential issue of having two legitimate big-league catchers—Vazquez and Swihart—is a happy one. It just didn't do the Red Sox any favors in 2015. Boston backstops finished with a 1.6 WAR, good for only 19th in the majors, which doesn't take into account the lost benefit of Hanigan's (not to mention Vazquez's) well-regarded pitch-framing ability. It's even uglier judging by Baseball-Reference's WAR. Sox catchers came in at -1.3, 24th in the bigs and better than only three AL teams.

Oh, but back to May 1 and the actual game. It was indeed nondescript, aside from the season-altering injury. The Yankees won, 3-2. Sabathia and Masterson got the job done, each throwing six innings of two-run ball. Sabathia scattered seven hits and two walks while punching out three. Masterson matched him with six hits allowed, three walks and two strikeouts.

The Red Sox led until Brian McCann's RBI single in the seventh. Alex Rodriguez's eighth-inning homer turned out to be the game-winner. Dellin Betances and Andrew Miller pitched a scoreless frame apiece to finish it off in Fenway's first look at Miller as a beardless, pinstriped mercenary.

The night turned out to be a harbinger of things to come for two Boston batters. Xander Bogaerts finished 1-for-3 with a walk and a run scored, the sort of night that became typical for him, while Hanley Ramirez went 0-for-4. There was also one effort that was very much not predictive of the next few months: Allen Craig homered, the only time he did so all season.

And then there was the freak Hanigan injury. It's a scenario that begs for ifs: *If* Teixeira managed to get out of the way; *if* Hanigan's bare hand was hidden behind his back; *if* the ball had deflected in a marginally different direction; *if* the bone was bruised instead of broken. The story of the 2015 Red Sox—and 2015 AL East— could have been an entirely different one.

10 Things You Should Remember About The 2015 AL East

1. Trade-deadline acquisitions Troy Tulowitzki and David Price helped fuel the Blue Jays' second-half surge to the franchise's first division title since 1993.

2. The Blue Jays' championship marked the fourth different AL East winner in as many years, continuing a run of unusual parity. All five teams have won the division at least once since 2010.

3. After a year-long suspension, Alex Rodriguez hit .250/.356/.486 with 33 home runs, 86 RBI and 2.7 WAR, his highest mark since 2011.

4. The Yankees infused youth (Greg Bird, Luis Severino) into their old lineup and fragile rotation to snag a Wild Card berth.

5. The Red Sox finished last for the third time in four years, bringing an end to the Ben Cherington era. The club hired Dave Dombrowski as president of baseball operations.

Wednesday, June 24: Jays Steal One from Rays in Extras

It's funny to consider now, knowing what we do about the Jays and the division and how it all went down in the end, but for a long time the AL East was very much up for grabs. June 24 offers a window into an alternate reality.

The Blue Jays got to Tropicana Field early for the getaway day matinee, a quick turnaround after getting shut down by Tampa Bay ace Chris Archer (eight innings, one earned run) in a Rays win the night before. The first-place Rays were 41-32 and two games up in the division, while the Jays were in fourth but only three games back—a reminder of how tight the AL East was as the season approached the halfway mark.

6. New Jays third baseman Josh Donaldson, acquired in an offseason deal with Oakland, rivaled Mike Trout for AL MVP honors with 8.7 WAR and Gold Glove defense.

7. Rays ace Chris Archer had a breakout year, matching or besting many career highs while pitching more than 200 innings for the first time.

8. Baltimore first baseman Chris Davis rebounded in a big way in his contract year, slashing .262/.361/.562 with 5.6 WAR and a major league-best 47 homers.

9. Xander Bogaerts and Mookie Betts, 22-year-old dynamos, established themselves as the gems of Boston's young core, which also includes left-hander Eduardo Rodriguez and catcher Blake Swihart.

10. Baltimore's Manny Machado, still just in his age-22 season, returned from injury and broke out in a big way, hitting 35 homers and posting a 134 wRC+ while playing in all 162 games.

June 24—a 1-0, 12-inning Blue Jays win—marked the beginning of the Rays' descent. Tampa's chances of winning the division, according to FanGraphs' division odds, fell from 25.2 percent—the club's high-water mark of the season—to 21.4 percent. A game later, 17.2. A week later, 9.1. The Rays were effectively a non-factor the rest of the way. The Jays, meanwhile, saw a small jump with the extra-innings victory, from 19.7 to 21.9 percent, though it got worse before it got better. (Toronto's low point came a month after this, July 28, the day it acquired Tulowitzki.)

The game itself was a good one. Tampa Bay's Nate Karns no-hit Toronto into the sixth, but Jays starter Marco Estrada bested him by staying perfect through seven and a third. The Blue Jays' long-unsettled bullpen did some tightrope walking—Bo Schultz and Brett Cecil combined to put five runners on base in their two scoreless innings—but righty Steve Delabar was impressive when it counted most, striking out two in a 1-2-3 12th inning to end it.

Chris Colabello afforded Delabar that save opportunity when he homered in the top of the 12th, someone at last breaking through after well over three hours of scorelessness. Colabello, a 31-year-old former independent league regular turned Toronto standout, got hold of a Brandon Gomes fastball left out over the plate and deposited it over the wall in left-center. It ended a stretch in which the Blue Jays' potent lineup scored just four times in 24 innings.

The contest was representative of the teams' soon-to-be-divergent seasons. Tampa's pitching was effective—excellent, even—but a hapless lineup did it no favors. The club finished the season with a 3.74 ERA (fourth-best in the AL) but only 4.0 runs scored per game, better than only one other AL team (White Sox).

On the Blue Jays' side, this was Estrada's second consecutive no-hit bid. He held the Orioles hitless into the eighth five days prior. It was the first time a pitcher carried a no-hitter as far as the eighth inning in back-to-back starts since Dave Stieb (also pitching for the Jays) in 1988. In a big-picture sense, it was part of a yearlong effort that validated Toronto's belief in Estrada, whom they acquired as a homer-prone 31-year-old the November prior from Milwaukee in exchange for Adam Lind. Estrada produced a career-best 3.13 ERA and 1.04 WHIP, plus a 6.7 hits-per-nine-innings mark that led the American League. He started Game 3 of the ALDS against the Rangers, a Toronto win in which Estrada allowed one run in 6.1 innings.

A fun footnote is that this was the game—or one of the games—when Donaldson ended up in the stands to make a highlight-reel catch. The play came in the eighth inning, with Estrada's perfect game still alive, and nobody out. David DeJesus lofted a pop-up down the third-base line, and it drifted deep into foul territory. Donaldson tracked it all the way, met the waist-high wall and leaped three rows into the stands to make the backhanded grab. While he wasn't hurt on the play, he did faceplant into the stomach of a Jays fan sitting up close at Tropicana.

Maybe we should've known the Blue Jays were doing something special.

Saturday, Sept. 12: Blue Jays Sweep Bronx Doubleheader, All But Lock Up Division

The further removed we get from 2015, as the details blur and the memories fade, the easier it will be to wrap the Blue Jays in a simple, tidy narrative: A largely mediocre club acquired David Price and Troy Tulowitzki right before the trade deadline, then went on an incredible run to catapult from fringe contender to dominant AL East champion, advancing to the postseason for the first time since 1993.

In reality, we know it was much more complicated than that. For one, the Jays boasted the majors' best offense from beginning to end, and their run differential was a largely positive one, suggesting they were much better than the .500 record they owned the day they added Tulowitzki to the active roster.

Then there is the matter of Toronto's second-half run, which benefits from a layer of nuance beyond "the Blue Jays won a lot." To be short: A division title was far from a given. The Jays lost, actually, on Aug. 1, when they were six games back. An 11-game win streak followed, but as late as Aug. 22 the Yankees were the statistical favorites in the AL East, according to FanGraphs' division odds.

Let's jump ahead a couple of weeks to the date in question, Sept. 12, when the Blue Jays woke up with a 2.5-game lead in the division. They had a 78.9 percent chance of finishing out front, the Yankees 21.1. For context on that, think about 2015 Stephen Drew stepping up to the plate and getting a hit. Unlikely? Sure. Impossible? Definitely not. The Yankees had approximately a Drew batting average's chance of winning the division at this point.

That changed considerably by night's end. A storm had moved through New York two days prior, setting up a pivotal Saturday doubleheader in front of a packed house on a warm, wet day in the Bronx. Over the course of eight hours, 20 innings, 31 runs, 692 pitches and—most significantly—two Blue Jays wins, the Yankees' deficit nearly doubled from a let's-chip-off-one-game-per-week 2.5 games to a far more intimidating 4.5. Their odds of winning the division plummeted to 7.3 percent, while the Blue Jays' shot up to 92.7.

A scouring of the box scores, play-by-play logs and on-site reports reveals several crucial moments that carried great weight within the games—and the season as a whole, given the significance of this day to the bigger picture—and developments that helped shape the Blue Jays down the stretch and into the playoffs. Here are a few.

- Game One, a 9-5 Blue Jays win that required 11 innings, very nearly never got that far. The Yankees pulled even at 5-5 in the bottom of the eighth and put Brett Gardner on third base with one out. Roberto Osuna entered and induced a pop out from Chase Headley and groundout from Greg Bird, stranding Gardner and paving the way for extra innings.

- A bout of wildness from Bryan Mitchell, a rookie reliever for New York, gave Toronto its first win. He faced four batters in the 11th: walk, hit by pitch, walk, strikeout. His three baserunners scored, and the Jays added another run (charged to Chasen Shreve) to take control.

- This was the game Tulowitzki suffered a fractured shoulder blade—a potentially brutal blow for a club known for its bats. But the state of the standings, aided greatly by that day's sweep, allowed Tulowitzki to rest until he was ready. He returned to play in two regular-season games.

- Game Two was a 10-7 Toronto win, and there weren't really any backbreaking plays—just relentless pecking away, as the Blue Jays do. Every starter except Edwin Encarnacion recorded a hit. Four Jays had multiple runs batted in. And then there was the man on the mound...

- Marcus Stroman made his season debut, an impressive feat considering he was ruled out for the season when he tore his ACL in March. At this point, with the playoffs only a handful of turns through the rotation away, Toronto wasn't sure what Stroman could give them or whether he'd be a factor in the postseason. His start gave an optimistic bend to that discussion. He gave up three runs in five innings, carrying a no-hitter into the fifth. He made one bad pitch, a three-run home run to Gardner (his third of the day). In three more starts, Stroman removed any doubt about whether he could help in October by allowing two runs in 22 innings. He was Toronto's No. 2 starter in the ALDS, and was lined up to start Game Seven of the ALCS, had the Jays forced that game.

Forgive the Blue Jays decision-makers if they started planning such things before the weekend was out. After his doubleheader, the division race was all but over, and postseason planning—lining up the rotation, resting whoever needed to be rested—could commence.

"Huge day, I'm proud of these guys," Blue Jays manager John Gibbons said afterward. "It was a long day. It wasn't an easy day to play. The first one to extras and they gutted it out. We basically used everybody and we came out on top two games. That's huge."

The American League Central View

by August Fagerstrom

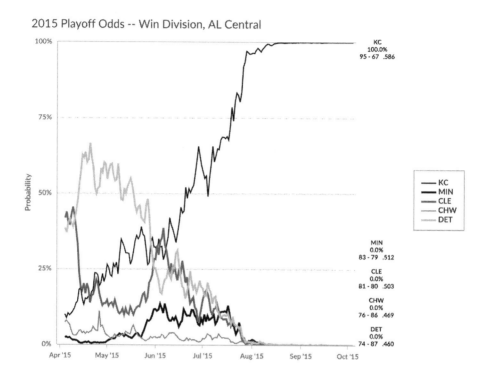

2015 Playoff Odds -- Win Division, AL Central

Parity ran deep in the American League in 2015, and the Central Division was no exception. The Central was largely viewed as a four-way tossup before the season began. And the team that was largely ignored—the Minnesota Twins—stuck around until the end and nearly made the playoffs.

Heading into the season, the Detroit Tigers were coming off their fourth consecutive division championship but also their earliest postseason exit in that stretch, a three-game sweep at the hands of the Baltimore Orioles in the Division Series. The Kansas City Royals played more baseball than any AL club in 2014, falling one game shy of their first World Series championship in 30 years. The Cleveland Indians were preseason darlings, with *Sports Illustrated* infamously picking them to win the World Series. Each of the three were viewed sensible picks to be found atop the throne at year's end. Yet, despite the apparent parity, the division race was essentially wrapped up by July. Let's go over three of the biggest swings in the division race throughout the season.

May 27-30: Are the Tigers Good?

The Tigers in recent years had developed something of a habit of getting out to hot starts. In 2013, they were 19-11 after the first 30 games. In 2014, it was 20-10. This year was no different, as the Tigers had their sights set on a fifth consecutive division title after another 19-11 start that had them in first place.

On May 27, the Tigers were one game back of the division-leading Royals with a division-leading 48 percent chance to make the postseason. Then they traveled to Los Angeles, and their season began to unravel.

It started with a 12-2 beatdown at the hands of C.J. Wilson and the Angels on a cloudy Thursday night at Angel Stadium. The starter for the Tigers was Buck Farmer, who gave up seven earned runs in five innings. That Farmer went on to appear in 13 more games after that one, including four more starts, highlights the main reason the Tigers finished with the highest team ERA in the American League and scuffled toward a last-place finish: quality starting pitching depth.

Detroit began the year with what appeared to be a formidable, albeit thin, rotation. Ace David Price fronted the staff, backed up by a well-above-average Anibal Sanchez and former ace Justin Verlander. The team acquired veteran Alfredo Simon in an offseason trade with Cincinnati, and while Simon didn't have a long track record, he was coming off a laudable season with the Reds in which he threw 196.1 innings with a 3.44 ERA. Even with some regression, he looked like a serviceable fourth starter.

The problem, though, was that the team lacked options beyond those four. Shane Greene, another offseason trade acquisition, had shown promise in his rookie season with the Yankees the year prior, but was already 26 years old and never achieved much in the way of prospect status. By June 10, he had posted a 5.82 ERA that got him not just booted from the rotation but also demoted to Triple-A.

Sanchez got off to an equally troubling start, Verlander opened the season with his first career trip to the disabled list, and Simon proved his 2014 was a fluke. Price was the only constant in the Tigers' rotation, and in the absence of Verlander and Greene, Detroit was left relying on a stable of shaky, inexperienced starters, including Farmer, with none experiencing anything in the way of success.

Throughout much of the season, the back end of Detroit's rotation was a revolving door that featured Farmer, Greene, Kyle Lobstein, Kyle Ryan and veteran Randy Wolf, a group that racked up a combined 45 starts with a collective 6.53 ERA in 227.2 innings.

Two days after Farmer's clunker in Los Angeles, Greene lasted just 1.1 innings after allowing seven earned runs on five homers by the second inning. That deflating loss dropped the Tigers' division odds below the Royals, marking the final time all season Detroit was not considered the division favorite.

The Tigers were swept by the Angels in a four-game series on the road before returning home and being swept in three games by Oakland. After eight consecutive losses—punctuated by a walk-off against the White Sox in Chicago—the Tigers had fallen to 28-28. They sat in third place, and any memories of their hot start were firmly in the past.

The final dagger didn't come until July 3, when star slugger Miguel Cabrera hit the disabled list for the first time in his career, costing him six weeks of action. It wasn't until Cabrera's injury that the Tigers conceded the division, throwing in the towel and going into sell mode approaching the trade deadline, but the slide that lead them to that point began with a four-game series in Los Angeles more than a month prior.

June 8-10: Royals Sweep Twins, Never Look Back

Despite much of the roster from their World Series run just months prior still intact, the Royals were not viewed by many as a true threat in the American League in the preseason. Look no further than the FanGraphs staff predictions, in which exactly zero of 38 polled writers picked the Royals to make the playoffs, much less win the division.

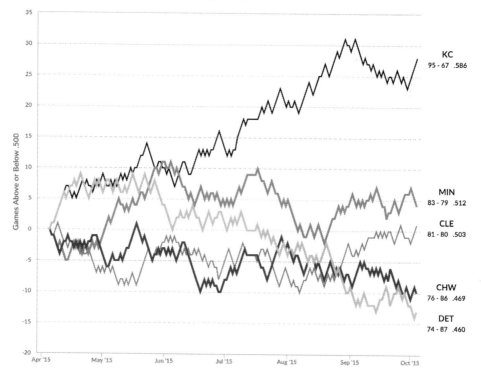

2015 Games Above or Below .500, AL Central

KC 95 - 67 .586

MIN 83 - 79 .512

CLE 81 - 80 .503

CHW 76 - 86 .469

DET 74 - 87 .460

Don't we look silly now. The Royals won their first seven games and continued to go toe-to-toe with the red-hot Tigers atop the Central over the season's first month. By May 23, Kansas City was 28-14 and already had stretched out a three-game lead in the division.

But two weeks later, they trailed the shocking first-place Minnesota Twins by one game with the Twins coming to town for a three-game series. After it was over, the Royals never looked back.

In all three games, the Royals played their individual brand of baseball, taking an early lead within the first two innings and holding it the rest of the way with their combination of good defense and a lights-out bullpen. There were no lopsided victories—the wins were by scores of 3-1, 2-0 and 7-2—but there rarely were any blowouts. The Royals just found ways to win.

Kansas City's starters for the three-game sweep were Jason Vargas, Chris Young and Edinson Volquez, a typically underwhelming on the surface trio who pitched admirably for the Royals in 2015. And that sentiment essentially sums up Kansas City's rotation all year: "good enough." The starting pitching never overwhelmed, but it kept the Royals in games long enough for the offense to steal a couple bags and get a few clutch hits and for the bullpen to shut things down. The rotation did its part in keeping Kansas City in first place, putting the team in a position to acquire ace Johnny Cueto at the trade deadline from Cincinnati, just as it did its part in the midseason battle for the division with Minnesota.

> # 10 Things You Should Remember About The 2015 AL Central
>
> 1. Melky Cabrera, Adam LaRoche, David Robertson, Jeff Samardzija, Zach Duke, Emilio Bonifacio and Geovany Soto, whom the White Sox signed in the offseason for a combined $53.89 million, produced just 3.0 WAR.
> 2. From late May to late June, Chris Sale struck out at least 10 batters in eight consecutive starts. Sale and Pedro Martinez are the only pitchers in baseball history to accomplish this feat.
> 3. After four straight seasons in either fourth or last place in the divison, the Twins finished over .500 and remained in the playoff chase until the end.
> 4. The future of the Twins—Byron Buxton and Miguel Sano, ranked as the No. 2 and No. 15 prospects in all of baseball by FanGraphs—arrived.
> 5. The Royals went all in, making major moves to acquire ace Johnny Cueto and the dynamite Ben Zobrist in hopes of a repeat World Series run.

The standout game of the series was the second, a 2-0 victory in which Young, Franklin Morales, Kelvin Herrera, Wade Davis and Greg Holland combined to one-hit the Twins while striking out just five. Subtle domination.

After the sweep, the Royals had a two-game lead in the division and had increased their division title odds to 45 percent. From that point, the Royals led the division for the rest of the season and essentially had it clinched by the end of July, with 97-percent division odds by Aug. 1.

June 5-11: Indians Can't Get Over the Hump

The Indians and Royals couldn't have had more different beginnings to their seasons. Kansas City had proven itself to the world the season prior, yet KC was slept on in the preseason before proving everybody wrong with a sensational opening month. Cleveland, on the other hand, missed the playoffs in 2014 and did very little to improve its roster in the offseason, yet the Tribe was seen as the favorite in the American League Central by experts nationally.

6. In the 2014 playoffs, Lorenzo Cain hinted at stardom, and in 2015 he proved he was a star, as he finished in the top 10 in position player WAR.

7. The Indians, behind rookies Francisco Lindor (shortstop) and Giovanny Urshela (third base), completed one of the most drastic statistical defensive 180s in baseball history.

8. Francisco Lindor debuted like whoa. Lindor, the No. 14 prospect in baseball according to FanGraphs, had one of the best rookie seasons by a shortstop in major league history, posting 4.6 WAR in just 99 games.

9. The White Sox were terrible on defense again, and while they were slightly better than they were in 2014, they were much worse compared to their peers. They finished last in the AL by Ultimate Zone Rating (UZR) and next-to-last in Defensive Runs Saved (DRS).

10. Joe Mauer's fade continued unabated, as he posted career worsts in OPS (.718) and WAR (0.3).

Despite that, as good a start as the Royals got off to, that's how poor a start the Indians had. While Kansas City came out of the gates with a 25-14 start that put them in first place, the Indians by that time were 15-23, in last place and already 9.5 games out of first.

Cleveland won six in a row in mid-May to claw back into things, and by June 4 the Indians had won 14 of their last 20, pulling their division odds all the way up to 38 percent. On Friday, June 5, the Tribe began a six-game homestand against Baltimore and Seattle with their spirits high after taking consecutive road series from the Royals and Mariners.

Alas, the homestand didn't go as Cleveland had hoped. The Indians lost four of the six games, and their division odds would never again eclipse the odds with which they began this stretch.

The final two losses of the series, each to the Mariners, encapsulated the Indians' struggles in 2015. On June 9, reigning American League Cy Young Award winner Corey Kluber took the mound for Cleveland and turned in a strong performance, holding the Mariners to two runs in seven innings. The Indians lineup, however, was stymied by Roenis Elias over six innings, plating just one run on a solo Yan Gomes homer in the second inning.

Kluber's lack of run support was already a story by that point in the season and continued to be one for the season's remainder. Despite throwing 222 innings with a 3.49 ERA and a strikeout-to-walk ratio that was in the top five in the major leagues, Kluber finished the season with a record of just 9-16 thanks to his American League-low run support of 3.38 runs per nine innings.

The Indians offense had a hard time scoring for any of the team's starters in the first half, but something about Kluber's outings seemed to render them especially punchless. It wasn't for a lack of getting on base, as the next day's game showed. The night after Kluber's start, Trevor Bauer and the Indians took on Taijuan Walker and the Mariners, with the Indians out-hitting Seattle, 12-10. Those 12 hits turned into just three runs, though, with the Indians losing, 9-3.

Cleveland went 1-for-17 with runners in scoring position that night, a single-game performance that would seem like an outlier if not for the entire season being something of an outlier.

The team's weighted runs created plus (wRC+) of 100 at season's end indicates the Indians had a league-average lineup, one that was tied with the first-place Royals in that regard. The difference between the Royals and the Indians, though, was clutch hitting. Kansas City's OPS with men on base was .778, the fourth-best adjusted OPS in the league. Cleveland can be found on the other end of the spectrum, posting a paltry .713 OPS with men on, giving the Indians the largest disparity between their overall adjusted OPS and their men-on adjusted OPS of any team in baseball.

That the Indians routinely got men on base showed their offense was capable. As they routinely failed to drive them in, the frustration mounted. Cleveland began the homestand with Baltimore and Seattle one game under .500, a mark the Indians hadn't yet reached to that point in the season. After dropping four of six while looking no different than the sub-.500 team they'd been to that point, they didn't pull back within a game of .500 for another three months. They finally reached the .500 mark by Sept. 13, with a record of 70-70, but by that point it was too late. The Indians ended up finishing a game above .500—the only time they'd gotten over that hump all season—but it was the early-season clutch hitting woes that dug them the hole too deep to climb out of.

The American League West View

by Miles Wray

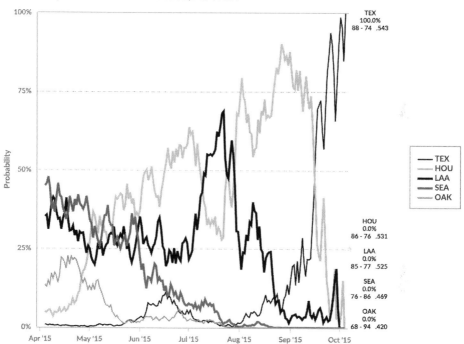

2015 Playoff Odds -- Win Division, AL West

The American League West has just wrapped up a doozy of a season. Over the last 12 months, from October to October, each of the division's five teams had at least a moment when it looked like the division favorite. The Oakland A's followed up their 88-win 2014 campaign with last winter's most prolific maneuvering, Billy Beane juking tiny steps forward and back, forward and back, moving ambiguously but perhaps still brewing another transcendental statistical alchemy. The Seattle Mariners were nothing if not bold over the winter. They won a single game fewer than the A's in 2014, which they followed up by doubling down on power and signing free agent Nelson Cruz to a contract that signaled a willingness to pay out an albatross in the future in exchange for playoff wins in 2015.

Then the season started, and the Houston Astros didn't grow up so much as they rocketed up three feet in a single night—voice hesitantly cracking at bedtime, a full, knotted chest of hair upon rising. After years of unmitigated losing—only some of those seasons lost in the name of rebuilding—Houston led the division with a 15-7 record at the end of April, an early-season mirage that grew more and more concrete with each subsequent game. When the All-Star break hit, the region's grumpy adults smacked the lights on and put the kibosh on what was a positively groovy party at the top of the division.

Nothing if not emboldened by the cloaked, House of Cards-style excommunication of their own general manager, the Los Angeles Angels rode their roster of 24 un-thrilling players and the one most thrilling player to the division lead in July. But then, when the dog days hit, the Texas Rangers—in flagrant defiance of any projection system, whether data- or gut-based—simply began winning heaps and heaps of ballgames, rousing at their leisure from what in hindsight appears to have been approximately an 18-month nap. After a year-plus of languid directionlessness, the Rangers' two months of fury was enough to take them to 88 wins and the division crown.

This is a division that beat up on itself. The division's third- and fourth-place teams, the Angels and the Mariners, were actually the best intra-division performers. The Astros finished with a dominant 16-4 record in interleague play compared with .500 play in their division. The Rangers finished 23-11 against the AL East—and below .500 within the AL West. As such, the story of this division hinges on three series sweeps, all of them involving the Astros.

April 30-May 3: The Astros' Revolution Dawns

On the last day of April, the Seattle Mariners arrive in Houston for a Series that will turn the teams' division chances upside down. At the time of this series, Houstonians do not yet know the revolution is being televised on their infamously low-rated local 'Stros broadcast. The best-attended game in this series is the Sunday matinee finale—which will turn out to be the Astros' 10th victory in a row—played in front of just over 25,000 fans. But, hey, who could really expect the fans to emerge automatically after they were more or less forced to bury their fandom underground for the last, oh, decade or so?

Houstonians eventually do get the picture—the average attendance on the season will top 26,500, even with these sleepy early weeks taken into consideration—but a look back at this series after watching the Astros play real-live October baseball shows just how rapidly the organization is growing its own success. On a passed ball, hometown catcher Jason Castro receives scattered, cynical boos, his usefulness as a regular starter on a playoff-bound team not yet established. In the series opener, the Astros' starting left fielder is Robbie Grossman, who was very recently mentioned alongside names like George Springer as a player hesitant to sign the type of extension I'll call The Jeff Luhnow Deluxe. (The Jeff Luhnow Deluxe is an extension offered to a player who has just appeared or has yet to appear in the majors for many years at a-skosh-above-minimum rates.) With 24 games played and a .467 OPS in 2015,

Grossman's lack of staying ability at the major league level is considerable evidence The Jeff Luhnow Deluxe is not guaranteed to be a team-friendly proposition.

Grossman's presence in this winning Astros effort goes a long way, I think, in underscoring what was perhaps Houston's most important strength in turning its fortunes from dour to brilliant: overwhelming organizational depth. Instead of riding a formerly-more-promising prospect like Grossman into the ground, the Astros are always and swiftly prepared with an even younger and even more promising prospect. Grossman's underwhelming performance will cue the promotion of previously unheralded Preston Tucker. And also: The Astros frequently will slide career center fielder Colby Rasmus to the corners, clearing the way for Jake Marisnick to eviscerate Tal's Hill. Lack of performance from any one Astros player almost doesn't register as cause for concern in Houston because the next man is already up.

Witness Houston's starting pitchers in this series. While veteran Scott Feldman and prized reclamation project (or was it just a clamation project?) Collin McHugh locked down two starts, the second and fourth games were handled by Samuel Deduno (two starts for Houston in 2015) and Roberto Hernandez (11 starts), neither of whom remained in Houston come time for the stretch run.

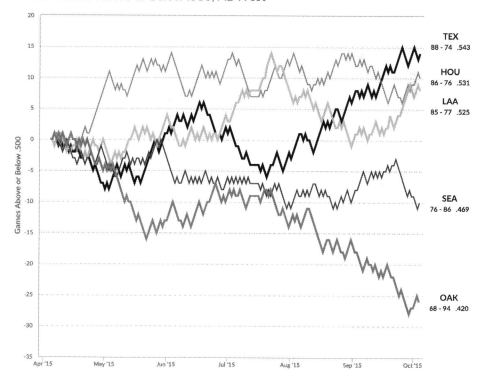

2015 Games Above or Below .500, AL West

The Mariners, also, relied on considerable contributions from players who did not end the season in Seattle. But while the Astros' deployment of so many players felt like the energetic pursuit of the best talent combinations possible, the Mariners' use of, uh, depth, smacked of Rolodex-twirling desperation. Bearded Dustin Ackley starts in this series, eventually traded to the New York Yankees in humble admission that the shadow of Stephen Strasburg—Strasburg being the player selected directly before Ackley in the 2009 draft—carried so much more weight and heft in Seattle than Ackley's own accomplishments ever did. Austin Jackson, who seemed to be suddenly sucked marrow-dry of his youth upon arriving in Seattle in the middle of the 2014 season, gets some sleepy starts in here as well—the Mariners cannot figure out how to use him and eventually trade him to the electrifying Chicago Cubs for that most popular of trade targets—the player to be named later. Rickie Weeks, gamely trying to press on outside a Milwaukee Brewers uniform and sans dreads, makes some of his forgettable 37 Mariners appearances here and eventually is cut. The consistent and slow cycling in and cycling out of mismatched veteran options just might be the facet of Jack Zduriencik's tenure that history best remembers.

True, few shed tears over the end-of-season dismissal of Mariners manager Lloyd McClendon—and, in fairness, he probably cycled through

10 Things You Should Remember About The 2015 AL West

1. Mike Trout exerted world-class effort in dragging the rest of the team above .500; his best comp is no longer another ballplayer but, tragically, Sisyphus.

2. The A's posted an elite first-half run differential but forgot to collect the real wins along with the Pythagorean ones.

3. Carlos Correa inspired breathless and genuine Hall of Fame discussion after nearly dozens of career games played.

4. The Angels more or less paid the Rangers to take Josh Hamilton, a sunk cost all the way down to the pitch-dark ocean floor.

5. Even after Royals-mania overwhelmed All-Star voting, the AL West accounted for four of the nine starters (Mike Trout, Albert Pujols, Nelson Cruz, Jose Altuve), plus its starting pitcher (Dallas Keuchel).

Seattle's plentitude of barely distinguishable relievers as well as anybody could. While pitcher wins and losses are flawed at best, it feels entirely fitting that Seattle's 36 bullpen losses on the season were the second-most in the majors (Tampa Bay had one more). This series would be bookended by reliever losses—Dominic Leone losing the opener in walk-off fashion and Carson Smith losing on a homer to Evan Gattis in the finale.

In winning three of the series' four games by a single run, with one blowout in the middle, the Astros were not following their usual status quo. Houston posted a +111 run differential on the season, third-best in the majors (trailing only the

Toronto Blue Jays and St. Louis Cardinals) but only finished with the 10th-most wins, indicative of the Astros' many blowouts when their whole lineup seemed to sizzle with homers.

The series began with the Mariners holding a 38.2 percent chance of winning the West, the Astros 23.8. The series ended with the odds almost perfectly reversed.

July 28-30: Astros Beat Back Angels with Meaningful Depth

The Angels spent the entire first half of their season trying—and succeeding—to keep pace with the Astros, eventually taking over the division lead on July 12 and arriving in Houston for this series with a one-game edge and a 54.7 percent chance of winning the division to the Astros' 43.7 percent. Although the atmosphere in Houston by now had shifted from library-esque to comfortably raucous, this series played out with the exact same script as the Mariners series described above, just with much higher stakes: meaningful depth triumphing over necessary depth. The Astros won all three games and emerged with a better than two-in-three chance of winning the division.

At the beginning of July, the baseball world was briefly titillated by the power play that went down in Anaheim, with manager Mike Scioscia triumphing over general manager Jerry DiPoto, who was shown the door less than a full season after putting together the winningest team in baseball (the Angels' 98-win 2014). I say briefly titillated because, after a lack of pot-stirring gossip followed the story, what quickly became clear is that the Angels didn't really have much of a plan in mind after releasing DiPoto—or, if they did, it wasn't a great one. While other playoff contenders swung momentous deals for star players in these taut days before the trade deadline, the Angels were content with gathering as many veteran utility players as they could from around the league. It was extremely easy for the Angels to do—and also just as ineffective.

6. The Astros rode the three true outcomes to their philosophical limit, as they led the American League with 34.7 percent of their plate appearances ending in a walk, strikeout or home run.

7. The Astros and Rangers shoved their chips in at the trade deadline, acquiring Cole Hamels, Scott Kazmir, Carlos Gomez and Mike Fiers, and set the stage for premiere decade-long rivalry.

8. Demoted on May 8 after hitting .144/.252/.233, 21-year-old Rougned Odor returned to the majors on June 15, and hit .292/.334/.527 for the rest of the season.

9. Switch-pitcher Pat Venditte made his major league debut for the A's, tossing 28.2 innings of slightly below league-average innings, though he was death against lefties (11.57 K/9 in 14.0 innings).

10. Led by Delino Deshields, the Rangers were the majors' best baserunning team; dragged down by Robinson Cano, the Mariners' were the majors' second-worst.

In marched Conor Gillaspie, Shane Victorino, and the Davids Murphy and DeJesus from their underwhelming squads around the majors, ready to apply copious amounts of veteran wisdom and experience. They joined a lineup that was, well, not very robust. This year, there were 38 major league players who received at least 100 plate appearances and hit under .200. So about one per team, right? Well, five of them appeared for the Angels. It's hard to know whether to be incredibly impressed or incredibly depressed that the Angels actually made it to the last day of the regular season with what basically amounted to a National League lineup—that is, with at least one spot serving as something of a break in the action for the opposition. Should Angels fans be depressed at the organization's puzzling inability to procure depth or impressed at the top half of the team's lineup for being able to grimly pull what should be a cellar-dweller above water?

I'll go with depressed. Not only do players like Mike Trout come around once in never, but contracts as valuable as Trout's don't, either. Not that I'm totally sure how they'd do it, but it sure would be nice to see a sense of urgency from the Angels as they team-build, what with a real contender for title of Best Player Ever getting a nearly threefold raise to Elvis Andrus-level money next season ($15.25 million). Perhaps that red-and-white 27 jersey will look like a relic 20 years from now, the Millville Meteorologist having long ago decided to leave for greener pastures. Trout missed three games all season; two of them came in this series, and when he played in the series finale, the Angels were shut out. From time to time Mr. Trout can pretty much do it all on his own—but alas, not every time.

Like a Michael Bay Transformer flipping an internal switch and going from pick-up truck to flying, justice-wielding robot, the Astros fundamentally changed their form in the nearly three months since the Mariners series. Rotation stopgaps are gone, replaced by 21-year-old wunderkind Lance McCullers and pricey trade deadline investment Scott Kazmir, who makes his scoreless Astros debut in this series finale. Houston also has a new hitter who locks down the three-hole in the lineup, a spot that will remain his for the foreseeable future. At 20 years old, Carlos Correa appears in only 99 major league games in the 2015 season, yet still leads all shortstops in home runs (22). Always playing with the preternatural equanimity of the aged veteran, Correa quickly justifies his first overall selection in the 2012 draft.

Sept. 14-17: Rangers Turn the Tables on the Astros

At the July 31 non-waiver trade deadline, the Texas Rangers traded for Cole Hamels from the Philadelphia Phillies, and it felt like a weird trade. It didn't feel like a bad trade, mind you, from either side's perspective, but it felt weird because the Rangers were clearly tooling up for future years, when ace Yu Darvish would not be lost to Tommy John surgery. Trades in which both the seller and the buyer trade with the future in mind tend not to happen at the trade deadline. In interviews just after the trade, Rangers general manager Jon Daniels focused on the advantageous nature of Hamels' contract—three full years after this one, plus a one-year player option to follow—instead of the pitcher's present-tense contributions. Which was only sensible; at the time, the Rangers were 50-52 and had a 1.6 percent chance to win the division, well behind the dueling Angels and Astros.

From then on out, the Rangers put together the third-best record in the majors (behind the Toronto Blue Jays and Chicago Cubs, and tied with the Pittsburgh Pirates). In a year when preseason predictions turned out to be especially useless, the Rangers had the distinction of being a playoff team that showed hardly any inclinations of being one until the final few weeks of the season.

Even after watching what can only fairly be called their dismantling of the Astros, I'm still not totally sure how they did it. Shin-Soo Choo and Adrian Beltre had sublime seasons, yes, but the Mariners have their Cruz and Kyle Seager and the Angels have their Trout and Kole Calhoun. Two star players does not a contender make. The theories of the Rangers' instantly scorching stretch drive will no doubt be thrown in statisticians' faces—as with Buck Showalter's monumentally clutch Baltimore Orioles of a few seasons ago—and will also no doubt include the good chemistry cheer spread by perpetual front-of-dugout celebrants Rougned Odor and Hanser Alberto. Whatever the reason, this much is true: Whenever the Rangers needed somebody to extend their extensive parade of singles, they got it, whether it was Will Venable or Drew Stubbs or Mike Doggone Napoli, who would be serenaded with chants of his own name during his surprisingly sweet return to Texas.

This series was pretty simple: The Astros held a half-game lead heading into Arlington, and then the Rangers dismantled them single by single. In the second game of the series, they tallied 14 hits in a 6-5 walk-off win, and 13 of them were singles, including two that set up the winning run. They would hit some home runs too, including two in a six-run first inning against Dallas Keuchel in the series' third game, but Texas' ability to move the procession one base at a time was helpful. The Rangers outscored the Astros 33-13 over the four games, and rapped out 33 singles in the process. They won all four games of course, and with two and half weeks left in the season, moved their division-winning odds from 32.3 percent to 69.5. As lost as last year's 67-win Rangers looked, perhaps that wasn't a sign of things to come but rather a quick aberration for a franchise that routinely puts together 90-win seasons.

You are forgiven if you thought the AL West would finish in something like the exact opposite order it eventually did—and you are not alone, either.

The National League East View

by Alex Remington

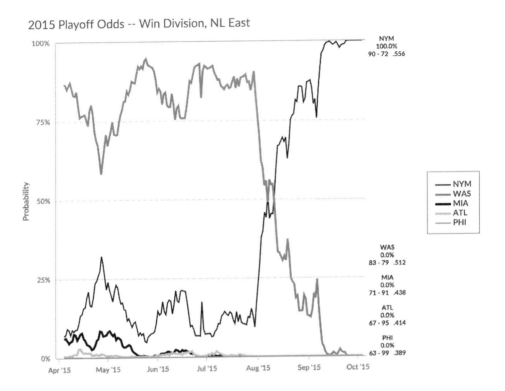

2015 Playoff Odds -- Win Division, NL East

The 2014 National League East was arguably the weakest division in baseball, with only one team, the 96-win Nationals, above even the .500 mark. The division in 2015 was inarguably worse. Teams from outside the division went 246-184 against Eastern teams, a .572 winning record, which would have led the division.

The East was paced by the 90-win Mets, who were expected to be decent thanks to the pitching of Matt Harvey and Jacob deGrom and the near-readiness of highly rated young pitchers like Noah "Thor" Syndergaard and Steven Matz. Their fortunes were seemingly dealt a major blow when Zack Wheeler was forced to undergo Tommy John surgery in March. Ultimately, his injury wouldn't be a factor.

For many, the story of the year was not how the Mets won the division, but how the Nationals lost it. After spending $210 million to acquire Max Scherzer, the best free agent pitcher on the market, the Nationals had won the offseason. The defending division champions were coming off a 96-win season and were loaded for bear. Yet they won 13 fewer games in 2015 than they had in the previous year.

After travelling through an ocean of games, three days stick out.

June 28: A Harbinger of Things to Come

As dawn broke on Sunday, June 28, the Washington Nationals had a 41-33 record and were in first place by three games over the New York Mets. It was a two-team race at that point: the Braves, Marlins and Phillies had already effectively been eliminated.

In other words, three months into the season, all was pretty much as expected. A few writers had picked the Marlins as a dark horse to win the World Series, and many viewed the Mets as a pretty good team, but after the Nationals added Max Scherzer while retaining virtually their entire core, most people expected Washington to win the division and perhaps the World Series.

So in late June, as the Nationals stood atop the division, three games ahead of the Mets, 6.5 games ahead of the Braves, 11 games ahead of the Marlins, and 15.5 games ahead of the Phillies, all looked roughly as it should have—which is why Washington had a 92.9 percent chance of winning the division, while the Mets were at 6.8 percent.

It was a big day for the Mets, as top pitching prospect Steven Matz was about to make his debut against the struggling Reds. Meanwhile, the Nationals had a double-header scheduled with the cellar-dwelling Phillies. On paper, it might not seem like a turning point for the season, but the outcome of those three games on June 28 resulted in the biggest one-day swing in division odds all season.

Here's what happened.

The Nationals were in Philadelphia for a three-game set. On Friday, June 26, they won the first game 5-2, behind Scherzer's dominant pitching. Saturday's game was postponed due to rain, and the teams agreed they would make it up immediately after the Sunday afternoon game.

Nationals manager Matt Williams moved his players around a great deal between the two games: the only Nats who started both games were Ian Desmond, Yunel Escobar, Clint Robinson and Michael Taylor. The latter two were supposed to be bench players, but they got pressed into service following injuries to Jayson Werth, Anthony Rendon and Ryan Zimmerman. Despite the offense being stretched thin, Stephen Strasburg managed to eke out a victory over Kevin Correia in the first game, 3-2.

But the Nats were less lucky at dusk. Tanner Roark came out of the bullpen for a spot start and got shellacked, giving up 12 hits and eight earned runs and getting yanked in the middle of the fourth. He was rusty, having pitched just two innings in the preceding 12 days. It was one of several instances of questionable pitching management by Matt Williams during the season. The Phillies won, 8-5.

In their 19 meetings with the Phillies, the Nationals went 12-7—a perfectly respectable record, but those losses to the Phillies constituted the margin between the 83-79 Nats and the 90-72 Mets.

As for the Mets that Sunday: After losing two years to Tommy John rehab immediately after getting drafted, Matz blew through the minor leagues. He spent 2012 in rookie ball, 2013 in Single-A, ended 2014 in Double-A, and before his call-up he had a 2.19 ERA in 90 innings in Triple-A Las Vegas—a desert ballpark that is famously unfriendly to pitchers. He wasted no time getting to work in the majors, yielding just five hits and two runs in 7.2 innings. At the plate he was 3-for-3 with four runs batted in. The Mets won 7-2.

As a result of the day's games, the Nationals' odds of winning the division fell from 92.9 percent to 82.1 percent and the Mets' odds rose from 6.6 percent to 17.6 percent, nearly a 22-point swing. It wasn't a permanent swing by any means—after a Mets loss and Nats win on Tuesday, July 1, the odds went back to 90.6 percent for the Nats and just 8.9 percent for the Mets—but it was a clear sign of things to come. The Nats' frustrating offense and the Mets' indomitable pitching would monopolize the storyline for the rest of the summer.

Aug. 12: Aces Dominate

The Nationals and Mets fought for the division lead all year. The Mets had it for all of April and much of May, the Nats had it for parts of May and June and all of July, and the Mets took the lead back for good on Aug. 3. Entering games on Aug. 12, the Nats were 2.5 games out of first place and just four games above .500.

They were in Los Angeles. After losing to Zack Greinke on Aug. 11, the Nationals' odds of winning the division dipped below 50 percent for the first time all season. It now stood at 48.7 percent, and while it's hard to say that a game in mid-August is a must-win, the Nationals' playoff dreams were already starting to slip away. Unfortunately for them, their opponent on Aug. 12 was Clayton Kershaw.

For their part, the Mets had a frustrating June and July, going 25-30 in those two months and allowing the struggling Nationals to stay in contention. But at the turn of the month they finally started to turn it around. After a walk-off victory against the Nationals on July 31, the Mets went into a two-week stretch where they won 11 out of 13 games. On the 12th, they were hosting the Rockies, a bad team that was trying to avoid a 100-loss season.

Their rotation took over. On the 11th, Matt Harvey blanked the Rockies, 4-0. On the 12th, they sent up 2014 NL Rookie of the Year Jacob deGrom, arguably the staff ace. As Kershaw carved up the Nationals, allowing three hits in eight shutout innings, deGrom did roughly the same to the Rockies, allowing two hits and no runs in seven innings.

It was a difficult summer for the Nats offense. While Bryce Harper was easily the best hitter in the league, his teammates struggled to put the bat on the ball during the rare moments when they managed to stay on the field. All six of their other returning starters—first baseman Zimmerman, left fielder Werth, infielder Rendon, center fielder Denard Span, shortstop Ian Desmond, and catcher Wilson Ramos—performed far below their standards.

Ramos and Desmond managed to stay healthy but had arguably the worst years of their careers. Werth, Rendon and Zimmerman couldn't stay on the field, averaging just 76 games played among them, and each also had the worst year of his career. Span had a nice season with the bat—a wOBA of .348, his best since 2009—but he played only 61 games.

The Nationals got badly bitten by the injury bug, but what was even worse was the way their key players performed when they were on the field. And after the domination of aces Kershaw and deGrom on this day, Washington's division odds had slipped down to 40.2 percent. It was the last day it would remain over that 40 percent threshold.

2015 Games Above or Below .500, NL East

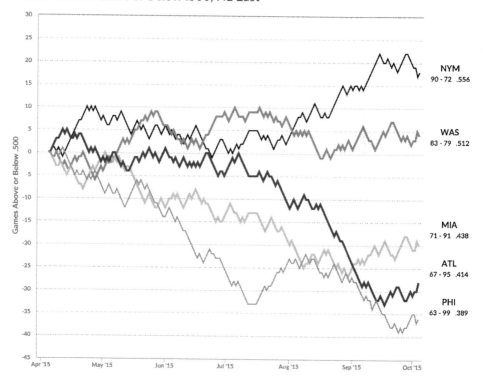

Sept. 7: The Death Blow

After spending much of the summer barely above .500, the Nats knew the Wild Card was likely out of reach. Their only path to the playoffs was a divisional pennant.

After a four-game sweep of Atlanta, they were six games above .500 and only four games back of first-place New York as the Mets came to town.

The last time they'd faced each other was July 31-Aug. 2, and the Mets had broomed them. That had been a shock: The Nationals had been a first-place team watching their divisional lead evaporate. Now they were fighting for their lives, knowing that anything less than a sweep of their own would make their playoff dreams almost impossible.

The first game's match-up seemed awfully favorable for Washington, as Mets holdover Jon Niese hooked up with Nationals ace Scherzer. Niese came into the game with a 9.92 ERA in his previous three starts and whispers suggesting that he was about to lose his rotation spot (he would), while Scherzer was a former Cy Young winner who had one of the richest contracts ever given to a pitcher.

Scherzer blinked first, though, giving up solo home runs to Michael Conforto and Kelly Johnson in the third inning as the Mets ran out to a 2-0 lead. Niese would give them all back and then some, yielding a Ramos grand slam and a Werth RBI double in a five-run fourth. But Scherzer could not hold the line, allowing single runs in the fourth, fifth and sixth, finally departing after six innings with the teams tied 5-5.

10 Things You Should Remember About The 2015 NL East

1. The Marlins' Dee Gordon bested his seemingly fluky 2014 breakout season, leading the National League in batting average (.333) and steals (58), and leading NL second baseman in WAR (4.6).

2. Shelby Miller posted the best season of his career, one that included his first All-Star nod, but because of the Braves' anemic offense, he went 24 straight starts without being credited with a win.

3. Atlanta's Andrelton Simmons once again led NL infielders in Ultimate Zone Rating (UZR). He is now third all-time in shortstop UZR despite not having played in most of the UZR era (2003-2015).

4. After a very disappointing 2014 debut with the Mets, Curtis Granderson posted his best season since 2011, and tallied his third 5+ WAR season.

5. Top prospects Aaron Nola (starting pitcher) and Maikel Franco (infielder) successfully broke in to the majors with Philly.

In retrospect, Scherzer's exit was probably the last time the Nationals had a plausible chance at winning the division, as manager Matt Williams kept making the wrong bullpen moves. His choice to start the seventh inning was Blake Treinen, who immediately gave up a leadoff single to Wilmer Flores. The next batter, Ruben Tejada, bunted, but Treinen managed to get the leading man, so there was a man on first base with one out and a double play opportunity. But Williams did not believe in the ability of the man he'd chosen to start the inning to get the second out of the inning.

So he yanked Treinen in favor of Felipe Rivero, a rookie lefty, to face lefty batter Curtis Granderson, who walked on seven pitches. Williams then brought in Casey

Janssen, a righty who had given up eight earned runs over his previous six appearances, to face right-handed David Wright. Wright singled on a 1-2 pitch, scoring the go-ahead run. Williams then called for lefty Matt Thornton, who had been selected off waivers a month earlier. He faced the left-handed-hitting Daniel Murphy, and induced a sacrifice fly, giving up a run and getting the second out of the inning.

Williams had been ignoring recent performance and track record with these relievers, but at least he had the platoon advantage. But then he went ahead and ignroed that too, and left Thornton in to face a second man, Yoenis Cespedes. Cespedes hit better against righties than lefties this season, but that is besides the point. Thornton was a 38-year-old who lost two mph on his fastball this year, and who had recorded just one shutdown in the month leading up to this plate appearance. Cespedes, meanwhile, had entered the game having homered in four of his past five games, and he had homered earlier in the game off of Scherzer to make it five of six. This situation called for one of the Nationals' best. Instead, Williams left Thornton in to dance.

6. Giancarlo Stanton of Miami bashed 27 homers by the end of June, and while a hamate bone injury ultimately limited him to 74 games, he still finished 10th in the NL in homers.

7. Jose Fernandez and Matt Harvey had their innings watched carefully, but their results—a 2.24 FIP for Fernandez and 3.05 for Harvey—were exemplary.

8. It was a good year for Rule 5 draft picks, and the NL East was no exception, as the Phillies' Odubel Herrera (3.9 WAR) and the Mets' Sean Gilmartin (0.9 WAR, 2.75 FIP) were pleasant surprises.

9. Marlins general manager Dan Jennings became the first non-player or manager to run a major league game since Ted Turner in 1977. It went poorly.

10. The Braves are rebuilding, so they traded away 13 relief pitchers, but the relievers who did suit up were worse than expected. So much worse, in fact, that team president John Schuerholz had to assure season ticketholders that the team would try to achieve a .500 record in 2016.

Cespedes predictably hit an RBI double, extending the lead to three runs. Jonathan Papelbon and Drew Storen would remain in the bullpen, as the Nationals lost by that same 8-5 score. They would proceed to lose their next four games as well, their season all but over except for one sad epitaph. That came in the eighth inning of the game on Sept. 26, when Papelbon choked Harper in the dugout. After the fracas subsided, Williams sent Papelbon out to pitch the ninth. Later, he said he wouldn't have let Papelbon keep pitching if he had realized how bad the dugout fight had been.

On Monday, Oct. 5, the day after the season ended, the Nationals fired Matt Williams. It was hard to blame them.

The National League Central View

by Greg Simons

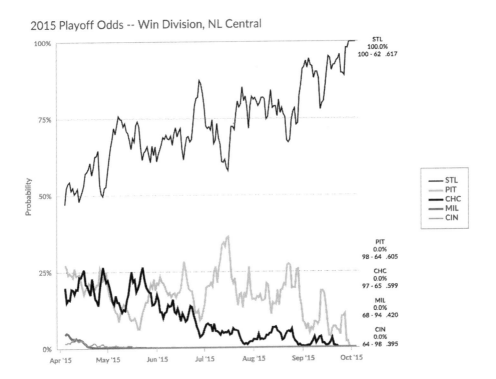

2015 Playoff Odds -- Win Division, NL Central

We all know the National League Central produced three playoff teams and the three best records in baseball in 2015, with each team winning 97 games and making the 2015 NL Central the first division to claim three 97-win teams, which also were the best three records in the game. But what were the key moments throughout the year that provided each with the biggest push on their way to greatness? Let's look.

July 9-12: Pirates, Cardinals Renew Hostilities

In 2011 and 2012, the Pittsburgh Pirates started their season well, only to fade badly during the second half, though the '12 dropoff was postponed a few weeks compared to the previous year. In 2013 and 2014, Pittsburgh stayed strong all season long and claimed a Wild Card berth, announcing to the baseball world that the Pirates' long stretch of disappointment was over, and that they were—and would continue to be—a team with which to be reckoned. In 2015, Pittsburgh used its July 9-12 four-game series with St. Louis to put the Cardinals on notice that this renewed rivalry was going to be tightly contested once again.

The first game of the series actually was a St. Louis victory. Young Redbirds hurler Carlos Martinez was excellent over 7.1 innings, out-dueling veteran mediocrity Jeff Locke, 4-1, thanks to a messy fifth inning for the Pirates. However, the remaining games would be decidedly different.

The June 10 game featured Pittsburgh's 24-year-old ace, Gerritt Cole, against Lance Lynn. Cole wasn't great on this occasion, but he was more than good enough, while Lynn put on a Jekyll-and-Hyde performance that ended up making Cardinals fans want to hide their faces. While striking out the side in the first, Lynn also allowed two singles and a double, leading to the Pirates' first run.

St. Louis grabbed a brief lead in the top of the third on a Matt Carpenter two-run homer, but Pittsburgh immediately plated two runs of its own to retake the lead. Then Neil Walker ended the scoring with a fourth-inning, two-run homer. After, neither team mounted much of a threat, and the Bucs had knotted the series.

Then things *really* started to get interesting. The next night, John Lackey and A.J. Burnett were solid if unspectacular, both pitching into the seventh frame. The Cards used a solo home run, a sacrifice fly and a run-scoring error to build a 3-0 lead through 4½ innings. Burnett helped his own cause (because that's what all pitchers must be said to have done) with a homer in the bottom of the fifth. Trailing 3-1 going into the home half of the eighth, the Pirates used a walk-error-single-error-single sequence to tie things up, and that's where things remained through regulation.

Mark Reynolds' second solo home run of the game gave the lead back to St. Louis in the top of the 10th. It would have been a two-run shot had Yadier Molina not been picked off following a leadoff single. To make his blunder more shameful, it was Molina's own patented catcher-to-first pickoff that nailed him. That mistake proved costly, and Pittsburgh bounced back against Cardinals closer Trevor Rosenthal with a triple and a single to square the game at four runs apiece. The game meandered on.

And on, and on, into the 14th inning, when the Redbirds again moved ahead. This time it was via a small-ball approach, with Carpenter walking, stealing second, taking third on Francisco Cervelli's throwing error, and scoring on a Jhonny Peralta single.

Nick Greenwood was brought in to try to save the game, but he was nowhere close to being up to the task. Walker greeted him with a single before Andrew McCutchen ripped a home run to deep center field to secure the walk-off, 6-5 victory. Pittsburgh had cut the Cardinals' lead to 3.5 games, and the Pirates looked for more in game four.

St. Louis rookie Tim Cooney was something less than stellar in the finale, serving up three runs in five innings, but the bullpen held Pittsburgh scoreless over the next four frames. Francisco Liriano was his usual self, with a healthy number of strikeouts (six) and an unhealthy number of walks (four) in his 6.1 innings pitched. But he gave up only two runs, exiting with a chance at victory.

Tony Watson pitched the eighth for Pittsburgh, and he gave up a walk and a single before an error loaded the bases. A groundout scored a run, but a liner and strikeout limited the damage, though St. Louis had tied the game, which is how things would stay until the fateful 10th inning.

Sporting one of the best names in baseball, Arquimedes Caminero came into the game and was promptly knocked around. Two singles, a groundout and a hit-by-pitch loaded the bases. Randal Grichuk followed with a deep blast to center field, and two runs scored. Reynolds tried to chug all the way around from first base, but he was gunned down at the plate thanks to two strong relay throws. Grichuk was left at third by a lineout, but St. Louis had taken a 5-3 lead.

The Cardinals turned to their closer for the second straight night, and for the second straight night Rosenthal was lit up, this time throwing gasoline onto a bonfire. A Jordy Mercer leadoff single was followed by a fly ball and groundout, leaving a runner on second with two outs and the Cardinals with a two-run lead, so things seemed secure. However, consecutive singles by Starling Marte, Jung Ho Kang and Cervelli tied the game. A walk to Travis Ishikawa set up a force out everywhere, but that out wouldn't come. Instead, Gregory Polanco laced a liner to right, providing Pittsburgh with its second consecutive 6-5, extra-inning, walk-off victory.

With this three-game run, the Pirates trimmed their division deficit to 2.5 games, the closest they'd been to first place since late April. Their odds of winning the division surged 12.4 percent in those three days. And by getting to Rosenthal in back-to-back games, they exposed some weakness in the Redbirds' fireman. The Pirates claimed victory in this battle and announced to St. Louis and everyone else that they'd be ready to go toe-to-toe with any team all year long.

Aug. 6-9: Cubs Make a Statement

With their four star rookies—Kris Bryant, Jorge Soler, Addison Russell and Kyle Schwarber—all up to stay, the Chicago Cubs used an Aug. 6-9 four-game home series with the San Francisco Giants to demonstrate just how good their young squad was. This was a key series, because they were battling San Francisco for a Wild Card berth.

The series' first affair saw Jason Hammel and the Cubs batters square off against Chris Heston, who came into the game with a 1.64 ERA in his previous five starts. He didn't have his best stuff this day, however.

In the bottom of the first, a base on balls, hit-by-pitch, and another free pass allowed the North Siders to load the bases without putting the bat on the ball, but then Soler did just that, driving a two-run single to left. The Cubs' offense was much more demonstrative in the second, as back-to-back singles by Hammel and Russell were followed by a bomb by Schwarber, and just like that, they had a 5-0 lead.

The Giants used the long ball to claw back into the game, with Brandon Belt, um, belting a two-run homer in the fourth and Brandon Crawford doing the same in the sixth to get San Fran within a run. However, the Giants were held hitless the rest of the game, and the Cubs brought it home.

The second game featured the Cubs' $155 million man, Jon Lester, against former Japanese league reclamation project Ryan Vogelsong. This matchup was a case of "follow the money," though it took a while to work out that way.

Each team plated a run early on using a double-single combo, and it stayed 1-1 through 4½. But then the wheels fell off for San Francisco. Three singles, two doubles, a walk and two stolen bases later, it was 6-1 Chicago. Again, the Giants cut into the lead, scoring single runs in the seventh and eighth, but the Cubs got a run back in the eighth and finished off a 7-3 victory.

The third game offered up some offensive fireworks, and the Cubs faced their first deficit of the series, though only briefly. Matt Cain and Kyle Hendricks both struggled, as Belt homered again—a two-run shot that put the Giants up, 2-1—and Crawford doubled in a run, while Bryant accounted for Chicago's first three runs.

2015 Games Above or Below .500, NL Central

The Cubs seemed to seal the game with two runs in the fifth and three in the eighth for an 8-3 lead. However, relievers James Russell and Jason Motte made things interesting, allowing three runs on three singles and a double. Justin Grimm would come on and induce a groundout for the final out, and give Chicago a 3-0 series lead.

Who better to toe the rubber as the Cubs went for the sweep—and likely play-off death knell for the Giants—than Jake Arrieta? This start was early in Arrieta's second-half reign of terror on opposing hitters, and while it wasn't his best start, it was pretty darn good. Another Jake, Peavy that is, tried to counter Arrieta—an unenviable task to be sure—though he acquitted himself pretty well.

The Cubs struck early, and were up 2-0 at the end of the second. The Giants got runners into scoring position in three of the first four innings, but none crossed the plate. After making quick work of San Fran in the fifth and sixth, Arrieta allowed two more base runners in the seventh. After two quick outs and a single, Grimm came in to finish the eighth frame. If only the ninth inning were as uneventful.

Hector Rendon came in to close out the win, but it wasn't pretty. Belt led off with a single, and Crawford (the duo were seemingly San Fran's only hitters this series) doubled Belt to third. Rendon then plunked Ehire Adrianza to load the bases with no outs. However, the closer buckled down and fanned the next three batters to preserve the shutout victory that gave Chicago its third four-game sweep of the year.

Emotionally, this domination had to energize the Cubs. Mathematically, it gave them a big boost, as their play-off odds jumped from 56.3 percent before the series to 80.6 percent afterward. While many expected 2015 to be a chance for Chicago's young players to get used to the big leagues and build toward 2016, things clicked sooner than expected. The team parlayed the big contributions from its rookies—and, of course, many of its veterans—into a 97-win campaign and a playoff spot. This four-game series of domination was a terrific demonstration of the things that put the Cubs ahead of their original timeline.

> ## 10 Things You Should Remember About The 2015 NL Central
>
> 1. The Cubs' rookie class—led by Kris Bryant, Jorge Soler, Kyle Schwarber and Addison Russell—was simply outstanding.
>
> 2. Chicago postponed Bryant's major league debut until two weeks into the season to delay his free agency a full year, a decision that might have cost the Cubs the chance to host the Wild Card game.
>
> 3. Rookie starters made 110 starts for the suddenly rebuilding Reds, including 70 of 76 second-half starts. Anthony DeSclafani (3.46 FIP) and Raisel Iglesias (10.45 K/9, 3.66 FIP, 2.92 xFIP) stood out.
>
> 4. From June 21 through the end of the season, Jake Arrieta went 16-1 with a 0.86 ERA, 0.70 WHIP and 147 Ks in 147 innings pitched (20 starts).
>
> 5. The Cardinals got 28 innings pitched from Adam Wainwright, 229 at-bats from Matt Holliday, 175 ABs from Matt Adams, and couldn't find a steady center fielder all year long. It didn't matter.

Sept. 28: St. Louis' Denouement

The St. Louis Cardinals clinched a playoff spot relatively early, but didn't want to settle for merely making the postseason. Avoiding the one-and-done Wild Card game certainly is plenty of incentive to keep pushing until a division title is in hand, and that was the situation the Redbirds found themselves in Sept. 28.

Heading into Pittsburgh up three games with only six to play, St. Louis certainly was in the driver's seat, but the division was far from assured. Despite the Cardinals having sole possession of the NL Central lead since April 17, the Pirates had proven extremely difficult to shake, trimming the deficit to 2.5 games multiple times throughout the summer. Were Pittsburgh to sweep the upcoming series on its home field, the division would be knotted up, and the pressure would be mounting for the two-time defending division champs from the Gateway City.

Monday's series-opening matchup wasn't exactly a showdown between aces, instead featuring Lance Lynn against J.A. Happ. Lynn may be a three-time 15-game winner, but that has as much to do with strong run support as it does with his pitching skills. He's certainly an above-average pitcher, but he's not someone the Cardinals want to lead their staff. Happ's career 61-61 record and 96 ERA+ heading into the contest were good evidence of his thorough mediocrity, though he pitched quite well for the Pirates after they acquired him from Seattle at the trade deadline, finishing the year 7-2 with a 1.85 ERA and 209 ERA+ in 11 Pittsburgh starts.

6. Cincinnati's Joey Votto was essentially the hitting equivalent of Jake Arrieta. In the second half of the season, Votto posted a .359/.532/.618 line.

7. Milwaukee's Ryan Braun bounced back from two down years to post one of four 20-20 seaons in the majors and earn All-Star honors once again.

8. Acquired in trade for a middle reliever, Pittsburgh catcher Francisco Cervelli's batting line of .295/.370/.401 was a pretty nice approximation of the .290/.402/.430 triple slash Russell Martin provided the Pirates in 2014.

9. The Brewers' Francisco Rodriguez just kept chugging, logging 38 more saves to become the active career leader with 386, which is also good for seventh all time.

10. The Reds traded Johnny Cueto, but they failed to move Votto, Aroldis Chapman or Todd Frazier. The latter's hot first half built his trade value to its peak, but his ice-cold second half made the Reds look foolish for not dealing him.

The Cards had a fairly representative lineup, one that finally contained Matt Holliday—his quadriceps nominally healed—but Tony Cruz was filling in for the injured Yadier Molina. The Buccos countered with their eight regulars, though that now meant Jordy Mercer at shortstop instead of Jung Ho Kang after the latter's leg was torn up on a contentious slide by the Cubs' Chris Coghlan a week and a half earlier.

The game got off to a lethargic start, the first nine batters being retired in order. But starting in the bottom of the second frame, it became a bend-but-don't-break outing for Lynn. Given the number, severity and significance of the injuries the Cardinals suffered throughout the 2015 campaign, this just-enough approach typified their entire year. A free pass, double, and one-out intentional walk loaded the bases before Lynn escaped the inning unscathed thanks to a flyball/out-at-home double play started by center fielder Jason Heyward. The details were a bit ugly, but the result was positive for the Redbirds.

The next few innings were largely uneventful, the exception being a heady play by shortstop Jhonny Peralta following a leadoff double by Gregory Polanco in the fifth. Peralta fielded Josh Harrison's grounder and threw in the direction he was moving, tossing the ball to Matt Carpenter to get the lead runner at third base instead of taking the routine play at first. A groundout followed that might otherwise have scored a run, but instead it and another punch-out of Marte finished the inning.

St. Louis once again offered no threat in the top of the sixth, while Steve Cishek came on to pitch the bottom of the frame and followed Lynn's pattern of wildness and then some. Cishek alternated walks with outs for the five batters he faced, leaving the bases loaded for groundball specialist Seth Maness. Going against the grain, Maness got Polanco to fly out to right.

The Redbirds used the powerhouse combination of a one-out walk, groundout and infield single to get Stephen Piscotty to third in the top of the seventh, but Joakim Soria's strikeout of Peralta stranded the runner. The first play following the seventh-inning stretch is probably the most memorable of the game. Harrison drove a Kevin Siegrist pitch to deep left-center, and defensive replacement Peter Bourjos ranged over to make a terrific sliding catch. However, in the process, his knee slammed into the head of a diving Piscotty, leaving Piscotty flat on his back for several minutes while he received medical attention. Once play resumed, the Pirates again loaded the bases, but two additional flyball outs snuffed the rally.

In the ninth, with closer Mark Melancon in for Pittsburgh, Carpenter laced a one-out single to right. Jon Jay, who had replaced Piscotty, dumped a single to right-center. First Polanco, then Andrew McCutchen, failed to field the ball cleanly, allowing Carpenter to score from first. Mark Reynolds gave St. Louis breating room by following with a two-run home run. This was only the second loss of the year for Melancon, who led the majors with 51 saves. Trevor Rosenthal made things interesting by allowing a leadoff walk and a single to start the bottom half. But a whiff and two lineouts ended it and put the Cardinals firmly in control of the NL Central.

The Cardinals allowed the fewest runs in baseball in 2015, with their 525 mark far clear of the second-place Dodgers' 595 total. While the details of this game show the dangers of relying on the pitching and defense to bail out a team time and time again, it once again worked for St. Louis, and this particular victory all but sealed the division. The Cards' division odds jumped more after this game than any other, rising 9.1 percentage points, from 88.9 percent to 98.0 percent. It jumped all the way to 100 percent just two games later thanks to a 11-1 thrashing in the final game of the series.

The National League West View

by Dustin Nosler

2015 Playoff Odds -- Win Division, NL West

A side from the Washington Nationals, no team was a bigger favorite before the season to win its division than the Los Angeles Dodgers. All the projection systems loved them, and the competition in the National League West wasn't projected to be as tough as in others.

On the surface, that seems like an odd thing to say. The defending World Series champions resided in San Francisco, and the team 125 miles to the south in San Diego—with an eager young general manager—made about every trade imaginable in the offseason, attempting to dethrone the Dodgers as division champions. Despite that, the Dodgers' odds of winning the National League West were 73.8 percent before a pitch was even thrown. Their worst odds to win the division were 68.1 perecent, and that came on April 11—six days into the season. Clayton Kershaw took his first of seven losses on the season, and the Dodgers were a pedestrian 2-3.

After that, their odds sat firmly in the 80-percent range and first touched 90 percent on May 5.

This was in contrast to the last couple of years, when the Dodgers started slowly and had to play very well in the second half to ensure the division title. But they were mostly consistent throughout the entire 2015 season. That's not to say it wasn't tough for them at times. Their NL West odds dipped as low as 76.4 percent on July 26, when they suffered a 3-2 loss to the Mets in New York.

July 23-26: Mets Make Dodgers Sweat

The Dodgers traveled to New York for what would be the first of two times (see: 2015 National League Division Series) with a three-game lead on the Giants. San Francisco was in Oakland and riding an 8-1 stretch.

Los Angeles was set to start Clayton Kershaw, Ian Thomas (!), and Zach/ks Lee and Greinke, the latter of whom was in the middle of a 43.2-inning scoreless streak.

Kershaw was dominant in the first game: He had a perfect game going through six innings. While he didn't record the 24th perfect game in major league history, he pitched a three-hit shutout to extend his own scoreless streak to 29 innings. These were the pre-Yoenis Cespedes Mets, but it was still a team that was only three games out in the NL East. This was also Kershaw's highest win-probability-added (WPA) game of the season at 0.60 (he finished at 4.92 on the season, third-best in baseball behind Greinke and Cubs ace Jake Arrieta).

Thomas was making his first major league start and just his second appearance with the Dodgers, who acquired him on May 27 from the Braves in a deal that included Juan Uribe—who'd wind up with these same Mets. Thomas was able to pitch five scoreless innings en route to a 7-2 Dodger victory. Justin Turner paced the Dodgers' offense with three hits—a home run and two doubles—and they chased Mets starter Jon Niese after three innings.

Then came Lee's start. The Dodgers' first-round draft pick in 2010 and $5.25 million-bonus man was finally going to make his major league debut. At 23, that isn't uncommon, but he had been built up—likely because of that bonus—to be in the same ilk as Kershaw. Nothing could be further from the truth. If he were more like former Dodger first-rounder Chad Billingsley, the organization would have called that a win. While making one's debut in New York isn't optimal, making it against one of the worst offensive teams (at the time) was favorable. So, as baseball is wont to do, the Mets tagged Lee for seven runs and 11 hits in 4.2 innings. The Metropolitans would win 15-2 in a game that obviously was never close.

Still, the Dodgers had already taken two of three from the Mets and were sending Greinke to the mound on a Sunday morning/early afternoon. He was being opposed by Mets' ace Jacob deGrom in what promised to be a low-scoring affair. And it was. Greinke was good but not great, going seven innings and giving up two runs on four hits. His scoreless innings streak ended at 45.2, and the Dodgers went on to lose 3-2 in 10 innings on a Uribe RBI single (typical Hollywood scriptwriting, really). The loss dropped the Dodgers to 56-44.

Meanwhile in the Bay area, a Giants sweep of the Athletics catapulted San Francisco's odds of winning the NL West to a season-best 22.7 percent. Considering they—the defending World Series champions—started at 7.2 percent, it was a significant moment. Despite losing six of their first seven games in the month, the Giants finished July with a 14-10 record. That, coupled with the Dodgers' identical win-loss record, gave the Giants some hope.

To begin August, San Francisco had a 14.1 percent chance of winning the division. Not impossible, but when you consider the Texas Rangers had a 1.4 percent of winning the American League West on the same date, it wasn't really that unrealistic.

2015 Games Above or Below .500, NL West

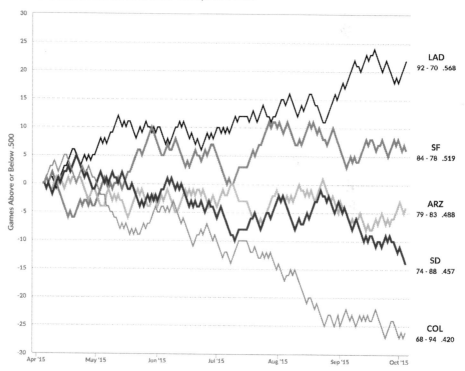

In August, a five-game losing streak at the hands of the A's and Houston Astros dropped the Dodgers' odds to 82.9 percent. In the first game against the Astros, crafty righty Mike Fiers threw a no-hitter. Not Dallas Keuchel, not recently acquired Scott Kazmir...Mike Fiers. That's baseball. The Dodgers negated the losing streak by winning five in a row—three against the Cincinnati Reds and two against the Chicago Cubs. That streak ended with Arrieta's no-hitter on Sunday Night Baseball. Narratives flew about teams being no-hit twice in a season, and things were getting a little dicey among the fan base. So, what better to temper all that than a showdown with the Giants—a team that had, almost inexplicably, remained in the hunt for the division title?

Aug. 31-Sept. 2: Dodgers Broom Giants, Ice Division

The Dodgers and Giants were separated by 3.5 games when this series began. Simple math: If the Dodgers got swept, they'd have a half-game lead. If they did the sweeping, they'd be up by 6.5. The former did not happen. The latter did.

The series' first game, which pitted Jake Peavy against Brett Anderson, ended up being a 14-inning affair. Both starters lasted fewer than six innings, and as such both bullpens got quite the workout. Dodgers reliever Chris Hatcher was one of the stars of the game, throwing three scoreless innings of relief. Adrian Gonzalez, who had homered earlier, won the game with an RBI single, giving the Dodgers a 4.5-game lead.

The middle game featured the best pitching matchup of the series, Madison Bumgarner opposing Greinke. Each hurler went seven innings and put his team in position to win. The difference was one swing of the bat from Joc Pederson.

The rookie center fielder got off to a hot start in 2015, hitting .298/.461/.596 in the season's first month. Through 53 games, he had 17 home runs and nearly a 1.000 on-base plus slugging percentage. Unfortunately for Pederson, he would hit just .177/.319/.303 over the season's final 98 games. He had faced Bumgarner two times earlier in the game and put good swings on the ball with no positive box-score results. Leading off the seventh inning against Bumgarner, he fell behind, 0-2. He worked the count to 3-2 and then hit a 405-foot home run that left his bat at 106 mph. It was the game-deciding run and pushed LA's lead to 5.5 games.

The series finale pitted reigning NL Cy Young and MVP winner Kershaw against trade-deadline pickup Mike Leake. More often than not, Kershaw is going to be the star of any game he's a part of, and this was no exception. Finishing a sweep of San

---

10 Things You Should Remember About The 2015 NL West

1. Madison Bumgarner's arm didn't fall off after an incredible postseason run in 2014, and he pitched (and hit) splendidly in 2015 (5.1 pitching WAR, 1.2 batting WAR).

2. The Rockies finally traded Troy Tulowitzki, signaling a new direction in Colorado, though it's anyone's guess as to what that direction actually is.

3. The Arizona Diamondbacks basically gave away prospect Touki Toussaint, a first-round draft pick in 2014, to save $9.5 million—after signing a $1.5 billion telvision contract.

4. Clayton Kershaw and Zack Greinke formed one of the most dominant pitching duos in years (1.90 ERA combined).

5. Third baseman Matt Duffy came out of seemingly nowhere to almost save the Giants' season (116 wRC+, 4.9 WAR).

Francisco would be demoralizing, even to a persistent club. A 6.5-game lead with a month to play looked better than 4.5. Kershaw spun what would be tied for his fifth-best game of the season (by Game Score), a six-hit, one-run complete game in which he struck out 15 Giants and threw a career-high-tying 132 pitches. Manager Don Mattingly could have lifted Kershaw in the ninth inning when he ran into a little trouble, but he stuck with him, partly because the Dodgers bullpen (again) had its troubles over the course of the season, but mostly because he was Clayton Kershaw. The sweep improved the Dodgers' NL West odds by more than five percentage points with 30 games to play.

The Giants had dealt with injuries the entire season. It began with Hunter Pence's broken left forearm in spring training, which kept him out for the first six weeks. Center fielder Angel Pagan played 133 games, but he wasn't right, and his 81 weighted runs created plus (wRC+) was 16th-worst of any qualified hitter. Former rotation mainstays Tim Lincecum and Matt Cain were shells of their former selves, and second baseman Joe Panik, an NL All-Star, was hurt and played just four games from Aug. 1 on. There were a lot of injuries, but those are the ones that stood out most for the 2015 San Francisco Giants.

6. Nolan Arenado broke out by hitting 42 home runs, to go along with his usually stellar defense, and helped the Rockies mitigate the loss of Tulowitzki.

7. Arizona had two bright spots: Paul Goldschmidt continued to be amazing by hitting .321/.435/.570, and A.J. Pollock became a top-tier player by posting a 6.6-WAR season and a 132 wRC+.

8. James Shields' signing didn't pay off for the Padres. Despite pitching half of his game in pitcher-friendly Petco Park, he allowed home runs on 17.6 percent of his fly balls, a career-worst percentage.

9. Carlos Gonzalez returned from injury to tally his first 40-homer season, and quell fears that his career was trending aggressively downward.

10. The Yasmany Tomas experiment at third base ended quickly and poorly for Arizona, but while he didn't hit enough to be a starting outfielder, Ender Inciarte and David Peralta both topped 3 WAR, and with Pollock gave the D-backs the majors' most valuable outfield.

Despite all the injuries, they still were mathematically alive going into the final week of the season. But the series that bridged August to September against the Dodgers saw their division odds slip from 13.6 percent down to 2.0, and they never threatened LA again.

April 13: Padres' Hopes Dwindle Early

While the two-team race between the Giants and Dodgers rightly dominated the division's headlines, the Padres spent the winter announcing their presence. So, before we close the book on the division, it's instructive to go back and look at when their season began to fall apart. Unfortunately for San Diego, it happened early—April 13.

That Monday, the Padres hosted the Diamondbacks to begin a three-game series. The enigmatic Andrew Cashner was on the hill for the Friars, and he was good. Despite allowing seven hits and issuing a walk, he struck out nine in his six innings of work. And yet, the Diamondbacks had the game all but won in the second inning.

In that second inning, Yangervis Solarte would misplay a ground ball, allowing a run to score. Instead of potentially turning an inning-ending double play, there were runners on second and third and still just one out. Two batters later, Ender Inciarte would double to left, and then Chris Owings singled to right, and just like that it was 4-0 Diamondbacks.

The 2015 Padres had plenty of flashy, name brand talent—Justin Upton, Matt Kemp, Craig Kimbrel, James Shields, Wil Myers, Derek Norris, Tyson Ross, Cashner—but there were two problems. First, the majority of these players were more sizzle than steak, and second, the remainder of the roster left much to be desired.

Looking at this game, the middle infield combo of Solarte and Alexi Amarista was particularly regrettable. Solarte would actually end up the team leader in games started at third base, and his 1.6 WAR was good for fourth-best among Padres position players. If that sounds disheartening, it's because it is. Amarista would lead the team in starts at shortstop. He would total 357 plate appearances for the season, one of 268 players to clear the 300 PA bar. Of those 268, only 12 finished with a worse WAR than Amarista. Only three of them—Rene Rivera, Omar Infante and Mike Zunino—finished with a lower weighted runs created plus (wRC+) mark than Amarista's 49. Amarista managed to hit 51 percent worse than league average. And he started half of the team's games at shortstop.

There were other lowlights sprinkled across the roster on April 13. Will Middlebrooks started at third, on his way to a second consecutive sub-replacement level season. Frank Garces would mop up the mess. He would mop up a lot of messes on the season, which was about all he was qualified to do given his 5.21 ERA and 12.7 percent walk rate. And finally and most disappointingly, there was Matt Kemp. Kemp was brought in to resuscitate an offense that had finished dead last in the majors in runs scored in 2014. But the offense-carrying Matt Kemp is no more, and his slightly above average offense and far-below average defense left him essentially a replacement player for the third consecutive season. His 0.4 WAR was "good" for 12th among Padres position players.

Before this Monday game, the Padres' division odds had jumped up to 20.8 percent. Following an 8-4 loss in which they were never really in the game, they dropped back to 16 percent. By the month's end, they would drop under 10 percent, and wouldn't eclipse that mark for the remainder of the season. The Padres may have won the offseason, but they faceplanted once the season began, and new general manager A.J. Preller was left to face the reality that he had gutted the team's farm system to build a 74-win ballclub.

To Err Is Human, But Not Royal

by Brad Johnson

In many ways, this October felt like a continuation of the 2014 postseason, except that this time, the Royals would not be denied, taking the World Series in five compelling games.

Kansas City outscored the New York Mets by a margin of eight runs over five games. However, run differential fails to capture the stunning, late-inning reversals that sunk the Mets' season. New York closer Jeurys Familia blew three saves—only one of which can be attributed to his pitching. Meanwhile, over the entire postseason, the Royals scored an astounding 51 runs after the start of the seventh inning. Talk about clutch!

Speaking of clutch performances, we're here to talk about our pet statistic—Championships Added (ChampAdded). The stat has two components. First, the standard Win Probability Added (WPA). The outcome of a game is decided by each individual play. WPA measures the value of those plays by accounting for score, inning, base state (e.g. runner on first), and number of outs. The second ingredient is a leverage index for each game—the Championship Value. As a team moves deeper in a series, its chance to win (or lose) the series increases. Obviously, games take on greater significance in close series.

Let's turn to the numbers. Game Seven of the World Series is worth one full championship since it's winner-takes-all. ChampAdded assigns a value of 1.000 to the game since the winner will receive the Commissioner's Trophy. All other games are worth a fraction of a championship. For example, had we seen a Game Seven of a League Championship Series round this year, it would have been worth 50 percent of a World Series. Below is a table that notes the total ChampAdded for each game.

Championship Value of Playoff Games										
	0-0	1-0	1-1	2-0	2-1	2-2	3-0	3-1	3-2	3-3
Wild Card Game	0.125	X	X	X	X	X	X	X	X	X
Division Series	0.094	0.094	0.125	0.063	0.125	0.250	X	X	X	X
Championship Series	0.156	0.156	0.188	0.125	0.188	0.250	0.063	0.125	0.250	0.500
World Series	0.313	0.313	0.375	0.250	0.375	0.500	0.125	0.250	0.500	1.000

Once we know WPA and Championship Value, we simply multiply them together to derive ChampAdded. Each play can produce a positive or negative piece of a championship. The stat is expressed as a decimal like batting average and many other familiar stats. For example, San Francisco's Madison Bumgarner tallied a ridiculous .869 ChampAdded in the 2014 postseason. You should read that as 86.9 percent of a championship.

Starting with the Division Series round, every team had a 12.5 percent chance of winning the World Series. Teams that fail to win October glory are docked -.125 ChampAdded. In other words, they cede their 12.5 percent chance to another club. The World Series champion Royals contributed a total of .875 ChampAdded (1.000 minus .125 equals .875).

It is our tradition to use ChampAdded to identify a series MVP, a series goat, and the biggest play of the series. The MVP is the player with the most valuable series. The goat is the player who hurt his team the most. The biggest play of the series is the play with the highest ChampAdded.

AL Wild Card: Houston Astros vs. New York Yankees

Surprisingly, the Astros led the American League West for most of the season. Even more surprisingly, it was the Rangers who eventually leapfrogged to the top of the division. The late-season change in fortune forced the Astros into the Wild Card game against the Yankees. The Bronx Bombers also fit the theme of surprise. Their aging roster wasn't supposed to keep pace in a tough AL East, but they put up a good fight until the end.

The game itself was a straightforward affair. The Astros raced out to an early lead and then extended it. The Yankees failed to respond in any way. Dallas Keuchel spun six scoreless innings, holding New York to three hits and a walk. Tony Sipp, Will Harris and Luke Gregerson combined for three no-hit innings. Sipp allowed one walk—the only New York base runner in the final three frames.

Game MVP: Keuchel ruled the Wild Card round with his six shutout innings. His mastery took the New York crowd out of the game and helped the Astros to an easy victory. He earned .042 ChampAdded, or 4.2 percent of a championship.

Game Goat: The sixth inning was the Yankees' best opportunity to do damage. Alex Rodriguez came to the plate with two on and two out. He ended the inning with a fly out. It was his most damaging out in a 0-for-4 performance. He's "credited" with -.016 ChampAdded. Still, it was definitely a team loss.

Big Play: When your opponent fails to score, the first run is often the most important play of the game. Such was the case with Colby Rasmus' second inning home run. It was worth .014 ChampAdded.

NL Wild Card: Chicago Cubs vs. Pittsburgh Pirates

The Pirates and Cubs featured the second and third best records in the National League, but they were stuck behind the Cardinals in the NL Central. For the second straight year, a potent Pirates roster was eliminated by an unhittable pitcher.

Kyle Schwarber singled home Dexter Fowler in the first inning against Pirates ace Gerrit Cole. It was all the Cubs would need with Jake Arrieta on the bump. If you thought Keuchel pitched well, Arrieta was masterful. He did his best Bumgarner impression, with a complete game shutout. He allowed just five hits and struck out 11 Pirates.

Game MVP: Shutouts ruled the Wild Card round. Arrieta was the game MVP with .037 ChampAdded. You may notice he's given less credit than Keuchel despite a better outing. He shared too much of the credit with Schwarber (.031 ChampAdded) and Fowler (.017). Also, Arrieta was 0-for-2 at the plate; Keuchel didn't have to bat.

Game Goat: This was supposed to be a battle of aces, but Cole looked decidedly mortal. He made several mistakes—especially to Fowler and Schwarber. By virtue of allowing all four Cubs runs, Cole earned goat honors. He was dinged for -.028 ChampAdded.

Big Play: Schwarber's two-run blast opened a three-run lead for the Cubs. It was worth .022 ChampAdded.

AL Division Series: Houston Astros vs. Kansas City Royals

The Royals may have won the World Series, but their young "ace," Yordano Ventura, had a difficult October. The struggles began in Game One of the AL Division Series against the Astros. Houston jumped to a quick 2-0 lead in the first inning, and Ventura was fortunate to escape at that point. When the Astros coasted to a 5-2 win, it looked like a Wild Card team might once again surge through the playoffs.

The narrative mutated in Game Two. For the third straight game, Rasmus drove in the first run. More work by George Springer and Rasmus led to a 4-2 Houston lead through the first three frames. Kansas City turned the tables in the sixth inning with a rally. It was the first of many late-game rallies for the Royals, who won 5-4.

Following a Game Three win, the Astros nearly pulled off the best-of-five series victory in Game Four. After feasting on reliever Ryan Madson, Houston held a 6-2 lead heading into the eighth. That proved to be a season-wrecking half inning for the Astros. The Royals refused to make outs. They tapped five consecutive singles against Harris and Sipp.

That set the stage for a critical error by shortstop Carlos Correa. The Astros still had a 6-4 lead, but the bases were loaded with no outs. Kendrys Morales hit a chopper back toward the pitcher. The ball tipped Sipp's glove on the way past the mound. Correa was perfectly positioned to field the ball and turn a double play. Instead, the last hop took a Super Ball bounce over Correa's glove. Houston should have escaped that play with two outs, a runner on third, and a 6-5 lead. Instead, the game was tied and the Royals still had no outs.

The Astros were forced to call on their closer early. Gregerson held the Royals to just one more run, but the damage was done. With Josh Fields in for Gregerson in the ninth inning, Eric Hosmer padded the lead with a two-run homer.

Game Five once again started in the Astros' favor, as Luis Valbuena popped a two-run home run in the second inning. But the Royals responded with seven unanswered runs to secure the win.

Series MVP: Kendrys Morales had a solid series. He went 5-for-19 with three home runs and six runs batted in. All told, he produced .060 ChampAdded. But that's not the whole story, is it? Our ChampAdded stat doesn't adjust for errors. No matter what happens in the field, the credit goes to the pitcher and hitter.

Morales' double-play-turned-error in Game Four was worth .039 ChampAdded by itself. That probably should be docked from Correa rather than credited to Morales. The Royals might still have won the game if Correa had made the play, but it would have been a different contest. Without the error, catcher Salvador Perez would have earned the series MVP with .051 ChampAdded.

Series Goat: Even if we properly adjust for Correa's error, he still isn't the series goat. In fact, he would have still posted a positive ChampAdded. Goat honors belong to Evan Gattis. He went 4-for-19 with no extra base hits. His only run batted in came on a ground out. Houston needed more pop from their designated hitter. His -.049 ChampAdded hurt.

Big Play: Based purely on psychic value, Correa's error was probably the biggest play, but ChampAdded uses different criteria. When Valbuena kicked off the Game Five scoring with a two-run home run, he notched .054 ChampAdded. Unfortunately for his team, the Royals were undaunted by the deficit.

AL Divison Series: Texas Rangers vs. Toronto Blue Jays

Not to be outdone by the other ALDS, the Rangers and Blue Jays also went the full five games. The first two contests were both exciting. The Rangers touched up David Price for five runs over seven innings in Game One. The Jays tried to claw back, but lost, 5-3.

Game Two went 14 innings. Mike Napoli tied it at 4-4 in the eighth inning. The bullpens held the line until LaTroy Hawkins and Liam Hendriks combined to allow a two-out rally in the 14th. Texas won 6-4.

With a 2-0 series lead, the Rangers were in the driver's seat, but the Blue Jays tied the series with low-stress wins in Games Three and Four. With everything on the line, Game Five in Toronto was an epic.

The score was tied 2-2 in the seventh inning. With two outs and the Rangers' Rougned Odor on third base, we were treated to the quirkiest error of the postseason. With Shin-Soo Choo at the plate, Jays catcher Russell Martin attempted to throw the ball back to the pitcher, and it tipped off Choo's bat down the third base line. Because Choo was in the batter's box and didn't intentionally interfere, it was a live ball. Odor scampered home to score the go-ahead run. Or did he?

The play resulted in chaos. The home plate umpire initially called it a dead ball and sent Odor back to third. However, that was the wrong interpretation of the play. The umpire crew huddled and corrected the call. After a slew of arguments, a player ejection, and a rain of beer cans on the Rogers Centre turf, the smoke cleared with the Rangers ahead 3-2. Choo struck out shortly thereafter.

Toronto struck back in the home half of the seventh inning by using the secret weapon of the 2015 postseason—errors. Martin reached on a miscue by Elvis Andrus. Then Kevin Pillar reached on an error. Then Ryan Goins bunted and reached…on an error. With the bases loaded and one out, Josh Donaldson tied the game with a fielder's choice. Then it was Jose Bautista's turn.

Bautista sent a Sam Dyson pitch deep into the night. His bat flip heard 'round the world led to more extracurricular shenanigans. When the smoke cleared this time, the Blue Jays held a 6-3 lead. The Rangers threatened again in the eighth but never got back on the board.

Series MVP: Who else? Bautista turned a tie into a win in Game Five. He went 6-for-22 over the series with two home runs and five runs batted in. He tallied .101 ChampAdded—mostly via his series-breaking blast.

Series Goat: Aside from one particularly bad pitch, Rangers reliever Sam Dyson had a solid series. Alas, Dyson doesn't get a mulligan for that game-losing home run he allowed. That one pitch clinched him a spot among the worst performers of the postseason, with -.074 ChampAdded.

Big Play: Bautista was the obvious MVP, Dyson the obvious goat, and Bautista's Game Five home run the obvious top play. The three-run bomb was worth .087 ChampAdded. The Martin throwing error (credited to Odor) was the third-biggest play at .043 ChampAdded.

NLDS: Chicago Cubs vs. St. Louis Cardinals

Of the four Division Series, the Cubs and Cardinals matchup was the tamest. There were still moments of drama, but they weren't anything like the Correa error or Bautista bat flip bomb.

Game One was a duel between former Red Sox teammates Jon Lester and John Lackey. The Cardinals expanded on a 1-0 lead in the eighth inning and locked down the win. Cardinals third baseman Matt Carpenter led off Game Two with a solo home run, but it was all downhill from there for St. Louis. A five-run rally including a key error by Jaime Garcia put the Cubs ahead in the second inning. They held on to tie the series.

While the Cardinals fought the whole way, they struggled to keep Cubs hitters from going yard. Game Three was tied after four frames, but back-to-back fifth-inning home runs by Kris Bryant and Anthony Rizzo furnished a 5-2 lead. Chicago ultimately won, 8-6, with the help of five home runs.

In Game Four, the Cardinals once again hit the accelerator in the first inning. This time, the damage came via a Stephen Piscotty two-run home run. The two teams juggled the lead until the sixth inning, when Rizzo hit a solo home run to give Chicago a 5-4 edge. Schwarber later added an insurance run via a long ball. In total, the Cubs hit eight home runs over the last two games of the series.

Series MVP: Jorge Soler may have had a disappointing season, but he did some serious work in the postseason. Against the Cardinals, he went 4-for-7 with three runs, four runs batted in, a double, two home runs and six walks. That's a .571/.769/1.571 triple slash. He totaled .041 ChampAdded.

Series Goat: In his only start, Michael Wacha allowed four runs (and three home runs) over 4.1 innings. Combined with an out at the plate, his performance measured -.047 ChampAdded.

Big Play: Even without playing much, Javier Baez rated well by ChampAdded. Most of his total is courtesy of a three-run home run he hit in the second inning of Game Four. The blast gave the Cubs a 4-2 lead in the deciding game.

NL Divison Series: New York Mets vs. Los Angeles Dodgers

The Mets went into their series against the Dodgers as a steep underdog. They had to somehow scrape past Clayton Kershaw and Zack Greinke, two of the league's top starters.

But Jacob deGrom outdueled Kershaw in Game One, and Game Two, with Greinke pitching, also started in the Mets' favor. After Yoenis Cespedes and Michael Conforto popped solo home runs in the New York first, Noah Syndergaard cruised through six frames with just one Dodgers run allowed. Syndergaard returned to start the seventh, but he allowed two of three batters to reach base. Bartolo Colon and A.J. Reed were summoned to put down the rally, but they threw fuel on the fire. Los Angeles scored four runs in the inning and won, 5-2.

Game Three got sloppy. The Mets dismantled Brett Anderson and Alex Wood en route to a 13-7 win. Then, a second chance against Kershaw in Game Four did not go in the Mets' favor. He held New York to three hits and a walk over seven innings. Steven Matz failed to keep pace despite a laudable effort.

With everything on the line in Game Five, the two clubs manufactured a nail-biter. It was Greinke versus Game One hero deGrom. The Dodgers led 2-1 after the first inning. A Travis d'Arnaud sacrifice fly tied it in the fourth. It was a special sac fly (more in a moment). In the sixth inning, Daniel "Babe" Murphy gave the Mets a decisive 3-2 lead with his third home run of the series. New York clung to the one-run advantage all the way to the NLCS.

Series MVP: Game Five was Daniel Murphy Day. A series-winning home run is often enough to earn the ChampAdded MVP all by itself. Murphy also drove in the first run with a double and scored the second run. That special run I mentioned? Murphy reached base with a single. The infield shifted for the next batter, Lucas Duda, but he drew a walk. Murphy strolled to second then swiped an uncovered third base. Without the heads-up baserunning, he doesn't score on the sac fly.

Those three run-scoring plays accounted for .107 ChampAdded. Incidentally, Murphy's .110 ChampAdded total for the series wasn't much higher. He was the most valuable player of the Division Series round.

Series Goat: Brett Anderson had a terrible Game Three start. He allowed six runs over three innings. Along with an out at the plate, he posted -.070 ChampAdded.

Big Play: Murphy's game-winning homer in Game Five was a .048 ChampAdded play. Murphy's double in the first inning was the second biggest play at .038 ChampAdded.

AL Championship Series: Toronto Blue Jays vs. Kansas City Royals

In retrospect, if any team was going to beat the Royals, it would have been the Blue Jays. Their offensive power was capable of burying any opponent well before the late innings. But Toronto certainly entered the series quietly; Edinson Volquez and friends shut out the Jays in Game One.

Game Two also went the Royals' way, but at least the Jays put up a little fight. Through six innings, they scraped together three runs against Ventura. When the Royals came to bat against David Price in the seventh, they performed their now-familiar brand of late-inning sorcery. Five singles, a double and an RBI ground out contributed to a five-run rally. Kansas City tacked on an insurance run in the eighth to win, 6-3.

In Game Three, with the series moved to Toronto, the Blue Jays chased Johnny Cueto after just two-plus innings. They added six runs in the third inning to produce a 9-2 lead. It was just enough. The Royals scored four runs in the ninth inning, but still lost, 11-8.

With a chance to tie the series in Game Four, the Blue Jays wilted. Starter R.A. Dickey failed to escape the second inning, allowing five runs. The game was so lopsided that Toronto eventually called on infielder Cliff Pennington to finish the ninth inning. It was a 14-2 victory for Kansas City.

In the Division Series, the Blue Jays were undefeated in elimination games. That trend continued for Game Five. They ran away with a 7-1 win. It was a tight contest until the sixth inning when a bases-clearing Troy Tulowitzki double gave Toronto a 5-0 lead.

After the first five games featured few dramatic moments, Game Six was unequivocally the best of the series. The Royals jumped to a 2-0 lead after two innings with two solo home runs. Jose Bautista answered in the fourth with one of his own. In the seventh, Alex Rios singled home Mike Moustakas to open up a 3-1 lead.

In the top of the eighth, Bautista went yard for the second time, a game-tying, two-run shot. But despite his best efforts, Bautista couldn't carry the team to victory. In the bottom of the eighth, Lorenzo Cain scored from first on an Eric Hosmer single to right field. This one requires explanation.

The hit forced right fielder Bautista to range to his left. Typically in this situation, the outfielder's job is to assume the runner from first will take third and hold the hitter to first. When Bautista fielded the ball, he immediately fired to second base without pausing to judge Cain's intentions. Usually, it's the right play. Not this time. Cain took advantage to score the winning run. It's hard to blame Bautista for making the strategically correct decision, but it was a tactical disaster.

Series MVP: Bautista's timely heroics at the plate earned him the Series MVP award, even though his team was eliminated. He hit .316/.500/.684 in 26 plate appearances with two home runs, four runs and six runs batted in. He's credited with .114 ChampAdded.

But hold up, what about the play that allowed Cain to score? If we penalize him for that mistake—the play was valued at .056 ChampAdded—Bautista falls to fourth most valuable. Royals relievers Wade Davis (.068 ChampAdded) and Kelvin Herrera (.062 ChampAdded) were next best.

Series Goat: Ryan Madson narrowly edged out Ben Revere as the series goat. The Game Six blast off him by Bautista accounted for nearly all of the damage he allowed. He graded out at -.089 ChampAdded. Revere went 5-for-24 with three walks and seven strikeouts. He netted -.086 ChampAdded.

Big Play: Bautista's two-run blast was worth more than eight percent of a championship (.082 ChampAdded). The Blue Jays may have fallen short of the World Series, but Bautista had a huge October at the plate.

NL Championship Series: Chicago Cubs vs. New York Mets

We were treated to an excellent postseason with many hard-fought series. This was not one of them. The Cubs never held a lead. They fought back to tie a couple of games, but that was it.

Daniel Murphy kicked off the scoring with a solo home run in Game One. It was his third straight game with a homer. Starlin Castro tied it at 1-1 with a run-scoring double in the fifth inning. From there, the Mets took control, winning 4-2.

With Cubs ace Arrieta on the mound, Murphy homered again in the first inning of Game Two. David Wright had already opened the scoring. Murphy extended the lead to 3-0. It was a drama-free 4-1 Mets win.

Game Three, with the play shifted to Chicago, was probably the best of the series. Yoenis Cespedes was instrumental to the Mets' regular season success, but he disappeared for most of the postseason. This game was the exception. He went 3-for-5 with two runs batted in and a run scored.

In the third inning, Murphy homered in his fifth straight game to give New York a 2-1 lead. After Jorge Soler tied it 2-2 with a solo shot in the fourth, it was time for Cespedes to create a run. He singled to start the sixth inning. Lucas Duda sacrificed him to second base. Cespedes then stole third base. With two outs, Michael Conforto struck out swinging, but the ball reached the backstop. Conforto reached first and Cespedes scored on the play. The Mets eventually won, 5-2.

The final contest was a lopsided Mets win. With New York up 6-1 in the eighth inning, Murphy popped another two-run home run. He's the first player to homer in six consecutive postseason games. And he's not even the series MVP.

Series MVP: That honor belongs to Cespedes. He dragged the Mets to victory in Game Three, burying the Cubs in the process. He posted .052 ChampAdded, even though he had just one hit in the other three games.

Series Goat: Arrieta may have channeled Bumgarner earlier in the postseason, but he lost his touch in the NLCS. His Game Two drubbing cost -.045 ChampAdded. It wasn't a terrible start; he allowed four hits and two walks, with eight strikeouts, in five innings. It just happens he also allowed four runs.

Big Play: Sweeps don't produce many big plays. We have to reach all the way back to Game One, when Castro tied the game with a fifth inning double. It was a .031 ChampAdded play. And it was quite inconsequential to the series.

World Series: New York Mets vs. Kansas City Royals

The NLCS may have been dull, but the World Series once again lived up to the hype. The series began and ended with extra-inning theatrics. Even though they won only one game, the Mets held frequent leads.

The Royals kicked off the scoring in Game One in Kansas City with Alcides Escobar's inside-the-park home run. Fast forward to the bottom of the eighth, and the game was tied 3-3. Juan Lagares kicked off an unlikely two-out rally with a single and a stolen base. Next, Wilmer Flores grounded to first, but an Eric Hosmer error allowed Lagares to score the go-ahead run.

The Mets entered the ninth inning with closer Jeurys Familia against the bottom of the Royals order. Alex Gordon bashed a one-out home run to tie the game. It would stay tied until the 14th inning. Against Bartolo Colon, Escobar reached on an error by David Wright. Ben Zobrist singled and Cain was walked to set up a force at home. Hosmer hit a walk-off sacrifice fly to redeem his earlier error.

Game Two belonged to the Royals. The Mets took the first lead then closed shop. Kansas City scored seven unanswered runs, winning 7-1.

The third game, in New York, was an early-innings battle. The Mets fell into a 3-2 deficit after allowing Alex Rios to score on a passed ball in the second inning. They tightened up defensively and piled on seven runs against Yordano Ventura, Franklin Morales and Kelvin Herrera. The 9-3 victory was the only time the Royals didn't overwhelm the Mets in the late innings.

Game Four looked to be going the Mets' way. Through five frames, New York nursed a 3-1 lead. Lorenzo Cain singled in a run in the sixth and forced Steven Matz from the game. The Mets still held a 3-2 lead in the eighth. When New York setup man Tyler Clippard allowed two of three batters to reach base, Mets manager Terry Collins summoned his top reliever, Familia.

With runners on first and second, Hosmer hit a soft chopper to second base. The ball took a weird, dead short-hop under Murphy's glove, allowing the tying run to score on the error. Had the ball been fielded cleanly, the Royals would have had runners on second and third and two outs. The next two batters hit weak singles, giving Kansas City a 5-3 lead.

The Mets' Matt Harvey was masterful for most of Game Five. Through eight innings, he allowed just four hits and walk, with nine strikeouts. Would Harvey return for the ninth inning? The TV camera panned to the dugout where Harvey had just been told he was done—yet was successfully lobbying Collins to stick with him.

Cain led off the ninth with a tough at-bat that ended in a walk. After he stole second base, Hosmer doubled him home. The score was 2-1 with no outs and a runner on second. Once again, Collins belatedly turned to Familia.

Mike Moustakas grounded out to first base, moving Hosmer to third with one out. A fly ball could tie the game, but Salvador Perez hit an easy ground ball to Wright. The Mets' partially injured third baseman took a peek at Hosmer then slung the ball to first for the out. Hosmer took off for home and beat a wild throw from Duda. Had the throw been on target, Hosmer would have been an easy out. Instead, he's credited with a gutsy run-scoring play. The game headed to extra innings.

In the 12th, Mets reliever A.J. Reed had two outs and a runner on third. The Royals turned to Christian Colon to pinch hit for Luke Hochevar. The last time Colon had come to the plate was in the final game of the regular season—Oct. 4, almost a month earlier. Reed had a huge matchup advantage, but he made two consecutive terrible pitches. Colon laced the second of them for a go-ahead single, and the two-out deluge was on. The Royals tacked on another four runs to take a decisive 7-2 lead.

Series MVP: Hosmer earned the top mark with .181 ChampAdded, but let's do a little deconstruction of his series. The Game One error was a -.083 ChampAdded play. Let's subtract that from his total. He also made an error in Game Four that led to the Mets' second run. Let's dock another .021 ChampAdded. Finally, should Hosmer get credit for Murphy's critical error? That was a .128 ChampAdded play. If we remove these three plays, Hosmer posted -.051 ChampAdded. Even if we take credit for his Game Five baserunning play away from Perez (.025 ChampAdded), Hosmer is still in the negative.

If you want a cleaner MVP, it's Ben Zobrist. He was a tenacious presence at the plate all postseason long. He went just 6-for-23 with three walks in the World Series, but he also scored five important runs. All told, he posted .154 ChampAdded.

Series Goat: The goat was Familia. He blew three saves, so how could it be anyone else? Still, you have to feel sorry for him. There's no doubt Game One falls on his shoulders, and it was a devastating blow. But it's hard to blame him for errors and weak hits in Game Four. He actually should have escaped Game Five with the lead despite inheriting a difficult situation. That one is on Wright and Duda. His -.247 ChampAdded was the single goatiest performance in any series.

Big Play: That Game One blown save really hurt. Gordon's game-tying home run was the biggest play of the series at .148 ChampAdded. Honorable mention goes to Murphy's Game Four error (.128 ChampAdded).

Playoff MVP: Now this gets interesting. As previously noted, our ChampAdded stat is designed to award plays to hitters and pitchers. Defenders get no credit for majestic snags or costly blunders. Hosmer tops the list of MVPs, though as we just discovered, a defensive adjustment could leave him off this list entirely.

And if Hosmer weren't here, the MVP of the entire postseason didn't even reach the World Series. Bautista came through with timely blasts in the ALDS and ALCS. Of course, we can make a defensive adjustment for Bautista too. And that would move him down the list, although he would still remain in the top 10.

Once we remove defensive miscues, we're left with Wade Davis as the postseason MVP. In 10.2 innings, he allowed no runs, six hits, and three walks. He fanned 18 of 39 batters faced. He recorded a win and four saves.

So who's the true MVP? It's up to you to decide.

Honorable mention goes to Curtis Granderson, who did his best to carry the Mets in the World Series. Murphy helped New York get that far, but he mostly disappeared on the biggest stage. And, well, there's a defensive adjustment to be made for him too. Jon Niese and Chris Young deserve a shoutout for excellent long relief work in the World Series.

2015 Postseason Heroes	
Player	ChampAdded
Eric Hosmer	0.265
Jose Bautista	0.215
Wade Davis	0.195
Alex Gordon	0.181
Curtis Granderson	0.171
Ben Zobrist	0.165
Daniel Murphy	0.164
Jon Niese	0.140
Luke Hochevar	0.114
Chris Young	0.096

The Royals won the World Series, but that doesn't hide Ventura's ugly postseason. He's the prime protein in this goat stew. Familia is a tough-luck inclusion here. Even though Cespedes was the MVP of the NLCS, he still shows up on the goat list.

The Blue Jays had three of the goats. It makes sense. To counterbalance Bautista's dominance, somebody had to struggle. Those somebodies were Revere, Tulowitzki and Price.

2015 Postseason Goats	
Player	ChampAdded
Yordano Ventura	-0.171
Jeurys Familia	-0.146
Ben Revere	-0.127
Travis d'Arnaud	-0.083
Troy Tulowitzki	-0.083
Addison Reed	-0.080
Sam Dyson	-0.074
Yoenis Cespedes	-0.071
Brett Anderson	-0.071
David Price	-0.070

References and Resources

For more on WPA:

- Dave Studeman, The Hardball Times, "The One About Win Probability," *hardballtimes.com/main/article/the-one-about-win-probability*

Commentary

The Year in Frivolity

by John Paschal

The 2015 baseball season arrived on a kind of timer, with a variety of settings for a variety of situations. First, newly minted Commissioner Rob Manfred mandated a series of pace-of-play rules designed to shorten games to something less than *Ulysses*-type length. A batter would now have to keep at least one foot in the batter's box during an at-bat, and, perhaps more importantly, it would need to be his foot and not someone else's. In addition, the new rules called for a prompt return to play after TV commercial breaks, meaning viewers would now have less time to weigh the relative merits of Viagra and Cialis while the pitcher tried to remember precisely where he had concealed the pine tar.

On a separate setting, the Washington Nationals were said to be right on time. Having added free agent ace Max Scherzer to an already stellar staff, the team from D.C. would defy contemporary status to make its mark on posterity—"one for the ages," experts claimed, "right there with the all-time teams." Meantime, the once woeful Astros were thought to be "a year away," still gathering markers en route to their long-awaited arrival. As for the defending American League champion Royals, they were just soooo last year.

The Cubs, meanwhile, boasted a stable of young talent and a hot new manager to guide it. The timing of Joe Maddon's hire, however, seemed curious if not alarmingly convenient. Following an investigation, Major League Baseball would clear the Cubs of tampering, but not before observers formed enduring opinions about the synchronized clocks of team and manager. Did Cubs fans care? Of course they didn't. They had been waiting since the year 1908.

With regard to those Cubs, the timing of Kris Bryant's debut fell beyond the rookie's command. Owing to a provision in baseball's service-time rules, the Cubs would gain an additional year of control if they delayed his arrival by the length of a fortnight. And so they did, despite the predictable protests—"like *clockwork*," you might have said—of Bryant's agent, the persistently loud Scott Boras. On a separate timetable stood Alex Rodriguez, returned to the Yankees' Opening Day lineup after a year-long suspension for the use of performance-enhancing drugs. Upon getting off to a surprisingly hot start, A-Rod would learn that boos are brief when replaced by the memory that flags fly forever.

And so continued another season of baseball, its games shorter but its months as ponderously, maddeningly and wonderfully long as ever.

April

On Opening Day at Wrigley Field, several malfunctioning restrooms force spectators to urinate in corners and into cups. As the Cubs-Cardinals game moves along, fans address the situation with shouts of "Bladder up!" and "We are seriously number 1!"

In his first start for the Marlins, newly acquired Matt Latos surrenders seven earned runs on six hits and two walks in less than an inning against the Braves. Asked later what he likes most about pitching for Miami, Latos says, "Frankly, it's the short work days."

Following his Opening Day shutout of the Phillies in Philadelphia, Red Sox starter Clay Buchholz receives a warning letter from Major League Baseball that he violated the new pace-of-play rules by stepping out of the batter's box after each at-bat. Later, all nine Phillies starters also receive letters, each praising the player for helping to reclaim the lost time by "stepping so efficiently from the batter's box and then returning so briskly to the dugout."

On April 11, Angels starter C.J. Wilson tells a reporter that team owner Arte Moreno hired a private investigator to follow him after he signed a five-year, $77.5 million contract in 2011. Asked how he detected the investigator, Wilson replies, "It was the British accent, plus the deerstalker hat emblazoned with the Angels logo."

In a newspaper interview, former minor leaguer and current NFL quarterback Russell Wilson claims he has considered returning to baseball, saying, "You never want to kill the dream of playing two sports." Later, Wilson maintains his chummy relationship with the press by telling reporters that his favorite part of baseball is reading coverage.

On April 13 in Chicago, newly signed Cubs ace Jon Lester attempts his second pickoff throw since 2013 and promptly launches it down the right field line, providing additional evidence that he suffers an unfortunate case of the yips. Asked repeatedly afterward if he suspects that his problem is uncorrectable, Lester offers an unfortunate case of the yeps.

In mid-April the commissioner's office launches an investigation into the increase in players testing positive for the anabolic steroid Stanozolol. Upon hearing the news, chemists alter a single molecule and change the name from Stanozolol to Stanozolmao.

In Cincinnati, Reds manager Bryan Price issues a public apology for his rant a night earlier, stating, "In my pre-game conversation with reporters yesterday, I used wholly inappropriate language to describe the media coverage of our team." Linguistics experts later agree, saying, "Instead of using the modern lingua franca of English, Price should have used Adai, Crowlitz Karkin or any of dozens of extinct North American languages so that no living person would be subjected to his potty-mouthed balderdash."

On April 23 in Chicago, benches clear and punches are thrown after Royals starter Yordano Ventura shouts at Adam Eaton upon fielding the White Sox outfielder's comebacker. Later, lip-readers determine Ventura told Eaton about the ending of this week's *Fresh Off The Boat* after the outfielder specifically asked him not to.

In late April, the Orioles give consideration to boycotting a game at Toronto's Rogers Centre because the new turf there is "too spongy." Asked to elaborate, Orioles outfielder Adam Jones says the turf "always seems to forget its wallet when we go to lunch."

On April 23, Marlins ace Jose Fernandez becomes a naturalized U.S. citizen during a ceremony in Florida. To honor the event, Fernandez grabs a bag of Funyons, plops onto the couch and watches six straight hours of pre-preseason football coverage.

Washington ace Max Scherzer tells a reporter in late April the National League should adopt the designated hitter, asking rhetorically, "Who would people rather see, a real hitter hitting home runs or a pitcher swinging a wet newspaper?" Asked to respond to Scherzer's comment, several teenagers reply non-rhetorically, "What's a newspaper?"

On April 27, after playing the season's first 19 games in domed stadiums, the Tampa Bay Rays finally prepare to play in an outdoor venue, Yankee Stadium. In the lead-up to the game, reporters scramble to FanGraphs.com when they hear Tampa Bay manager Kevin Cash describing what they believe is "Al Fresco's debut."

Following days of discussions, the Angels and Rangers agree to a trade sending Josh Hamilton from Los Angeles, where the outfielder has become a persona non grata, back to Texas, where, in 2012, many fans turned on him for what they considered derogatory statements. After the trade, Hamilton agrees to resolve an age-old California vs. Texas debate as to "whose boos are friendliest and whose condemnations are most laid-back."

May

In the midst of a Dodgers-Brewers game at Miller Park, play-by-play man Bob Uecker is trapped in the broadcast booth after a door malfunctions. Asked afterward to describe his whereabouts during the incident, Uecker deadpans, "Juuuuuuuuuuuuuuust a bit inside."

In Nashville for his first injury-rehab game, former AL MVP Josh Hamilton finds himself facing former AL Cy Young Award winner Barry Zito of Oakland's Triple-A affiliate, the Sounds. To honor the moment, famed country musician Merle Haggard rejiggers one of his biggest hits by singing "if we make it to September."

On May 14, former Yankees catcher Jorge Posada texts an apology to Alex Rodriguez after telling an interviewer that A-Rod and other PED users do not belong in the Hall of Fame. Rodriguez later says he would have texted back "but my thumbs are too bulky."

After Rangers closer Neftali Feliz blows his third save, in a game against the Indians, skipper Jeff Banister declares there are no defined roles in the Rangers bullpen. Later, Feliz says he's happy with the decision, as he is tired of the role of the Titanic in the movie *Titanic*.

Having fired Mike Redmond, the Marlins choose general manager Dan Jennings to move into the managerial role despite the fact that Jennings hasn't managed a team since he did so at a high school 30 years ago. Once in uniform, the new manager decides his first order of business is to tell his players to stop parking in the teachers' lot.

On May 18 in Houston, Astros right-hander Lance McCullers Jr. wears Batman cleats in his major league debut in a game against the A's. Later, when an attendant points to the thing on the locker room floor, not a single player will lay claim to the Joker jockstrap.

On May 22, Brewers pitcher Will Smith is suspended for having a foreign substance on his arm during a game against Atlanta. Later, the commissioner decides to increase his punishment by making him sit through the entirety of his namesake's movie *After Earth*.

In late May, Phillies manager Ryne Sandberg complains about the soft-rock music—Carole King, Eric Carmen, Kansas—played at Nationals Park whenever they take batting practice there. Observers later suggest Sandberg will eventually realize "it's too late" and that he's "all by myself" if not "dust in the wind."

In a poll released in late May, 55 percent of respondents reveal they prefer that a pitcher bats, as opposed to the DH. Per the same poll, 55 percent of respondents also prefer that rock stars create public policy and teenagers make key medical decisions.

Owing to torrential rains in the Houston area, Minute Maid Park suffers significant flooding during the Astros-White Sox game on May 30. Making conditions worse for Minute Maid is that rival operatives manage to stir in five metric tons of powdered Tang.

June

In response to critics who cite his .219 batting average and .673 OPS, Boston's David Ortiz tells a reporter, "I'm not washed up...I can wake up and hit, bro." Mindful, the critics agree to call him Rip Van Single, then, thinking the better of it, Bloop Van Single.

After Oakland's Pat Venditte suffers a right shoulder strain in early June, the Athletics place the ambidextrous pitcher on the 15-day disabled list. Dismayed, Venditte's most ardent supporters question why the A's can't place him on the 7 ½-day disabled list.

On consecutive nights, Boston's Wade Miley and Philadelphia's Ken Giles get into heated disputes with respective managers John Farrell and Ryne Sandberg. While many observers attribute the outbursts to "the millennials' tendency toward entitlement and narcissism," others attribute them to the Red Sox and Phillies being truly terrible teams.

Early in a flight to Dallas/Fort Worth, the Dodgers' charter plane is forced to make an emergency landing at LAX because of a mechanical problem. Reports later indicate that when the plane skidded to the end of the runway, several Dodgers, most notably Yasiel Puig, expressed fear that they "over-flew the cutoff, man."

News arrives in mid-June that eight of the top nine vote getters in AL All-Star balloting are Royals. Though most observers respond with skepticism, Kansas City manager Ned Yost calls it a "great example of North Korean-style democracy in action."

During a 17-3 rout at the hands of the Orioles, Phillies outfielder Jeff Francoeur takes the mound for mop-up duty but is forced to throw extra pitches because the Phillies bullpen phone is off the hook. In search of a solution, manager Ryne Sandberg attempts to email the bullpen but is thwarted when he can't fit the envelope into his cellphone.

Ranked last in team batting average and 28th in runs scored, the Mariners reassign hitting coach Howard Johnson and appoint seven-time All-Star Edgar Martinez to replace him. After the hiring, Martinez's first advice to the team is to "hit better and score more runs."

In Chicago versus the Rangers, White Sox third baseman Gordon Beckham strokes a walk-off home run on Father's Day just six weeks after hitting a walk-off homer on Mother's Day. Providing guidance, White Sox hitting coach Todd Steverson later pulls Beckham aside to say, "We shouldn't think about our fathers only on Father's Day, and our mothers only on Mother's Day, but on every day throughout the season."

Per an ESPN report on June 22, newly obtained documents prove that all-time hits leader Pete Rose bet on baseball games despite his protestations to the contrary. At breakfast the next day, Rose continues to claim innocence and then orders his eggs over-under.

Days after tossing his first no-hitter, Washington's Max Scherzer is cruising with a 5-1 eighth-inning lead when light-hitting Phillies outfielder Ben Revere slams just his fourth career homer. Inspired by the unlikely event, Pete Rose bets $5,000 that he, Pete Rose, will someday sport an attractive haircut.

In late June, burglars enter the home of the Rangers' Adrian Beltre and steal several keepsakes. Asked if the burglary angers him, Beltre replies, "Yeah, it really rubs my head the wrong way."

July

After Jerry Dipoto resigns as Angels GM, a California newspaper reveals Dipoto's Newport Beach house is for sale, and it includes a media room with padded walls. Left unreported is that the $2.9 million home also includes a suddenly empty doghouse.

In a poll conducted by ESPN, a majority of players choose the Cubs' Joe Maddon as the manager they'd most like to play for. Given a follow-up question, players are unanimous in selecting "no one" as the manager they'd most like to sit on the bench for.

In early July, a group of University of Toronto engineering students introduce a pitching machine that delivers knuckleballs. Following the machine's debut, several Blue Jays suffer second-degree electrical burns after dousing the thing with celebratory Gatorade.

After starting his career 0-for-66 at the plate, Chicago's Jon Lester finally registers a hit, an infield single off Cardinals starter John Lackey. Lester's journey to first base is delayed, however, when he must consult Google Maps to find it.

In early July, the Braves demote outfielder Joey Terdoslavich to Triple-A while calling up pitcher Mike Foltynewicz to replace him. GM John Hart later explains, "Despite our belief that Terdoslavich will become a really big name, we needed to call up Foltynewicz right now because we have a position open on a triple-word score."

In the sixth inning of a game at Wrigley Field, Cardinals catcher Yadier Molina begins arguing with plate umpire Pat Hoberg in the midst of a play. Asked later to identify the play, Molina replies, *The Importance of Being Earnest But Also Somewhat Irrational.*

After the Twins give teammate Torii Hunter a pair of adult diapers in honor of his 40th birthday, on July 18, the Minnesota outfielder promptly begins wearing the diapers inside the visitors' locker room at O.co Coliseum. Upon getting word of the scene, officials at the notoriously sewage-plagued stadium ask Hunter "to go ahead and wear them throughout the remainder of the series."

On July 19, the Angels experience their first home rainout in 20 years. Meanwhile, about 100 miles south, the Padres are taking the usual steps to continue their 46-year drought.

In St. Louis, injured Cardinals starter Adam Wainwright is pressed into mound duty one day when the pitching machine at his eight-year-old daughter's softball game malfunctions. After the game, Wainwright reports his velocity was down, his control spotty, but his knowledge of *Frozen* and *How to Train Your Dragon* "much improved."

Just prior to a July 26 game against the Nationals, the Mets discover a baby raccoon in their clubhouse. Because urban raccoons are known to root around in garbage, the Mets later do the humane thing by relocating the little guy to the Detroit Tigers farm system.

In late July, PETA releases its list of the top 10 vegetarian-friendly ballparks, and at No. 3 is Nationals Park. Observers are surprised at the ranking, not because the stadium isn't veggie-friendly but because the disappointing Nats continue to cannibalize themselves.

With Houston leading the AL West, music superstar Taylor Swift announces she will move her Minute Maid Park concert from Oct. 13 to Sept. 9 to clear a playoff date for the Astros. Taking heed, the A's inform what's left of Lynyrd Skynyrd that they can visit plumbing-challenged O.co Coliseum "at any time" to play their song "That Smell."

On July 28, Mets reliever Jenrry Mejia receives a 162-game ban for a second failed PED test. Mejia later tells the press, "I rreeally, rreally rregrret getting caught rred-handed."

In late July, Mike Hill, the Marlins' president of baseball operations, tells the press, "I would hope our fans are educated enough to see what we're doing here." Afterward, fans respond by saying that what Marlins management is apparently doing is waking after naptime, going potty, having a juice box and watching cartoons.

Having made a flurry of offseason deals, Padres GM A.J. Preller shocks baseball by standing pat at the trade deadline, claiming the team can contend despite its losing record. Inspired, Padres fans stick to their own approach by shrugging and heading to the beach.

August

On Aug. 1 against the Nationals, the Mets' Lucas Duda hits home runs in each of his first two at-bats, meaning his last eight hits have been homers. In the eighth inning, his RBI double puts an end to his streak but does secure his new nickname, Octobomb.

A day after calling Jose Bautista a "nobody" via Twitter, Royals starter Yordano Ventura apologizes, calling the Toronto slugger "a great human being." Thinking his apology inadequate, Ventura later issues via Instagram a Photoshopped image of Bautista's head on a body that includes Ghandi's legs, Mother Teresa's torso, St. Francis of Assisi's hairshirt and the L.A. Dodgers' checkbook.

In the eighth inning of a game against the Giants, Braves catcher A.J. Pierzynski attempts to frame a David Aardsma pitch that bounced about three feet in front of the plate. Inspired, former major leaguer and prison inmate Lenny "Dude" Dykstra attempts to cash a check that bounced about three feet in front of the bank.

After the hard-hitting Blue Jays score 26 runs in a sweep of the Twins, outfielder Torii Hunter says Toronto's hits "sound like car crashes." In response, a National Leaguer claims soft-hitting San Diego's hits "sound like Priuses idling on a grassy lawn."

On Aug. 4, three days after handing the general manager position to Al Avila, Tigers owner Mike Illitch finally informs Dave Dombrowski he's out of a job. Local pundits respond by saying they haven't seen so egregious a lame duck since 2012, when Johnny Damon last threw to home plate at Comerica Park.

In the ninth inning of a game in Kansas City, Tigers catcher James McCann glares at the Royals' Alex Rios because he thinks Rios is stealing signs at second base. Claiming innocence, Rios later explains he wasn't stealing signs so much as borrowing them.

Upon returning to the Marlins after his demotion to Triple-A, outfielder Marcell Ozuna tells reporters the minor leagues were "like a jail." Later, after toiling for one of the worst teams in the major leagues, Ozuna tells the same reporters that playing for the Marlins is "like a Stalin-era gulag but with worse decor."

On Aug. 18 the world's No.1 golfer, Jordan Spieth, throws out the ceremonial first pitch prior to the Mariners-Rangers game in Arlington. After allowing three earned runs on two doubles and a homer in the first inning, Rangers starter Chi Chi Gonzalez finds a measure of inspiration by asking for, but being denied, a mulligan.

After allowing two home runs to Yankees rookie Greg Bird during a game in New York, Twins starter Ervin Santana calls homer-friendly Yankee Stadium "a joke." Upon reflection, Santana admits that he also calls his hanging slider "a good straight man."

In the aftermath of Mike Fiers' no-hitter against the Dodgers, photos emerge on social media that appear to show a foreign substance on the Astros starter's glove. Fiers takes immediate issue with the "foreign substance" claim, saying he got it at a local Wal-Mart.

After his trade to the Dodgers, Chase Utley takes out a full-page ad to thank the Phillies franchise and its fans, ending his missive with "WFC forever!" Those who recall the Phillies' 2008 World Series parade know immediately what "WFC" means, while others need reminding that it stands for "we (frigging) choked" in 2011.

Following a 6-3 loss to the Rockies on Aug. 26, Atlanta starter Shelby Miller sees his record fall to 5-11 despite maintaining a 2.62 ERA. In response, several old-school observers claim Miller simply lacks "the will to win," while several new-school observers claim Miller simply lacks "the ability to leave the Atlanta Braves."

On Aug. 27 in Seattle, the White Sox take the field in 1976 throwback uniforms that include collared jerseys. For further period authenticity, the players also form Apple Computer, release *Frampton Comes Alive!* and, finally, create the Toronto Blue Jays.

A newspaper account on Aug. 27 reveals that Nationals pitcher Max Scherzer gave catchers Wilson Ramos and Jose Lobaton expensive Hublot watches for catching his recent no-hitter and one-hitter, respectively. Ramos and Lobaton later report that though fancy, the watches do not indicate when it is time for the Nationals to panic.

Per reports in late August, Athletics president Mike Crowley asks MLB to alter the team's 2016 schedule due to the extreme amount of travel the Athletics will have to undertake. In response, the commissioner's office tells Crowley, in effect, to take a hike.

On the same day Jack Zduriencik is dismissed as general manager, the Mariners also demote catcher Mike Zunino to Triple-A. Afterward, local pundits observe that while it's a bad time for Z's in Seattle, the games themselves are still a good time for zzz's.

To rally his team in the 14th inning of a game against the Giants, L.A.'s Kiké Hernandez arrives in the dugout wearing a banana-shaped jacket. Later, having joined teammates in a wild celebration of L.A.'s 5-4 win, Hernandez is placed on the DL with "bruising."

September

News arrives on Sept. 1 that a chickenpox outbreak has hit the Royals and at least two players are infected. Reacting to the news, several observers point to Yordano Ventura as the probable disease vector, as he has been acting like a five-year-old all season.

In early September, reports indicate Hanley Ramirez's failed outfield experiment has ended, and the former infielder will move to first base. Immediately after the announcement, experts are not surprised the news went completely over Ramirez's head and he later he had trouble relaying it to teammates.

Owing to Atlanta's 8-2 loss to Washington on Sept. 5, starter Shelby Miller sees his winless streak reach 20 games. Afterward, Miller is surprisingly upbeat, saying he's thrilled about his shot at the Washington Generals Award For Achievement In Futility.

On Sept. 8, Major League Baseball releases its 2016 regular season schedule. Key dates include Jackie Robinson Day on April 15; the All-Star Game on July 12; and New York Yankees On National Television Day on dates too numerous to print with expensive ink.

After Washington's crushing 8-7 loss to the Mets on Sept. 8, Nationals fans gather to boo manager Matt Williams at the conclusion of his postgame press conference. For the sake of convenience, the Nationals front office responds by scheduling what it calls a "boo conference," a "hiss conference" and, lastly, an "applaud his inevitable firing conference."

On Sept. 8, Royals pitcher Johnny Cueto disappoints hundreds of fans by failing to show up for a scheduled meet-and-greet that was to include a Johnny Cueto look-alike contest. Upon staging a second Johnny Cueto look-alike contest the next night, organizers are obliged to declare a first-place tie when no one shows up.

As part of a lottery for postseason tickets, the Cubs post a survey that asks, "Which of the following words would you use to describe yourself as a Cubs fan: casual, loyal, partier, passionate?" In answering a follow-up question, 100 percent of fans check the box reading, "Of *course* I wouldn't lie about my passion and loyalty; why would you even ask that?!"

After losing a bet on the University of Texas-Notre Dame football game in early September, White Sox pitcher John Danks is forced to wear a leprechaun costume during warm-ups prior to a game against the Twins. Inspired, Danks later decides to form a brotherhood with two other mythical creatures: 1998 McGwire and 1998 Sosa.

After blowing leads in consecutive games against the first-place Mets, Nationals reliever Drew Storen suffers a broken thumb when he punches his locker in frustration. Later, Storen advises embattled manager Matt Williams to avoid the same fate "because you're gonna need that thumb when Lerner tells you to hit the road."

When L.A.'s Adrian Gonzalez reaches into the stands for a foul pop-up during a game against the Rockies, a fan in the first row tugs violently on the first baseman's arm in an apparent effort at a souvenir. Afterward, the man explains he was indeed trying to add his collection of players calling him a douchebag.

Upon his first visit to Philadelphia following his trade to the Nationals, closer Jonathan Papelbon tells the media he was "one of the few (Phillies) that wanted to actually win." Later, having allowed a game-tying homer in the bottom of the 10th only to see the Nationals reclaim the lead in the 11th, Papelbon amends his statement by saying he "was one of the few (Nationals) that wanted to actually blow the save before notching the statistical win."

On Sept. 14 in Atlanta, the AL East-leading Blue Jays use an open date to attend the season-opening Monday Night Football game between the Eagles and the Falcons. Midway through the first quarter, the Blue Jays look on as the referee returns from a video replay and flags the Toronto offense for unnecessary roughness.

After Mike "Moose" Moustakas sets a Royals record with nine runs batted in in a win against the Orioles, executives at Warm Springs Ranch—home of the famed Budweiser Clydesdales—give their newborn foal the name "Moose." In recognition of the season-long antics of Kansas City's most temperamental pitcher, they also name the horse's ass "Yordano."

In announcing the creation of the Esurance MLB Awards, on Sept. 15, Major League Baseball introduces 24 award categories that include Best Social Media Personality, Best Fan Catch and Best Celebrity Fan. Experts agree, however, that the most hotly contested category will be The Award For The Fan Who Most Quickly Mutes Christopher Russo.

In mid-September, Toronto pitcher David Price divulges via Twitter that team-mate Munenori Kawasaki uses the name "Michael Jordan" when ordering coffee at Starbucks. He also divulges that teammate Troy Tulowitzki uses the name "oft-injured Sam Bowie."

After Kansas City's Alex Rios homers in the fifth inning of a game in Cleveland, the Progressive Field pyrotechnics operator surprises fans by igniting the fireworks normally reserved for Indians home runs. Later in the inning, the operator surprises fans again when he throws confetti and blows a celebratory bugle while showing a scoreboard replay of the Cuyahoga River fire of 1969.

During a Phillies home date, fans at Citizens Bank Park receive Pope Francis baseball cards in honor of the upcoming papal visit to Philadelphia. Upon turning to the back of the card, the fans are delighted to see that Pope Francis boasts a fielding percentage of 1.000, owing in large part to quick hands and papal infallibility.

In mid-September, Gatorade introduces a pair of virtual-reality goggles that allow each user to experience an at-bat from the perspective of Washington star Bryce Harper. At the same time, Gatorade also reveals plans for similar goggles that allow each user to experience a want ad from the perspective of current Washington manager Matt Williams.

News arrives on Sept. 17 that former big leaguer Rafael Palmeiro has signed with the independent Sugar Land Skeeters to play with his 25-year-old son, Patrick. In a press conference, the elder Palmeiro explains that he is looking forward to joining "the millennials," but only later does he discover, upon learning that "Skeeters" is an idiomatic term for "mosquitoes," that he is joining what experts call "the malarials."

After Pedro Strop halts a ninth-inning rally to close a 5-4 victory over the Cardinals at Wrigley Field, the Cubs reward the reliever with a "beach vacation" that includes fruity drinks, sun block and a lounge chair in a sand-filled kiddie pool next to his locker. Meanwhile, across town, the White Sox reward closer David Robertson—he of the seven blown saves and four losses—with a "Siberian vacation" that includes bootleg vodka, fingerless mittens and a straight-backed chair in a peat bog inside the meat freezer.

On Sept. 19 the Angels lose primary set-up man Joe Smith to a sprained ankle after he stumbles on some steps at the team hotel in Minneapolis. Asked how it happened, Smith replies, "Contrary to the corporate catchphrase, they did not leave the light on for me."

According to a report in late September, an investment group has proposed building a new spring training facility for the Braves on a former garbage dump in Florida. In related news, a separate group has proposed building a new Phillies facility atop a garbage barge in the Subtropical Convergence Zone of the North Pacific.

In efforts to end the Curse of the Billy Goat and send the Cubs to their first World Series title since 1908, organizers in Chicago invite five competitive eaters to devour an entire goat at a public event. Afterward, many observers declare the effort a success while others express misgivings that they just ate Bill Buckner.

After Jonathan Papelbon hits Baltimore's Manny Machado with a fastball in the ninth inning of a game in Washington, MLB suspends the Washington closer for a period of three days. On the fourth day, and even more so on the fifth, Papelbon is dismayed that no one—not even a teammate—has come to get him down.

In Chicago for a key series against the Cubs, Pittsburgh's Andrew McCutchen arrives at the team hotel to find his room has not undergone housekeeping service. The Pirates later learn a lesson in irony when, in the second inning of game three, Cubs ace Jake Arrieta slams a homer off of A.J. Burnett's room-service fastball.

After Bryce Harper fails to effusively hustle on his eighth-inning pop-out in a game against the Phillies, closer Jonathan Papelbon confronts him in the dugout and wraps a hand violently around the outfielder's throat. Afterward, Papelbon tells the press, "Well, in my defense, I'm new here, and I just thought the Nationals enjoyed choking."

In the aftermath of the Papelbon-Harper incident, the Nationals suspend the closer for the rest of the season and also remove Papelbon jerseys from the team store at Nationals Park. To replace the Papelbon jerseys, the store begins stocking Harper Protective Turtlenecks And Fortified Bowties.

After getting hit by a pitch in a game against the Reds, Cubs first baseman Anthony Rizzo joins Don Baylor as the only players in major league history to notch 30 hit by pitches and 30 homers in a season. Asked how he feels about the achievement, Rizzo says, "Sore."

In advance of the Dodgers' trip to New York to face the Mets in the National League Division Series, LA Metro taunts the New York Mass Transit Authority by tweeting, "(P)lease tidy up the 7 train, @Dodgers blue is coming to town." Meanwhile, Citi Field parking attendants taunt their Nationals Park counterparts by tweeting, "You can go ahead and tidy up your lots for next year."

One Draft or Two?

by Kiley McDaniel

Major League Baseball makes tweaks to the rules for the domestic draft and international signing process with each new Collective Bargaining Agreement (CBA). The current CBA expires on Dec. 1, 2016, and this next set of rule tweaks is the most anticipated in recent memory because MLB's recent hints and moves may bring an international draft to fruition.

Your reaction to those words depends on how closely you've been following this story. For casual fans, the concept of all the players entering pro ball through the same mechanism, like the National Basketball Association and National Hockey League drafts, seems equitable, exciting and easier to follow. For fans following this multi-year arc more closely, the experience is more like raising a puppy: constantly hoping to avoid a mistake and ultimately powerless to stop whatever is going to happen.

The Current Draft System

Before I jump into possible changes, I'll first lay out the current rules for the draft and the international system. The latter is commonly called July 2, referring to the first day 16-year-old players are eligible to sign.

Draft picks and corresponding bonus pool money are handed out in reverse order of the standings, with 12 competitive balance picks added to smaller-market clubs after the first and second rounds and compensation picks moving among teams based on free-agent signings. Clubs can trade only the competitive balance picks, and some teams already have shown an affinity to acquire those picks. Apart from the dozen competitive balance picks that are new to this current CBA, this is essentially how picks have been dispersed for a long time.

The big difference in the most recent CBA into how players are drafted and/or signed as a whole is the bonus pool. Picks used to have a suggested slot bonus amount that was used largely for negotiation purposes, whereas now the slot amounts for each pick accumulate into a pool that comes with a soft cap. The penalty for going more than a few percentage points over the cap is a loss of one or multiple future first-round picks. Clubs have deemed this too big a penalty to go well over their pool. The one loophole to spend much higher is an unlimited number of $100,000 or lower bonuses permitted after the top 10 rounds, but that level of player isn't enough to move the needle, strategically speaking.

Effectively, MLB has instituted a hard cap on draft spending, which is exactly what it wanted to do. Owners want certainty and cost controls for (mostly) financial and (also) public relations reasons, while the MLB Players' Association (MLBPA) doesn't want to start allowing salary caps at any level, for fear it could spread to the big leagues and limit earning power for the top players. MLB did a good job setting the incentives and penalties in the draft system so that a soft cap the MLBPA would agree to would effectively be treated like a hard cap.

The Current July 2 System

MLB was looking to replicate this sort of result with the international signing rules but slightly misfired, and the free market ran a semi truck through the hole, which will certainly be patched in the next CBA. The July 2 market used to be completely open in every sense of the word: background checks, confirming identities and ages of players, steroid tests, open prospect games for all 30 teams to scout, policing of contact between teams and players, and any sort of spending limits or controls were all essentially absent, so MLB made a concerted effort in the last five to 10 years to clean that up.

MLB has done a great job with confirming identities, steroid testing, registering players and holding open, MLB-run showcases and games for prospects. The process now runs more smoothly, and the only real downside is that the teams with big networks don't have the opportunity to hoard or hide players from the smaller-budgeted teams with smaller international staffs.

Where the industry as a whole feels MLB has gone wrong is in its attempt to put in a soft spending cap system with penalties, which it did successfully in the draft. The bonus pools are, like the draft, done in reverse order of the standings but without any compensatory or competitive balance considerations. Teams are able to trade up to 50 percent of their pool or trade for up to 50 percent more to adjust their pool to fit their spending needs, with a handful of teams still opting to spend something close to a theoretical minimum on players each year and leaving bonus pool money on the table.

MLB ran into some unintended consequences when it turned out the penalties weren't harsh enough to dissuade teams from going over their spending pools. With a two-year ban on signings over $300,000 for going well over the pool, teams can simply roll three years of spending into one year and get the added benefit of having those player mature faster than if they signed 16-year-olds over a three-year period. It's simply a matter of moving budget money from one year to the next.

For teams that used to spend freely and now have limits, it's a way for them to spend whatever they want, just condensed into a smaller window. A couple of teams have done this each year of the new CBA. In last year's period, the Yankees and Red Sox both set new standards for spending. It looks like the Dodgers may have joined that club, having spent roughly $40 million in the first few months of the 2015-2016 period and almost assured to spend more.

Another unforeseen by-product of this new rule comes from the 20 or so teams that treat the spending pools like a hard cap. When teams have a hard cap they can't go over, they have to find more creative ways to generate value. In the past, teams could spend their budget, then find an exceptional player and lobby ownership for extra money to sign him, but now many owners won't allow their teams to incur penalties. The way to get around this is to reach verbal deals with players well ahead of time, to lock in discounts for the risk of committing to a 14-year-old. In the old system, verbal deals were common, but normally only for top players who found a high bid a few months early or lesser players who would be packaged with top players.

Early in the current CBA, teams so routinely locked in players eight to 12 months early for a discount that players now are getting locked up that early for no discount, or even a premium. Since the practice is so widespread and so many teams were willing to take on the risk of the player changing/maturing in that eight to 12 month period, it became a market risk almost all teams began assuming at some level, so the practice of seven figure discounts is now rare. This practice always has been illegal, but it almost never has been enforced since it's so common, so it is hard to prove and, until recently, wasn't seen as a problem.

Recent July 2 Rule Changes Map MLB's Course

The downside of these early deals is that teams can try to wiggle out of a deal if a player gets hurt and just hope the bad buzz in the industry for doing so won't affect future signings. The Yankees are one prominent team that spent huge in the 2014 period, incurring more than $30 million in bonuses and penalties, a stark contrast to a just over $2 million bonus pool. The Yankees had a verbal deal with Dominican shortstop Chris Torres for $2.1 million; he was set to be one of the top players in their 2014 spending spree. After an injury dampened excitement about the player, the Yankees got out of the agreement, but after all the other big spending teams had already allocated their money. Torres ended up signing for $375,000 with the Mariners, which looks like a nice value buy for Seattle, but the youngster may have only one payday in his life, and the process betrayed him. There was a trail of messages from Torres' representative and the Yankees to corroborate his story, so the Yankees paid a fine of $20,000 to MLB.

Some teams saw this and similar situations as an opportunity to wait until closer to July 2 to lock up any players or shop in bulk at lower price points in an effort to find more bargains. One example was Venezuelan righty Alvaro Seijas, who is rumored to have turned down multiple seven-figure offers before the offers dried up when money was allocated, ultimately settling for $725,000 with St. Louis.

MLB's response to this epidemic was to pass a new set of rules to discourage the practice, akin to the "nudge" in social science, since the action was already illegal but basically unenforceable. It barred using major league team facilities for non-MLB-run events if the players hadn't already turned 16, in an effort to cut down on early evaluations of players in prospect leagues with organized showcases and games, giving scouts extra game looks they didn't get five to 10 years ago.

This approach merely moved those workouts to poorer quality fields rather than stopping them and the evaluations that precipitate early deals. MLB also barred players under 16 from going to team academies for private workouts. Players can stay for up to 30 days at an academy to give an interested team a long, private look, but smaller-budget teams often have trouble getting top players into their academies; the agents give the teams that often spend big money a better chance at private evaluation. The change hasn't done much so far, as the top handful of players who are eligible to sign on July 2, 2016 were locked up to multi-million dollar deals before July 2, 2015, and in some cases months before it.

While both of these rules, along with more MLB-run events, will make early evaluations and thus early deals less prevalent, teams wonder if the cost is worth it. Some players who turn 16 earlier but are eligible to sign the same day as kids who turn 16 just before the signing date have an advantage. For players who turn 16 later in the period, Jan. 1 is the day they can take part in academy visits and non-MLB events held at MLB academies. To curb a practice (early verbal deals) that happened due to a system MLB created (bonus pools), the league is making it harder for teams to evaluate players as a method for fixing the problem it created.

This seems like a half-measure by MLB, which has a larger vision for where July 2 can go. Scouts are starting to see that vision when they connect the dots of MLB's actions in Latin America. MLB would like the July 2 season to start—meaning teams start evaluating players in earnest and target players for deals—on Jan. 1. Presumably, verbal deals made in that six-month period are acceptable for MLB, and it would be a more streamlined, equitable process in which a domestic scouting director could fly down for a few events and, until Jan.1, have nearly as much knowledge about the class as an international scouting director.

Clubs don't like this direction for July 2, as they value an open market with freedom for the savviest teams when it comes to strategy and scouting to get an edge. Big-budget teams would like no spending restrictions and small-budget teams would like a hard cap, but they all tend to agree MLB should let teams scouts players as they see fit and not obscure the process with rules enacted only to pave over a mistake MLB made.

Possible Changes

That was quite a windup to set the stage for where the new CBA could take us, but it seemed appropriate to cover the big issues, which tend to be mostly on the international side. The short version of the buzz about possible changes is that the owners and MLB want it and, given its actions in the last two CBAs, the players' union will ask for some minor concessions to approve the changes, like expanding Super Two arbitration or raising the minimum salary.

The union represents amateur players in CBA negotiations only because the draft is tied to big league free agency via compensation picks. The union likes having this power as a bargaining chip to get something it wants for big leaguers, while owners like that the union will let them do almost anything they want to the draft and July 2 short of a formal hard salary cap.

The two broad ways MLB could approach this issue are to have two separate drafts for international and domestic amateur players or combine them into one draft, akin to the NBA and NHL.

The two-draft system would run similarly to how things run now, with the main difference being that instead of having a bonus pool of money with which to go out and sign players, teams would have a certain number of picks with which to draft them. And those picks would probably come with hard, required slots that couldn't be negotiated up or down. Since some teams, like Miami or Baltimore, typically spend $1 million or so on international players each year and the top pick in the draft would come with a required bonus around $4 million, MLB would also have to include either the trading of picks (the likely choice and the simplest solution) or a soft slot on each pick that would allow a lower budgeted team to spend only $1 million on a non-consensus player with the first pick. There are other things to work through. Can players declare for the draft or opt to wait a year? What happens to undrafted players? But this option is logistically feasible, and those are smaller details.

A one-draft system is much more complicated to pull off. MLB would have to create an even playing field in negotiations for the 16-year-old Dominican player with limited game experience and no college options versus a 21-year-old player at an SEC school whom teams have watched for four or five years at the top amateur levels. That is the main challenge of this configuration, because, at some point, either a team's domestic or international director will have the final choice of whom to pick, and the domestic player will almost always win out due to familiarity and level/quality of information. To put a 16-year-old kid from a third-world country into a hard-slotted draft with no negotiation leverage from a college commitment seems destined to sell those kids out even further. It sounds like the owners like this idea in theory for the broad optics, but executives think the aforementioned and other complications make this a secondary option.

One solution would be to move the international signing age to 18 years old and create teams and leagues run by MLB to mirror the high school/college system in the States. The problem there is you'd have to cover a number of countries with this system, not just the Dominican Republic and Venezuela. That's a long way to go and a lot of money to spend changing the culture and training process of a pretty efficient system—mostly for PR reasons—just so you can have one draft.

The Big Questions

I didn't go into extreme depth in the last section, since it's all speculative at this point, and it seems more important to address the underlying assumptions that would drive this decision rather than the potential details.

Should July 2 be run like the draft?

This gets at the question that will decide if there's one draft or two. At a deeper level, it's asking if kids in third-world countries without a high school/college team system should be treated the same as domestic players. You can probably guess that I think it's silly to jump through all these hoops to try to make the two markets as similar as possible when they're clearly two completely separate markets that should be treated as such.

Could the Dominican turn into another Puerto Rico?

If there's one draft, and maybe even if there are two, scouts have speculated that MLB—in an effort to streamline and control the signing process—could move the international signing age to 18, coinciding with the draft. International scouts point to Puerto Rico as a cautionary tale about a baseball hotbed which, due to being added to the domestic draft pool, had its signing age jump from 16 to 18 a few decades ago. The talent dropped off significantly.

Upon further inspection, it appears the age shift happened after a historic wave of talent, and we may be coming into another one, including Astros shortstop Carlos Correa, Indians shortstop Francisco Lindor and Twins pitcher Jose Berrios, and 2016 may be the best draft class from the island in some time.

While the example is weaker now with Puerto Rico's resurgence, the case for Dominican talent drying up always was weak. Puerto Rico has options for young people, like basketball or advanced education, various industries, etc. In the Dominican, baseball is still almost the only way for most young boys to get ahead through sports, and the economy depends on MLB's money. Changing the signing age would shift incentives and the development process, but that process is efficient now and would be efficient then. The free market has teams paying players who are trained by buscones—agent-prospectors—who put resources toward players as young as 12 years old. The Dominican Republic will always be a power in producing players, regardless of slight rule changes.

More developed countries with strong economies and more diverse sports cultures, like Venezuela, may see a shift if the signing age changes and buscones become less aggressive in developing players at a younger age. That said, since we're starting with the secondary countries and not the Dominican or Cuba, the effect would be lessened. I think MLB should try to dictate as little as possible about the broad parameters of how/when teams can scout and sign players, since unintended consequences have caused more problems than they solve.

How do you get every country to buy into a draft system?

This is the biggest logistical question surrounding the international draft. A number of countries have unique systems for their amateur players to enter MLB. Mexico runs its teenagers through its pro league, and those teams keep the majority of the bonuses MLB pays the players. Japan drafts its teenagers into its pro system and keeps them until at least their mid-20s. South Korea and Taiwan generally put kids through high school and allow them to sign at 18. Most Latin American and European players sign at 16.

Then there's Cuba. In short, I would assume Cuba would get a cut of what's paid any player it allows to leave the country (at least 10 percent), and some age/experience benchmark would be set to allow certain players (think White Sox first baseman Jose Abreu) to become a free agent rather than subject to the draft.

Cuba has a steady flow of multi-million dollar bonus caliber teenage players emerging every year and a diluted, but still existent, pool of players in their mid-to-late-20s with big league potential. The country is in the awkward position of having no way to benefit from Cubans getting MLB money, as the players escape the country and legally aren't allowed to send money back due to the U.S. embargo.

The Dominican government doesn't get money directly from July 2 prospects (it waives the income tax for these deals), but the money comes back to the island in many ways. With Cuba-U.S. relations improving, Cuban players (and their money) may be allowed back in the country soon, but given the high profile nature of the recent wave of Cuban players, their government could negotiate a cut of any player that signs. MLB would like a formal, more cost-controlled way for these players to enter the league and it would also greatly reduce of eliminate unsafe defections.

These relationships are all at equilibrium, and a draft would disrupt each situation. Venezuela allows MLB to sign its prospects but has put new restrictions on when MLB scouts can come into the country. Asking a country, especially one with a semi-hostile government, to allow its players to enter MLB only through a hard-slotted draft with no negotiation power would be a hard sell. Scouts think the economic reality in Venezuela is weak enough to work out a deal, and the Dominican relies on MLB to boost its economy, so both eventually should get done.

That said, the concept of an international draft is to keep spending down, and that works only if every country is included, because one exception (think 20-year-old Cuban second baseman Yoan Moncada, whom the Red Sox spent $63 million to sign last year) is enough to undermine the whole process. Do you think MLB can convince Mexico and Cuba and Venezuela and the Asian and European countries all to submit to a new, more stringent system of rules?

I would tend to say no, but MLB has a trump card: money. The upside for MLB of all these teams going over their bonus pools is that the penalty money—expected to be a smallish, seven- or low eight-figure slush fund once the CBA expired in 2016—is already around $80 million and likely ends up around $100 million. Paving over political and economic differences can be done when there's an unexpected nine-figure pile of money sitting around. The rules state this penalty money goes to a general international fund to be used at MLB's discretion. Ironically, the penalty money teams are sending to MLB so they can stockpile talent before a draft is instituted may actually be speeding up the process of a draft being created.

Does an international draft solve a problem?

I've given you all the information to make your own choice here. If you like controlling spending with an effective hard cap, then you'd take a step toward yes. If you like having every player in the world in a set system for signing with as few exemptions as possible, then that's another step toward yes. There also are plenty of things that would lead you toward no, like MLB's rules often having unintended consequences that muddy the waters in amateur markets rather than making things easier. Some clubs have complained that MLB should be more transparent with its rule-making and the international draft creation process, but since this is a small part of revenue to owners versus big league payrolls, there probably won't be much heat from ownership to MLB to be more open to suggestions.

To answer my question, I would lean toward no, but there's certainly a way to implement a two-draft domestic and international system that is a net positive for all involved (or, at least, not any worse than it is now). MLB hasn't tipped its hand yet. It appears to be working behind the scenes to get buy-in from all the involved countries, but it undoubtedly will float its proposal in the media before negotiations on the next CBA are closed.

Return of the Run

by Jeff Sullivan

R ob Manfred inherited a game in a crisis. Baseball wasn't dying, but it was in an increasingly bad way. As discussed as a daily occasion, game lengths were getting out of control, surging beyond the three-hour mark. And of at least equal concern: run-scoring was in a slump. It didn't get the attention of the game-length issue, but the commissioner certainly realized strikeouts were rising and offense was sinking. While there's no such thing as a specific point at which baseball becomes unwatchable, more time spent with less happening wasn't in the game's best interests in terms of gaining popularity. The game needed to speed up, and the game needed runs.

I'm not going to sit here and talk to you about pace of game. That's a good topic, but a different topic, and the early results are moderately encouraging. I just want to focus on the offense, and below is a plot of what Manfred was looking at when he took over the job. Here are the runs scored per nine innings, league-wide, on a month-to-month basis from 2000 through 2014.

Runs per 9 Innings by Month, 2000-2014

The trend in more recent years is clear. Curiously, starting around when PITCHf/x systems were installed everywhere, offensive levels started to drop. Some people pointed to the harsher anti-PED policies, but never mind the reasons – all that really mattered were the results. Teams stopped scoring. In September of 2014, the league average dropped below four runs per nine innings in a month for the first time this millennium. That was the last month of pre-Manfred baseball.

How do you fix offense, with pitchers only throwing harder and harder? It wasn't an easy question to answer. The point a lot of people would come to was that the strike zone would need to be adjusted, reduced. The called strike zone has gotten bigger every year for which we have data, and of course that works to the pitchers' advantage. Manfred did speak a few times about how he would monitor the size of the zone in 2015. So that issue was on his radar from the outset. It's something that might indeed be revisited.

The thing is, something unexpected happened. Manfred took over a game without enough runs, and on the surface, he didn't change anything. But let's go back to that first plot, only this time extending through 2015. The course of the trend was interrupted.

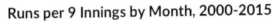

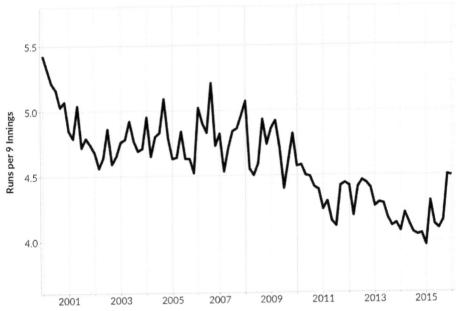

On the right side, the recovery is obvious, and it's sharp. In no month in 2015 did offense finish below four runs per nine, but it spiked later in the summer. Through the All-Star break, the league averaged 4.14 runs per nine, almost an exact match for the previous first half. But in 2014's second half, the average dropped to 3.98. And in the most *recent* second half, the average instead jumped to 4.45, the highest mark since the first half of 2010. This year's August saw run-scoring leap to 4.50 runs per nine, and then it stayed there in September. For much of the season, it felt like baseball's new normal. But then rather suddenly, runs returned, as under-the-radar as runs can ever be. Quietly, offense in baseball reached a level it hadn't seen in years.

It's one thing to observe something in the numbers, but it's quite another to explain it. And now this occurrence has some real significance, because if Rob Manfred wants to understand what's happening in the game today, it's important to know where the runs came from. What was behind the offensive resurgence?

To take something off the table early, it wasn't the strike zone. According to research by Jon Roegele, at no point did the zone shrink, so it's not like there was a midyear umpire conversation. The zone stayed as big as it's been, so as much as the nature of the strike zone is a story, for our purposes it's not a relevant story.

There's not much to be gleaned from strikeouts and walks. They stayed around the same levels. And though there was a slight hike in batting average on balls in play (BABIP), it was well within normal boundaries. It couldn't explain the magnitude of what took place down the stretch. The big explanation here is probably the obvious one: dingers. The home run is the most valuable type of hit, and as 2015 went on, home runs surged.

Here's an over-simplification: After major league teams hit close to 4,000 home runs in 2014, they ended 2015 much closer to 5,000. The total increased by 723. To get more precise, consider the rate of home runs on contact, where contact is defined as at-bats plus sacrifice flies minus strikeouts. Below is a plot of how that stat has fluctuated over 16 years.

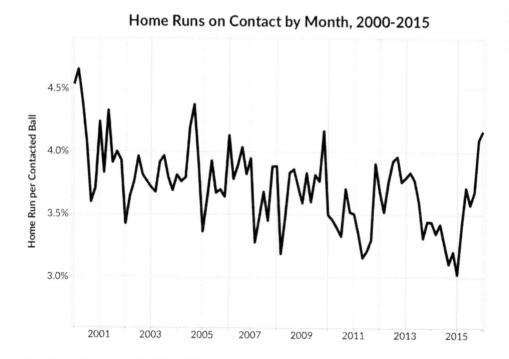

Home Runs on Contact by Month, 2000-2015

You can see the spike at the end, mirroring what happened with general run-scoring. Though strikeouts didn't meaningfully decline at any point in 2015, the quality of contact by hitters was improved. Home runs came back. And though this isn't shown, doubles and triples also increased. The suggestion is that balls were just hit harder. When they were hit, they were hit with greater authority.

If you take the All-Star break as dividing the season into "halves," then, since 2000, here are the top halves in rate of home runs on contact.

Highest HR/contact%, Season Halves, 2000 – 2015		
Half	Season	HR/Contact%
1st Half	2000	4.52%
2nd Half	2004	4.16%
1st Half	2001	4.10%
2nd Half	2015	4.08%
2nd Half	2001	3.96%

This most recent second half finished with the highest such rate since 2004. And though other halves are in the vicinity, the two halves from 2014 rank third-to-last and last in the sample. More recent years have tended to feature fewer home runs on contact. In that sense, 2015 was a throwback. September's rate of homers on contact was the highest rate in a month since August of 2004.

Our question has an explanation, itself asking another question. Why were there more runs? There were more home runs. So, why were there more home runs?

It's a difficult question to answer. Maybe that's surprising to you; maybe it isn't. I talked to a handful of front-office members, and they couldn't offer anything definitive. There are some theories, and some partial explanations, but it's hard to get all the way there.

Just to pick the low-hanging fruit, the 2014-2015 offseason did see some ballpark modifications, but nothing dramatic. The Mets made the biggest changes, at Citi Field, bringing in a part of their wall anywhere between five and 11 feet. When that was first confirmed, Mets general manager Sandy Alderson figured it would mean somewhere around 25 extra home runs, so that can be only a tiny part of this. The Padres brought in a Petco Park wall, but by only 34 inches. That would be difficult to even notice.

Two front-office members suggested, half-jokingly, "global warming?" There's a clearly understood relationship between air density and fly-ball distance, and this was a summer of warm temperatures. However, as compelling as the explanation would be, the average game temperature increased from 72.5 degrees in 2014 to just 73.8 degrees in 2015. Warmer, yes. More hitter-friendly on balance, yes. But physics-of-baseball authority Alan Nathan figures this doesn't get you too far. He wrote in a message: "I doubt one can account for an increase in HR production by a change in the mean temperature, certainly not one that small." He calculated in an earlier work that an increase of one degree Fahrenheit would boost home runs around 0.6 percent. In reality they increased more than 15 percent.

One thing I haven't mentioned yet: This was an incredible season for rookies, and especially for rookie hitters. Year over year, the league population remains similar, but it doesn't remain identical. This season saw one of the better collective rookie performances ever. After hitting 471 homers in 2014, rookies in 2015 surpassed 700. Without question, some of the home-run surge came from an improvement in hitter quality. Batters who played in 2014 but didn't play in 2015 averaged, in 2014, a 2.7 percent rate of home runs on contact. Batters who played in 2015 but didn't play in 2014 averaged, in 2015, a 4.1 percent rate of home runs on contact. League numbers will respond to the presence of guys like Kris Bryant and Miguel Sano. Again, it's a partial explanation. Now take all the other players, the players who played at least a little bit in each of the last two seasons. For each of them, I calculated their 2014 home-run-on-contact rates. Then I applied those rates to their 2015 numbers, weighted for playing time. At 2014 rates, those players would've been expected to hit almost 3,700 homers. Instead, they hit about 4,300. It works the same for pitchers, too. Based on 2014 numbers, the carryover pitchers would've been expected to allow a hair over 3,400 homers. They instead allowed 4,000.

In short, it isn't just about new talent. Rookie hitters were responsible for about 200 more home runs than usual. Rookie pitchers were responsible for about 50 more home runs than usual. But the total home-run increase was in the vicinity of 750. Carryover hitters hit more home runs than expected. Carryover pitchers allowed more home runs than expected.

At this point, to explain everything else, I think you consider two competing options. One is something you never can dismiss entirely: randomness. Sometimes things just happen, without rhyme or reason, because ultimately we're dealing with samples of data. It's possible the effect could be nothing. But then, one of the front-office members figured the effect is real, and another specifically said he didn't think it's random noise.

Which takes you to the other option, the one that sounds like a conspiracy theory. To directly quote one of the front-office people: "I'd guess it's the ball." To be absolutely clear, it's a guess, as noted. It's not that this individual knows anything in particular, and in fact, he couldn't say what about the ball might've changed. But you can't *not* think about it.

Obviously, small differences in the ball could have significant effects on where the ball goes. And obviously, small differences in the ball could presumably go by unnoticed, pitch to pitch. We'd be talking about something quite subtle. It's also not anything we could prove, and MLB itself would deny anything and everything. I wouldn't have even included these paragraphs if it weren't for someone in the industry making the same suggestion. It's a little out there. It could be taken as a real accusation. But it's not difficult to come up with a motive—more runs = good—and it's not like there are easy and obvious alternative explanations for the data. The ball started to fly. It's natural to be curious, and it's not all about the rookies.

As is often the case, we won't know more until we have more information. We won't know the real significance of this trend until we see how or whether it keeps up, which means we'll be waiting into 2016, trying to figure out if there's still offense in the game. We've been offered some relief from the lows of 2014, but this could have been a fleeting thing. It wouldn't be the first time.

But at least we get to wonder about this now. One year ago, it looked very well like offense was dying, and dying irreversibly. Like it would take a wholesale change to the strike zone to restore some semblance of balance. One year ago, strikeouts and pitchers were out of control. Strikeouts are still high, and velocities are still high, but in 2015 the hitters had a potent counter-attack: the dinger. They didn't make more contact, but it seems they made *better* contact, and that made the game more like how the game ought to be. There was more suspense in the moment, because the result of an at-bat wasn't a foregone conclusion.

Maybe MLB had something to do with that. Maybe it didn't. Ultimately, I can't know who's most responsible for the home-run increase. But one way or another, Rob Manfred now has a game that's taken some steps forward from where it was when he took office. So much for baseball moving glacially.

References and Resources

- FanGraphs & Baseball-Reference
- Jon Roegele, The Hardball Times, "Why is Run Scoring Depressed in September, and What Just Happened in August?," *hardballtimes.com/why-is-run-scoring-depressed-in-september-and-what-just-happened-in-august*
- Adam Rubin, ESPN.com, "Mets Tweaking Stadium Dimensions," *espn.go.com/mlb/story/_/id/11898412/new-york-mets-announce-tweaks-citi-field-dimensions*
- Corey Brock, MLB.com, "Padres poised to begin renovation plan at Petco," *m.padres.mlb.com/news/article/100668432/padres-poised-to-begin-renovation-plan-at-petco*
- Alan M. Nathan, Baseball Prospectus, "Baseball ProGUESTus: Global Warming and Home Runs: Is There a Connection?," *baseballprospectus.com/article.php?articleid=17249*

Random Developments

by Phil Birnbaum

What's the most famous sabermetric discovery since the *Bill James Baseball Abstract* era ended more than 25 years ago?

Most sabermetricians would probably say Voros McCracken's "DIPS" discovery. In 2001, McCracken published an article on the Baseball Prospectus website in which he made the claim that pitchers don't vary much in their ability to prevent hits on balls in play that stay in the park.

Sure, pitchers give up varying proportions of hits, but almost all of the variation in pitchers' long-term success is based on their strikeouts, walks, and home runs allowed. Once the ball is put into play, any differences are minimal—and those differences, small as they are, need to be reduced even further by factors outside the pitcher's control, like the defense behind him and the effects of the park.

I'd agree that the DIPS finding is one of the most important of the recent sabermetrics era. But I'd argue it for a different reason. In my view, McCracken's discovery is most significant not because of what it tells us about pitching and defense—important as that is—but because it ushered in an environment where sabermetrics started taking randomness seriously. DIPS started the "Luck Era."

You can phrase McCracken's hypothesis another way, as some do:

"Differences in outcomes among pitchers, on balls put into play, are largely a matter of luck."

Randomness is only one of the causes of the differences, but, as we will see, it is indeed the largest. And, because of that, the "luck" perspective on DIPS is the one that proved to be most useful. Because, if luck is the main reason Pitcher A allows a .340 batting average on balls in play (BABIP) while Pitcher B allows only .270…well, then, we can infer that Pitcher A's pitching statistics are going to be worse than his talent would suggest, while Pitcher B's stats are going to be "too good."

That's an important thing to know when forecasting next year's performance. If you can see that a pitcher's 4.70 ERA is really only 4.25 plus 0.55 points of "bad BABIP luck," that tells you he's probably going to be quite a bit better next year.

In other words: Voros McCracken's DIPS theory was an early—and very successful—attempt to separate the "signal" of a pitcher's talent from the "noise" of the randomness that affected his balls in play.

Dealing with randomness, in order to separate the signal from the noise, has been the focus of much of the important sabermetric work since then.

Some players have hit exceptionally well in clutch situations, while others have hit significantly worse. How much of that is random, and how much is real "clutch talent"?

What about hitting streaks (which Mitchel Lichtman explores elsewhere in this book)—real, temporary variations in talent, or just noise? Or unusual platoon splits, or how some players appear to "own" certain opposing pitchers? In the post-DIPS era, we are more willing to accept the influence of randomness, and we have developed methods to separate it from whatever real effect might exist.

Here's one prominent indication of how even mainstream sportswriting has accepted the idea that luck is a big factor in winning or losing. In *Moneyball*, Oakland A's GM Billy Beane famously says:

> *"My shit doesn't work in the playoffs. My job is to get us to the playoffs. What happens after that is fucking luck."*

What's impressive is not just that Beane recognized this, but how it's now almost the consensus wisdom in mainstream sportswriting—how short playoff series are pretty much a crapshoot.

This is now a popular subject even outside sports, how to separate luck from skill. Nate Silver published *The Signal and the Noise* in 2012. More pertinently, that same year saw the release of Michael Mauboussin's *The Success Equation—Untangling Skill and Luck in Business, Sports, and Investing.* His book is aimed at the business market, especially the finance industry–Mauboussin is a Wall Street investment specialist–but his examples draw heavily on the "luck" literature from sabermetrics, with Tom Tango's contributions (some of which I'll get to shortly) among those most prominently discussed.

And that literature, as far as I can tell, began in response to the debate about pitchers and balls in play.

McCracken's DIPS theory, so contrary to intuition, sparked a vigorous debate. Adherents said, "Look, the BABIP correlation from year-to-year is low, so Voros was right." Skeptics said, "Look, knuckleball pitchers seem to generate low BABIPs over their entire careers, so Voros was wrong."

Of course, those arguments are extremist caricatures. The question isn't black and white: "Do pitchers have control, or don't they?" The question is, "What proportion of observed variation in pitcher BABIP represents real differences in talent?"

In other words: *How much?* How much of BABIP is luck, and how much isn't?

Well, how do you figure that out? I'll get to the math in a bit, but let's start with a more intuitive explanation of how you can separate luck from skill.

Suppose you get 20 people to each toss a different fair coin 10 times each, and count the number of heads. One guy winds up with eight heads, and one guy winds up with only three. How much of that difference is because of luck, and how much is because of skill?

Well, clearly, 100 percent of the difference is luck. Fair coins don't differ in "skill," and, presumably, neither do tossers.

Now, you get the same 20 people to solve 10 easy calculus problems (if there is such a thing). Half of them solve them all; the other half, never having taken calculus, get none of them. In this case, the difference is, clearly, 100 percent talent.

Now, you combine the two into one test. After the combined 20 trials—half coins, and half calculus—one competitor has 16 successes, another has only three, and the rest are in the middle. Now, how much of the difference is skill, and how much is luck?

Well, it's more skill than luck. Because, the range of observations for the coin tossers is small, from three to eight, or some such. But the range of observations of the calculus is larger, from zero to 10, with nothing in between.

You measure the range by calculating the "standard deviation" (SD) of the set of observations. If the data forms a bell-shaped curve, you can just eyeball the SD—it's half the horizontal distance, symmetrical around the peak that contains about two-thirds of the observations. Basically, the SD is "approximately" the typical distance from the center.

If we were to calculate the SD for the combined test, we might get something like, 5.3.

In this case, we might not have a perfect bell curve for the coin tosses, and the calculus results certainly don't form a curve (everything's either zero or 10). But you can calculate the SD mathematically. It turns out that for the calculus problems, the SD is exactly five (which makes sense, since the average is five, and every solver is exactly five points away from average, one way or the other). You can also figure out that, typically, the SD of the number of heads in 10 coin tosses is about 1.6. (That may not be the exact case every time, because every set of coin tosses is random, but if you try it at home, you should get something close to that.)

So, for the total 20-trial experiment, we can say that:

- SD(coins) = 1.6
- SD(calculus) = 5.0

  Or,

- SD(luck) = 1.6
- SD(skill) = 5.0

So, skill is about three times as important as luck, in one sense.

This works fine for our contrived example, where we knew that half the task was coins, and half was calculus. But what about real-life tasks, like preventing hits on balls in play? How do we decompose that?

"Solving DIPS" is the title of a paper released in August of 2003, itself a summary of prior discussion on the now-defunct Baseball Primer website. There, three saber-metricians—Erik Allen, Arvin Hsu and Tom Tango—did the hard work of figuring out how big a difference in luck you'd expect, and also figuring how big the differences are in pitcher talent, fielder talent, and park effects. For the record, here's what they got. For a pitcher who gives up 700 balls in play:

Expected Differences	
Factor	SD
Park Effects	.004
Team Defense	.006
Pitcher BABIP skill	.010
Luck	.016

So, that's why pitchers appear to be so inconsistent in their observed BABIP—by far, the largest contributing factor is random chance.

Now, why was this DIPS study so important in how sabermetrics treats the evaluation of luck? Because it was the first—that I know of—to figure out the easy way do to the decomposition.

That method is based on one of the most basic relationships in the field of statistics. If two variables are independent—that is, the value of one of them doesn't give you any information that helps you guess the value of the other—they form a pythagorean relationship. Since talent and luck are indeed independent—you don't expect good players to be an more or less lucky than bad players—you can get:

$$SD (luck + talent)^2 = SD(luck)^2 + SD(talent)^2$$

And, since observed performance results from that sum of luck and talent, you can say:

$$SD (observed)^2 = SD(luck)^2 + SD(talent)^2$$

And things are easy from there. In fact, right now, we can quickly figure out how to split major league season records into luck and talent.

First: If you gather team W-L records from the last couple of decades, you'll find that the SD is about 11 games. In other words, a "typical" variation from 81-81 is 92-70, or 70-92.

Second: From statistical theory, you can calculate that if you treated a major league season as a series of 162 coin tosses, the SD of team records would be around 6.4 games.

So:

$$11^2 = 6.4^2 + SD(\text{talent})^2$$

And so:

- SD(talent) = 9.0 games, approximately, and:
- SD(luck) = 6.4 games, approximately.

Note: The square of the SD is called the "variance." So, you can say that Var(observed) = Var(luck) + Var(talent). After rounding, that works out to "121 = 40 + 81". Since luck comprises 40/121 of the total variance, and talent 81/121, statisticians might say "Luck is 33 percent of the variance of team records, and talent is the other 67 percent." While that's a good (and perhaps the only) way to get the numbers to add up to 100 percent, I'm not a big fan of this kind of variance breakdown. As we will see, for "regressing to the mean" for projection purposes, the proportion before squaring makes more sense than the proportion after squaring, even if you can't easily get to 100 percent that way.

It's a quick and easy result. What does it mean, though? Well, leaving aside the details and quibbles:

- In an average season, two thirds of teams have a talent level within nine games of .500 (that is, between 72-90 and 90-72). Ninety-five percent of teams are within 18 games. But, five percent of teams are either horrible (worse than 63-99) or great (99-63 or better).

- To get a team's final record from its talent, you have to add its luck. Of course, luck is random, by definition. Two-thirds of teams will be lucky (or unlucky) by 6.4 games or fewer. But one or two teams a year will be very lucky or very unlucky, by 13 games or more. In other words, you might see a highly-touted team, seemingly destined to go 93-69, wind up at 79-83, just by random, dumb luck.

- Teams that wind up with great records probably were somewhat lucky. Teams that wind up with poor records probably were somewhat unlucky. When teams go 98-64, you should expect they weren't really that good and got lucky some-how—maybe their players had lucky career years, or they outperformed their Pythagoras, or they hit well in the clutch, or some such.

- But: how much lucky is "somewhat?" Well, talent and luck vary by a ratio of about 9.0 to 6.4. So, for every discrepancy of 15.4 wins, probably nine of those wins came from talent, and 6.4 from luck. That works out to 58 percent talent, 42 percent luck. So, on average, 42 percent of the difference from the mean is just random chance, and 58 percent is real.

That team that won 98 games? That's 17 games over .500. Fifty-eight percent of 17 is 10 games...so, on average, a team that goes 98-64 is really a 91-71 talent that got lucky.

If you don't believe this...well, you can verify for yourself. Find a bunch of teams that won between 97 and 99 games. Then, check how they did the following year. You'll find that they probably actually did win around 91 games. (Actually, I'd bet it's even fewer than 91, because they're not the same team the following season. Because of aging, and loss of talent for other reasons, good teams tend to collapse towards .500 in talent even after accounting for luck.)

It's very important to keep in mind that randomness varies with sample size—the shorter the season, the more luck you're going to have to put up with. If you cut the season in half, luck increases by 1.4 times (the square root of 2), proportionately per game. So you're going to wind up with luck and talent being almost exactly equal!

In other words: "how much of the variation in baseball outcomes is attributable to luck?" depends heavily on what kind of outcomes you're interested in. A season has a certain amount of luck; a game has proportionately more, and an inning even more than that. On the other hand, if you were to group a decade's worth of records together to form 1,620-game seasons, that gives luck more time to even out, and talent would become proportionally more relevant.

That's part of the reason that the professional sports differ in how much they're affected by randomness—they have different numbers of games in a season. But, there's another, perhaps more important, reason—the structures of the sports themselves differ significantly in how easily talent can overcome luck.

In baseball, where the differences in team talent are small compared to the length of the game—a good team might be expected to get as few as one or two additional hits more than an inferior team—it takes 69 games until luck evens out enough that talent becomes more important.

In basketball, however, the game is structured so that the better team is much more likely to be able to overcome the effects of random chance. Tom Tango calculates that in the NBA, it takes only 14 games for talent to become more important than luck.

Similarly, in the NFL, it takes only 12 games. Which is a good thing, since the pro football season is only 16 games long, in total.

So that's why accounting for luck is so useful: it can tell you things like, "...so, on average, a team that goes 98-64 is really a 91-71 talent that got lucky."

That obviously is valuable information to have. If you're the GM, you'll know that you're probably not as good as your record. If you're an opposing GM, of a team with 89-73 talent, you might be more willing to stand pat knowing you're really competing with a 91-win team instead of a 98-win team. And so on.

Except...those teams are 91-71 teams only *on average*. There will be wide variations. You could easily be looking at a 97-65 team that missed by a game, or an 81-81 team that got *really* lucky. Usually, you have lots of other evidence to help you figure out which it is—preseason projections, historical performance, evidence of career years or variations in pythagorean projection, and so forth.

But, even so, this kind of calculation gives you a good anchor point at which to start—at 91-71 instead of 98-64.

I would argue...15 years ago, this simple methodology had barely been appreciated, if it had been noticed at all. It's one of the most obvious results in statistics, and its applications went ignored. But once it was seen how easily useful it was, suddenly there sprouted applications everywhere.

"Regression to the mean" is the term used to describe the phenomenon where if you measure something, and then measure it again, the second time is likely to wind up less extreme in that direction than the first one. ("Regression *toward* the mean" is more accurate, since the second reading doesn't go all the way back to the mean, just partway back. But "regression *to* the mean" is nonetheless the more common phrase.)

For instance, one game, a batter goes 3-for-4. If you measure again tomorrow, he's likely to hit worse than .750, regressing back towards the league mean of .270 or whatever.

But you also can use regression to the mean to describe the phenomenon where the *talent level* is less extreme than the measurement. So, if a batter hits .750 today, not only is he likely to *hit less than* .750 *tomorrow*—it's also more likely that his *talent* is less than .750 *today*.

So this technique by which you split observed values into luck and non-luck... that's really a method of figuring out how much you regress an observation to the mean to get an estimate of the talent that produced it. And, in so doing, you are better able to project future performance, which is an empirical benefit that everyone cares about, even casual fans.

As we saw, to estimate a team's talent after a 162-game team season, you regress its actual wins by 42 percent. For starting pitcher BABIP, you regress a lot more—according to "Solving DIPS," 72 percent. And, of course, for a fair coin, you regress

---

"number of heads" by 100 percent—because no matter what, the "talent" of a fair coin is 50 percent heads.

————————

Does clutch hitting talent, in general, exist? Do some players improve their normal performance when the game is on the line, while others "choke" instead?

The consensus, for a long time, was, no, there's no evidence of clutch or choke players. Then, in 2005, Bill James published his famous essay, "Underestimating the Fog," in which he changed his mind on the issue. Bill argued we really don't have conclusive evidence. How do we know we didn't just miss the signal within the "fog" of noise?

It was a valid point, but some of the reactions were predictably unwarranted. To create a straw man caricature—"Derek Jeter wins five games a year for the Yankees just by being clutch. You can't argue with me, because Bill James said clutch hitting is real!"

That's what happens when you ask "Does it exist?" instead of "How big might it be?"

Tom Tango, Mitchel Lichtman and Andy Dolphin fixed that in *The Book*. They took the raw data, crunched variances, calculated randomness, and found that to estimate clutch hitting talent, you have to regress observed clutch hitting by...98 to 99 percent. And that's only if you combine four years' worth of player data to get rid of half the noise!

From 2000 to 2004, Bret Boone hit for a wOBA of .458 in clutch situations and .349 otherwise. That's a difference of .109. What's *The Book's* actual estimate of Boone's clutch ability? .0018.

In the same study, Frank Thomas was the worst "choke" hitter, his wOBA .177 worse in the clutch than in normal situations. His estimated clutch skill? -.0019.

Now, the 98 percent regression is an overall average. It could be, of course, that some players are legitimately clutch and some not at all, in a ratio of two percent "yes" to 98 percent "no." But, either way, we've found a limit on how many, or how skilled, clutch players there can be. If you think Bret Boone's +.109 clutch performance is real, you have to postulate 49 others, adding up to the same +.109, whose clutch performance is zero.

Many of the findings in *The Book* are in the same vein. One of the most surprising, to me, is that some pitchers are better from the stretch, and some from the windup.

But while the observed differences look significant...well, those, too, are mostly luck. Even after observing pitchers for five years, you still have to regress their observed differences by 80 to 90 percent. Which means, when you look at a five-year veteran's "stretch vs. windup" differential, only 10 to 20 percent of it is real, and the rest is random noise.

————————

And, one more, that's among the most important—platoon splits.

From 2000 to 2004, some players hit for as much as .100 better in wOBA with the advantage, while others had a *negative* platoon differential of as much as -.041. But after filtering out the effects of luck, Tango/Lichtman/Dolphin found that the range of true talent was much narrower, from .050 to .003 (with no player actually appearing to possess a true negative platoon advantage). It seems that over a four-year sample, a typical batter would need to be regressed somewhere around 80 percent to the mean. That is, only around 20 percent of a player's observed platoon tendencies—as measured against league average—is real.

So, signal vs. noise, luck vs. talent—I'd argue that's the biggest advance in sabermetrics since McCracken. We've made big strides in how we measure luck, estimate the underlying talent from the raw numbers, and improve our forecasts. Those advances go largely hidden, secondary to the particular subject at hand. But look below the surface, and there they are.

In the early days of sabermetrics, Bill James taught us how to measure performance. Now, we are more able to evaluate how much of that performance is real—and how much is random.

References & Resources

- Voros McCracken, Baseball Prospectus, "Pitching and Defense: How Much Control Do Hurlers Have?," *baseballprospectus.com/article.php?articleid=878*
- Tom Tango, Mitchel Lichtman, Andrew Dolphin, *The Book: Playing the Percentages in Baseball*
- Nate Silver, *The Signal And The Noise: Why So Many Predictions Fail—But Some Don't*
- Michael Mauboussin, *The Success Equation—Untangling Skill and Luck in Business, Sports, and Investing*
- Erik Allen, Arvin Hsu, and Tom Tango, Baseball Primer, "Solving DIPS," *tangotiger.net/solvingdips.pdf*
- Jon Terbush, The Week, Why doesn't Moneyball work in the playoffs?," *theweek.com/articles/458933/why-doesnt-moneyball-work-playoffs*
- Tom Tango, Inside The Book Blog, "True Talent Levels for Sports Leagues," *insidethebook.com/ee/index.php/site/comments/true_talent_levels_for_sports_leagues*
- Bill James, *SABR Baseball Research Journal No. 33*, "Underestimating the Fog," *sabr.org/research/underestimating-fog*

The Coming Fight: Why the Next CBA Won't Be So Easy

by Dave Cameron

For over 20 years, Major League Baseball has enjoyed nearly unprecedented labor peace among the major American team sports. Since the last time MLB had a work stoppage, the NBA and NHL have both had two lockouts that saw games canceled (with the NHL losing an entire season in 2004-2005), while the NFL went through a contentious fight with its players in 2011 that lasted over five months, wiping out most of each team's training camps. The sting of losing the 1994 World Series has seemingly motivated both the owners and the players association to find common ground, and with the league prospering, both parties have been content to keep the ball rolling. With the current collective bargaining agreement set to expire on Dec. 1, 2016, however, there is some concern that baseball may be in for a more difficult path to compromise this time around.

The primary issue, of course, is likely to surround player compensation. Most labor negotiations hinge on the distribution of income between corporate profits and the salaries and benefits received by the workforce that creates those profits, and MLB is a profit-seeking corporation, incentivized to retain as much of its own income as it can. And over the last few years, the shifting media landscape has swelled MLB's income-streams in a dramatic way.

The rise of DVR and streaming services like Netflix have led to a generation of so-called "cord-cutters," who are uninterested in paying inflated monthly cable subscription prices for the right to spend a half hour trying to find interesting content across a couple of hundred segregated channels. The ability to time-shift our viewing choices onto our own schedule is destroying the value of advertising during live television, leaving the business model that helped create some of the largest companies in America trying to figure out how to keep their income streams afloat while their industry pivots around them.

To this point, their answer has been live sports; people are generally less interested in watching a game after its conclusion, leaving sports leagues as one of the few remaining holders of content that people demand to watch as it is aired. And because major league baseball is a daily sport, providing content for television networks seven days a week for seven months a year, cable companies have bet big on it, rapidly increasing the rights fees for both national and regional programming.

Just among the league's national programming contracts with ESPN, Fox, and TBS, the league reportedly will be paid an average of $1.5 billion per year for the rest of the decade, as well as the start of the next decade. And that's just the national rights fees; each team strikes its own deals with its regional sports network, or in some cases, owns part or all of that network and uses it to generate income. Since the current CBA went into effect, the Dodgers reset the market for local television contracts, landing a deal that paid them in excess of $300 million per season for the rights to broadcast their games locally.

Since that deal, smaller-market rivals have been able to lock in big raises in annual fees received from the deals that they were under previously, often pushing up from $10 or $20 million annually to closer to $100 million per year. The explosion of television rights money has dramatically altered the financial landscape in MLB since the last CBA was negotiated, and makes it unlikely that the players are going to be satisfied with salary raises that are not keeping pace with the growth in league revenues.

According to research from Maury Brown at *Forbes*, MLB's revenues have grown from roughly $1.4 billion in 1995 to around $9 billion in 2014, which represents about a 650 percent increase. During the same 20-year period, player salaries have grown from around $900 million to $3.5 billion, a significantly smaller increase of a little under 400 percent. And MLB doesn't plan to take its foot off the gas, telling Eric Fisher of the *Sports Business Journal* that it is working toward a goal of $15 billion in annual revenues. While no exact date is set for that goal to be accomplished, Fisher reported that this isn't a long-term project, and mentioned a "half decade" as a potential window for the league to get to that lofty platform.

The upcoming CBA is the players association's chance to fight for a larger share of that ever-growing pie, and it seems likely that the union is going to want to ensure that the league's dramatic growth doesn't disproportionately end up as ownership profits. But while the publicly reported and discussed figures of MLB's revenues get larger, it remains to be seen how much of that total MLB will be willing to stipulate is baseball-related income generated directly by the performance of the players on the field.

In Fisher's *SBJ* article, for instance, he quotes Giants CEO Larry Baer saying the following:

> *"We are uniquely positioned to take advantage of the opportunities out there when it comes to digital," said Larry Baer, San Francisco Giants president and chief executive. Baer will be part of a newly merged board of directors encompassing MLBAM and MLB Enterprises. "The digital world is changing really fast, but it also presents a huge array of opportunities. And I think we're now set up as well as anyone to change with it and exploit that. Digital's the big area where I see us getting to $15 billion," Baer said.*

You're probably familiar with MLBAM—the league's Advanced Media wing—which has been responsible for products like MLB.tv, the At-Bat app, and the implementation of tracking technologies like Statcast. There's no question that baseball has been at the forefront of pushing technological advances, and its app has been the highest grossing sports application in the Apple ecosystem for six consecutive years. But when Baer and others talk about MLB's opportunity in digital, they aren't just talking about the opportunity to separate consumers from $20 for a mobile app, or $140 for an MLB.tv subscription; they're talking about the opportunity to turn their first-mover advantage into a business that profits from other companies attempting to get up and running in the digital streaming environment.

Over the last two years, MLB has pushed heavily in this direction. After starting out as primarily a hosting provider for other networks—most notably ESPN's World Cup coverage, but also providing the technology for NCAA's men's basketball tournament to be streamed online—MLB struck deals with HBO and World Wrestling Entertainment (WWE) that saw it co-develop apps to provide so-called Over-The-Top networks. Both of these products were new services, designed from scratch, and showed that MLB could provide full support for a partner that wanted to provide content (both on television and mobile) without going through a traditional cable operator.

But then, last August, MLB struck a deal with the National Hockey League that signaled an even more aggressive direction for its digital division. Instead of simply being a technology partner, MLB acquired the NHL's digital streaming rights, paying $100 million per year for ownership of the hockey league's digital broadcast rights, making MLB a full-on rights-holder. That agreement signaled that Major League Baseball expects to be a player in the market providing live sports (besides just baseball) to the cord-cutting generation. The NHL deal gives MLB three sports—already cemented was an agreement with the PGA to provide early-round coverage of events, since traditional networks cover only the weekends—that it theoretically could package together in a bundle, and positions MLB to become a supplemental option for the Netflix crowd.

As part of the deal with the NHL, MLB sold it an equity stake in BAM Tech—the working name for the the new division of MLBAM that is developing these partnerships—that will amount to seven to 10 percent of the new company, at a price that puts BAM Tech's valuation in the $4-$5 billion range. Given that this arm of MLBAM is already worth as much as many famous technology startups based in Silicon Valley, there have long been rumors that MLB will look to spin off BAM Tech as its own company. An IPO of this new division would bring in a big windfall for each team, each of which owns approximately a three percent stake in BAM Tech. If an IPO priced the new company at $5 billion, each major league club would reap about $150 million in exchange for liquidating its ownership, and that kind of flood of cash would likely see the MLBPA pushing for significant raises in player salaries.

However, MLBAM CEO Bob Bowman said they are not currently anticipating an IPO, and instead are looking for a strategic partner to take a minority stake in the company. The expectation is an announcement of an investment from an outside party at some point in 2016, with MLB continuing to grow BAM Tech internally in the short term, potentially exploring even more deals to acquire content rights. It is certainly easy to speculate that with an upcoming CBA negotiation, MLB might not want to be sitting on $5 billion in cash as it negotiates the size of the increase in salaries players should receive going forward.

But it's not even clear that the players have much of a claim to these revenue streams. In many ways, BAM Tech isn't so different from a company like Uber or Snapchat, and if MLB owners had individually gotten together to form a venture capital firm that funded the growth of one of those companies, no one would be clamoring for those owners to then plow the returns from a smart investment into the sports team they also happen to own.

Perhaps a comparable example would be Mark Cuban, owner of the NBA's Dallas Mavericks, who also operates as a venture capitalist, including appearing on ABC's hit TV show "Shark Tank," where he finances startups that often have nothing to do with basketball. When one of Cuban's investments turns into a big success, he's not expected to split that money with Dirk Nowitzki, because his ownership of the Mavericks is tangential to his technology investments.

MLB's investment in BAM Tech is more complex, because it did grow out of the original premise of providing live-streaming of major league games directly to consumers. Most of MLBAM's revenues still come from its baseball products, and players should be compensated for revenues generated by the league's activities in monetizing their product. But the growth of BAM Tech as a partner with companies like HBO and WWE, plus its ability to generate revenues by selling access to hockey games, muddies the waters of how much of the increase in MLBAM's revenues should trickle down to the players. Should baseball players really profit from MLB's ability to sell hockey games or golf tournaments? It's likely the two sides are going to have differing opinions on that, and sorting out the amount of future revenues that should be included in the discussion of player wages is likely to be a very complex negotiation.

Even beyond the size-of-the-pie argument, the implementation of increased player compensation is also not exactly straightforward, and could end up providing some major sources of disagreement as well.

The MLBPA, like most unions, has agreed to compensation arrangements that push the flow of wages toward employees with more tenure. Veterans receive a disproportionate share of the money teams spend on their player payrolls, while more productive young players earn something close to the league minimum for their first few seasons, then work up towards a market-wage in their fourth, fifth, and sixth years in the majors. But in recent years—perhaps not coincidentally coming during the drug-testing era—the relative production of veterans has fallen, with the game skewing more heavily toward young talent.

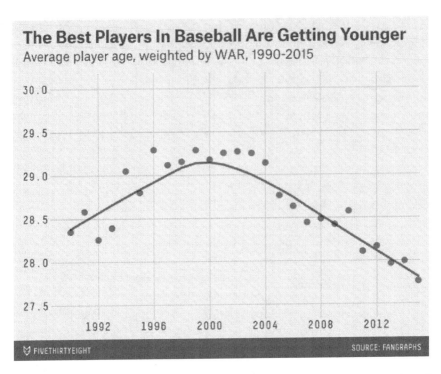

The Best Players In Baseball Are Getting Younger
Average player age, weighted by WAR, 1990-2015

SOURCE: FANGRAPHS

Led by generational talents like Bryce Harper, Mike Trout, and Clayton Kershaw, the game is being dominated by players in their 20s, and in some cases, their early 20s. But because players have limited ability to negotiate significant raises in the first few years of their careers, the majority of salary dollars still go to older players.

Percentage of Salary, by Age Group, 2004-2013				
Year	25 & under	26 to 30	31 to 35	36 & up
2004	3%	35%	40%	22%
2005	3%	33%	41%	22%
2006	3%	32%	48%	18%
2007	4%	30%	47%	19%
2008	4%	28%	47%	21%
2009	4%	32%	50%	15%
2010	3%	33%	50%	14%
2011	4%	36%	44%	16%
2012	4%	40%	41%	15%
2013	4%	42%	38%	16%

The final numbers aren't in for 2014 and 2015 yet, but given there were more than 30 position players age 36 or older with 100 or more plate appearances in 2012 and 2013, and just 22 in 2014 and 18 in 2015, this trend does not appear to be abating.

The recent rise in allocation of salaries towards players in the 26-30 age-bracket is due in part to the trend towards signing key contributors to long-term deals during their pre-arbitration years; teams have taken advantage of individual player's desires for financial security, reducing their overall expenditures by keeping a larger share of premium players out of the free agent market. With more guaranteed contracts for younger players, teams are ending up with more money committed to a wider range of players in their peak years; when the player doesn't work, the team is out $10 or $20 million it wouldn't otherwise have spent. But when the player has a big breakout after he signs the deal—Paul Goldschmidt, for instance—the team often comes out way ahead, with the franchise paying far less for premium production than the open market would have forced it to.

So it's not enough for the MLBPA simply to say it's time for the league to start sharing a larger portion of the pie with the players; there likely will have to be a plan in place for either getting more players to the open market or pushing more dollars toward players who aren't eligible for free agency. Both paths come with significant obstacles.

The most direct way to get more players to the open market would be for the MLBPA to fight for a shorter path to free agency. Currently, teams get a minimum of six years of team control, but given how easy it is to keep a player in the minor leagues for the brief time required to avoid giving him a full service year in his rookie season, most impactful players end up playing closer to seven years before becoming eligible for free agency. And if they opt for early-career security, as many of the game's best young players have, the actual term with their original organization is more often upwards of 10 years.

When the system is set up to restrict costs before free agency, expecting that market rates will make up for the early-career shortfalls later on, that becomes a real problem; teams are becoming less willing to overpay for aging players, especially as their production has fallen, and the money that was supposed to make up for the underpaid years is simply getting allocated to keep the next generation of players from reaching free agency after six or seven years. For a significant portion of the major league population, the vast majority of the productive portion of their career will come during the years in which they have limited abilities to be compensated for their performances.

The MLBPA could propose reducing the amount of service time required to reach free agency, but that would be a dramatic structural change that ownership would likely strongly oppose. And with baseball currently celebrating unprecedented parity, with lower revenue teams achieving unprecedented success, reducing the number of years before free agency would likely be seen as a step back in the fight for competitive balance MLB has spent a few decades attempting to create. The more quickly players are valued at their market wages, the less important scouting and player development become, and MLB will likely hesitate to institute policies that give teams with significant payroll advantages an easier time turning that cash into a larger ability to buy premium players.

This is the same issue the league would likely raise if the players asked for a higher league minimum salary. A significant increase in the minimum salary would act as a regressive tax, increasing the marginal costs for the lowest-spending teams more than the teams in large markets with plenty of disposable income. While the minimum salary is likely to increase in a significant way, using a league-wide increase in the baseline salary of all players would make it more difficult for the league to sustain the current level of competitive balance; the Dodgers and Yankees can absorb an extra $10 or $15 million in mandatory spending a lot easier than the A's or Rays can.

From a competitive balance standpoint, the league has been successful in part because the luxury tax has worked as a constraint upon the top tier of payrolls—with the notable exception of the current iteration of the Dodgers, anyway—while the rise in television revenues has allowed the bottom tier teams to spend enough to retain their best players, rather than simply acting as a farm system for developing players who get paid by the big boys in free agency. But with the revenue growth of television contracts going disproportionately to larger market teams, it's unrealistic to expect the teams with the lowest payrolls to drive a large increase in the share of the pie going to the players.

If the players are going to get a significantly larger portion of the pie, they're going to have to figure out how to get the league to extract it from the higher-revenue teams, but without ignoring the league's concerns about maintaining the smaller spread in team payrolls that we've seen in recent years. And that's no easy task.

Perhaps that involves asking for another expansion in revenue sharing along with a big bump in the the league minimum; if the higher-revenue teams were essentially underwriting most of the increase in costs across the majors, it could push more money to the players without dramatically altering the current spending ratios between teams with different revenue streams. But franchises with a long history of success—and the revenues that come with an entrenched fanbase—are probably going to be reticent to use their financial advantages to subsidize their competitors. With a new commissioner in place—one whose election was contested by a reasonably-sized bloc of owners, it should be noted—it isn't clear that Rob Manfred will have the political capital to push increased revenue sharing on the teams that produce the most revenue for the league.

If an increase in revenue sharing proves too difficult, the MLBPA may have to get creative. One interesting suggestion I've heard bandied about, albeit as a long-shot possibility, is that MLB could fund a comprehensive insurance plan for all players—similar to worker's compensation—providing a significant benefit to players whose careers are prematurely derailed by injury. Currently, players are able to buy individual insurance policies, but they are prohibitively expensive and often don't provide payouts unless it is proven that the injury sustained is career-ending. These policies are often of little help to a pitcher who undergoes Tommy John surgery, missing out on years of prime-aged earnings, but has no desire to retire after one elbow problem.

With the significant increase in Tommy John surgeries, pitchers are particularly harmed by a system that limits their earnings until the second half of their careers, so a comprehensive insurance plan that paid out a percentage of expected earnings while a player is rehabbing may be one way to not only distribute a higher percentage of revenues to the players, but to compensate the players who carry the most risk.

Additionally, a comprehensive insurance plan would limit the needs of players to self-insure by signing early-career extensions that keep them from reaching free agency after six or seven years. With a systematic safety net in place, individual players would not be carrying as much personal risk, and would have more incentive to try to maximize their earnings through arbitration and reaching free agency in the shortest time possible. Beyond just the actual payouts to players who become disabled, a worker's compensation agreement would push more players into the open market, and theoretically drive an increase in wages by reducing the number of star players playing at wages that don't reflect their contributions on the field.

Of course, the logistics of introducing a worker's compensation program would be no small matter, especially since player compensation is much more variable in major league baseball than it is within most unions. Not only would both sides have to agree on how it would be funded—which would again lead to the question of how strongly MLB wants to push the highest-revenue teams to bear the burden of increased player compensation—but the union itself would likely have to have some long discussions about who would be eligible for the program. The players who would benefit the most from a comprehensive insurance program would be those with few years of service, but they usually wield the least power within their association, and the MLBPA would have to make an intentional decision to negotiate primarily for increased wages for their most junior members.

That's probably why the idea has been described as far-fetched, but it also speaks to the difficulties of expanding the proportion of league revenues that go to the players. There is just no simple way to facilitate payments from owners to workers that doesn't have ramifications on some other aspect of the sport, which is why this upcoming CBA negotiation may prove more difficult than the others.

And we haven't even touched on the non-monetary aspects of the negotiations. Beyond simply dividing up revenues, both sides have their own separate agendas. MLB is likely going to push for some kind of unified player-entry system, (which Kiley McDaniel covers elsewhere in this book) most likely by advocating for an international draft to replace the failed bonus-slotting program currently in place. There will likely be additional discussions of the Joint Drug Agreement, and how the enforcement of the penalties handed down are enforced.

The players are rumored to be pushing strongly for limitations on media access, and might want a greater say in how pace-of-play changes are implemented. There will likely be discussions regarding the public reporting and sharing of health information, especially now that MLB is consolidating medical information into a central database. As biometric analysis (including systems that purport to measure a player's physical degradation in real-time) grows as an industry, the players may seek some greater measure of control over how that information is disseminated.

Finally, there's the matter of the length of the season. Commissioner Manfred has openly spoken about considering reducing the regular season to 154 games; an eight-game reduction for each team would either allow for an expansion of the postseason or for more frequent off days during the year, or both if done correctly. This would be a hit to the owners' pockets, both in terms of gate revenue and of existing television contracts—which are based on a 162-game season and would need to be reworked—and thus isn't highly likely. The negotiations will be complex as is. But players may view the reduced wear and tear as a big positive. More importantly, trading a few April or May midweek games for a best-of-seven Division Series is tantalizing, and that possibility makes the commissioner's public statements intriguing.

In the end, though, these negotiations will mostly boil down to figuring how to spread the wealth from a very lucrative business. The last few negotiations have seen both sides not wanting to rock a boat that was bringing prosperity to everyone on board, but with players eyeing an increasing pile of gold on the ownership side of the boat, this could prove to be a significantly more difficult series of conversations. Add in a new union head in Tony Clark—a former player, who will bring a different perspective to the negotiations than former executive director Michael Weiner—and the current commissioner perhaps possessing less power than Bud Selig, and there are enough variables in play that an easily-worked-out agreement is probably not in the cards this time.

If Commissioner Manfred is going to use walk-up music as he enters the negotiating room, I will humbly suggest a little tune from The Notorious B.I.G.: "Mo Money, Mo Problems." Indeed.

References & Resources

- Rob Arthur, FiveThirtyEight, "Baseball's Kids Are All Right," *fivethirtyeight.com/features/baseballs-kids-are-all-right*
- Eric Fisher, *Spors Business Journal*, "MLBAM moving swiftly to pursue spinoff," *sportsbusinessdaily.com/Journal/Issues/2015/06/01/Leagues-and-Governing-Bodies/MLBAM-spinoff.aspx*
- Shalani Ramachandrian, *The Wall Street Journal*, "MLB's Tech Unit Wins NHL Streaming Business," *wsj.com/articles/mlbs-tech-unit-wins-nhl-streaming-business-1438715135*
- Peter Kafka, re/code, "Pro Baseball's Streaming Video Unit Gets Ready for a $3 Billion Spinoff by Adding Pro Hockey," *recode.net/2015/08/04/pro-baseballs-streaming-video-unit-gets-ready-for-a-3-billion-spinoff-by-adding-pro-hockey*

GM in a Box: Dan Duquette

by Alex Skillin

Record and Background

Age: 57

Previous organizations

Dan Duquette cut his teeth in the industry with the Milwaukee Brewers, where he started as a scout after graduating from Amherst College. Following his seven years in Milwaukee, the Expos hired Duquette as their director of player development. In that job, he helped continue the organization's strong track record of cultivating talented youngsters.

In 1991, Duquette took over as general manager in Montreal (for the departing Dave Dombrowski) before being handed the opportunity to work in the same position with his hometown Red Sox four years later. Duquette served as GM in Boston through 2002 but was dismissed when the current ownership group took over. Afterward, he was out of major league baseball for nine years.

Years of service with the Orioles

Four. After a long search for their next GM, the Orioles hired Duquette in November 2011 in a move few expected to pay any dividends. Baltimore hadn't made the playoffs since 1997, but Duquette helped guide the team to a surprising 93 wins in his first season and a Wild Card berth.

Following Baltimore's respectable third-place finish a year later, Duquette proved that playoff run was no fluke, leading the Orioles to 96 wins in 2014 and the organization's first division title in 17 seasons. Despite a disappointing finish in 2015, under Duquette, the Orioles have enjoyed their best four-year run since the mid-1990s.

Cumulative record

With the Orioles: 355-293, including one AL East crown and trip to the American League Championship Series (2014), and one Wild Card appearance (2012).

With the Red Sox: 656-574 from 1994 to 2001, including one AL East title (1995) and trip to the ALCS (1999), and two Wild Card finishes.

With the Expos: 181-143 from 1992 to 1993.

Overall: 1,192-1,010.

Playing career

Duquette never played professionally, but he was a catcher on the varsity baseball team at Amherst.

Personnel and Philosophy

Notable changes from the previous regime?

Duquette's biggest departure from the previous regime, led by long-time baseball executive Andy MacPhail, has been his ability to build adequate pitching and depth throughout the Orioles' roster. Through a series of good trades, most notably the deal that brought Adam Jones and Chris Tillman to Baltimore for Erik Bedard, MacPhail built up a solid stock of position players. Additional trades for J.J. Hardy and Chris Davis left Duquette with more to work with than many realized at the time he was hired.

What's separated Duquette from MacPhail has been his creativity and the nontraditional avenues he's used to bring valuable contributors to Baltimore. MacPhail comes from a family of long-time baseball executives, and his strategy as GM was certainly more by the book than Duquette's has been. Since taking over the Orioles, Duquette hasn't been afraid to pick up just about any player off the scrap heap and find a role for him at Camden Yards.

The biggest change has been the success Duquette has brought to a franchise that rarely played competitive baseball for over a decade prior to his arrival.

What characterizes his relationship with ownership?

The Orioles didn't win much before Duquette's hiring, and many observers attributed all their losing to team owner Peter Angelos, who, fair or not, has developed a reputation for being difficult to work under. That a number of candidates turned the job down before Duquette took it only lent credence to this notion.

And despite his success with the Orioles, Duquette seemingly wanted to leave the organization for greener pastures (and a promotion) with the Blue Jays last offseason. That Duquette felt Toronto was a better situation than his present job in Baltimore could say a lot about how he feels about the potential for sustained success under Angelos. Or perhaps Duquette just wanted a cushier position with a higher salary.

Nevertheless, Duquette has achieved more working with Angelos than any Orioles GM had in 15 years. Their relationship, at the very least, must function well enough for the club to continue excelling on the field. With Duquette and manager Buck Showalter the clear leadership pair, the team is enjoying a rare period of stability during the Angelos era.

What type of people does he hire?

Upon arriving in Baltimore, Duquette remade much of the team's scouting department. He hired Gary Rajsich (with whom he'd worked in Boston) as the club's director of scouting and reassigned former top lieutenant Lee MacPhail IV, who has since left the organization. Duquette also brought in longtime major league pitching coach Rick Peterson to serve in a new role as Baltimore's director of pitching development.

Perhaps Duquette's biggest move was hiring former Orioles standout player Brady Anderson, first as a special assistant and now as the team's vice president of baseball operations directly under Duquette. Anderson has taken a big role in Baltimore's front office and was even rumored to be the next man in line as GM if Duquette had departed for Toronto last offseason.

Duquette also hired Sarah Gelles to be the club's director of baseball analytics and has certainly made more use of advanced stats than his predecessor.

Further back during his time with the Expos, Duquette was open-minded enough to hire a statistical consultant named Mike Gimbel in an era when such thinking was anything but the norm. Gimbel followed Duquette to Boston and consulted with the Red Sox until 1997.

Has he ever been outspoken in the media?

He did have a couple conflicts with John Valentin while in Boston. Valentin grew angry when the team decided to move him to third base and play Nomar Garciaparra at shortstop as a rookie in 1997, though Duquette remained largely silent and let manager Jimy Williams handle the matter.

A few years later, Duquette grew angry when Valentin underwent knee surgery with a doctor the team hadn't authorized. The Red Sox released a statement criticizing Valentin's decision, which angered the player and his agent. Again, however, Duquette stayed mostly silent and avoided getting into any war of words through the media. Valentin missed the rest of the season, and the media scrutiny soon subsided.

Having experienced the worst of what media scrutiny has to offer in Boston—especially after the now infamous "twilight of his career" comments about Roger Clemens following the 1996 season, which were taken out of context and used against Duquette as Clemens enjoyed success with Boston's AL East rivals—he has little appetite for providing reporters with juicy quotes for their stories in Baltimore. He's far more comfortable allowing Showalter to soak up the media spotlight and serve as the public face of the Orioles.

Is he more collaborative or authoritative?

Collaborative. Duquette's the man in charge, but he seeks help from any number of avenues in his front office. Having a voice like Gimbel's around in Montreal and Boston speaks to Duquette's willingness to listen to an alternative viewpoint.

In Baltimore, Anderson is an influential voice in the team's decisions, and so too is special assistant Lee Thomas, a long-time executive who helped lead the Cardinals and Phillies to success in the '80s and early '90s. Rajisch continues to run the scouting department, and Gelles provides input from her analytical perspective.

What kinds of managers does he hire?

Duquette hasn't hired a manager since taking over as GM, and Showalter's success is the reason. Working for a GM who likes to raid the waiver wire and give castoffs a chance, Showalter has proven the perfect manager for his ability to squeeze the most out of limited talent and build a solid sum from spare parts.

Given his previous managerial hirings—Jimy Williams and Grady Little in Boston, Felipe Alou in Montreal—Duquette does seem to prefer someone with many years of baseball experience in the manager's chair.

How closely does he work with the manager?

Duquette and Showalter have been the duo at the center of Baltimore's revival these past few seasons. The two work closely to manage the club's roster and find the perfect roles for undervalued players.

Showalter likely has as much influence as any manager not named Mike Scioscia, though rumors suggest he'd like to have a little more power within the organization.

Player Development

How does he approach the amateur draft?

The Orioles haven't had a good track record in the draft for many years, and outside of a few picks, that's pretty well continued under Duquette. He hired Rajsich in part to lead the club's efforts in the draft, and while the Orioles have made some decent picks near the top, Baltimore's farm system still ranks among the worst in baseball.

Drafting Kevin Gausman and Hunter Harvey, the Orioles have shown a willingness to target high-level pitchers from both the high school and college level in the first round. Outside of those two, however, Baltimore hasn't drafted anyone over the last four years who can realistically be expected to turn into an above-average major leaguer. And Harvey didn't pitch in 2015 due to injury.

Duquette did decide to forfeit the team's first two picks in the 2014 draft when the Orioles signed Nelson Cruz and Ubaldo Jimenez in free agency.

Does he prefer major league-ready players or projects?

A little of both, though Duquette has always been adept at finding projects from whom he can extract previously unseen value. The likes of Miguel Gonzalez, Ryan Flaherty, Steve Pearce and David Lough, among others, have flourished at one time or another during Duquette's time in Baltimore.

His greatest trick is unearthing legitimate major league value from players few other organizations have interest in. Finding Brian Daubach, during his time in Boston, is perhaps the best example of this.

Tools or performance?

Performance. The Orioles haven't been married to one or the other under Duquette, but they've probably been a little more conservative than most teams. Gausman and Harvey have stuff that screams top-of-the-rotation potential, yet they also came with solid track records of success on the field. The same goes for 2015 first-rounder D.J. Stewart, who doesn't necessarily have standout tools but put together solid numbers in college at Florida State.

High school or college?

High school. The Orioles haven't leaned heavily either way, but they've taken more high schoolers at the top of the draft than college players. Their first three picks in 2013 were all high schoolers, and after drafting Stewart from college in 2015, they took Ryan Mountcastle, an 18-year-old from Florida, with their other first-round selection.

Pitchers or hitters?

Pitchers. Despite taking outfielder Stewart with their first pick in 2015, the Orioles have usually targeted pitching early in the draft. Baltimore has taken Gausman (first round, fourth overall pick), Harvey (first round), Branden Kline (second round) and Brian Gonzalez (third round) all near the top of the draft recently.

Does he rush players to the majors or is he patient?

Both. The Orioles famously promoted Manny Machado all the way from Double-A during the 2012 season, and they handed Jonathan Schoop the starting job at second base a year ago when he was just 22.

But they've also been conservative with pitchers like Gausman, whom they've handled too cautiously. Other top prospects like Chance Sisco and Christian Walker have been given plenty of time to take their lumps at each level in the minors.

In the past, Duquette has shown a tendency to give youngsters a chance. He handed Nomar Garciaparra the Red Sox's starting shortstop job at the age of 23. With the Expos, Duquette gave everyday opportunities to Larry Walker and Marquis Grissom when they were just breaking into the majors.

Roster Construction

Is he especially fond of certain types of players?

Duquette loves players who can fill a role—any role—on the cheap. In Montreal, he stayed patient with a young roster and was eventually rewarded, though that was largely because he had few other options. Yet even in Boston, Duquette took flyers on players other organizations didn't want, with Daubauch, Reggie Jefferson and Troy O'Leary coming to mind.

During his time with Baltimore, Ryan Flaherty has stuck around for years because of his versatility and minimal cost. Duquette found a valuable bench/platoon role for Delmon Young after the rest of the league had given up on him. Pearce, Lough, Alejandro De Aza and Jimmy Paredes are all prime examples.

He's also regularly turned castoffs and failed starters like Darren O'Day, Zach Britton, T.J. McFarland, Tommy Hunter and Brian Matusz into solid relievers.

Does he like proven players or youngsters?

Neither, really. Duquette loves finding unproven players who can succeed (because he can get them cheaply), and he doesn't especially care what age they are. Gonzalez was a 28-year-old Double-A reject when the Orioles signed him back in 2012, and he's gone on to make just under 100 league-average starts for Baltimore ever since. Pearce and Lough aren't youngsters by any means either. When he signed Henry Urrutia out of Cuba in 2011, he was 26.

Although he led a youthful team in Montreal (mostly due to the Expos' team-building philosophy at the time), Duquette built a veteran squad in Boston, signing players like Manny Ramirez and Johnny Damon to big free-agent deals.

Offensive players or glove men?

Glove men, but partially because Duquette had the luxury of inheriting a team with strong offensive performers in Adam Jones, Chris Davis and Manny Machado. Duquette has been able to fill in the gaps with strong defenders such as Hardy, Lough, De Aza, Schoop and Caleb Joseph.

With the Red Sox, Duquette built an offensive juggernaut by the end of his tenure, bringing in the likes of Ramirez, Damon, Jose Canseco, Dante Bichette and Carl Everett. In a way, he's proven capable of adapting to the league-wide environment at the time, which favored lineups full of mashers during his tenure in Boston but now favors versatile players.

Power pitchers or finesse guys?

No preference. The Orioles have used power pitchers such as Chris Tillman and Bud Norris in recent years and also depended on soft-tossers in Gonzalez and Wei-

Yin Chen. They've leaned slightly more toward finesse guys but only because they're undervalued on the open market.

Does he allocate resources primarily on impact players or role players?

Role players. In 2015, Jones was Baltimore's highest-paid player and earned just over $13 million. Outside of Ubaldo Jimenez, Davis and Hardy, no other Orioles player made more than $10 million this past season. Duquette has built a roster filled with solid contributors without committing much in the way of money or years.

Besides Jones, Jimenez, Hardy and Chen, the Orioles don't have anyone signed to a long-term contract beyond 2015, though locking up Machado should be a team priority.

The one exception is his experience in Boston, where he invested big money in proven veterans. Even then, however, Duquette liked to supplement the team's roster with unknown role players who could contribute more than expected.

How does he flesh out his bullpen and bench?

By leaving no stone unturned. Duquette has converted numerous failed starters into successful relievers, with Britton, Matusz and Hunter particularly standing out. He traded Jim Johnson when he got expensive. The bench has been a revolving cast of characters, including Danny Valencia, Chris Dickerson, Wilson Betemit, Travis Snider and Young. The one notable exception to the bullpen strategy has been with Andrew Miller, who he sacrificed a premium prospect in Eduardo Rodriguez in order to obtain.

Does he often work the waiver wire, sign minor-league free agents, or make Rule 5 picks?

All of the above. The Orioles have made more waiver claims than just about any other team under Duquette, and they've also struck gold on minor league free agent deals with Gonzalez and Young. In addition, Baltimore has been one of the few squads to get anything out of the Rule 5 draft, with Flaherty and Jason Garcia both providing contributions.

When will he release players?

Duquette isn't afraid to release players and doesn't let recent history color his view on a player's overall value. He had little problem cutting the cord on both Young and De Aza after their production dipped in 2015 following successful tenures with the club. Trade acquisitions in big deals—like Jemile Weeks, who came over for Jim Johnson—are also not given special treatment just to make it look like the team got something of value in return, as is often the case elsewhere.

On whom has he given up?

The one mistake Duquette would like to have back is the deal that sent Jake Arrieta to the Cubs in 2013. The Cubs also received Pedro Strop, with the Orioles getting back Scott Feldman and Steve Clevenger. Arrieta has since blossomed into an ace, and Strop remains a solid member of Chicago's bullpen. Meanwhile, Clevenger has earned his rep as a throw-in, and Feldman left in free agency.

Trading Eduardo Rodriguez may come to be a regrettable decision as well, as the young lefty had a solid rookie season with the Red Sox. On the other hand, Andrew Miller was a big reason why the Orioles made it to the 2014 ALCS.

Otherwise, Duquette hasn't been really been burned by giving up on anyone. He traded for Bud Norris at the 2012 deadline and had little issue with cutting him partway through the 2015 campaign after a series of poor outings.

To whom has he given a shot?

Just about anyone with a pulse. Few expected Chen to make an impact when the Orioles signed him from Korea in 2012, but he's proven to be one of Baltimore's most reliable starters ever since.

When Matt Wieters went down with an injury early in 2014, Duquette handed Joseph an opportunity at catcher despite an underwhelming minor league track record. Joseph has since turned into a valuable performer at little cost.

Finally, he gave Nelson Cruz a shot in 2014, when seemingly no one else wanted him. Baltimore only paid Cruz $8 million for a 40-homer season, which was a nice win for Duquette.

With the Expos, Duquette showed a willingness to throw youngsters right into the fire, handing full-time jobs to Delino DeShields, Grissom and Walker.

Does he cut bait early or late?

Early. He has shown devotion to some younger players, such as Schoop, even when they struggle for long periods of time, but those are exceptions.

Perhaps the best examples are Mo Vaughn and Roger Clemens. With Vaughn, Duquette was right on the money. Duquette let him leave in free agency following the four best years of his career, the last of which in 1998 was his career-best, 6.3 WAR. Over the next five seasons, he totaled only 3.5 WAR, and was out of the game after that.

Clemens, on the other hand, didn't work out too well. After Duquette was unable to re-sign him following the 1996 season, he would have to watch Clemens come back and post his career-best 10.7 WAR season in 1997. All told, Clemens posted 10 consecutive 3-WAR or better seasons after he left the Red Sox.

Is he passive or active?

Active. Duquette is always at work tinkering with his roster, raiding the waiver wire and searching for undervalued assets.

An optimist or a problem solver?

Both. One has to be an optimist to take so many chances on so many castoffs as the Orioles have done in recent years. But he's also proven to be a master at successfully running a club with limited resources and excelling under an owner just about no one else wanted to work for.

Does he want to win now or wait out the success cycle?

Given their poor farm system and restricted spending, the Orioles are seeking to win now under Duquette. With Adam Jones in his prime and Manny Machado just entering his, Duquette has done everything he can to build a competent roster around his best players. Considering Baltimore has few long-term commitments beyond 2015, there's no guarantee the current roster sticks together for much longer.

Trades and Free Agents

Does he favor players acquired via trade, development, or free agency?

Development and free agency, though the Orioles hardly ever dip their feet into the expensive waters of the open market. Instead Duquette has found roles for many in-house guys who were never considered top prospects. He's also signed numerous unheralded free agents (often on minor league deals) with consistent success. Even his inspired signing of Nelson Cruz came on a cut-rate, one-year, $8 million deal.

Duquette did spend plenty of money in free agency with the Red Sox. He signed Ramirez to a massive, eight-year, $160 million deal and gave out big contracts to Damon and others. He also twice traded for Pedro Martinez (first in Montreal, then in Boston), which he deserves obvious credit for.

Is he an active trader?

Not especially, though Duquette makes plenty of small deals that barely register on a national scale. Seemingly unremarkable trades for De Aza and Lough have borne some fruit, but they're just examples of Duquette tinkering with his roster. Unsurprisingly, the Orioles are often busy in July, trading for Gerardo Parra this season and striking deals for Andrew Miller, Bud Norris and Francisco Rodriguez prior to past trade deadlines.

Does he tend to move talent or hoard it?

Outside of Baltimore's three best young pitchers (Gausman, Dylan Bundy and Harvey), Duquette has shown little interest in hoarding talent. He traded away

Eduardo Rodriguez in 2014 for two months of Andrew Miller as the Orioles eyed a pennant chase. He sent Jim Johnson to Oakland after back-to-back 50-save seasons as the team's closer.

The biggest mistake he's made is dealing Arrieta to Chicago, but otherwise, he's proven adept at trading away assets that can easily be replaced. Every season, it seems, the Orioles will trade away a reliever who's proven dependable (in 2015, it was Tommy Hunter), before finding someone else on the roster who can fill in.

As his two deals for Pedro show, he has no problem trading away talent for the right price.

With whom does he trade and when?

Duquette's made deals with a wide variety of teams, both inside and outside the AL East and in the National League. He won't hesitate to make trades early in the season either, as he demonstrated when acquiring Nick Hundley in May 2014 after Matt Wieters went down with an injury. The Orioles made more trades in the first three months of 2015 (five) than they did in July, August and September (three).

Will he make deals with other teams during the season?

Yes, and Duquette's proven far more active on the trade market in-season than during the winter. He hasn't been one to strike a big deal during his tenure, largely due to the club's mediocre farm system. In a way, he uses trades as another type of waiver claim.

In one of the most successful trades in Red Sox history, Duquette famously landed Jason Varitek and Derek Lowe for Heathcliff Slocumb just before the trade deadline in 1997.

How does he approach the trade deadline?

Baltimore has made trades at the deadline in each of the past three seasons, and Duquette hasn't hesitated to aggressively add to his squad. With their playoff chances debatable in 2015, the Orioles still added Gerardo Parra from the Brewers on July 31. In 2014, the O's landed Miller to solidify their bullpen, and in 2013, Duquette dealt for Norris, Rodriguez and Scott Feldman leading up to the deadline.

Are there teams or general managers with whom he trades frequently?

Duquette's made a couple of deals with the Red Sox the past two seasons and has also worked well with Jeff Luhnow and the Astros. In addition, the Orioles have made multiple trades with the Brewers, Cubs and Royals.

Has he ever gone to any extremes with his free-agent signings?

The one extreme Duquette's gone to on the free-agent market is signing Ubaldo Jimenez to a four-year, $50 million deal, which, given Jimenez's history, came with a fair bit of risk. Still, the Orioles had already surrendered their first-round pick signing Cruz that winter, and neither the length nor overall price of Jimenez's deal were/are enough to sink Baltimore financially.

Instead, Duquette's proven far more willing to reward his own players, handing out lucrative extensions to Jones and Hardy, investments he likely saw as far less risky than paying top dollar on the open market.

In Boston, he handed Ramirez $160 million over eight years, a massive contract for MLB at the time in 2000. But you can't say that money was poorly spent given all the success Ramirez had with the Red Sox. Besides Jimenez, when Duquette has spent big, he's done so on the right player.

Under what circumstances will he sign free agents?

He had far more money to burn in Boston than in Montreal and Baltimore. Yet even then, he mostly got things right, signing the likes of Tim Wakefield, Jose Offerman, Ramirez and Damon.

He'll also sign a player when it's simply too good an opportunity to pass up. Signing Cruz to a one-year, $8 million contract is one of the best free-agent moves in recent memory. Even the Jimenez deal came when Baltimore had already surrendered its first-rounder in the 2014 draft.

Otherwise, Duquette has been more than happy to scoop up under-the-radar players for little money and add depth to a core that's already in place.

Contracts

Does he prefer long-term deals or short?

Short. Outside of Jones and Jimenez, Duquette has committed no more than three years to any player on Baltimore's roster. The only players who have even received multi-year contracts are Chen, Hardy and O'Day. Everyone else on the Orioles is still under initial team control or signed to a one-year deal.

Per usual, Manny Ramirez's contract is the one exception here.

Does he often backload his contracts?

Perhaps a little, but not to the extent we've seen big free-agent deals being backloaded in recent years. Jones will earn over half his contract in the final three years of the deal between 2016 and 2018. Jimenez's contract pays him roughly the same over all four years.

Does he lock up his players early in their careers or is he more likely to practice brinksmanship?

When Duquette has locked up players on extensions, he's made sure to pick the right guys. With the Red Sox, he signed Nomar Garciaparra to a five-year, $23.5

million deal in 1997, which, even at the time, was a great deal for the team. And certainly locking up young players to multi-year deals wasn't as common back then as it is now. Boston paid its star shortstop an average of $4.65 million per season for his prime years and benefited from two team options at the end of the deal that paid Garciaparra $10.5 million in 2003 and $11.5 million in 2004.

Jones is the only player Duquette has made sure to lock up long-term in Baltimore, but the outfielder clearly stands in a class of his own. In most scenarios, Duquette simply lets a player's contract run through to the end, as he did with Davis and Wieters. He locked up Hardy soon after netting him, and of course, he famously signed Pedro Martinez to the richest contract ever for a pitcher (at the time) shortly after acquiring him from the Expos.

Does he like to avoid arbitration?

Duquette's avoided arbitration with just about all his players in Baltimore. He's found common ground with Davis, Wieters, Tillman and Pearce, and even came to a two-year agreement with O'Day to avoid arbitration in 2013.

Anything unique about his negotiating tactics?

While currently averse to long-term deals, when he does sign them, Duquette likes to tack on club options at the end of the contracts, though that doesn't make him unique among major league GMs. Hardy, Chen and O'Day have all had team options at the end of their contracts, which gives a little extra benefit to the Orioles.

Back in 1997 with the Red Sox, Duquette added two years of club options to the end of Garciaparra's contract, a smart move that has proven to be ahead of its time.

Is he vocal? Does he prefer to work behind the scenes or through the media?

Duquette is anything but vocal and rarely says something of note to the media, especially involving player contracts. Jones' six-year deal in 2013 came with little fuss and so too did Hardy's extension last season.

Bonus

What is his strongest point as GM?

Duquette is a master at uncovering diamonds in the rough. He's also a bit of a chameleon. In Boston, he was able to adapt well to having a higher budget, but the lack of a big budget did not stop him from succeeding in Montreal and Boston.

What would he be doing if he weren't in baseball?

When Duquette was let go in Boston, he kept a very low profile, but he was still involved in the game. He founded the Dan Duquette Sports Academy in western Mass., which its website describes as a "sports camp, tournament facility and lakeside retreat for boys and girls who are interested in learning baseball, softball, basketball, and soccer from distinguished high school, college and pro coaches." They also are a popular venue for sports team retreats, and the facility has continued to operate since Duquette started working with the Orioles. He also purchased a team in the New England Collegiate Baseball League, and helped found the Israel Baseball League. That only lasted one season, but did help a lot of players get into the game. In one way or another, Dan Duquette will always be around baseball.

Rob Manfred: Year One

by Jack Moore

Rob Manfred is not the typical baseball commissioner. He is not a judge, a general or a politician. He is not a czar or a patriarch. Manfred is a CEO, his expertise built on nearly three decades working within the business machine that is Major League Baseball, first as a collective bargainer and an outside counsel for the owners. In 1998, when Bud Selig graduated from interim commissioner to the real thing, Manfred came on as his executive vice president of economics and league affairs. Since then, he has had the reins on some of MLB's most important projects, including the negotiation of the league's first drug testing agreement in 2002 and the Biogenesis investigation in 2013.

Manfred's job is not strictly business, of course. The commissioner of baseball spends far more time in the public eye than the typical CEO, his public statements given deeper reads in the mainstream media. Every move he makes has to be done with a eye on the public relations impact, all while ensuring he doesn't step too hard on the toes of the 30 owners who pay his salary. The major difficulty for Manfred in his time as commissioner will be navigating the constant pushing and pulling of these separate forces as he tries to keep baseball moving forward in what is the most volatile sports landscape America has seen in half a century.

Manfred's first year in office has given him a somewhat soft landing, at least. Biogenesis was squarely in the rearview mirror. The current Collective Bargaining Agreement runs through 2016, a buffer zone before labor strife kicks into high gear. This period of relative calm allowed Manfred to lay out a relatively wide-ranging platform for his early days in office, as spelled out in a letter to fans on the league's website as well as in an interview with ESPN's Jerry Crasnick shortly after he took office. That platform can be boiled down to five points, which I will examine in depth here.

1. Baseball Must Be Reinforced as the Game of the Children

Manfred's letter to fans spent by far the most space on this one, and understandably so, as the vast majority of baseball fans feel a deep connection between baseball and their childhoods. "This notion that baseball is the game of children is central to my core goals as Commissioner," Manfred wrote. Unfortunately, Major League Baseball's fan demographics suggest exactly the opposite. According to Bloomberg Business, roughly half the viewers of the 2014 World Series were over 55 years old, and a paltry six percent were under the age of 18.

Manfred cites his own Little League experience as critical to shaping him as a baseball fan. His primary approach to engaging with young people is to get them playing the game. It's a smart approach, but it may be harder than it sounds. More and more youth coaches are demanding year-round participation in a single sport. Particularly in cold climates where baseball can't realistically be played in winter, this means the popularity of football and basketball is siphoning participants away from baseball in the spring and summer.

In May, *The Wall Street Journal's* Brian Costa detailed the struggles Little League organizers encountered in even signing up enough kids to fill a roster. The Newburgh, N.Y. Little League featured in the story has seen participation drop from 206 players in 2009 to 74 this past year, nearly a two-thirds decline. According to the National Sporting Goods Association, this trend has been nationwide. Youth participation in baseball dropped from 8.8 million in 2000 to 5.3 million in 2013. Softball has seen a similar trend, with a drop from 5.4 million to 3.2 million in the same period.

The result has been the closing of some youth leagues and the consolidation of others with nearby cities. While these consolidation efforts keep baseball going in these areas, they also require far more travel, which has worked to price out children from lower-income families. Minority communities are hit particularly hard. As Costa wrote, "Roughly two-thirds of Newburgh's Little Leaguers are minorities. When youth baseball dries up in a place like this, it pushes the sport even further in the direction it has been headed for years: richer, whiter, smaller."

Manfred addressed these concerns in his letter. "Specifically, I plan to make the game more accessible to those in underserved areas," Manfred wrote, "especially in the urban areas where fields and infrastructure are harder to find. Giving more kids the opportunity to play will inspire a new generation to fall in love with baseball just as we did when we were kids. Expanding Little League, RBI and other youth baseball programs will also help sustain a steady and wide talent pool from which our clubs can draw great players and create lifelong fans."

Manfred is on the right track. Now we'll have to see if his words translate into action. Major League Baseball under Bud Selig made its own efforts to encourage minority participation, like the expansion of the RBI program and the construction of baseball academies like the one in Compton, Calif., in the late 1990s and early 2000s. But these programs have not translated into results on the field. African-American participation in baseball continues to decline, to the point where Selig put together another one of his famous blue ribbon committees to solve the problem back in 2013.

Baseball should be willing to throw money at this problem. Consider it an investment. Major League Baseball poured $3 million into its Compton academy in 2003, which sounds impressive until you realize $3 million was all of 0.07 percent of MLB's $3.9 billion revenue in 2003. MLB and the Players Association agreed to a $30 million joint investment in youth baseball growth and development in July. It's a good start. But again, MLB set a record with $9 billion in revenue in 2014. This program, which is set to invest $10 million per year, is still plowing only about 0.1 percent of league revenue into youth baseball.

Baseball's return on its investment in youth baseball will be proportional to the size of said investment. Not only is it the right thing to do for kids who want to play baseball—particularly marginalized and working-class kids—but it's something Major League Baseball needs to do if it wishes to maintain its fan base. As Manfred told *The Wall Street Journal*, "The biggest predictor of fan avidity as an adult is whether you played the game." Manfred is aware it isn't in baseball's best interests to be cheap when it comes to supporting youth baseball. Now, can he get the owners to open their checkbooks?

2. Baseball Needs to Market its Stars

It's a constant complaint among baseball commentators that baseball does a horrid job of marketing its stars. It's hard to argue when basketball stars like LeBron James, Chris Paul, Kevin Durant and James Harden are household names no matter where they play, while baseball's elite like Andrew McCutchen, Joey Votto, Evan Longoria, Giancarlo Stanton, Paul Goldschmidt and others outside the large markets are relative unknowns until they appear in a nationally broadcast playoff series. Even Mike Trout, playing in the Los Angeles market, hardly has the Q Rating one would expect from a phenom with three top-two MVP finishes in his first three seasons.

Adding more nationally telecast games on Fox Sports 1 and continuing to operate MLB.TV as the greatest sports streaming service in the age of cord-cutting will only help make players outside of the New York-Boston area more visible. But Major League Baseball still isn't boosting these players for a nation to see. Trout's biggest endorsement deal is from Subway. McCutchen, in a story for Yahoo! in April, practically begged to be made one of the faces of baseball going forward. "I want to be like Griffey," McCutchen told Jeff Passan, "And you can make that player. We can have that player in baseball. Part of the reason I like to be the way I am is because of baseball."

It's a lot harder to just make these things happen now, however. People take in their baseball and baseball news from a far wider variety of sources than they did in Griffey's day. Major League Baseball can't just run an advertising blitz on network TV and *Sports Illustrated* and think it will hit the whole fanbase, especially the young people baseball wants so badly to court. MLB will have to find ways to reach young people, and that means using the internet and social media and adapting to whatever killer app comes out between editing and publication of this book and makes the current flavor of the month obsolete.

But perhaps more critically, people within the game have to be willing to let these players become stars. With the energy he exudes on the field, Yasiel Puig was practically begging to become a superstar in 2014, but baseball men from all corners of Los Angeles—his Dodgers teammates, his coaches, and the people who tell his stories as journalists—instead insisted on reining him in and shackling all the enthusiasm that made him so compelling. This is all too common a pattern with young star players. The constant criticism lobbed at Bryce Harper this season as he destroyed the National League in one of the greatest seasons in recent memory, regardless of age, is just the latest and greatest example.

Harper, however, is the rare white star to draw this kind of ire, whether it's because he's too brash or too beautiful or whatever other nonsense reason people have found to resent him. Usually it's players like Puig or Hanley Ramirez or Justin Upton who get this treatment, who get dismissed as "attitude problems" and discarded as potential faces of baseball. If Major League Baseball wants to appeal to all children, it will need to embrace these players and at least learn to work with them rather than constantly fight these respectability battles in the media.

If Manfred wants to speed up the process of embracing these players, he needs to continue to support the hiring of blacks and people of color in managerial and front office positions. He has already issued a warning to clubs in the wake of Milwaukee's quick hiring of Craig Counsell as its manager that failures to follow the Selig Rule and interview at least one minority candidate for these positions will be punished. He needs to keep that promise, because it is critical to have people who will identify with minority stars in these organizations if the kinds of culture clashes we have seen are to be avoided.

I would offer one more suggestion to make the marketing of players easier: Stop considering them enemies in the war on performance-enhancing drugs. This doesn't mean dropping the war. It means ending the absurdity of protecting a man like Tony Bosch in order to pursue suspensions for major league stars. The distributors are the real bad guys in this situation, but baseball has put an absurd amount of resources into protecting these people in order to remove its own stars from the playing field. As long as players are adversaries to be caught, suspicion will permeate the game, and there won't be a record set or a star born without somebody speculating about steroids, and that does nothing but hurt baseball's ability to create stars and connect with fans.

3. Baseball Needs to Modernize Itself

The idea of baseball as a leader in modern technology may have seemed silly as few as 10 years ago, but behind the efforts of Major League Baseball Advanced Media, it has become not just a tech leader in sports but in entertainment as a whole. MLB.TV continues to be the highest quality sports streaming offering around. The system is so advanced that MLBAM has been hired to oversee digital streaming services for WWE, and most recently HBO as part of its HBONow platform.

"When HBO decides it's going to offer an over-the-top product for the first time in history, other than sports, where do they go? They go to MLB Advanced Media to provide the streaming for that product. That's an astounding development," Manfred told Crasnick, and it's difficult to argue with his conclusion. He continued, "I think it's important we take that great technology company and make sure we apply that technology in ways that enhance the experience of fans in the ballpark, but maybe more importantly, when they engage on television."

MLB is already working on using its technology to enhance broadcasts with Statcast, but the technology is still young, and its use on air this past season was little more than showing off a fancy toy. It will take some time for broadcasters to figure out the best way to use the mountain of data Statcast dumps into their laps, so perhaps that's to be expected. But there are still valid concerns about MLB's chokehold on the Statcast data and questions about how much of it will be available to the kind of enterprising researchers who have made sabermetric breakthroughs happen.

Of greater concern should be the number of people these broadcasts are actually reaching. MLB.TV is great, but blackout rules prevent people from watching teams in their own markets. And in certain markets, like Las Vegas or Iowa, viewers are blocked from as many as six different markets and can be blacked out for over 33 percent of games, as SB Nation contributor and Iowa resident Mike Bates documented in a running count on his Twitter feed throughout the 2015 season. While all this may be necessary to keep cable companies happy and the rights fees flowing into team coffers, it's not helpful for getting people, particularly the young people who figure to make up most of the cord-cutting population, into baseball.

Under Manfred, Major League Baseball has made some slight progress against the blackout rules, which serve the cable companies far more than they serve baseball. MLB came to an agreement with Fox to set up local streaming options for 15 markets in the 2016 season. Unfortunately, this would still require a cable subscription that includes the regional Fox network, but it's a step in the right direction. Manfred and MLBAM head Bob Bowman have made in-market streaming a priority, according to an August report from Sports Business Daily.

Giving fans access to the game from anywhere, "in-market" or not, would be as modern as it could get in today's media world, and it's encouraging to see baseball working to that end. The only question is how hard the cable companies are going to work against it.

But baseball is not always fighting the good fight when it comes to restricted content. MLB continues to aggressively scour video sources like YouTube for highlights and has aggressively filed DMCA copyright takedown requests, even to the extent of removing animated .GIFs from Twitter. Baseball's desire to control its own image is understandable, but in eliminating fans' ability to spread highlights and other videos, it cuts off many avenues of engagement for the game. People don't hear about baseball only through mass media like television and newspapers anymore. Personal sharing can be just as important, but as long as MLB continues to be a copyright troll, it will miss out on a gigantic number of opportunities to create new fans.

4. Baseball Needs to Strengthen Player Relations

"I am a player guy—all the time," Manfred told Crasnick. We all know better than that by now. Manfred works for the owners, and he represents them in collective bargaining. He is not a partner of the players. As Marvin Miller wrote in his autobiography, *A Whole Different Ball Game*, "It's always amazed me that so few baseball writers have grasped this obvious fact, opting instead for a romantic view of the commissioner as some kind of Socrates or Solomon whom baseball people flock to for an objective view of a current crisis. The owners select the commissioner and pay his salary, and they do not pay him to be objective."

That said, Manfred has inherited a strong position in what have been the owners' biggest battlegrounds with the Players Association in recent years: salaries and drug penalties. As FanGraphs' Nathaniel Grow detailed before the 2015 season, the player's share of baseball-related revenues has dropped from 56 percent in 2002 to 38 percent in 2014. And the union has knuckled under to all of ownership's demands on performance enhancing drugs, having agreed not only to HGH testing but also increased penalties for steroids, penalties designed to save MLB from the embarrassment of players who tested positive making big impacts in the playoffs.

Manfred's focus has been on increasing access to players, not only for fans but for advertisers and business partners as well. "For a product to be popular, people want access. They want to be able to get at stars," he told Crasnick. "The way you get them to accept that is to build on the positive relationships we've been able to establish over the last 20 years." He continued, "The players have to understand, when I go to them and say, 'I need you to do X, Y or Z today,' it's not because I'm looking to generate $200,000 more of revenue from that appearance to put in my pocket. It's so we have the people who are going to replace Derek Jeter, so our sport attracts the kind of media companies that are so crucial to our business."

This all ties into Manfred's previous point about marketing the game's stars, and it's true, the access demanded in today's environment is far broader than in the television or radio age. But I think it's interesting Manfred cites Jeter, because Jeter and his website, The Players Tribune, are proving on a daily basis this access doesn't have to be provided by the leagues. Players like Andrew McCutchen and David Ortiz have used The Players Tribune to tell important and compelling stories about the struggles of baseball players in low-income communities and the racist assumptions of baseball reporters pursuing PED stories.

Manfred recognizes players have valuable stories to tell. While he is selling his plan as one to provide more access to fans, it sounds to me like an attempt to make sure those valuable stories fall under MLB's umbrella rather than somewhere by players and for players. It bears resemblance to the promotional wars the Players Association and the league fought in the late 1960s, in which the union owned the rights to players' likenesses but the league owned the rights to the logos. The league formed Major League Baseball Promotions and would lobby groups signing deals with the Players Association to ditch the players and take the logos instead. So maybe Manfred isn't looking to put money in his pocket, but he may wind up restricting the players' ability to market themselves.

Manfred has at least recognized that the idea of baseball's commissioner as a neutral arbitrator is absurd and one that would not hold up in court. This is the mistake Roger Goodell and the NFL has been making in recent years. Their plans to handle domestic violence and other disciplinary cases (including DeflateGate) have insisted Goodell serve as final arbitrator, despite the fact he, like Manfred, is an employee of the owners. This insistence on the commissioner's total control over the players has cost the NFL in the courts; DeflateGate marked the fifth consecutive case with Goodell as a neutral arbitrator the league has lost to the NFL Players Association. Now, the NFL's entire disciplinary system is in doubt, as any long suspension upheld by the commissioner as arbitrator can be challenged under that precedent.

Major League Baseball did not make the same mistake with its domestic violence policy, which includes an appeal process with a neutral arbitrator. This both allows for action to be taken before the criminal process is complete and ensures the player's right to due process—important not just for the player's labor rights to check against abuse of power but also for ensuring the suspensions of guilty players will hold up in court. It was a sign Manfred and his MLB can see the players as a group to be worked *with* rather than *against*, and such cooperation and respect will be critical to ensuring baseball doesn't fall back into the constant labor strife it endured in the 1970s, 1980s and 1990s.

5. Baseball Needs to Become a More Unified Business Operation

It's easy to forget now, with MLBAM serving as the engine of baseball in the internet age, that its beginnings were humble. MLBAM began as a way to consolidate baseball's digital resources and run all its internet content—originally just websites and mobile apps in the early 2000s—from one place in a uniform fashion. It has gotten so big that its other engagements—the aforementioned HBO, WWE and other non-baseball streaming services—are slated to be spun off into a separate company called BAM Tech.

Bob Bowman has been promoted from MLBAM's leader to Major League Baseball's president of baseball and media, and what remains of his project after the spinoff will be fully integrated into the MLB machine. It's great that Major League Baseball is buying into the power of technology, but it's important to recognize that an important part of MLBAM's success was its freedom to experiment. One of those experiments turned out to be MLB.TV, the result of noticing baseball's gigantic inventory of games was a resource waiting to be tapped.

This is the real question. Unification will undoubtedly lead to more efficiency, but will it allow the same kind of creativity? "Everything was designed to make baseball one business," Manfred told Crasnick. "Whether you're dealing with [MLB

Advanced Media] or [MLB Network] or 245 Park Avenue, we are one organization. There's one-stop shopping." This process is for sponsors and advertisers first and foremost, and fans just have to hope it doesn't lead to the elimination or obsolescence of a quirky project like MLBAM that could revolutionize the way fans watch, experience and access the game.

Manfred appears to understand the differences between his commissionership and those of men like Kenesaw Mountain Landis, Bowie Kuhn and even Bud Selig. His job isn't to control baseball. His job is to moderate disputes within ownership and negotiate with the players in a way that leads baseball to its healthiest future.

Make no mistake, Manfred's first job is ensuring baseball continues to make money hand over fist. But he has at least shown in public that he realizes this requires cooperation with the players and reaching out to fans to make the game as accessible as possible. His real test—a new CBA—is yet to come, and we will see how many of these principles from his first year hold up when he takes to the negotiating table as baseball's patriarch for the first time.

References & Resources

- Jerry Crasnick, ESPN, "Rob Manfred's Top Five Priorities," *espn.go.com/mlb/story/_/id/12218054/new-mlb-commissioner-rob-manfred-top-five-priorities*
- Rob Manfred, MLB.com, "Commissioner Rob Manfred's Letter To Fans," *m.mlb.com/news/article/107424384/new-mlb-commissioner-rob-manfreds-letter-to-fans*
- Brian Costa, *The Wall Street Journal*, "Why Children Are Abandoning Baseball," *wsj.com/articles/why-baseball-is-losing-children-1432136172*
- Bob Nightengale, *USA TODAY*, "Bud Selig to create task force on blacks in baseball," *usatoday.com/story/sports/mlb/2013/04/09/mlb-african-americans-in-baseball-jackie-robinson-42/2069119/*
- *Milwaukee Journal Sentinel*, "Baseball builds youth academy," *news.google.com/newspapers?nid=1683&dat=20030811&id=lhofAAAAIBAJ&sjid=Y44EAAAAIBAJ&pg=6393,338860&hl=en*
- Jeff Passan, Yahoo! Sports, "Baseball's greatest challenge? Convincing people it's still cool," *sports.yahoo.com/news/baseball-s-greatest-challenge--convincing-people-it-s-still-cool-230449039.html*
- Matt Snyder, CBS Sports, "Report: Local streaming coming to 15 MLB markets next season," *cbssports.com/mlb/eye-on-baseball/25272459/report-local-streaming-coming-to-mlb-next-season*
- Nathaniel Grow, FanGraphs, "The MLBPA has a Problem," *fangraphs.com/blogs/the-mlbpa-has-a-problem/*

- Jason Abbruzzese, Mashable, "Major League Baseball's digital arm will live-stream hockey games," *mashable.com/2015/08/04/mlb-live-streaming-hockey*
- Maury Brown, *Forbes*, "The Biggest Media Company You've Never Heard Of," *forbes.com/sites/maurybrown/2014/07/07/the-biggest-media-company-youve-never-heard-of/*
- Mike Bates, Twitter, *https://twitter.com/MikeBatesSBN/status/651065337199362048*
- Mike Bates, Twitter, *https://twitter.com/MikeBatesSBN/status/651499169866207237*

All This Has Happened Before: The Mets' Rotation, Then and Now

by Erik Malinowski

Coming into the 2015 season, most experts would have wholeheartedly agreed that the New York Mets had a good, promising pitching staff that was on the upswing but far from a sure thing—talented but unproven starters, an ace who was coming back from 18 months of rehab, and a bullpen that had a chance of inching its way to some consistent measure of respectability. There weren't question marks so much as there were blank spaces scattered about. Whether those would be filled in (and by whom) were a mystery as February dawned.

So when closer Jeurys Familia struck out Cincinnati's Jay Bruce on Sept. 26 to officially clinch the National League East title for the Mets, there was almost no part of this scene that wasn't surprising at a core level. Before the season, ESPN had polled 88 baseball writers and asked who they thought would win the N.L. East: 85 said the Washington Nationals and two said the Miami Marlins. A single person picked the Mets, who will now get to raise their first new flag at Citi Field next season.

How did they get there? The offense, which had been downright abysmal over the first half and even past the All-Star break, found its stride thanks to myriad trade deadline acquisitions: Yoenis Cespedes (57 games, .942 OPS), Kelly Johnson and Juan Uribe all stepped up after their arrivals. Travis d'Arnaud and David Wright finally got healthy, and Wilmer Flores wasn't *actually* traded (and it's a good thing, too, with his .808 OPS in 44 games after the non-waiver deadline). Michael Conforto (.841 OPS in 56 games) provided a steady middle-of-the-lineup bat even while jumping right from Double-A to the bigs, and his defense in left (six assists) was one of the best in the National League after his call-up. Yes, the offense in the second half (a league-leading 5.82 runs per game after July 23) played a pivotal role in securing the Mets' first division crown in nine years—but not *the* most pivotal role.

From start to finish, it was the Mets' pitching staff that set the tone and gave a less-than-stellar offense a chance to win every night out. From a 4.5-game lead in May to a 4.5-game deficit in July and back again, pitching coach Dan Warthen kept the staff focused and motivated and pitching better than anyone could have ever expected.

So when Familia unleashed his 94-mph splitter to strike out Bruce and clinch the division, it was the culmination of months of buildup and years of development. The thing is, that sort of thing is not uncommon for the Mets. The franchise, 54 seasons old, has gone through this cycle before with pitchers. All the really successful Mets teams over the years have been built on pitching—the 1999 and 2000 teams that went to the playoffs and remain the highest and fourth-highest scoring teams in Mets history are the glaring exceptions. Sometimes it flames out before it starts (Generation K, anyone?) but often it comes in waves of several years at a time. There's a crescendo to it. You can often see it happening for a couple of seasons before it finally crests.

That's the identity of the 2015 Mets staff, one that sits at the start of a rising wave. Before we look at how this current crop of young Mets hurlers (and one old exception) made history, let's look back at some organizational comps, because what occurred in 2015 had a very distinct Mets feel, and if that holds true, it'll be a bad sign for National League opponents through 2016 and beyond.

An Amazin' Season (1969)

Remember this about the Mets when they made their run in '69: They had finished every season in their (albeit brief) history in either last place or next-to-last place. And then they won 100 games—completing a 27-game turnaround from the previous season—and knocked off the 109-win Baltimore Orioles in a five-game World Series. There has likely never been a more stunning single-season turn of events than what that Mets team pulled off, and it was done, more than anything, with pitching.

Primary Mets Pitchers, 1969										
Player	Role	Age	W	L	ERA	SV	IP	SO	ERA+	FIP
Tom Seaver	Starter	24	25	7	2.21	0	273.1	208	165	3.11
Jerry Koosman	Starter	26	17	9	2.28	0	241.0	180	160	2.67
Gary Gentry	Starter	22	13	12	3.43	0	233.2	154	106	3.63
Don Cardwell	Starter	33	8	10	3.01	0	152.1	60	121	4.03
Jim McAndrew	Starter	25	6	7	3.47	0	135.0	90	105	3.35
Ron Taylor	Closer	31	9	4	2.72	13	76.0	42	134	3.59
Tug McGraw	Closer	24	9	3	2.24	12	100.1	92	163	2.86
Nolan Ryan	Reliever	22	6	3	3.53	1	89.1	92	104	2.70

Tom Seaver had already become a rising star by winning 32 games over his first two seasons, but he was otherworldly in 1969, ripping off 25 wins, a league-low 6.7 hits per nine, and a 165 ERA+ over 273 innings. Seaver was only in his age-24 season and would go on to post even better numbers over the next couple of years as he matured, but he was already a much-needed ace when the Mets were ready for their unexpected but welcome growth spurt that year.

His supporting cast was excellent, as well. Jerry Koosman was a 6-foot-2 lefty who was also just coming into this own as a major leaguer. Koosman went 19-12 for the 1968 season, his first full one in the bigs, and he and Seaver formed a powerful one-two punch at the front of the rotation. Rookie Gary Gentry, all of 22, was a physically unimpressive (6-foot, 170 pounds) but surprisingly effective No. 3, logging 35 starts and three shutouts. There was quite a dropoff after that triumvirate, but the bullpen had some dominant arms, including 24-year-old closer Tug McGraw and a 22-year-old flamethrowing setup man named Nolan Ryan.

Sure, a whole mess of things had to go *just* right for the 1969 Mets to pull up the unthinkable and win the World Series, but it was all made possible by the duo of Seaver and Koosman, plus the collective efforts of the other pitchers, many of whom were still far off from their career peaks.

Don't Call It a Comeback (1973)

After the events of 1969, the Mets won 83 games a season for the next three years and finished third in the NL East every time out. So it was quite a jolt when they won only 82 games in 1973 yet won the National League pennant and scraped out a 3-2 World Series lead before blowing the final two games in Oakland to MVP Reggie Jackson and his A's. Once again, the Mets' pitching staff was the overwhelming reason why they advanced as far as they did, and the peripherals, if not as gaudy as they were four years earlier, were still enough to make for a deep postseason run.

Primary Mets Pitchers, 1973										
Player	Role	Age	W	L	ERA	SV	IP	SO	ERA+	FIP
Tom Seaver	Starter	28	19	10	2.08	0	290.0	251	175	2.57
Jerry Koosman	Starter	30	14	15	2.84	0	263.0	156	128	3.18
Jon Matlack	Starter	23	14	16	3.20	0	242.0	205	114	2.98
George Stone	Starter	26	12	3	2.80	1	148.0	77	130	3.56
Jim McAndrew	Starter	29	3	8	5.38	1	80.1	38	68	4.35
Tug McGraw	Closer	28	5	6	3.87	25	118.2	81	94	3.87
Ray Sadecki	Reliever	32	5	4	3.39	1	116.2	87	107	3.38

Seaver was sublime in the three years following the 1969 season—he averaged 20 wins a year and would record single-season career-bests in ERA, FIP, Ks, and WHIP—and he was the anchor again in '73. Still only 28, he led the league in ERA, complete games (18), ERA+, FIP, WHIP (0.976), and hits per nine (6.8). Koosman, again, was the left-handed complement to this equation, even as his win-loss record belied the underlying peripherals, which remained solid. Jon Matlack, a 6-foot-3 lefty, was now the designated No. 3 starter; he allowed more baserunners that would've been preferred (1.28 WHIP) but could get a strikeout when needed. George Stone, acquired before the season in a trade that sent Gentry to the Atlanta Braves, was a lifesaver No. 4 down the stretch: From Aug. 27 to Sept. 19, Stone won five straight starts, posting a 2.10 ERA in them.

With McGraw once again the closer, the Mets made the A's sweat right up until the very end of Game Seven, but the 1973 season would, in the end, only mark the start of an era of futility—10 straight years of finishing double-digit games out of first. The fact that the Yankees shook off the doldrums of a long playoff-less streak shortly thereafter made things more painful.

Teamwork to Make the Dream Work (1986)

From a pure talent standpoint, the '86 Mets staff remains, top to bottom, the most talented collection of pitchers the club has ever assembled. Four starters logged more than 30 starts and boasted a winning percentage above .700. Since 1901, they are the only team ever to do that. For context, the 2001 Seattle Mariners are the only other team ever to have *three* starters pull off the feat. (Incidentally, the 2015 Houston Astros joined the fraternity of 40 teams that have had exactly two such starters.)

Primary Mets Pitchers, 1986										
Player	Role	Age	W	L	ERA	SV	IP	SO	ERA+	FIP
Dwight Gooden	Starter	21	17	6	2.84	0	250.0	200	126	3.06
Ron Darling	Starter	25	15	6	2.81	0	237.0	184	127	3.43
Bob Ojeda	Starter	28	18	5	2.57	0	217.1	148	140	3.05
Sid Fernandez	Starter	23	16	6	3.52	1	204.1	200	102	3.01
Rick Aguilera	Starter	24	10	7	3.88	0	141.2	104	93	3.59
Roger McDowell	Closer	25	14	9	3.02	22	128.0	65	119	3.22
Jesse Orosco	Closer	29	8	6	2.33	21	81.0	62	154	3.61

There was not a weak spot to be found in the Mets rotation, and Dwight Gooden stood atop that collection of young, lethal pitchers. Still only 21, Gooden (like Seaver before him) had already thrown two dominant seasons of big-league ball before his World Series year, winning 41 games over that time. In fact, across the board, Gooden's numbers were down from his 1985 totals (which would've been just about impossible to replicate anyway) but he was still the undisputed ace on the staff. His reputation, built up over two magnificent seasons, was secured, even as his numbers went from otherworldly to merely great.

Ron Darling, Sid Fernandez and Bob Ojeda, all more than competent hurlers with strikeout-inducing stuff, were a formidable trio backing up Gooden. The 23-year-old Fernandez, acquired for practically nothing after the 1983 season in a trade with the Dodgers, was arguably the most important counterpart to Gooden's heat. Armed with a devastating, looping curveball, Fernandez posted the best FIP of any starter on the team, and he logged just as many strikeouts as Gooden but in 46 fewer innings. But he and Gooden and Darling and No. 5 starter Rick Aguilera all gelled during the 1985 season, when the Mets won 98 games but finished three games out of first to the eventual World Series champion St. Louis Cardinals.

The Mets bullpen was an all-time assortment in 1986. Four pitchers (Aguilera, Jesse Orosco, Randy Myers and Roger McDowell) would go on to save 968 games over their combined careers. But in '86, it was either McDowell, who didn't start a game all year but still finished with a 14-9 record to go with a team-high 22 saves, or Orosco who was called on to secure one of the Mets' team-record number of wins.

The memorable seven-game World Series win over Boston secured this team's place as the gold standard in Mets history, the one by which all others shall be measured. But there was also a blueprint drawn up with the '86 team, a schematic that built off the '69 and '73 seasons and showed how you can build a winning staff from within that can find success over a period of years. The Mets would win at least 87 games in each of the next four seasons, including a 100-win 1988 campaign that saw them go as far as Game Seven of the NLCS before bowing out to the Dodgers.

After the development exhibited in 1984 (90-72) and 1985 (98-64), no one was surprised the '86 Mets rocketed to first class when they did. Whether this current Mets team can make good on a similar arc is a more interesting proposition.

Harder, Faster, Better? (2015)

Perhaps 2014 wasn't a lost season for the Mets' pitching staff, but it was a mixed bag. Matt Harvey was absent from the active roster while rehabbing from the Tommy John surgery he underwent in October 2013. Bartolo Colon and Jon Niese were the stalwarts, starting 61 games between them. Zack Wheeler, all of 24, surprised by leading the staff in games started. Wheeler used his dazzling array of pitches (four-seamer at 96, slider at 90, curve at 80) to post 9.1 K/9 and a 3.55 FIP over 185 innings. Wheeler had a solid prospect pedigree, though—he was a top-100 prospect four years running and was Baseball America's 11th-ranked prospect in 2013. The real shocker, though, was 26-year-old Jacob deGrom stepping in to go 9-6 over 22 starts, post a 2.67 FIP over 140 innings, and win the National League Rookie of the Year Award. The Mets went 79-83, but combine Wheeler and deGrom with the returning Harvey, and things were looking up for 2015.

And then the Mets lost Wheeler to his own Tommy John surgery near the end of spring training, and the staff was once again left with questions. How would this rotation be able to compete with the pitching of, say, the Washington Nationals? Could Harvey hold up over an entire season? Was deGrom a fluke? And would the Mets be able to maintain some semblance of increased improvement over the last season? Would this season stand as a modern-day analog to '84 or '85 when the Mets were on the precipice of greatness? Or more akin to '73, when everything aligned for only a brief moment before scattering into the ether?

Primary Mets Pitchers, 2015										
Player	Role	Age	W	L	ERA	SV	IP	SO	ERA+	FIP
Bartolo Colon	Starter	42	14	13	4.16	0	194.2	136	89	3.84
Jacob deGrom	Starter	27	14	8	2.54	0	191.0	205	145	2.70
Matt Harvey	Starter	26	13	8	2.71	0	189.1	188	136	3.05
Jon Niese	Starter	28	9	10	4.13	0	176.2	113	89	4.41
Noah Syndergaard	Starter	22	9	7	3.24	0	150.0	166	114	3.25
Steven Matz	Starter	24	4	0	2.27	0	35.2	34	164	3.61
Jeurys Familia	Closer	25	2	2	1.85	43	78.0	86	200	2.74
Tyler Clippard	Reliever	30	4	1	3.06	2	32.1	26	122	4.65
Addison Reed	Reliever	26	1	1	1.17	1	15.1	17	322	2.74
Sean Gilmartin	Reliever	25	3	2	2.67	0	57.1	54	139	2.75

This much is clear: There were no more question marks about the Mets' prowess by the time the curtain fell on the 2015 regular season. Even without Wheeler, Warthen's staff leaned on Harvey, deGrom, Colon and rookies Noah Syndergaard and Steven Matz to reel off 90 wins for the first time in nine years. Throw in Familia, who saved 43 games and developed the fastest and perhaps nastiest splitter ever seen, and the Mets' collection of pitchers, from top to bottom, was better than anyone else's in baseball.

Even amid all the innings-limit talk that plagued the final quarter of his season, Harvey was the rock that held up this staff, making his absence in 2014 even more glaring in hindsight. Over 29 starts, Harvey struck out 188 batters in 189.1 innings, walked only 37, and posted a 136 ERA+. His four-seamer averaged 96 mph, with a 91-mph slider, 88-mph change, and 84-mph curve to boot. It's perhaps not surprising that he became less dependent on his four-seamer and slider as the season progressed and moved more toward the change, owing to the increased workload from which he was two years removed.

In the end, Harvey's peripherals weren't as gaudy as they were during his breakout 2013 season (2.01 FIP, 191 Ks in 178.1 innings), because of the slight increase in walk rate and more noticeable drop in his strikeout rate and fastball velocity. Still, Harvey provided as much a psychological boost as a tangible. His mere presence—reminiscent of Seaver or Gooden—was that of a power ace, a clear No. 1 who led off every rotation cycle with a bang. With him firmly entrenched atop the staff, the trickle-down effect guided everyone else in their roles.

Only slightly less important than Harvey's return was that of deGrom, proving that his exceptional 2014 Rookie of the Year campaign was not a fluke, especially considering deGrom was not a highly touted prospect like those immediately surrounding him. With a four-seamer sitting at 95 and a 90-mph slider, deGrom could then drop in either the 86-mph change or 82-mph curve if he so chose. Across the board, the lanky, 6-foot-4 deGrom improved in just about every metric over his 2014 numbers.

Noah Syndergaard wasn't called up until June, but his presence was undeniable and pretty historic. Over 150 innings, the man called Thor had a 9.96 K/9 and 1.86 BB/9. Only 17 pitchers in baseball history have done that in a season (minimum 150 innings). His 166 strikeouts were the fifth-most ever by a Mets rookie, eclipsed only by some names already mentioned: Gooden (276), Koosman (178), Seaver (170) and Matlack (169). The average velocity on his four-seamer (97.1 mph) was the highest ever recorded by FanGraphs for a single season, going back to 2002 (minimum 100 innings pitched per season). His 1.05 WHIP was a Mets rookie record.

By season's end, the 6-foot-6 Syndergaard possessed a complete arsenal of pitches, mixing in the heat with a high-80s change and low-80s curve. Hitters were defenseless when he had command. "This guy throws a lot more strikes than you would think a young man with that kind of arm and that size," Mets manager Terry Collins said after the season. "It's surprising how much he pounds the strike zone. That's where I was most impressed as he went through the season. He throws strikes and he makes you swing the bat. That's why I think he's going to be a good pitcher. His stuff speaks for itself." With the loss of Wheeler, Syndergaard was everything the Mets could've hoped for. On any other team, he'd likely be the No. 2 if not the ace, but on this team he'll slot in behind Harvey and deGrom.

Steven Matz was another late-season bright spot, especially when other starters were struggling through to the season's finish line. But the biggest (in more than ways than one) season-long boost came from fastball-happy Bartolo Colon, who made 31 starts, throwing that 90-mph "heater" more than 83 percent of the time (second-highest clip in baseball, behind St. Louis' Lance Lynn), and ended up leading the Mets in innings pitched. Posting a decent 3.84 FIP in his age-42 season, Colon was more than an instant attraction wherever he went. He was a stabilizing force through August and September, and insofar as clubhouse chemistry can have a real impact on games, he appeared to provide it in spades.

Backing up all of this dominance up front was the closer Familia, who developed the fastest splitter in history. FanGraphs clocked its average velocity at 93.6, which makes it just about unhittable. After prospective closer Jenrry Mejia was caught using PEDs and suspended in early April for 80 games, Familia stepped into the role without a hitch, and Warthen helped refine the splitter as the season progressed. It wasn't quite Mariano Rivera/cutter level of unhittable, but it was certainly a kindred spirit. (When Mejia was suspended yet again in July, this time for 162 games, barely any Mets players or fans blinked.) And relievers such as Sean Gilmartin, Tyler Clippard and Addison Reed all were fairly reliable down the stretch, posting above-average ERA+ and strikeout rates comparable to the rotation.

As a collective, the Mets staff exhibited not only impeccable command and historically high heat. This was the first team in major league history to boast four starting pitchers (Colon, deGrom, Harvey, Syndergaard) who threw at least 150 innings and had a strikeout-to-walk ratio higher than 5.0. (The only other team ever to have three such starters was the 2005 Minnesota Twins, with Brad Radke, Johan Santana and Carlos Silva.)

Part of that excellent strikeout-to-walk ratio can explained by the Mets' infatuation with throwing first-pitch strikes, and throwing some very hard cheese. Among starters throwing 150 innings in 2015, the Mets had those same four starters all rank in the top 20 in the majors, with Harvey leading the way (68.2 percent, sixth overall). According to Baseball Savant, the Mets threw 4,948 pitches that were 95 mph or higher, a whopping 41 percent more than the next closest team, Kansas City, which threw 3,498 such pitches. Syndergaard (1,421), Harvey (1,258), and deGrom (901) accounted for 72 percent of that total and their efforts combined tallied 82 more than the *entire* Royals team. Familia had the highest single percentage of any Mets pitcher, with 758 of 1,137 (a full two-thirds) reaching that speed. It's no wonder deGrom (12.7 percent), Syndergaard (12.2 percent), and Harvey (11.6 percent) were all in the top 20 in swinging-strike rate among starters with 150 innings pitched.

Overall, a full 22 percent of all Mets pitches in 2015 clocked 95 mph or higher. For comparison's sake to the other recent league leaders, that's 29 percent higher than the 2014 Royals, 63 percent higher than the 2013 Cardinals, and 45 percent more than the 2012 Rays. And among all pitchers (minimum 150 innings), deGrom (.574), Harvey (.609), and Syndergaard (.645) were in the top 15 in lowest OPS allowed. You can't hit what you can't hit, and the Mets proved that simple maxim truer than any club in recent memory.

For next year, the Mets can look forward to essentially swapping out Colon, a free agent, for the 6-foot-4 righty Wheeler, who is expected to be back at full strength in time for spring training. And when they do, they'll have a Harvey-deGrom-Syndergaard-Wheeler-Matz starting five. If that doesn't give you some serious '69 or '86 vibes, you are incapable of human emotion: Harvey as the Seaver-Gooden power pitcher archetype; deGrom using an above-average fastball and offspeed stuff to keep hitters off balance, like Sid Fernandez or Jerry Koosman; Syndergaard the eye-bulging fireballer, not unlike a young Nolan Ryan.

And it's not just next year. Harvey and Familia are under team control through the end of the 2018 season. Wheeler is under contract through the end of 2019. He may already be 27, but deGrom is also under team control through 2020. And Syndergaard and Matz are under team control through 2021. This gives the Mets at least a three-year window at utter domination, and if Harvey and Familia can be coaxed back into the fold, potentially even longer. In 2019, the oldest of the group will be deGrom at 31, and 31 may be less a concern for him than most at that age given that he has fewer major league innings on his arm than most pitchers.

There are other roles to be filled as time goes on, but the one constant with the Mets has always been pitching. The Miami Marlins, in their brief 22-year history, have already developed one more lethal hitter—Miguel Cabrera and Giancarlo Stanton—than the Mets have in 54 seasons, with their lone achievement being Darryl Strawberry (and Strawberry was the first overall pick in 1980). Pitching is what the Mets do well, and now they might actually have the best collection they've ever corralled. You can make a case that each of next year's starting five could improve on his previous year of service. For the rest of the National League, that's a terrifying prospect.

References and Resources

- Eno Sarris, FanGraphs, "Jeurys Familia in Context Is Unfair," *fangraphs.com/blogs/jeurys-familia-in-context-is-unfair*
- Anthony DiComo, MLB.com, "Syndergaard dominates with complete arsenal" *mets.mlb.com/news/article/153044274/noah-syndergaard-becoming-a-complete-pitcher*
- SABR Baseball Biography Project, sabr.org/bioproject
- Baseball-Reference Play Index, FanGraphs & Baseball Savant

2015, The Better in Verse

by Joe Distelheim

In 1949, *Sport* magazine published poet Ogden Nash's "Lineup for Yesterday," a tribute to the stars of modern baseball's first half-century. In that spirit, we offer a similar look at the recently concluded season.

A is for Astros
The season's surprises
Their talent will serve them
For years, one surmises

B's for BA
A stat we ignore
The sabermetrician
Prefers to use WAR

C is for Cubs fans
Whose stout hearts did gladden
Watching the youngsters
Come through for Maddon

D is for Denver
Tulowitzki took flight
And the Rockies' poor fans
Are left with Coors Light

E is for Ernie
Great star of his era
Why must we lose Banks
And also Y. Berra?

F is for Fielder
Who found a re-charge
What a comeback he made
In his pants extra-large

G is for Greinke
Some think there's no better
But I pined for a Cy
For Jake Arrieta

H is for hackers
That dastardly crew
Who plundered the Astros
On behalf of St. Loo

I is for injuries
That rose up to smite
Such sluggers as Miggy
And Stanton and Wright

J is for Johnson
To the Hall he did go
With Smoltzy and Pedro
And Craig Biggio

K is for Kang
The fine first-year Pirate
But the best rookies going
Were Correa and Bryant

L is for last
That's the Phils, to their sorrow
And the farm crop is thin
It's said, "That's Amaro"

M is for Mattingly
Let's offer a toast
To an oft-maligned manager
(And also Ned Yost)

N's for no-hitters
You count seven? I heard ya
But few ever matched
The two from Max Scherzer

O is for ousted
Early given the sack
Goodbye Mr. Roenicke
Redmond, Ryno and Black

P's for predictions
"Gentlemen, your bets?"
How many had Royals,
Cubs, Blue Jays and Mets?

Q is for quicker
Games we were promised
Why didn't much change?
It's TV, to be honest

R's for Ramirez
The Sox' acquisition
Hanley's value was zapped
Playing out of position

S is for strike zone
Can you tell me, please
Why balls are called strikes
When they're thrown 'neath the knees?

T's for Toronto
Who looked dead in July
Did you see this coming?
No? Neither did I

U is for umps
Sure, they're earning their pay
But aren't they embarrassed
Overruled on replay?

V's for most valuable
This year there's some doubt
But my votes would go to
Harper and Trout

W's for Washington
And its season of drama
The Nats wound up scorned
More than Bush and Obama

X is in Texas
(See it there in the middle?)
Adding Cole Hamels
Helped more than a little

Y is for Yoenis
Detroit's contribution
As the Mets grabbed him up
With but small restitution

Z's for Zduriencik
From Seattle he'll go
He thought "We can win"
But the Mariners Cano

History

The 1904 World Series

by Adam Dorhauer

Sept. 15, 1994: My father sat at the breakfast table with the morning's Kansas City Star laid out in front of him. A quick glance at the headlines confirmed what we had been speculating for weeks. Commissioner Bud Selig had made it official: There would be no World Series.

As I picked the discarded pages up off the table and began to skim through the sea of articles on the strike, one particular headline caught my eye: "Ninety years ago, ego got in the way." It was about the 1904 Giants, about John McGraw and owner John T. Brush, and about the only other time in major league history the World Series had been cancelled.

The first modern World Series was played in 1903 between the Boston Americans and Pittsburgh Pirates. A year earlier, Pittsburgh had defeated a team of American League all-stars (two wins, one loss, one draw) in an exhibition series, but tensions between the American League and National League prevented anything more official.

Starting from the AL's declaration as a major league in 1901, the two leagues had engaged in a constant series of disputes over player contracts and market rights that left organizations financially strained and fans disillusioned. After two years, both sides were eager for a truce. Each league sent a delegation to Cincinnati to broker a peace. The result was the 1903 National Agreement, which ended the disputes and established the National Commission (the equivalent of today's Commissioner's Office) to mediate between the leagues and rule on future issues.

Among the provisions outlined in the initial peace deal was a note that the leagues could schedule a series of championship games between teams from the AL and NL. Specifically, the peace deal said "[The scheduling] committee shall be authorized, if they deem the same advisable, to provide for a series of championship games between all of the clubs of both Leagues." This led not only to the World Series between Pittsburgh and Boston, but to nine different interleague series following the 1903 season, including city championships in Philadelphia, St. Louis and Chicago, and an Ohio state championship between Cleveland and Cincinnati.

Fans who had grown tired of the fighting between leagues responded with greatly improved attendance from 1902. Particular interest was taken in the Boston-Pittsburgh series. World Series crowds overflowed the capacity of both Boston's Huntington Avenue Grounds and Pittsburgh's Exposition Park, and sections of the outfields were cordoned off to accommodate the extra demand.

Spectators filling the outfield of Huntington Avenue Grounds before Game 3 of the 1903 World Series, *Boston Globe*, Oct. 5, 1903

The peace agreement proved stable, forging the groundwork for the modern Major League Baseball organization that remains to this day, but the World Series almost didn't last. While the agreement was welcomed by almost every organization, there was one notable exception: the New York Giants, owned by John T. Brush, the most avidly anti-AL figure left in the game. Brush vehemently opposed the peace agreement, and even attempted to break the agreement by signing George Davis away from the American League, where he had been assigned to Chicago (Davis played four games for the Giants before pressure from the rest of the NL forced him to sit out most of the 1903 season and return to Chicago in 1904).

When Brush's Giants won the pennant in 1904, they refused to face the AL champion and the World Series was called off. After just one year, the postseason institution that would grow into baseball's crown jewel was in danger of fading away.

The Other John

The headline I saw during the 1994 strike was actually referring not to Brush, but Giants manager John McGraw. The legend, as I've since heard repeated over the years, was that McGraw stubbornly refused to accept the upstart American League as the National League's equal, and refused to participate in a championship series that would acknowledge its status as a rival major league. In truth, the 1904 World Series was a casualty of a broader feud stretching back before McGraw ever joined the Giants. McGraw certainly got caught up in it and played a role, but far more important was Brush.

The backstory and details of the feud among Brush, the American League, and the other NL owners that led up to the 1903 agreement were covered in more depth in the Hardball Times article "The Birth of the American League and How it Transformed the Game," which I recommend reading as a complement to this piece, but the gist of it was that, for various reasons, Brush wanted no part of any agreement between the AL and NL.

Unlike most other owners, Brush had the resources to outbid AL teams for players and to withstand a protracted dispute with the AL. He personally hated American League president Ban Johnson, dating back to Johnson's career as a sportswriter in Cincinnati, where Brush at the time owned the Red Stockings. (In fact, Brush was indirectly responsible for Johnson's rise to power—when the Western League was looking for a president in 1894, Brush recommended Johnson for the job to get him out of Cincinnati, unaware that Johnson would eventually build the struggling minor league up to the American League.)

Then, as if Brush couldn't get any more opposed to the idea (actually, probably at least in part because Brush couldn't be any more opposed regardless), the most significant concession the NL gave the AL in the agreement was to allow the AL to relocate its Baltimore franchise to New York. This, of course, meant competing directly with Brush's NL team for the market share. (To be fair, though, the reason Baltimore needed to relocate so badly was that Brush had bought the Baltimore franchise the year before and released all its players in an effort to bankrupt the organization.)

So Brush was never really on board with any kind of working relationship with the AL. Where McGraw comes in is during the 1902 Baltimore saga.

McGraw was, in some ways, an unlikely ally for Brush. While he later became publicly dismissive of the junior circuit, McGraw was actually one of the first big stars to sign with the American League in 1901. He had strong personal and business ties to Baltimore, a city occupied by the AL. He had even twice refused to report to Brooklyn as a player before joining Brush's Giants in New York.

McGraw's path to the AL began in 1899, when the owner of Baltimore's NL franchise, Harry Von der Horst, bought a share of the Brooklyn Bridegrooms (subsequently rechristened the Superbas) and transferred several of Baltimore's stars, along with manager and co-owner Ned Hanlon, to Brooklyn. As arguably Baltimore's biggest star, McGraw was among the players Brooklyn most wanted. However, McGraw and teammate Wilbert Robinson refused to report to their new team. The two had opened a successful sports bar called The Diamond Cafe in Baltimore and elected to stay and operate the business, even if it meant walking away from the game. Rather than risk losing the two entirely, Von der Horst agreed to keep them on the Orioles roster.

This was a rare victory for a player fighting ownership for control over his own destiny, but it was short-lived. The Orioles folded after the 1899 season, and McGraw and Robinson were again assigned to Brooklyn. Once again, they refused to report. The two managed to successfully engineer a trade to St. Louis on the condition that they would be free to leave at the end of the year, scoring yet another rare victory, this time against the reserve clause. (Ironically, despite twice refusing to report to Brooklyn as a player, Robinson is best known for his later career as Brooklyn's manager, where he was so influential and beloved the team was actually named after him for a while.)

The idea behind getting the reserve clause stricken from their contracts was that the American League was beginning to make its move and would be putting a team in Baltimore the following year. After playing out the 1900 season in St. Louis, McGraw and Robinson both quickly signed with the new AL Baltimore franchise as free agents.

Robinson was at this point 36 years old and near the end of his playing career, but McGraw was in his prime and still one of the game's premier third basemen. He had also established himself as a capable manager after taking over the 1899 Orioles in Hanlon's absence. As one of the game's most valuable commodities, McGraw was offered partial ownership of the Baltimore franchise as part of his deal with the AL.

So McGraw was, at least on the surface, one of the last people Brush would have counted on to help him take on the AL. And this was before McGraw married Blanche Sindall, a Baltimore native, following the 1901 season. The one thing that McGraw and Brush had in common, however, was a strong, shall we say, distaste for Johnson.

McGraw repeatedly clashed with Johnson during his time in the AL. Johnson was particularly renowned for cleaning up professional baseball and did not tolerate dirty play or disrespect toward umpires. McGraw was nicknamed "Muggsy." It took only until May for McGraw to earn his first suspension. By mid-summer, there were rumors McGraw was so frustrated with Johnson he was planning to pull his Baltimore team out of the AL entirely and enter the NL. McGraw, and Baltimore, made it through the 1901 season, but things got worse in 1902.

Seven games into the 1902 season, McGraw was involved in, at least to that point, the ugliest incident in the AL's short history. Umpire Jack Sheridan ejected McGraw for arguing a call, and, following the game, fans stormed the field in anger. Police had to escort Sheridan to safety, and one officer was struck by a brick that had been thrown at the umpire. Johnson suspended McGraw five games for his role in inciting the incident.

Less than two months later, McGraw was ejected from another game and refused to leave the field. He and teammate Joe Kelley continued to hold up the game, shouting insults at the umpire until the ump forfeited the game to Boston. Johnson was fed up. He suspended McGraw again, this time indefinitely. McGraw would never play another game in the American League.

Within a few weeks of his final suspension, McGraw had left Baltimore for New York, and he and fellow owners Kelley and John Mahon had pooled their shares to create a majority stake and sold the team to Brush. (Well, to be technical, the sale was actually to Brush and fellow NL owner Andrew Freedman, who had been Brush's primary ally in opposing interleague relations. Freedman actually still owned the Giants in 1902, with Brush still in Cincinnati, but by the end of the year, Freedman had sold his team to Brush and left professional baseball.)

As mentioned above, Brush deliberately ran the team into the ground and sent most of its decent players to either New York or Cincinnati. Baltimore was effectively crushed, and moved to New York under new ownership the following season to rebuild.

1904 World Series Cancelled

The 1903 Series had been a huge success. The games were the best attended of the year and attracted national media attention. Fans had clearly taken an interest in seeing the World Series continue. Midway through the summer of 1904, however, the future of the Series was beginning to come into doubt.

The Giants had emerged as the clear favorites in the National League. From late June to early July, they went on an 18-game winning streak that put them 10 games clear of the rest of the league, and from there they pretty much coasted to the pennant. Around that time, plans for an overseas tour at the end of the season were leaked to the papers, and fans began to question whether Brush's team intended to face the AL champions at all. The overseas tour never came to fruition, but the worries were well-founded nonetheless.

It didn't help that the New York Highlanders were in a tight pennant race with Boston for the AL title. This was the very team Brush had tried to bankrupt in Baltimore and its move to New York the most bitter sticking point from the 1903 National Agreement. Furthermore, the Highlanders were competing for the same market base as the Giants, and Brush was concerned the new AL team would have more to gain from the interest generated by a World Series.

That July, McGraw made public statements denouncing the AL and Johnson, which Johnson believed had been motivated by Brush. In response, Johnson issued a statement urging the National League to participate in the World Series, to put the good of the game ahead of personal squabbles and bow to the overwhelming demand of the fans.

Johnson's appeal was largely ignored. With the season drawing to a close and the issue pressing, McGraw told the press his team wouldn't face an American League challenger. Brush called the AL a "minor league" and compared it to the Eastern and Southern leagues, saying he had no obligation to put his team's championship honors on the line against such lesser opposition. Brush was duly lambasted in the press for this statement, even by NL supporters. Critics were quick to point out that the supposedly "minor" AL had won the previous World Series (and gone 35-27 overall against the NL in the nine series after the 1903 season), had outdrawn the NL in total attendance that year, and occupied more populous cities than did the NL.

The Evening World, Sept. 28, 1904

The Highlanders and Boston Americans both issued formal challenges to the Giants in the event that their team won the AL pennant (the race went down to the final day, with Boston and New York playing back-to-back doubleheaders against each other to close the season and decide the championship). Neither McGraw nor Brush responded to either challenge. When it became clear the Giants would not voluntarily enter into a World Series, Johnson appealed to NL president Harry Pulliam as a last resort.

At the heart of the issue was the question of whether a World Series had been agreed to by the leagues beforehand, or whether it was incumbent upon the teams involved to organize a series themselves at their own discretion. Johnson believed the scheduling committee had arranged the Series at the previous offseason meetings. Pulliam, who may have been quick to appease Brush after rumors the latter was gathering support to oust him as league president in the next election, disagreed. Pulliam argued that while the committee may have endorsed a series, it didn't have the authority to actually arrange it. He ruled Pittsburgh had negotiated its series with Boston on its own and New York was free to do, or not do, the same.

Pittsburgh president Barney Dreyfuss sided with Johnson, saying his team had represented the NL in the 1903 World Series as part of league-wide effort, as evidenced by the eight other postseason interleague series, and that he was under the impression the arrangement had been renewed. His team, having finished fourth in the NL in 1904, challenged Cleveland, fourth in the AL, to a postseason series, keeping with what Dreyfuss believed the leagues had agreed to ahead of the season.

Pulliam's decision to uphold New York's stance was central not only to the 1904 World Series, but to the integrity of the World Series going forward. The World Series was modeled after various postseason exhibitions from the 19th century, none of which really managed to elevate the postseason to the status of a league pennant. A World Series that existed only as a private and optional arrangement between teams, as Brush and Pulliam saw it, would likely have been relegated to the same historical footnote as its predecessors.

The First "World Series"

The concept of a postseason series between the two reigning league champions dates all the way back to 1882, the first year there even were two concurrent major leagues. As champion of the newly formed American Association, Cincinnati challenged NL champion Chicago to an exhibition series. The teams split two games at Cincinnati's Bank Street Grounds before the remaining games were cancelled at the request of the American Association (and by "request," I mean the American Association threatened to kick Cincinnati out of the league if the series continued due to animosity over the NL signing away players contracted to AA teams).

While this was the first time two reigning major league champions met, postseason exhibitions themselves were not new. Teams of the era would extend their schedules as long as they could after the season ended to supplement their revenue, traveling around playing exhibitions against anyone from fellow major league teams to minor league teams to local amateur clubs. Teams would even schedule additional exhibition games on off days during the season to bring in extra money and promote their clubs.

The Cincinnati/Chicago series was much in the spirit of these exhibitions, and was clearly not sanctioned by their respective leagues. In 1883, however, the American Association and the National League signed the first National Agreement. Also known as the Tripartite Agreement due to the inclusion of the minor Northwestern League as a third signatory, the negotiations dealt mostly with expanding the reserve clause and ensuring each team's contract claims would be honored by clubs from other leagues.

The following year, the AA champion New York Metropolitans invited the NL champion Providence Grays to the Polo Grounds for a three-game series, this time with the blessing of league officials. Newspapers billed the matchup as the World's Championship Series, or, in a more headline-compatible form, the World's Series.

Note: There is a legend that the term "World Series" came from the sponsorship of the New York World newspaper. While there were cases of newspapers creating or sponsoring sporting events as promotional stunts (the Tour de France, for example, was created by the French newspaper L'Auto), there is no evidence such an arrangement ever existed with the New York World, and that etymology is considered apocryphal.

The idea and the name stuck, and the series became an annual tradition that continued through the 1890 season, when AA-NL relations once again broke down and the American Association withdrew from the National Agreement.

Early historians sometimes considered these AA-NL match-ups as part of the lineage of the modern World Series. For example, Francis Richter's History and Records of Baseball (1914), Ernest Lanigan's Baseball Cyclopedia (1922), and Hy Turkin and S.C. Thompson's Official Encyclopedia of Baseball (1951) all list the AA-NL series alongside the AL-NL series in their postseason registers. The Turkin/Thompson encyclopedia even includes the 1882 Cincinnati/Chicago series.

Modern sources, however, invariably distinguish between the AL-NL World Series begun in 1903 and earlier postseason efforts. The Macmillan Baseball Encyclopedia (first published in 1969) gives a brief mention of the AA-NL series in the introduction to its World Series register, but does not include them. Baseball-Reference presents the series with the disclaimer "Post-season games prior to 1903 were considered exhibitions." Major League Baseball does not officially consider the AA-NL matchups as World Series championships, and fans of teams like the Cardinals, Giants and Cubs will almost never include their teams' victories in these series when counting World Series titles.

Why, though, are these series held in lower esteem than the modern World Series, to the point that they are dismissed as exhibitions? Let's contrast the 1884 Series between New York and Providence with modern expectations.

While the leagues gave their tacit approval for the 1884 series, they had little to do with actually organizing it. The series was organized by the teams themselves after the season had ended. The Providence team stopped in New York on its return trip from Philadelphia, where it had just finished its season, to negotiate the terms for the series.

It is even possible that a similar meeting between the AA champion Philadelphia Athletics and NL champion Boston Beaneaters had been intended as the first World Series the year before, but simply never came to fruition. Baseball-Almanac.com claims that this was the case, and that Philadelphia pulled out of the Series due to poor performance in its postseason tour leading up to the Series. I can't find any direct evidence supporting a planned 1883 World Series, but it is plausible. The AA and NL had already signed the National Agreement, and Philadelphia did cut short its postseason on Oct. 15, citing fatigue and injuries to several key players requiring rest.

In 1884, Providence and New York played in separate exhibition series against other major league teams between the end of the season and their World Series meeting, similar to the tours Philadelphia and Boston had undertaken the year before. Both teams had already received their championship parades/receptions in their home cities before they met in the World Series. The series was simply not approached with the same reverence it is today, and was treated as something more akin to a typical postseason exhibition with a bit more glamour.

The games themselves did nothing to dispel this assessment. Largely due to miserable weather, attendance was poor, with the final game drawing just a few hundred spectators. Two of the three games were called before the full nine innings. The Providence Morning Star wrote that the final game was called after six innings due to darkness, but the New York Sun says the Metropolitans simply gave up after falling behind 11-2. It's possible the start of the game was delayed long enough for darkness to become a factor (Providence initially didn't want to play due to the weather and low fan turnout, and had already won the series by taking the first two games anyway), but the game lasted only an hour and 20 minutes from start to finish.

New York used Buck Becannon, a local semi-pro pitcher whom it had signed to pitch the final game of the regular season, in the lopsided Game Three loss. While that alone is something you'd never see in a competitive postseason game, the reason Becannon was used is even more startling: New York's ace pitcher, Tim Keefe, was unavailable because he umpired the game.

Game 3 box score from *Providence Morning Star*

While the series did pick up in popularity and attendance over the ensuing years, it never completely lost the air of an exhibition. Twice (in 1885 and in 1890) the series ended in a tie. The format was constantly changing, ranging anywhere from three games played in one city (1884) all the way up to a 15-game tour across nine different cities (1887). Teams would continue playing all scheduled games even after the series was decided. Other teams would stage their own exhibitions while the World Series was going on, and local papers sometimes gave more coverage to their own team's game than to a World Series game on the same day.

The games were generally umpired not by professional AA or NL umps, as we see today, but by players or managers from neutral (Keefe aside) teams. This isn't as crazy as it might sound. During the 19th century, it was common for players to have experience umpiring, as amateur clubs umpired their own games and routinely trained their players to do so. At least one game (Game Four of the 1885 series) was delayed because the two teams could not agree on an umpire and had to select a new one on the spot.

Players who didn't play for a team during the season sometimes appeared for that team in the World Series. For example, Tom Forster played for Pittsburgh in 1884 and appeared in the Series for New York, Sy Sutcliffe spent the 1887 season in the Northwestern League and appeared in the Series for Detroit, and Jumbo Davis split the 1889 season between Kansas City and St. Louis but appeared in the Series for Brooklyn.

The practice was that teams would start signing new players as soon as the season ended, and then would begin using those players immediately in any postseason exhibitions to try them out, get them experience with their new teammates, etc. More notable than any of these appearances, though, was that of Bug Holliday in the 1885 World Series. Chicago manager Cap Anson recruited Holliday during the Series to fill in a game in right field so he could rest one of his starters. Holliday would eventually make his official major league debut in 1889 and go on to a solid career with Cincinnati, but at the time, he was just an 18-year-old local amateur who happened to be present.

This is the kind of stuff you saw in exhibitions. The AA-NL games were, by and large, treated less seriously than regular season games, let alone comparable to today's postseason.

After the withdrawal from the National Agreement (and subsequent collapse) of the American Association, the NL experimented with a couple more post-season formats. In 1892, the league declared a first- and second-half champion and then held a championship series between the two, much like the playoff format in the strike-split 1981 season. From 1894-1897, the second-place team faced the pennant winner in a series for the Temple Cup, a trophy created and donated for the event by Pittsburgh team president W.C. Temple. Neither attempt lived up to the AA-NL series, and the idea of an official postseason was dropped until 1903.

New World Series Regulations

The World Series was at a critical juncture. On the one hand, you had the majority of franchises eager to capitalize on the fervent popularity of the 1903 event to grow it into something bigger. On the other, you had the contingent backing Brush's actions that saw it as nothing more than a continuation of the exhibition-like affairs of the 1880s, with the teams free to treat it as they wished.

In the end, it wasn't the magnates on either side who decided the issue. Rather, it was the overwhelming response from the fans and the press that managed to do what Johnson nor Dreyfuss nor any of the other owners could: It changed Brush's mind.

It was too late for the 1904 Series. Brush had already successfully dodged that. Once he did, though, he took the full brunt of the country's frustration. Sportswriters intimated that Brush and McGraw simply thought they couldn't beat the Americans or Highlanders. The New York World called the Highlanders "New York's real Giants." The Salt Lake Herald profiled Clark Griffith and Jimmie Collins (New York's and Boston's managers, respectively) under the headline "two American League managers Brush was afraid to play."

Even Brush's own players were unhappy with him. They didn't appreciate being tagged "quitters" for Brush's stunt and were not happy about foregoing the bonus money they would have earned in a World Series. They even considered organizing themselves under the management of infielder Jack Dunn and taking on Boston without Brush or McGraw's involvement, but decided against it because they hadn't kept in practice since the end of the season and felt they were not in top form by the time they met to discuss the possibility.

The Evening World, Sept. 28, 1904

Brush was undoubtedly fazed by his sudden pariah status, but he also quickly realized his actions were genuinely against the best interests of baseball. America, as it still does, loved the game best when the actions on the field were unmarred by the ugliness of the business off it, and the sudden catharsis emerging across the country in the wake of the cancelled Series convinced Brush he had pushed that line too far.

Thus it was Brush himself who took the lead in moving forward. Brush sent a letter to Pulliam recanting his opposition and pledging to support a future World Series if certain regulations could be guaranteed. While this sort of conditional support might sound a bit dodgy, Brush's recommendations were in fact legitimate improvements designed to prevent future hang-ups or snags from halting another World Series.

That offseason, the National Commission approved a new set of regulations governing the World Series based heavily on Brush's suggestions. The "Brush Rules," as they were called, standardized the various minutiae teams used to negotiate on their own. Things like the number, location and schedule of games, the selection of umpires, the division of gate receipts, etc., were explicitly defined or delegated to the National Committee to resolve.

Most importantly, the new regulations did two things. One, they placed the World Series clearly under the jurisdiction of the National Committee. Two, they compelled the champion of each league to participate. This obviously solved the 1904 problem, but it also addressed the major shortcomings of the AA-NL series of the 1880s. No longer would the quality or nature of the Series be dependent upon the whims of the teams involved. By ensuring proper administration and consistent standards, the new rules established a framework that allowed the World Series to build and sustain its elevated stature.

The newly stabilized World Series would run uninterrupted for another 90 years, weathering challenges such as the Federal League, the Black Sox scandal and multiple wartime drafts. That's not to say Brush was necessarily responsible for this success; he was, after all, the main threat in the first place. His eventual contribution essentially amounted to ceasing to obstruct something everyone else wanted.

Still, Brush's response in the wake of his own destruction was a critical step forward. After the owners called off the 1994 World Series in an attempt to force a salary cap onto the league, federal judge (and future Supreme Court justice) Sonia Sotomayor was there to set them back on track. In 1904, baseball's heads of state were on their own. There wasn't going to be anyone to bail them out if Brush or his allies continued to push the issue.

Instead, he, and his ego, got out of the way.

References & Resources

- Adam Dorhauer, The Hardball Times, "The Birth of the American League and How it Transformed the Game," *hardballtimes.com/the-birth-of-the-american-league-and-how-it-transformed-the-game*
- Digital Commonwealth: Massachusetts Collection online, *digitalcommonwealth.org/search/commonwealth:sf268762j*
- Chronicling America, Library of Congress, *chroniclingamerica.loc.gov/lccn/sn83030193/1904-09-28/ed-1/seq-8/*
- Google Newspaper Archives
- Baseball-Reference.com
- John F. Green, SABR, SABR Baseball Biography Project: Bug Holliday, *sabr.org/bioproj/person/5b06bc9d*
- Don Jensen, SABR, SABR Baseball Biography Project: John McGraw, *sabr.org/node/23303*
- Francis Richter, *History and Records of Baseball*, 1914
- Ernest J. Lanigan, *Baseball Cyclopedia*, 1922
- Hy Turkin & SC Thompson, *The Official Encyclopedia of Baseball*, 1951

- Macmillan Publishing, *The Baseball Encyclopedia*, 1969
- Doug Pappas, SABR Business of Baseball Committee, *roadsidephotos.sabr.org/baseball/data.htm*
- Dave Johnson, *Kansas City Star*, "Ninety years ago, ego got in the way," Sept. 15, 1994
- *The Evening World*, "Brush Places Ban on Post-Season Series," Sept. 26, 1904
- *The Evening World*, "It Looks as if the Highlanders are Now the Real New York 'Giants,'" Sept. 28, 1904
- *The Evening World*, "Dreyfuss Insists That Teams Should Play," Oct. 11, 1904
- *The Evening World*, "No Truth in Reported Story that Giants Will Be Taken Around the World if They Win the Pennant," July 12, 1905
- *The Minneapolis Journal*, "Another War in National League," Aug. 26, 1904
- *Evening Star*, "Sports of all Sorts: Postseason Games," Oct. 6, 1904
- *Evening Star*, "Giants Dissatisfied," Oct. 13, 1904
- *Lancaster Daily Intelligencer*, "All Around the Bases," Oct. 12, 1883
- *Providence Morning Star*, "Home Again: Great Reception to the Victorious Providence Grays," Oct. 18, 1884
- *Providence Morning Star*, "Base Ball," Oct. 27, 1884
- *The Sun*, "The National Game," Oct. 22, 1884
- *The Sun*, "The National Game," Oct. 26, 1884
- *New-York Tribune*, "A Poor Game Closes the Season," Oct. 26, 1884
- Jeffrey Kittel, This Game of Games, "The 1885 World Series: Game 4," Aug. 9, 2010 (quoting St. Louis Globe-Democrat, Oct. 18, 1885), *thisgameofgames.blogspot.com/2010/08/1885-world-series-game-four.html*
- *Salt Lake Herald*, "Two American League managers Brush was afraid to play," Oct. 31, 1904
- *The Reach: 1903 Official American League Baseball Guide*, p 33
- *The Reach: 1904 official American League Baseball Guide*, p 49

There's Always a Reason to Go

by Frank Jackson

I have a soft spot in my heart for the tail-end of the major league season. I probably see more games in September than in any other month. After all, I can watch movies, drink beer, read, write, or travel all year around, but baseball is seasonal. So as summer glides into autumn, the realization sinks in that attending baseball games—one of the key elements of my hedonistic lifestyle—is about to go on hiatus. Remember those last precious days of summer vacation—haunted by those ubiquitous "Back to School" signs in store windows—when you were a kid? It's kind of like that with the waning days of the baseball season.

Most of the games I see at season's end are of little consequence to pennant races, but 49 years ago, I saw a doozy of a doubleheader. The last day of the 1966 season was Oct. 2; the teams were the Dodgers and the Phillies, the place was Connie Mack Stadium in Philadelphia. At stake was the National League pennant, and the Game Two starting pitcher for the visitors was Sandy Koufax.

Going into the final weekend of the 1966 season, the Phillies had a respectable 85-74 record, but they had been eliminated from the pennant race. The last three contests of the season were not without interest in Philadelphia, however, as the Los Angeles Dodgers were coming to town with a magic number of one. The Giants and the Pirates were still in contention, and they were going head to head in Pittsburgh. Mind you, this was a couple of seasons before divisions were introduced in each league, so all three teams—Dodgers, Giants and Pirates—were competing for the same crown.

Unfortunately for the Dodgers, on Friday night, Sept. 30, Chris Short went the distance for the Phillies and came away with his 19th victory, besting Claude Osteen, who finished the season at 17-14. But Saturday was another day—one that produced almost an inch of rain and necessitated a doubleheader on Sunday.

Saturday would have been Don Drysdale's spot in the rotation, so he was the obvious choice to start the first game on Sunday. He was well rested, as he had last pitched on Sept. 27, when he shut out the Cardinals 2-0. His record at that point stood at 13-16, so it was something of an off year for him. If he could win this game, however, that would clinch the pennant and leave Koufax to lead off the World Series starting three days later in Los Angeles. And if Drysdale didn't win the game…then Koufax would take the mound for the second game of the doubleheader. So said Dodger manager Walter Alston, then in the 13th year of a 23-year string of one-year contracts.

So on this Sunday afternoon in early October, the possibilities at Connie Mack Stadium were intriguing for a 16-year-old fan. I called up my friend Paul to see if he was interested in one last day at the ballpark. He agreed to go, postponing the writing of a paper—due the next day—about Aeschylus' play *Agamemnon* in favor of a day of unscripted drama at the ballpark.

The theater where this drama would be played out had become déclassé. by 1966. The local consensus was that Connie Mack Stadium, now considered a "classic" ballpark, had outlived its usefulness. The theater manager for most of the venue's final decade was Gene Mauch, who was just 34-years-old when he took over the Phillies in 1960 and managed the team into the 1968 season. His best-known production was the infamous 1964 season, which was still a sore subject two years later.

The Phillies were nominally the home team among a crowd of 23,215, but Dodger fans were much in evidence. When the Dodgers first moved to Los Angeles, plenty of Brooklyn fans came down to Philadelphia to see their beloved Bums. The crowds dropped off a bit after the Mets entered the NL in 1962, thus making it more convenient for former Dodgers (and Giants) fans to see their old teams. But on this day, both Drysdale and Koufax—who started their careers in Brooklyn (Koufax in 1955, Drysdale in 1956)—would be on display in Philadelphia.

Since the fortunes of Drysdale and Koufax had been intertwined for so long, it made sense they would hold out as a unit before the 1966 season. Drysdale had signed for $80,000 in 1965, Koufax for $85,000. They were seeking a three-year deal at $500,000 each (in other words, $166,666.67 per man per year). Of course, the reserve clause was still in effect in those days, so it was basically a staring contest with owner Walter O'Malley to see who blinked first.

Koufax and Drysdale hired J. William Hayes, a Hollywood lawyer, business manager, and former airline pilot (he was married to movie actress Nancy Gates), to handle the negotiations. In regard to Hayes' involvement, O'Malley uttered the famous last words, "I have never discussed a player contract with an agent and I like to think I never will."

The dual holdout lasted 33 days, officially ending on March 31. The end result was that Koufax signed for $125,000, and Drysdale for $110,000.

The difference between what they asked for and what they got seems laughably insignificant today—especially given the attendance bump the Dodgers got whenever either of them pitched. Ironically, while Koufax and Drysdale were holding out, a fellow by the name of Marvin Miller was touring spring training camps and campaigning for the position of executive director of the Major League Baseball Players Association.

Beyond the one-two punch of Koufax and Drysdale at the top of the rotation, the Dodgers had the reliable Osteen and a rookie by the name of Don Sutton. Their bullpen ace was Phil Regan, who went 14-1 with a 1.62 ERA and a league-leading 21 saves in 116.2 innings.

With these great pitchers in tow, the Dodgers led the league in ERA (2.62), fewest hits allowed (1,287), fewest home runs allowed (84), fewest walks allowed (356), and strikeouts (1,084), and tied the Giants and Phillies for the complete-games crown (52). The stand out was home runs—they allowed 39 fewer homers than the second-place Pirates. Said another way, the Pirates were closer to eighth place in homers allowed than first place.

The only notable category in which the Dodgers didn't finish at the top was saves. Their 35 saves placed them in a tie for third with the Cincinnati Reds (behind first-place Pittsburgh with 43). Of course, given the Dodgers' formidable starting rotation and their penchant for complete games, it is understandable that the bullpen might underachieve in racking up saves.

Offensively, the Dodgers were less intimidating, but they had a bit more punch than in recent seasons. Second baseman Jim Lefebvre led the team with 24 home runs and 74 runs batted in. Ron Fairly led in batting average with .288 (his 14 homers tied his career best to that point), while Willie Davis was the hits leader with 177. Outfielder Lou Johnson posted career bests with 17 homers and 73 RBI. Maury Wills was still around, but he didn't have his best year. His stolen base total dropped from 94 in 1965 to 38 in 1966, and he was caught 24 times.

This had been a decent but ultimately disappointing season for the Phillies, but there were some names of renown in the lineup. One was third baseman Dick (then Richie) Allen, who led the league in slugging (.632) and OPS (1.028). He hit 40 home runs (a career high), scored 112 runs and drove home 110.

Unlike a lot of sluggers, Allen generally sported a respectable batting average. In 1966, he hit .317, just one point shy of his career best during his rookie year of 1964. While he was often the subject of jeers from fans who considered him moody, no one headed for the restrooms or concession stands when he came to bat, as he was always a threat to hit one over the left-field roof.

The Phillies lineup also included first baseman Bill White, who hit 22 homers, drove home 103 and swiped a team-leading 16 bases. Another contributor was Johnny Callison, who led the majors with 40 doubles. Also noteworthy were center fielder Tony Gonzalez, steady offensively and defensively, former NL MVP Dick Groat, and fan favorite Tony Taylor.

The pitching staff featured Jim Bunning, Chris Short, Bob Buhl, Larry Jackson, and Rick Wise. The main catchers were veteran Clay Dalrymple, who had been with the team since 1960, and "Mr. Baseball," Bob Uecker, who had his busiest season. He tallied 207 at-bats (yes, that was really his career high) and seven home runs (half his career total). Despite a batting average of .208, 1966 might have been his career year.

So the Dodgers and Phillies both had a solid cast. But the play's the thing, is it not?

Unfortunately for the Dodgers, Drysdale was not at his best in the first game of the twin bill. He gave up two runs in the first inning and was taken out in the third inning after the first two batters reached base. The Dodgers responded with a three-run homer from Ron Fairly (off starter Larry Jackson) in the top of the sixth, but the bullpen couldn't hold the 3-2 lead. With the help of a couple of Dodgers errors, the Phillies manufactured a pair of runs in the eighth and three outs later, the Phillies had won, 4-3.

Notably, left-hander Short, who had started and won less than 48 hours before, was given the opportunity to win his 20th game. His scoreless eighth and ninth innings garnered him the victory and the only 20-victory season in his 15-year career.

Meanwhile, at the other end of the state, the Giants were still playing the familiar role of Dodgers nemesis. The Giants had won five in a row as they entered the last game of the season at Forbes Field, where they had eliminated the Pirates the day before when they swept a doubleheader. After the Dodgers lost the first game, there was nothing to do but watch the scoreboard until a final score in the Giants-Pirates game was posted. If the Giants lost, the pennant belonged to the Dodgers.

The Pirates led the Giants 3-2 in the top of the ninth, but pinch-hitter Ozzie Virgil Sr. singled (his last big league hit), bringing home the tying run. In the 11th, Willie McCovey pinch-hit and blasted a two-run homer. The Giants pushed across two more runs, and the Pirates could not respond in kind. Final score: Giants 7, Pirates 3.

Koufax hadn't waited to see the final score; he was already warning up. In fact, he had been in the bullpen during the first game in case his presence was needed then.

Now, though, the Dodgers had to win the second game of the doubleheader not just to clinch the pennant but to avoid giving NL President Warren Giles a panic attack over the worst-case scenario.

The Giants had one outstanding rainout against the Reds. If the Phillies won the second game, the Giants would be one-half game behind the Dodgers, so the rainout would have to be made up in Cincinnati, and if the Giants won that game, then there would be a playoff series with the Dodgers to decide the pennant. So the Giants hung around the Pittsburgh airport to see if they were going to take a short flight to Cincinnati or a long (and gloomy) flight to San Francisco.

It's worth noting that Koufax was not the only option the Dodgers had for the second game. One was Don Sutton, who had lost to the Cardinals on Sept. 28 to finish his rookie season at 12-12. So he would have been pitching with three days' rest on Sunday after pitching only four innings in his previous outing. Another was spot starter Joe Moeller, who had started eight games for the Dodgers that year. But it's doubtful Alston ever seriously considered anyone other than Koufax, who was better on short rest than anybody else with sufficient rest. (Koufax had beaten the Cardinals for victory No. 26 on Thursday, when he became the first pitcher to reach the 300-strikeout mark three times.)

Koufax had been pitching at Connie Mack Stadium for 11 seasons, and he had made his share of late-season history there. In fact, he had thrown the last pitch in Brooklyn Dodgers history when he pitched the eighth inning of a Sept. 29, 1957 Dodgers loss (2-1) at the Phillies' ballpark.

A bittersweet achievement took place there in his last start on Sept. 27, 1961. Koufax, working on short rest, gave up two unearned runs in another 2-1 loss to the Phillies. When he struck out Pancho Herrera in the the sixth inning, however, he surpassed Christy Mathewson's National League strikeout record, which had stood since 1903. Notably, Koufax had achieved the record in a "mere" 256 innings, 111 innings fewer than Mathewson needed.

That loss to the then-lowly Phillies was disheartening, but he responded by reeling off six consecutive victories against them. He made it seven in a row on June 4, 1964, when he threw a no-hitter in Philadelphia. This no-no was the third in a series of annual no-hitters Koufax threw from 1962 through 1965. By 1964 Koufax had become a big draw, and 29,709 were on hand to witness that year's gem, in which he faced the minimum of 27 batters, struck out 12, and fell one walk (to Allen, who was erased on an attempted steal) short of a perfect game. (That finally occurred on Sept. 9, 1965 against the Cubs at Dodger Stadium.)

Now, on Oct. 2, 1966, a mere victory would suffice, but Koufax would have to defeat Jim Bunning, who had won 19 games for the third season in a row. This was the second time in baseball history that two perfect-game pitchers had been matched up. The first time was earlier in the season (July 27) when the two had matched up for dual 11-inning no-decisions, won 2-1 by the Dodgers in the 12th. (Oddly, the first encounter between the two men was in 1954 while Koufax was playing basketball for the University of Cincinnati and Bunning, then a minor leaguer, had an offseason job as the freshman basketball coach at Xavier University.)

With Short, Bunning gave the Phillies a pretty good one-two punch of their own (the Phillies duo had 39 victories; Koufax and Drysdale combined for 40). He had won his 19th game in relief on Sept. 26, but missed his shot at a 20th victory on Sept. 28 when he started and lost a 2-1 contest to Steve Blass and the Pirates. So he was starting on his normal three days' rest and had every motivation to beat Koufax, even though he could achieve nothing for his team.

Unfortunately for Bunning, he just didn't have it on this day. The Dodgers scored one run on a base knock by Dick Schofield and two on a Willie Davis home run. They added another in the fourth on a sacrifice fly by John Roseboro.

Koufax, meanwhile, had problems of his own. He found his curveball wasn't working in the early going, so he stuck to his fastball—as he had done in shutting out the Twins in the seventh game of the World Series the year before. In the fifth inning, a back problem prompted an impromptu chiropractic adjustment in the clubhouse.

Five innings was all Bunning would get to give the Phillies. When his turn at bat came in the fifth, Mauch, down 4-0, lifted him for a pinch-hitter. It might have seemed like a decision of little consequence, but I think Mauch pondered it with care. The game meant nothing to the Phillies, but if he left Bunning in, there was a remote possibility the Phillies could score four runs off Koufax and give Bunning a fighting chance to get that 20th victory. On the other hand, Mauch might have felt he owed it to the National League to make his best effort to win the game, and perhaps he felt removing Bunning in favor of Wise was a sound decision.

Wise was only 21 years old and looked even younger. With his glasses on and out of uniform, he looked more like a high school science fair contestant than a major league pitcher. But appearance aside, Wise was well rested, and he vindicated Mauch's decision, giving up just one unearned run after errors by Allen and Taylor in the eighth. At that time, Wise was only in his second season. He would go on to enjoy good seasons with the Phillies, Cardinals, Red Sox and Indians in an 18-year career.

Koufax had held the Phillies scoreless through eight innings, so Wise's work appeared to have been in vain. When the Dodgers added a run in the eighth and another in he ninth, the game appeared to be over. After all, the Phillies had just three more outs to overcome a 6-0 deficit at the hands of Koufax. To their credit, they did not go quietly.

Dick Allen reached on an error and moved to second on the last base hit (No. 2,092) of Harvey Kuenn's career. Tony Taylor singled Allen home, and the unearned run erased the shutout. White doubled home Kuenn and Taylor. Uecker, who had once joked that an intentional walk from Koufax was one of his career highlights, was the next hitter. Reverting to form, he struck out for the first out of the inning. Bobby Wine, pinch-hitting, grounded out, and Jackie Brandt struck out for the final out of the game.

Though the Phillies had been dispatched, the hometown crowd erupted in cheers as the Dodgers poured out of the dugout to celebrate. The Phillies got a split on the doubleheader and won the series...but that was all but irrelevant. There would be no make-up game in Cincinnati, and there would be no playoff series between the Giants and the Dodgers. The season ended on schedule.

While the conclusion of the NL pennant race could not have been better scripted, the World Series was a great thud of an anticlimax, as the Dodgers were not only swept, but failed to score after the third inning of the first game. The Orioles threw three consecutive shutouts (for the first time since the 1905 Series), and their streak of 33 consecutive shutout innings remains a World Series record. The pitching staff's Series ERA was 0.50. For good measure, the Orioles played errorless ball.

Koufax pitched Game Two, but his efforts were thwarted by Willie Davis, whose three errors should have made him a goat, but the Dodgers' lack of offense made that a moot point. As a result, Koufax had to come out for a pinch-hitter after six innings. He yielded just one earned run, but in his last appearance on a pitching mound, he was hung with the loss, as Jim Palmer shut out the Dodgers by a 6-0 score. A few days shy of his 21st birthday, Palmer became the youngest pitcher in the World Series to throw a shutout.

What a difference a week makes! On Sunday, Oct. 2, the Dodgers were ecstatic in Philly; seven days later, about 100 miles to the south, they were shell-shocked. But an even greater shock lay in store for Dodgers fans a little more than a month later.

On Nov. 18, Koufax called a press conference at the Beverly Wilshire Hotel and announced his retirement due to traumatic arthritis in his pitching arm. The baseball world was shocked, but a few insiders knew the score.

The 1965 and 1966 seasons had wreaked havoc on Koufax's left arm. His teammates had seen his arm swollen to alarming proportions between starts. They had noted his heavy use of oral painkillers, the gobs of Capsolin slathered on his left arm, the cortisone shots, and the ritual postgame immersion of his arm in ice water. The side effects of his medication concerned him, and he was worried that his left arm would be permanently disabled. The Dodgers' team physician, Dr. Robert Kerlan, had advised him to retire.

Despite his spring holdout with Drysdale, Koufax knew 1966 would be his last season. In fact, the lingering effects of his preseason negotiations with management might have factored into his decision.

Before the '66 season, Koufax had made his upcoming retirement known to sportswriter Phil Collier, who covered the Dodgers and Angels for the San Diego Tribune before the major league Padres arrived in '69. It must have been difficult for a reporter to sit on a scoop for so long, but Collier did not betray Koufax's confidence.

Sutton, who heard the news while attending college in Mississippi, cried. He was not alone. The news was a shock to Dodgers fans, given the fact that the 1966 season marked Koufax's fifth straight ERA title—at 1.73, it was the lowest of his career. He also led the league (or tied to lead the league) in complete games (27), strikeouts (317), and shutouts (5). His 27th victory not only led the league, it was the highest total of his career. A minor statistic, but a telling one, which indicates his control is that he hit no batters in 323 innings, a National League record.

The result was his third Cy Young Award in four years—and this was when just one award was given for both leagues. In fact, the one year he missed out (1964) he was on course for the award (19-5, 1.74 ERA, 223 Ks in as many innings) but his injury-shortened season resulted in the award going to Dean Chance of the Angels.

For the second year in a row, Koufax had pitched the pennant clincher on two days' rest. His stats for 1965 and 1966 were remarkably similar: he was 26-8 in 1965 and 27-9 in 1966, and he started 41 games and completed 27 in each season. The results were great for the Dodgers, not so great for Koufax's left arm. Perhaps the fact that his string of annual no-hitters was broken in 1966 was an omen.

Given Koufax's stats, major league pitchers might have wondered where they could go to sign up for a sore arm like his. Pundits and fans wondered how good his record would have been if he'd had a healthy arm, or if he'd pitched for a team with a more potent offense. Latter day pundits wonder what Koufax could achieve today given the benefits of modern medicine.

The World Series aside, there was no doubt Koufax had gone out on top. Nearly half a century after he departed the stage, Koufax (who turns 80 in Dec. 2015) is a living legend. He is the ultimate poster boy for all those erratic left-handed pitchers who test the patience of their team's management. Since southpaws are fewer in number than right-handers and typically take longer to mature, most teams will stick with them longer. No team was rewarded more for its patience than the Dodgers in the later 1950s and early 1960s.

Whether Koufax would have lasted as long as Nolan Ryan or Roger Clemens is debatable. Pitching into one's 40s is remarkable, but so is an all-time great retiring at age 30. We expect the leading man to make it to the last act in the play; when he exits the stage early and doesn't return, it's a big surprise.

On Oct. 2, 1966, who would have guessed that moldering old Connie Mack Stadium would still be in business for four more years after Koufax had called it quits? But they had one thing in common. Koufax had burned out, but so had Connie Mack Stadium. On Aug. 20, 1971, a couple of kids sneaked into the shuttered park and started a five-alarm fire. Ironically, it was the same day a statute of Connie Mack, which had stood near the stadium, was re-dedicated at Veterans Stadium.

Of all the games I ever saw at Connie Mack Stadium, Koufax's swan song remains the most memorable. It might be the most memorable contest I ever saw. Another contender was Mike Witt's perfect game against the Rangers on Sept. 30, 1984—coincidentally, also the last game of the season. I guess the lesson is this: don't leave the theater till the curtain comes down on the final act.

As Yogi might have put it, the season ain't over till it's over. Unfortunately, as in Koufax's case, sometimes a career is over before it should be over.

References & Resources

- Baseball Almanac, Baseball-Reference and Retrosheet
- Jane Leavy, *Sandy Koufax: A Lefty's Legacy*, HarperCollins, New York, 2002
- Edward Gruver, *Koufax*, Taylor Publishing, Dallas, 2000
- William Morrow & Steve Delsohn, *True Blue*, New York, 2001
- Bruce Chadwick and David M. Spindel, *The Dodgers: Memories and Memorabilia From Brooklyn to L.A.*, Abbeville Press, New York/London/Paris, 1993

The Order Was Rapidly Fadin': The Tumult of 1965-1975

by Steve Treder

The 1960s, chronologically, began on New Year's Day of 1960 and concluded at the stroke of midnight on New Year's Eve, 1969. But from an American social/political/cultural perspective, it's often been suggested that what we understand to be "The Sixties"—that era marked by extraordinary turbulence, confrontation, and upheaval—really got going a few years later than 1960 and didn't burn out its fury until sometime in the mid-1970s. We might place the start of this period at precisely Nov. 22, 1963, when the gory assassination of President Kennedy shook the nation loose of any sense of innocence. As for the endpoint, such an exact time isn't obvious, but the dispiriting events of 1974-75—the resignation from office of President Nixon, and the capitulation of South Vietnam—can be seen as driving an exhausted culture into fully insular "Me Decade" mode.

Amid this national cacophony of urban riots, campus protests, counterculture, and constitutional crisis, major league baseball grappled with an interestingly similar torrent of profound change. Bob Dylan's iconic 1964 anthem "The Times They Are A-Changin'" proclaimed the spirit of the day, and within the realm of baseball just as beyond it, the battle between old and new was indeed raging, and it would indeed shake the windows and rattle the walls. Perhaps no other 10-year span in modern baseball history witnessed as much furor as that from the mid-1960s to the mid-1970s, and whether one welcomed the remaking of the sport or resisted it, all had to agree that by 1976 the present bore precious little resemblance to the recent past.

The Dome, the Turf and the Protractor

It was on April 9, 1965 that the first-ever indoor air-conditioned major league baseball game was played, in Houston's audacious brand-new Astrodome, touted "The Eighth Wonder of the World." The sellout crowd of 47,879 included President Lyndon Johnson, his wife Lady Bird, and Texas Gov. John Connally.

A domed baseball stadium had been dreamt of for some time; Walter O'Malley proposed one for his Brooklyn Dodgers in the mid-1950s. But the character with both the impudent vision and the political clout to render this particular dream a reality was Roy Hofheinz, the tireless, mercurial, big-thinking majority stockholder of the Houston Astros. A former Texas state legislator, county judge, and mayor of Houston (as well as campaign manager for LBJ in the 1940s), Hofheinz ensured that not only would the Astrodome building itself be the first of its kind, so would its scoreboard: a gigantic wraparound innovation that didn't merely log runs, hits, and errors, but presented flowing text, animated characters, and sound effects, including a snorting bull, lighted flags, and cowboy pistols firing ricocheting bullets in celebration of every Astros home run. No ballpark had ever been anything like this.

While the Astrodome was generally hailed as a grand success, it wasn't problem-free. In its original form, the domed roof was constructed of transparent glass panels, letting sunlight through to allow the playing field's grass to grow. However, this presented two unforeseen issues. First, the moisture in the grass was unable to fully evaporate, and water vapor would condense in the heights of the structure and periodically fall as indoor rain, to the point of interrupting and delaying games. Second, during daytime, the sunlit glass roof tended to blind fielders attempting to track fly balls.

To solve the second problem, early in the 1965 season the roof panels were painted white. This worked only too well: fielders were no longer blinded, but insufficient light penetrated the dome to keep the grass alive. So for the balance of 1965, the Astrodome's playing surface was dead grass, painted green.

New problems require new solutions, and cutting-edge technology was called to the rescue. Artificial turf (originally marketed as ChemGrass) had just been invented and patented by Monsanto in 1965, and the company suddenly had an eager (if not desperate) high-profile customer. The quickly rebranded AstroTurf product was installed in the Astrodome in 1966, providing the ballpark with yet another never-before feature.

The Astrodome's influence would resound. Multiple other stadiums quickly upgraded or augmented their traditional scoreboards with high-tech electronic "message board" systems (though few would ever be as extravagant as Houston's). And most interestingly, though no second domed baseball stadium would be introduced until 1977, many other major league venues opted to replace natural grass with artificial turf, even though they didn't face Houston's necessity to do so. By the early 1970s, synthetic playing surfaces were deployed in Chicago, Cincinnati, Kansas City, Philadelphia, Pittsburgh, St. Louis and San Francisco.

The motivation was economic. With no watering, fertilizing, weeding, or mowing, artificial turf was welcomed as a significantly less costly field to maintain. This was a particularly attractive feature for the many ballparks not owned and operated by the teams themselves, but instead by local municipalities, usually as multi-purpose baseball-and-football venues (as was the Astrodome). The rolling wave of such new facilities coming on board in the late 1960s and early 1970s included not just Cincinnati, Philadelphia, Pittsburgh, and St. Louis, but also Atlanta, Oakland and San Diego.

A striking feature of this large stock of new structures was the degree to which they resembled one another. As taxpayer-funded projects, they were designed with cost efficiency and multi-use flexibility as priorities over aesthetics and amenities. Nearly all employed an identical perfectly-round footprint (prompting critics to deride their architecture as protractor-driven) which, while accommodating both baseball and football, proved optimal for neither sport from the fans' (literal) viewpoint.

And without question, the sudden widespread imposition of synthetic turf impacted the style of baseball presented. The early versions of these surfaces were quite primitive: Fields were about as soft as a sidewalk, shooting grounders through infields at lightning speed, and prompting uncaught fly balls to bounce to comical heights. Defenses were befuddled, and so teams rapidly adapted by giving lineup preference to the fastest and nimblest players available. The resulting change in the manner of play was dramatic: Between the mid-1960s and the mid-1970s, the rate of major league home runs dropped by nearly 20 percent, while the rate of stolen bases jumped by nearly one-half.

Relocation, Expansion, Division and Television

The spate of new ballparks was a function not only of new construction, but simply of new cities. Six franchise relocations had occurred between 1953 and 1961, and after a few years of respite, the disruptive cycle began anew. Between 1966 and 1972 four clubs moved, and the San Diego Padres very nearly transferred to Washington D.C. following the 1973 season.

Wait: the San Diego Padres? Oh, that's right, they were one of the four newborn franchises, two in each league, inaugurated in 1969. Less than 10 years following MLB's first expansion in 1961-62, they were at it again, giving the big leagues a full 50 percent growth rate from 1960 to 1969.

As this second expansion created 12-team leagues, the Lords of Baseball were faced with the prospect of four of their brethren trying to sell tickets for a ball club mired in 11th or 12th place. This was felt to be a couple of places too far, and therefore, beginning in 1969 Major League Baseball adopted its very first-ever divisional structure, with two six-team divisions in each league.

Divisional play necessitated two profound alterations to the sport's long-settled seasonal arrangement. First, every team's schedule now became "unbalanced," requiring a different number of games (18) against each intra-division opponent than against opponents in the other division (12). Second, to determine each league's winner, a new playoff tier needed to be introduced: the League Championship Series. With this the concept of "postseason" play was born in big league baseball; until then it had just been the regular season and the World Series, and the "postseason" term was foreign.

Not just with the expanded postseason, but also with the All-Star Game, in these years MLB for the first time began to present its highest-profile games as not just locally popular events, but as nationally televised extravaganzas. The 1969 All-Star Game was the first scheduled to be played at night, and thus as primetime TV viewing. (A rainout required that game to be played the next afternoon, but beginning in 1970, every All-Star Game has been at night.)

On Oct. 13, 1971, Game Four of the World Series was the first ever under the lights. In the ensuing seasons, both World Series and LCS games began to be scheduled at night, for the advantage of televising networks. The era of baseball as a big-time TV show was begun. (This ended the decades-long era of World Series games being magnets for hooky-playing. This author well remembers suddenly coming down with mysterious vague illnesses and being unable to attend elementary school on the days of particularly crucial midweek World Series games. This author also now comprehends that his mom was a good sport.)

While the ongoing parade of relocations highlighted financial distress (or, at least, dissatisfaction) in specific locales, the expansions of the leagues themselves, as well as the investments in new ballparks and the more ambitious network television coverage, were indicators of a broadly healthy (or, at least, optimistic) professional sport. However, there was in this period an ominous development on the field of play that mounted to a crisis.

1.12 to 6.10

Across the decade of the 1960s, the rate of scoring in major league baseball distinctly declined. The causes of the trend were many (including bullpens, ballparks, and fielders' gloves), and were aggravated by an ill-advised rule change prior to the 1963 season that expanded the size of the strike zone. The dynamic reached an extreme in 1968, with offensive futility unprecedented in modern history. Its cavernous depth was illustrated by many metrics, but none more vividly than the major league-best earned run average posted by St. Louis Cardinals ace Bob Gibson: in 305 innings, a staggering, almost frightening mark of 1.12.

This ever lower-scoring product was not being happily received by the fan base. Writing in *The New Yorker* in October of 1968, Roger Angell captured the disquiet:

> The 1968 season has been named the Year of the Pitcher, which is only a kinder way of saying the Year of the Infield Pop-Up. The final records only confirm what so many fans, homeward bound after still another shutout, had already discovered for themselves: almost no one, it seemed, could hit the damn ball any more. ... Adding up zeros is not the most riveting of spectator sports and by mid-July of this year it was plain to even the most inattentive or optimistic fans that something had gone wrong with their game.

Ownership grasped the severity of the problem. For 1969 two rule changes were approved: the strike zone was returned to its pre-1963 dimensions, and a height limit of 10 inches was imposed on the pitchers' mound.

This delivered the intended effect of revitalizing hitting and scoring—but only temporarily. After rebounding in 1969 and '70, run production declined in 1971 and, especially in the American League, in 1972: Indeed, the '72 season saw just 3.47 runs per team/game in the AL, very nearly as low as the 3.41 bottoming-out of 1968.

This, in combination with the fact that American League attendance continued to significantly lag that of the NL, was seen as a crisis serious enough to prompt the sport's most dramatic rule change since the foul-strike rule in the very earliest 1900s: Rule 6.10, adopted by the AL in 1973, introducing the designated hitter to major league baseball.

Give Me a Head with Hair

Let's consider the realms of fashion and hairstyling. (You know you want to.) Few eras in American history burst forth with more brazen challenges to the status quo than the mini-skirted, bell-bottomed, Afro-headed mid-to-late 1960s. But few institutions refused the call to go "mod" more strongly than baseball. Into the first years of the 1970s nearly every big league organization still held to old-school grooming codes, enforcing a standard of closely trimmed, clean-shaven players in traditionally toned uniforms. Slightly long hair, sideburns, and tidy mustaches were dared by a few players in the late '60s, but such stylings encountered huffy resistance from management—or, as *All in the Family's* Mike "Meathead" Stivic would have put it, from "The Establishment."

One team, however, was different. First in Kansas City and then in Oakland, flamboyantly maverick owner Charles O. Finley's "Swingin' A's" were equally flamboyant in appearance. Consider uniforms: Finley introduced white kangaroo-leather shoes for his team as early as 1963—prompting Mickey Mantle to suggest, "They should have held hands and tippy-toed out there." Over the years Finley added ever more novel and brightly colorful looks to the rest of the club's uniform.

In 1972 he rolled out the most daring ensemble yet. In a bold innovation (that's since become standard procedure across all professional sports), the team didn't feature one static look, but instead rotated three different 100 percent polyester pullover jersey designs—one in white, one in Kelly green, and one in bright yellow—each with splashy green-and-gold sleeve bands and a large gothic "A" over the heart. It was, shall we say, a design not meant to appeal to an Archie Bunker.

Then there were Finley's players themselves. In that same 1972 season, Charley O. was the owner who decided to stop resisting the tide of players wishing to go hairy, and instead encourage it. He staged a "Mustache Day" promotion at the Oakland Coliseum on June 18, in which all fans entering the stadium sporting facial hair were admitted for free, and as a lead-in to the event, he offered a $300 bonus to any of his players who grew a mustache as well. More than half the roster took him up on the offer. Almost overnight it was not only the A's garish uniforms that made them stand out: They were "Finley's Mustache Brigade." Even manager Dick Williams got into the act, becoming the first mustachioed skipper since the very early 20th century. Catcher Dave Duncan and superstar outfielder Reggie Jackson not only grew mustaches but full beards as well. Duncan and ace pitcher Catfish Hunter grew long hair, flowing from under their caps and covering their necks. Ace reliever Rollie Fingers featured the most distinctive look of all, a spectacular waxed barbershop-quartet handlebar mustache. In the 20th century, at least, baseball had never seen anything like the look of this team.

The A's brazen anything-goes appearance was accompanied by a raucous, brawling mode of behavior that captured headlines and frequently upstaged their exploits on the field. But indeed it was the fact that they did win, consistently—grabbing a dramatic World Series victory in '72, and repeating in both 1973 and '74—while ardently defying traditional codes of appearance and decorum that made them much more than a curiosity or a sideshow.

The in-your-face success of the Oakland A's commanded respect, and their sassy look was an overnight trendsetter. Within a very few years, nearly all big league teams were sporting ever more gaudy uniform styles and allowing players to wear long hair, sideburns, mustaches and beards. It might well be the case that a baseball fan stranded on a remote island since the 1960s, rescued and attending a game in the mid-1970s, would find the simple visual appearance of the players the most shocking change, even more startling than the plastic grass and the digital message board.

Ball Four and Bowie

It was in 1970 that journeyman pitcher Jim Bouton's *Ball Four* was published. In concept, the book wasn't unprecedented: It bore significant resemblance to *The Long Season* by Jim Brosnan from 1960, a day-by-day first-person "diary" chronicling the bittersweet ups and downs of an individual non-star player's season, not just on the field but off it as well. Indeed, Bouton readily acknowledged he'd been inspired by *The Long Season*, having read it as a young minor leaguer.

But *Ball Four* was more candid in its depiction of off-field shenanigans, and far more graphically honest in presentation of vulgar language. Also, it's important to consider that *Ball Four* (in which Bouton received extraordinarily effective collaboration from his editor, Leonard Shecter) was a much funnier, better-paced read than *The Long Season*.

In any case, while Brosnan's book stirred up controversy in its day, it yielded nothing close to the impact of Bouton's. The bestselling *Ball Four* was a Richter-scale bombshell. The kerfuffle was such that even before its official June 1970 release, based simply on the ferocious reaction to pre-publication excerpts printed in *Look* magazine in May, Commissioner Bowie Kuhn felt compelled to call Bouton into his office and deliver a stern dressing-down.

To say the least, the meeting didn't go well for Kuhn. Bouton, accompanied by Marvin Miller, the executive director of the Major League Baseball Players' Association (MLBPA), was anything but apologetic, and refused to disavow a word he'd written. As a result, Kuhn's come-to-the-principal's-office meeting produced nothing but a mushily worded press release signaling that the party being forced to back down was in fact the commissioner.

And it was worse than that. As Bouton put it in his follow-up book (also edited by Shecter), *I'm Glad You Didn't Take It Personally*:

> I acknowledge a deep debt to Bowie Kuhn, our Commissioner. There are some who say it's a quarter of a million. I consider that an exaggeration.
>
> The reason for the debt is that he called me into his office to chat about Ball Four. As a result, there were headlines on every front page in the country. That's fame, and fame in the book business is fortune. If Bowie Kuhn and his public relations assistant, Joe Reichler, had entered into a conspiracy to sell copies of the book, they would have done nothing different.

To whatever degree Bouton overstated it for the sake of a good yarn, Kuhn's ham-handed attempt to intimidate the controversial ball-playing author and discredit his book had the opposite effect.

Ball Four was, of course, not only an immediate hit, but a work of enormous influence and enduring power; it would become the only sports-themed book to be listed in the New York Public Library's *Books of the Century* in 1996, and it would be honored by *Time* magazine as one of the 100 greatest non-fiction books of all time. Moreover, the commissioner's backfiring effort to squelch it not only served to make Kuhn look personally foolish, it fueled a growing "generation gap" sense among many players that baseball's traditional management authority deserved not obsequious respect, but instead direct challenge. *The Long Season* was suddenly a relic of a distant era.

Miller to Flood to Seitz

Jim Bouton's companion in the meeting with Kuhn was, perhaps, the single most impactful actor on the baseball stage throughout this pivotal period. Marvin Miller was a New York lawyer, an experienced, savvy negotiator, hired by the MLBPA in 1966 as the first labor professional to direct the union in its 20-year existence. Diminutive, dapper, with a calm demeanor that belied an intensely competitive drive, Miller brought erudite seriousness and a sense of focus and clarity to the MLBPA. Prior to Miller's arrival, ownership beheld the players' union in a bemused, condescending, paternalistic manner. Miller refused to be patronized, and while he achieved little of substance in his first few years, his mature, persistent presence fostered a palpable change in the temper of the players, who became far less compliant than before.

No player was more inspired by Miller than Curt Flood. The 31-year-old seven-time Gold Glove winning center fielder and four-time All-Star was traded by the St. Louis Cardinals to the Philadelphia Phillies in October of 1969 and decided to take that as his opportunity to challenge the Reserve Clause, the lynchpin of the asymmetrical employment bond between players and teams. Flood refused to report to

Philadelphia, and instead sued Major League Baseball for violation of federal anti-trust statutes.

Flood's lawsuit, it's important to note, was not undertaken at Miller's suggestion. Indeed, Miller counseled against it, expecting Flood would lose. But when Flood proceeded nonetheless, Miller aided him, and the union's player representatives voted unanimously in his support. Though Flood's claim was in fact denied, at the Circuit, Appeals, and Supreme Court levels, through the 29-month process his cause gained ever-stronger support from the rank and file of players, who'd been divided at the outset. Certainly it got the full attention of ownership, who agreed when negotiating the 1970 Basic Agreement to a new "10/5 Rule" granting the right to any player with at least 10 years of major league service, including the previous five years with one team, to veto a trade. This provision is often called the "Curt Flood Rule."

And without the rallying force of Flood's suit, it's highly unlikely the players would have been willing to go on strike as they did in the spring of 1972. That strike, the first in 20th century U.S. sports history, was also launched against Miller's advice, but by that point the players' militancy was self-propelled. The strike wasn't even over the issue of free agency; it stemmed instead from a dispute over ownership's level of funding of the players' retirement pension fund, and the sum in question was a mere $400,000 per year. In purely economic terms, the particular amount wasn't a big deal to the players, nor did it represent a significant expense to the owners. But, for both sides, this was no longer the issue. What was at stake was the principle of the matter. In just a few short years, relations between players and owners had reached a state in which "backing down" was, for both sides, an unacceptable option.

To reiterate, Miller did not encourage the players to strike over the pension fund. As the pension contract expiration date—March 31, 1972—approached, Miller met with the player representatives and conducted strike authorization votes, but he was considering the threat as just a bargaining ploy. Miller had been involved in labor disputes and negotiations for 30 years, and he knew a thing or two about the reality of strikes, in all their ugliness and difficulty. He didn't believe the pension fund was an important enough issue to warrant such a drastic step. Miller believed the players had no idea what they would be in for if they struck, and he knew the owners had far more money, far more legal resources, and the support of nearly all of the press on their side.

The owners made the very same calculation. Like Miller, they didn't expect the players would actually strike over this, and if they did, the owners didn't expect the union would retain solidarity. The owners perceived the strike threat as a bluff on Miller's part. They were correct in this assessment, creating the great irony of the 1972 strike: Miller and the owners shared an understanding of the situation—and both were mistaken.

Especially in the wake of the Flood lawsuit, ownership was fed up with Miller and the union. Believing the players had no right to behave as they were, the owners were spoiling for a fight. If the players were going to be foolish enough to strike over the silly pension issue, then ownership was eager to bring it on: This would be a gift, the opportunity to humiliate Miller and the MLBPA, and likely even break the union once and for all. St. Louis owner Gussie Busch put it plainly on March 22: "We voted unanimously to take a stand. We're not going to give them another goddamn cent. If they want to strike—let 'em.'"

On the eve of the strike deadline, Miller gathered the player reps in Dallas. In his low-key manner, he logically laid out the situation and presented his recommendation: Since the players had no strike fund, no field offices, no legal team, and no public relations resources, they should postpone the strike and continue to negotiate. But despite Miller's reasoning, they were resolute. Directly against the counsel of their hired labor negotiator, the players unanimously voted to strike.

So the historic work stoppage began. Opening Day was postponed. As Miller had anticipated, the striking players took withering criticism from the press and public. Even former star big league players blasted Miller and the striking players; one of them, Robin Roberts, had been instrumental in leading the early players' union.

But the players held firm. It was the owners, for all their bluster about busting the union, who immediately began to splinter. The players were losing salaries, but the teams were losing revenues—vastly more than the few hundred thousand dollars at stake in the pension dispute. Not expecting a strike, the owners had made no financial plans for it. Within just a few days, many were beginning to urge for a settlement. After less than two weeks, the strike ended, with the owners essentially agreeing to the players' demands.

Instead of being weakened, the union was vindicated, and the players were emboldened as never before. They had taken on the owners in an unprecedented direct confrontation and won, fully and convincingly. Though the particular issue at hand hadn't been a huge deal, the players' stunning success in pressing it gave them deep new confidence in plans to deal with their most central concern: the Reserve Clause.

Immediately following the strike, Ted Simmons of the Cardinals began to play the 1972 season without signing the contract he'd been offered. Under the 1970 Basic Agreement negotiated by Miller, if a player went the entire season without agreeing to terms, his case could be presented to an independent arbitrator, and the possibility existed that the arbitrator would rule that the old contract had become null and void, rendering the player a free agent. Simmons was the first player to begin to put this scenario to the test. Clearly fearing what might ensue if Simmons' case did go to arbitration, the Cardinals settled with Simmons in August by signing him to a two-year contract at a huge raise.

But players would keep pressing the issue. In 1973, five began the season without signing. None would remain unsigned all year, but in 1974 seven players took that route, and in 1975 six more did, and finally two of them—Andy Messersmith of the Dodgers and Dave McNally of the Expos—would finish the season unsigned. Their joint cases went to arbitration, and on Dec. 23, 1975, arbitrator Peter Seitz ruled that "there is no contractual bond between these players and the Los Angeles and Montreal clubs." Merry Christmas to the players. Free agency was born, and the fundamental nature of the business of baseball was changed forever.

The line, it was drawn. The curse, it was cast. The slow one now would later be fast.

References & Resources

- An excellent profile of Roy Hofheinz and his pivotal role in bringing major league baseball to Houston and building the Astrodome is in *Colt .45s: A Six-Gun Salute*, by Robert Reed, Lone Star Books, Houston, 1999, pp. 29-52, 203-211.
- A detailed brief on the Houston Astrodome can be found in *Green Cathedrals*, by Philip J. Lowry, Addison-Wesley, Reading, Massachusetts, 1992, pp. 46-48.
- "A Little Noise at Twilight," in *The Summer Game*, by Roger Angell, Popular Library, New York, 1972, pp. 196-197.
- The Mickey Mantle quote regarding the Kansas City A's white shoes is from the *1964 Official Baseball Almanac*, edited by Bill Wise, Fawcett, Greenwich, Connecticut, p. 8.
- "Finley's Moustache Brigade" was the term coined by David S. Neft and Richard M. Cohen in the 1972 season overview text in their iconic *Sports Encyclopedia: Baseball* series, St. Martin's Griffin, New York, annual.
- *Ball Four: My Life and Hard Times Throwing the Knuckleball in the Big Leagues*, by Jim Bouton, edited by Leonard Shecter, The World Publishing Company, New York and Cleveland, 1970.
- *The Long Season*, by Jim Brosnan, Harper & Row, New York, 1960.
- *I'm Glad You Didn't Take It Personally*, by Jim Bouton, edited by Leonard Shecter, William Morrow, New York, 1971, p. 67.
- A superb narrative connecting the Flood case, the 1972 players' strike, and the process leading to the Seitz decision can be found in *Lords of the Realm: The Real History of Baseball*, by John Helyar, Ballantine Books, New York, 1994, pp. 107-180.

A Win Amid the Losses: The '84 Detroit Tigers

by Joe Distelheim

In the hour after Larry Herndon caught Tony Gwynn's fly ball for the final out, we stood on the roof of Tiger Stadium and watched a police car and a taxi cab burn.

These were the 1984 Tigers, World Series champions. This was 1984 Detroit.

What baseball people remember most about the 1984 Tigers is the team's unprecedented hot start. The Tigers had an 18-2 April. They went 35-5 in their first 40 games. Detroit won 17 straight on the road, an American League record. Jack Morris threw a no-hitter on the first national Saturday game-of-the-week telecast. With that start, the Tigers became the first AL team since the 1927 Yankees (Ruth, Gehrig, those guys) to lead wire to wire; they were not out of first place one day all season.

What baseball people remember most about 1984 in Detroit is the ugly aftermath, seen as a confirmation of Detroit's popular, if one-sided, national image. A post-World Series national poll ranked it last in reputation for big American cities.

There's more to both story threads. I was sports editor of the *Detroit Free Press* at the time; with some help from my friends, I'd like to tell you the stories.

Detroit prided itself on being a good sports town. The slightly cynical might say that's because it was not a particularly good other-stuff kind of town. No Hollywood or Broadway diversions here. San Francisco is the City by the Bay. Detroit has the unglamorous Detroit River. There's no Bourbon Street, though plenty of bourbon, to be sure. It was a shot and beer kind of place. Sportswriters gleefully told the story of their new-to-town colleague who walked into the proudly disreputable bar the newspaper crowd frequented and asked for the wine list.

This was the sports scene in the early '80s: The NHL Red Wings were awful, but this still was a hockey town. The NBA Pistons were awful, but they drafted Isiah Thomas, just too late to play for fired coach Dick Vitale. The Lions were awful, but rookie Billy Sims led them to a 4-0 start in 1980. Bo Schembechler coached football at Michigan, in nearby Ann Arbor, but his longtime rival, Ohio State's Woody Hayes, was gone, dismissed after punching an opposing player.

And baseball fans revered the Tigers, but not so much the early-'80s middle-of-the-pack team. They talked about the real Tigers, the 1968 bunch that beat the Cardinals in the World Series and still hung around town, representing manufacturers (Bill Freehan and Jim Northrup), running a suburban doughnut shop (Mickey Lolich), running a fantasy camp (Jim Price), coaching at the fantasy camp (many of the rest), and acting as eminence grise (Al Kaline). This was the team that made the city feel good after the devastating 1967 Detroit riot that killed dozens. Recalls former *Detroit Free Press* baseball writer Bill McGraw, "the night the Tigers clinched the pennant in September, young people—both black and white—formed long parades of cars up and down (downtown streets) Woodward and Michigan, and some people yelled, 'Willie Horton, unite our city.'"

The official 1984 World Series program, a generic publication that went to press before anyone knew who'd be in the Series, had two pages on the American League West champion Kansas City Royals, one on the Tigers. The un-bylined latter article said "Members of that 1968 team still are worshipped like rock stars and like they rallied to beat the St. Louis Cardinals only last week instead of 16 years ago."

Quickly, though, Detroiters thought they might have something special in the 1984 team, managed and spoken for, often hyperbolically, by Sparky Anderson, who in spring training called this the most talented team he'd ever managed. This from the man who ran the 1970s Big Red Machine in Cincinnati.

It would be too glib to say this was a unique team. Just as every individual is unique, so is every team. But unusual? Yes. To wit:

- It was mostly home-grown, the product of some outstanding drafting acumen— and good fortune. Five of the regulars had been drafted by the Tigers: catcher Lance Parrish in 1974, second baseman Lou Whitaker in '75, shortstop Alan Trammell in '76, outfielder Kirk Gibson in '78, and third baseman Howard Johnson in '79. So had utility infielder Tom Brookens, who'd been part of the remarkable 1975 draft class that included Whitaker and three of the Tigers' starting pitchers: Morris, Dan Petry and Dave Rozema.

- The Tigers were young, especially in key spots. On Opening Day, Trammell, Whitaker and Gibson were 26, Parrish and Morris 28, center fielder Chet Lemon 29.

- How often does this happen? The Tigers struck lucky gold with a trade 10 days before the season began, getting reliever Willie Hernandez and veteran utility man Dave Bergman (from the Phillies for back-up catcher John Wockenfuss and outfielder/overmatched third baseman Glenn Wilson). Both acquisitions had superb seasons—28-year-old Hernandez with an MVP/Cy Young performance, Bergman becoming a Sparky favorite for good reason. But the deal wasn't considered a gimme at the time. "I'll be honest with you," Brookens told a *Free Press* reporter before the team's 30th anniversary celebration. "When we traded Wockenfuss and Glenn Wilson in the spring for a guy named Willie Hernandez and Dave Bergman, I thought, 'What the hell is going on here?'"

- If Sparky Anderson, didn't provide enough leadership color, there was the new man at the very top. McGraw, the *Free Press'* baseball beat writer that season, remembers:

It was Year One under the ownership of Tom Monaghan, an Ann Arbor pizza magnate. Despite his business acumen in building Domino's, he came across as kind of a goofy guy who exhibited a kind of messianic view of pizza—did you know it was nutritious for breakfast?—and he was reveling in his new-found wealth, buying Frank Lloyd Wright homes across the Midwest, assembling much of the real estate on Drummond Island in northern Michigan, throwing lavish parties for metro Detroit's elite. (Years later he sold everything and became a sort of secular monk.)

Monaghan put on a uniform in spring training and played catch with Al Kaline, and during the Tigers' season-opening series in the Twin Cities, he visited a regional Domino's office and led the staff in a cheer of "Eat more pizza, have more fun!"

- These Tigers were not a team of baseball immortals. Not one member of the team is in the Hall of Fame. Consider this: The Tigers won 104 of their 162 games. In major league history, every one of the other 32 teams that won at least that many has had at least one future Hall of Famer. (You'll excuse me for assuming Derek Jeter and Mariano Rivera of the 1998 Yankees and Albert Pujols of the 2004 Cardinals will be there once they've been retired long enough to become eligible.) Like McGraw, Mike Downey, the lead sports columnist for the *Free Press* that year, watched the '84 Tigers from spring training through World Series. (Downey went on to be a notable columnist for the *Chicago Tribune* and *Los Angeles Times*). Downey:

  All-time greats, well, maybe they weren't. Parrish, Whitaker and Chet Lemon got little Hall of Fame consideration, yet all three were in the 1984 All-Star Game's starting lineup for the American League along with George Brett, Rod Carew, Reggie Jackson, Cal Ripken and Dave Winfield. If that isn't 15 minutes of fame in baseball's universe, I don't know what is.

- This team was not a fluke of outlier years. Exceptions were Hernandez and Bergman, who came over in that key trade; they had never been and never would be as good as they were in 1984. By WAR, Trammell, Lemon and Petry were in the range of their career years. The other key players were normal-good. High-priced free agent Darrell Evans had about his least productive season in a long and outstanding career. There was also a now-forgotten one-and-almost-done surprise. Downey again:

  I remember a Tiger rookie from Cuba with the calypso-cool name of Barbaro Garbey Garbey, although I can't recall offhand if we used both Garbeys when alluding to him. I was not, alas, aware (until looking it up) that BGG had more RBIs that season than either Larry Herndon or Dave Bergman did, had more hits than Darrell Evans did and stole as many bases as Lou Whitaker did. (He did? He did.)

- Remember all the (fully justified) fuss over the AL champion Royals' 2014 bullpen? Greg Holland, Wade Davis, Kevin Herrera and Aaron Crow among them contributed 260 mostly strong innings pitched. Those four pitchers combined for a 20-9 record, 52 saves in 61 chances, and 5.3 WAR (8.7 RA9-WAR). People marveled at that four-man crew. In 1984, the Tigers got the job done with just two relievers—Hernandez and Aurelio Lopez. Between them, they pitched even more innings—278 to be exact—during which they posted a 19-4 record, 46 saves in 48 chances, and 3.6 WAR (7.4 RA9-WAR). Oh, and one MVP award and one Cy Young award.

- And then there was Sparky, not one to hide his emotions under the Old English D on his cap. It looked like the Tigers were coasting, but he took nothing for granted. From the diary he published after the season, on the day the team went from 35-5 to 35-6: "We stunk up the Dome (in Seattle)." Three weeks later: "We haven't played well in 20 games." July 1: "An ugly day. You couldn't put enough perfume on this game to make it smell halfway decent."

Tom Gage, inducted into the Baseball Hall of Fame's writers' wing in 2015, covered all 17 seasons of Anderson's tenure with the Tigers as the *Detroit News'* beat writer. From Gage, this story, recounting the night the Tigers moved their record to 34-5:

After a short bus ride from the ballpark, the Tigers were walking through the lobby of the team hotel when a baseball fan recognized Sparky by his silver hair and approached him.

Keep in mind that Anderson had been the Tigers' manager five years by then.

"Sparky Anderson!" the man said. "I'm from Dayton and I was a huge fan of the Big Red Machine that you managed in Cincinnati."

Anderson thanked the fan and kept walking. But so did the fan.

"No, really, I was a big fan of that team. You did a great job managing them, so when I saw you here, I wanted to say hello."

Anderson thanked him again. He was always very cordial with the fans.

"By the way," the man from Dayton then asked, "what are you doing now?"

Anderson stopped in his tracks. "If I'd been chewing gum," he said later, "I would have swallowed it.

Instant perspective.

Instant humility.

Call it what you will. But it served as a reminder that the Tigers' start was just that, a start—and hadn't been noticed by everyone.

When the Tigers were swept three straight in Seattle after leaving Anaheim with a 35-5 record, it was also a dose of humility.

There's much more to remember. For instance, a now-dated and clichéd ritual, described by McGraw.

> *It started slowly, as early as May, and we watched in stunned silence the first couple of times the wave slowly took form across the upper deck. We learned—and this is no definitive account—that the wave started at college football stadiums, perhaps even at the University of Michigan, which is why Tiger Stadium became one of the first major-league stadiums where it was seen.*
>
> *In any case, by summer the wave was cresting across both levels of the stadium, and bewildered visiting journalists and broadcasters were asking Detroit writers what was going on. I don't think I am imagining that I saw some waves go around the stadium's upper and lower decks in opposite directions.*

Meanwhile, as the Tigers were mowing down the American League, the Cubs, dormant since the 1969 Miracle Mets folded the Chicagoans like so many pieces of Wrigley's Spearmint, were almost as dominant in the National League. With general manager Dallas Green, late of Philadelphia, supplying a starting lineup that was five-eighths ex-Phillies, the Cubs scored more runs and won more games than anyone else in the NL—just eight fewer wins than the Tigers. Rick Sutcliffe arrived midseason and won 16 of 17 decisions. Chicago led the NL East by six games by the end of August and cruised from there. Meanwhile, the NL West was as weak as the newly ascendant Bud Light beer; among its six teams only the San Diego Padres cracked .500 for the year, and it was hard to take seriously a beach-town team clad in orange, brown and a shade akin to baby poop.

Motown and Chitown! An I-94 World Series! What a finale it was going to be. Two storied, original-16 franchises. Michigan and Trumbull to Clark and Addison. Two old parks full of history and sightline-impaired seats.

And then a ground ball rolled through the legs of Cubs first baseman Leon Durham in the deciding Game Five of the National League Championship Series. We had a San Diego-Detroit World Series.

Detroit. A couple of years after the Tigers' championship season, the city hung a huge black fist, sculpted of bronze, right downtown as a tribute to boxer Joe Louis. More than one wag observed that it was just as well the city didn't claim Casanova.

Memorably, when the Republican National Convention came to the city in 1980, *Time* magazine described Detroit as "Cleveland without the glitter." That remark might not have made the local newspapers; their unions were on strike that week. That kind of town.

The phrase "economically depressed city" is in the fourth paragraph of Sparky's diary of the season, written with the Tigers' PR guy. The first column of the Tigers profile in the World Series program notes that "Despite the economic upswing of the nation over the last couple of years, Detroit has still been mired in unemployment problems..." Tiger Stadium stood a dozen gritty blocks from downtown, in the kind of nondescript neighborhood that made you wonder if it had ever been descript.

In fact, the 1968 Tigers had made people feel good, but Detroit still had economic and racial woes. Michigan's governor joked wryly that his state didn't notice the early '80s recession because it had never recovered from the last one. If Michigan's situation was bad, Detroit's was worse. The Motor City was bleeding automotive jobs.

In 1984, as in 1968, this was a divided metropolis, maybe more so—city-suburbs, white-black, rich-poor, unions-bosses. The towering Renaissance Center, a gleaming office building named for the effect it was supposed to have on Detroit, sat isolated on the Detroit River, separated from the rest of the downtown by a multi-lane throughway no sane pedestrian wanted to cross.

These Tigers, at least, seemed to reflect a tough city, its mean winters, its quarrelsomeness. Morris was a glowering presence on the mound and a hothead who got called out publicly by his own pitching coach, Roger Craig, after a dugout tantrum. Gibson habitually wore a five-o'clock shadow, a slide-stained uniform and an attitude.

If there was a cause to unite the region even temporarily, it was the Tigers. Nuns painted their faces with tiger stripes. A just-married couple showed up in the left field general-admission seats during a game, the bride in a full white dress. A local TV sportscaster, Al Ackerman, ended each evening's report on the Tigers with the phrase, "Bless you, boys." It attained the 1980s equivalent of "going viral," and became the title of Anderson's book about the season. (It's now also the name of a prominent Tigers-centric blog.) Fans broke the 1968 team's all-time Tiger Stadium attendance record by 700,000.

Also rabidly following the team were the displaced Detroiters who were reversing the northward migration of the century's earlier years, when jobs were plentiful in the auto industry. Now...let Bill McGraw tell about his favorite bookstore:

> *Each Monday, there were stacks and stacks of papers from Houston, Dallas and others points southwest, and Detroiters flocked to the store to scoop them up. All they wanted were the help wanted sections, which were voluminous. And when the Tigers traveled to Dallas, there were so many expatriate Detroiters and Detroit fans in the park that it sometimes seemed like it was a home game.*

Sept. 18, Detroit, Game 151, Tigers 3, Brewers 0. From Sparky's diary:

WE CLINCHED IT!!!

I thought I had seen some parties in Cincinnati, but they were nothing like this. It was crazy. I was so happy for these fans. They're the greatest in baseball...

The clubhouse was packed after the game. Lance Parrish and Kirk Gibson came over to dump a bottle of champagne over me and accidentally cut my head. My uniform looked really good with a mix of blood and champagne all over it.

I'm not sure what time I got out of the clubhouse, but they were still party-ing on the streets outside the park...I've been involved in a lot of baseball celebrations, but I can honestly say that none of them ever matched anything like this.

Detroit was to match it, and beyond, for better and worse, because the Tigers would provide more to celebrate.

Now it was Oct. 14, Game Five of the World Series, Tigers up three games to one, leading 5-4 in the bottom of the eighth. A sacrifice bunt put runners on second and third, one out, Gibson coming up. He would of course be intentionally walked, load-ing the bases and setting up a double play with slow-footed catcher Parrish on deck.

Padres manager Dick Williams went to the mound to talk to his pitcher, future Hall of Famer Goose Gossage. Five years before, in his first major league at-bat, Gibson had struck out against Gossage on three pitches. Now, it turned out, Gossage would try to do that again. This time, he got one of those strikes.

Gibson hit Gossage's 0-1 pitch into the right field upper deck. The Detroit of old assembled whole cars faster than Gibson rounded the bases, slow-dancing. At the end of his saunter, the 51,901 jammed into the stadium stood cheering Gibson, his hat off, both arms in the air, screaming, delivering high-fives that would stun an NFL linebacker.

The ballgame was all over then except for the anticlimactic Padres ninth. But there was more to come that night in Detroit.

The Tigers won the division, pennant and Series at home. When they clinched the division title, fans broke through fences, ran onto the field and tore up pieces of turf as souvenirs. The Tigers mowed down the Royals in the best-of-five League Cham-pionship Series, winning three straight and holding Kansas City to four runs total. When the pennant-clinching 1-0 win was over, the authorities at Tiger Stadium had a plan; many fans got onto the field, but the police were in control. McGraw remem-bers the mounted police outside the stadium a couple of hours after that game, the horses' hooves crunching the glass from broken bottles.

For the Series clincher, there was, of course, a security plan. But, as McGraw remembers:

Late in the game, with the crowd jacked after Gibson's home run and his dance around the bases, the leather-jacketed cops took their positions again, and when the game ended fans poured onto the field and the police could do little about it. Outside the stadium, where ticketless young fans had gathered during the game, a riot was taking place in the streets, from the burning police car (and other vehicles) to looted stores to crowds shaking chartered buses filed with senior citizens.

When my work was done, I climbed the ladder from the third-deck press box to the stadium roof, and I walked along the Michigan Avenue side and looked down at the intersection with Trumbull. There was a light rain falling, and the scene looked like a revolution had taken place. The overturned cop car was still smoking, and the corner was filled with other debris. A good number of people lingered at the edges of the street.

The police later admitted they had erred in allowing all the young people without tickets to hang around for hours, boozing it up. They also blamed much of the ruckus on suburbanites, which was probably partially true.

There would be two iconic pictures from that night, of two young men, both with arms raised in furious joy. One was of Gibson, after his eighth-inning homer. The other was Bubba Helms, a 17-year-old suburbanite in a sea of them, who—holding aloft a World Series pennant—was caught at the intersection of a burning police car and an AP photographer.

Alex Cruden has been observing Detroit for some 40 years, mostly as an editor at the Free Press, more recently as an instructor at Wayne State University. His take:

People remember the 1984 Tigers as steady guys who played hard but fair, generally nice fellows. Which can happen when you start a season 35-5. But something that stands out to me was the two Tigers with more than a streak of meanness. Both were pitchers.

Willie Hernandez was new to the Tigers and new to closing and had a lot to prove. Jack Morris was the established ace and always was out to prove it.

The meanness was key to postseason success for the Tigers. So much of my memory film bank of that Series is the two of them just defying batters.

At its best, that kind of meanness refines itself into the resilience that has always been a characteristic of Detroit.

It was a time in southeast Michigan when some major hopes had hardened into major disappointments, and into major divisions. But those were also evidence of Detroit resilience: My meanness signifies I will prevail, and so will my team.

Persistence works. Today, downtown Detroit is cruising with positive energy that flows around the new ballpark—and an adjacent grand arena for the Lions. Similarly, midtown Detroit is warmly snapping back with practical gentrification, and creative rebuilding sparks glow all around the metropolis. And, for the Tigers, all we need now is a new bullpen.

References and Resources

- My thanks to former *Detroit Free Press* colleagues Bill McGraw, Mike Downey, Alex Cruden and Gene Myers (the paper's recently retired sports director, who provided a rare extant copy of *The Roar of '84*), and to former competitor Tom Gage.
- FanGraphs and Baseball-Reference are invaluable resources for baseball research.
- *The Roar of '84*, by Detroit Free Press staff
- *Bless You Boys*, by Sparky Anderson
- *World Series 1984*, by Major League Baseball

A Haphazard, Historical Examination of Pitcher & Team NERD Scores

by Carson Cistulli

To the naked eye, the editor of this publication, Paul Swydan, resembles—what with his friendly beard and friendly other features—a regular friendly person. And indeed, most of the time, that's entirely the case. Every year, though, right at the end of baseball's regular season, Swydan transforms from an amiable colleague into the Draconian editor of the Annual, whose taste for physical abuse is surpassed only by his even greater taste for *emotional* abuse.

Those familiar with the screen adaptation of Stephen King's *Misery* will have some idea of the basic arrangement. The Annual's contributors each play, in their own way, the James Caan character; Swydan, Kathy Bates. He stands above us ominously, motivated by one ambition only—to ensure the completion of his book. Each contributor, meanwhile, cowers in his respective chair, attempting to court inspiration even while Swydan's shadow stretches menacingly across our keyboards.

It's under those hostile circumstances that I've composed what follows.

"What follows," in this case, is a haphazard examination of both pitcher and team NERD scores over the last decade. And because the phrase "pitcher and team NERD scores" very possibly has no meaning whatsoever to the reader, what follows even sooner is a brief explanation.

In 2010, I was living in Portland, Ore. When not shopping for vintage t-shirts or bemoaning the newfound popularity of a formerly obscure indie rock band, I also spent some of my time in the company of the perpetually beflanneled Rob Neyer. During one of our conversations, I attempted to construct a list of those qualities that might render a baseball game most appealing to a neutral fan. Neyer responded by requesting the application of a "points system that would let us put a number on each game." NERD is the product of an attempt to create that points system.

On June 2, 2010, I introduced an early version of NERD at FanGraphs—in this case, for pitchers only. Combining four variables—expected FIP (xFIP), swinging-strike rate (SwStrk%), strike rate (Strk%), and luck (ERA-xFIP)—I produced a number between zero and 10 for every pitcher in 2010 who'd recorded more than 20 innings as a starter.

Instantly, the methodology required improvement—improvement that was aided considerably by the readers of FanGraphs. Within the year, I'd added nascent versions of NERD both for position players and teams. Over time, the effort has expanded, and now game scores—including a combination both of pitcher and team NERD, plus adjustments for postseason odds—appear at FanGraphs every day during baseball's regular season to assist readers in their viewing practices.

In essence, NERD represents an attempt to *reverse engineer baseball-viewing* tastes. Whose tastes, specifically, isn't entirely clear. At the start, it was mostly my own, probably—or, my own plus a foggy estimate of the public's, as well. Currently, it's probably still my own, but also with a less foggy and more substantial notion of that same public's.

The variables used in both the pitcher and team NERD algorithms are likely not the precise ones upon which every reader would settle. They're sufficiently acceptable for FanGraphs readers now, though, such that I don't receive constant suggestions as to how they might be improved. A small victory is how one might characterize this.

Pitcher NERD

We'll begin this examination with pitchers. And we'll begin the examination of pitchers, specifically, with a review of the components that inform pitcher NERD.

One note before we do: Pace scores—that is the average time (in seconds) between a pitcher's deliveries—are unavailable in a reliable form all the way back to 2006. Therefore, it's been omitted from the scores as calculated here. By definition, roughly 68 percent of pitchers will possess a pace mark within one standard deviation of league average (and 95 percent within two standard deviations). As such the omission of pace from the NERD formula is unlikely to greatly influence the final results.

That having been stated, here are the components of pitcher NERD:

1. League- and Park-Adjusted Expected FIP (xFIP-)
2. Swinging-Strike Rate (SwStrk%)
3. Overall Strike Rate (Strk%)
4. Average Fastball Velocity (Velo)
5. Age (Age)
6. Luck (ERA-xFIP)
7. Knuckleball Rate (KN%)

To calculate this edition of pitcher NERD, I found each pitcher's z-score (standard deviations from the mean) for categories one through five. I multiplied the xFIP score by two, divided both the swinging strike and overall strike percentage scores by two, and then added the Velocity and Age variables. Of note: The latter two are only included if they contribute a *positive* value—which is to say, a pitcher won't be penalized for throwing a fastball slower than league average or for having reached an age older than league average. Those are only bonuses. (As one might assume, both xFIP- and Age are calculated such that numbers *lower* than the league-average figure receive a positive z-score.)

The last two variables aren't z-scores. The first, Luck, is designed to credit pitchers who likely have positive regression awaiting them in the future. The Luck variable is calculated by subtracting the park-adjusted xFIP minus stat (xFIP-) from the ERA minus stat (ERA-) and then dividing by 20. So: (ERA- [minus] xFIP-) / 20. The highest possible Luck score is a 1.0 and, as above, only positive values are considered.

The Knuckleball bonus was added in 2012, mostly as a response to R.A. Dickey's excellent season. It's calculated merely by multiplying knuckleball rate by five (i.e. KN% * 5).

Adding a constant (around 3.8 for most years) gives all pitchers who've recorded at least 10 innings a score (roughly) between zero and 10, with average exactly at 5.0.

The final equation looks like this:

$$(XFIPz * 2) + (SWSTRKz / 2) + (STRKz / 2) + VELOz + AGEz + LUCK + (KN\% * 5) + C$$

The results then are capped at 10 (on the high side) and zero (on the low), although the majority of pitcher scores fit comfortably within that range.

As I say, all pitchers who've recorded 10-plus innings in a given season receive a NERD score during the daily edition of the NERD game scores that appear in the pages of FanGraphs.

Below is a collection of the top 20 NERD scores produced by starters who recorded somewhere between 10 and 162 innings. Below that is an assortment of unkempt thoughts regarding some of the names on that list. rNERD denotes "raw NERD"—which is to say, the score before being rounded down to 10 (or up to zero). While the table below is populated entirely by pitchers whose scores require rounding, this group represents a distinct minority relative to the entire population of pitchers since 2006 who've recorded 10-plus innings as a starter in a season. Were one in the mood, he or she might suggest these are the pitchers who've "broken NERD."

(Note: I have excluded "KN" for space considerations, as none of the pitchers here have a KN value other than zero.)

Name	Year	IP	XFIPz	SW STRKz	STRKz	VELOz	AGEz	LUCK	rNERD
Stephen Strasburg, WAS	2010	68.0	3.2	2.5	1.2	2.6	1.6	1.0	17.2
Francisco Liriano, MIN	2006	98.2	3.0	4.0	1.4	1.7	1.2	0.0	15.4
Jose Fernandez, MIA	2014	51.2	2.6	2.8	1.6	1.8	1.7	0.4	15.1
David Hale, ATL	2013	11.0	3.8	2.6	1.1	0.1	0.6	0.0	14.0
Danny Salazar, CLE	2013	52.0	1.9	3.3	1.9	2.2	1.1	0.4	13.9
Stephen Strasburg, WAS	2011	24.0	2.5	1.7	2.0	2.1	1.3	0.0	13.9
Hong-Chih Kuo, LAD	2006	29.1	2.9	2.1	1.9	0.9	0.8	0.6	13.9
Andrew Cashner, SD	2012	19.1	2.5	1.4	0.8	2.2	0.6	1.0	13.8
Jose Fernandez, MIA	2015	64.2	2.1	2.1	1.8	1.9	1.4	0.4	13.5
Ben Sheets, MIL	2006	106.0	2.5	1.9	2.1	1.1	0.1	1.0	13.1
Noah Syndergaard, NYM	2015	150.0	1.7	1.6	0.6	2.4	1.4	0.7	12.7
Randy Johnson, ARI	2007	56.2	2.5	2.0	2.0	1.1	0.0	0.9	12.7
Max Scherzer, ARI	2008	37.0	2.1	2.3	0.5	1.7	1.0	0.3	12.3
Carlos Carrasco, CLE	2014	91.0	2.1	2.3	1.6	1.8	0.2	0.2	12.2
Stephen Strasburg, WAS	2012	159.1	2.0	1.6	0.0	2.1	1.1	0.4	12.1
Chris Archer, TB	2012	23.2	2.2	1.0	-0.4	1.4	1.1	1.0	12.1
Stephen Strasburg, WAS	2015	127.1	2.0	1.1	1.3	1.7	0.4	0.9	11.9
Jenrry Mejia, NYM	2013	27.1	2.4	1.8	1.2	0.5	1.1	0.2	11.9
John Smoltz, ATL	2008	27.0	2.6	2.5	0.9	1.0	0.0	0.0	11.7
Brandon McCarthy, LAD	2015	23.0	2.0	1.4	2.1	0.9	0.0	1.0	11.5

Stephen Strasburg has pitched in parts of six seasons since 2010, and four of those seasons appear on this table. Here's the positive implication of that distinction: Strasburg, in two-thirds of his seasons, has produced among the most impressive collection of metrics among all major-league pitchers. Here, on the other hand, is the negative implication: Strasburg, in no *fewer* than two-thirds of his major-league seasons, has recorded fewer than 162 innings pitched.

The numbers illustrate objectively what human people have already probably felt with their emotions: Strasburg is a brilliant, and also somewhat flawed, talent. As a tragic figure, he hasn't quite reached the heights of an Oedipus or King Lear. A brief examination of the relevant literature, for example, reveals Strasburg almost certainly has never (a) killed his father nor (b) slept with his mother. One wouldn't be surprised, however, given Strasburg's combination of physical tools and actual skill, to find he'd won multiple Cy Youngs already. He hasn't.

The case of Strasburg illustrates one possible weakness of NERD (among its many possible weaknesses)—namely, that it doesn't account for pitchers who possess legitimate contact-management skills. And, conversely, it might actually credit pitchers who possess *below average* contact-management skills. Because here's why. Pitchers, by the methodology outlined above, receive a bonus in cases in which they produce an Expected FIP lower than their ERA. The logic: They're bound to regress positively. And most pitchers do regress positively under such circumstances. Thus, the elegance of xFIP as a simple ERA estimator.

Some pitchers' earned-run averages *don't* regress entirely to the marks otherwise suggested by their fielding-independent numbers, however, and Strasburg is quite possibly an example of such a pitcher. In nearly 800 career innings, he's produced an ERA (3.46) nearly a full run worse than his xFIP (2.69). That sort of discrepancy over that large a sample suggests some inability to prevent runs above and beyond those variables for which xFIP accounts. It's probable, in other words, that Strasburg's "bad luck" is actually a product, to some degree, of "bad skill." As for how that influences his watchability, that's a different question. On the one hand, competence is appealing; on the other hand, though, so are tragic flaws. In any case, there likely isn't a critical mass of people offended by how well Strasburg is acquitted by this methodology.

Moving on, here's a question: Did you open this book expecting to read multiple paragraphs in celebration of right-hander David Hale? In light of his 2015 campaign, very likely not—and yet, that's precisely what's happening right now. Following a trade last January from Atlanta to Colorado, Hale proceeded to record an ERA for the Rockies that was 33 percent greater (i.e. worse) than league average – this, even after having adjusted for the wretched influence of his home park. Not the tell-tale sign of a rousing success, that.

Hale's brief introduction to the majors in 2013, however, was markedly more impressive. Over two starts in September of that year, still with Atlanta, he produced strikeout and walk rates of 30.4 percent and 2.2 percent, respectively, in 11.0 innings. In fact, his actual debut was a nearly singular effort by almost any measure. During that debut, on Sept. 13, 2013, Hale faced 20 Padres at Turner Field, striking out nine of them while walking just one and also conceding no runs over five innings. As Baseball Reference's Play Index reveals, that strikeout total represents the sixth-highest such figure by a starter in his debut between 2006 and 2015.

Regard, all nine pitchers who have recorded nine or more strikeouts in a debut since 2006:

Nine or More Strikeouts, Major League Debut, 2006-2015						
Player	Date	Team	Opp	IP	TBF	K
Stephen Strasburg	06/08/10	WAS	PIT	7.0	24	14
Matt Harvey	07/26/12	NYN	ARI	5.1	23	11
Thomas Diamond	08/03/10	CHN	MIL	6.0	27	10
Johnny Cueto	04/03/08	CIN	ARI	7.0	22	10
Daisuke Matsuzaka	04/05/07	BOS	KC	7.0	26	10
David Hale	09/13/13	ATL	SD	5.0	20	9
Collin McHugh	08/23/12	NYN	COL	7.0	23	9
Wade Davis	09/06/09	TBA	DET	7.0	25	9

For such a simple criterion, debut strikeouts actually appears to represent an awfully effective means of predicting future success. Or, it *has* done for this sample of nine, at least.

Regard, by way of illustration, the career numbers of the eight pitchers on the table above who aren't David Hale:

Career Statistics, Selected Pitchers			
Player	IP	WAR	WAR/200
Matt Harvey	427	12.2	5.7
Stephen Strasburg	776	18.7	4.8
Collin McHugh	405	6.9	3.4
Johnny Cueto	1,420	22.8	3.2
Wade Davis	733	10.7	2.9
Daisuke Matsuzaka	790	8.2	2.1
Thomas Diamond	29	-0.1	-0.7
Average	654	11.3	3.5
Median	733	10.7	3.2

The only weak link within the group has been Diamond, a former 10th-overall pick of the Texas Rangers whose career was derailed by injury and (subsequent) ineffectiveness. The remainder—including even Matsuzaka, who produced some strong years before his decline—have developed into either (a) capable starters or (b) relief aces (mostly just Davis). Based only on this single data point, that is.

Is this intended to serve as a full professional endorsement of Hale's probable success in 2016 and after? No. Although, even if it were, the author's lack of credibility in that capacity would render it worthy of being ignored.

Let's move on now to NERD scores for qualified pitchers from 2006 to 2015. There are 830 such pitcher seasons during that interval. Here are the top 20 by pitcher NERD. Once again, rNERD denotes "raw NERD"—that is, a NERD score that hasn't been rounded down to 10 (or up to zero). Once again, KN is excluded for space reasons. Every value but one is 0.0. The exception, as you might surmise, is R.A. Dickey, who registered a 4.2 KN.

Top 20 Pitcher rNERD Scores, 2006-2015 (Qualified Pitchers)									
Name	Year	IP	XFIPz	SW-STRKz	STRKz	VELOz	AGEz	LUCK	rNERD
Chris Sale, CHW	2015	208.2	2.3	2.7	1.6	1.4	0.4	1.0	13.3
Clayton Kershaw, LAD	2015	232.2	2.8	3.3	1.6	1.0	0.1	0.2	13.2
Clayton Kershaw, LAD	2014	198.1	2.7	2.8	2.0	0.8	0.4	0.0	13.0
Felix Hernandez, SEA	2007	190.1	1.8	1.1	0.8	2.2	1.4	0.8	12.8
Felix Hernandez, SEA	2006	191.0	1.9	0.7	0.4	2.0	1.7	1.0	12.8
R.A. Dickey, NYM	2012	232.2	1.3	2.1	2.2	0.0	0.0	0.0	12.7
Carlos Carrasco, CLE	2015	183.2	2.2	2.4	1.6	1.4	0.0	1.0	12.5
Stephen Strasburg, WAS	2014	215.0	2.0	1.4	1.1	1.6	0.7	0.8	12.2
Matt Harvey, NYM	2013	178.1	1.9	2.1	1.2	2.0	0.9	0.0	12.2
Johan Santana, MIN	2006	233.2	2.2	2.9	2.1	1.3	0.1	0.0	12.1
Francisco Liriano, MIN	2010	191.2	2.1	2.5	0.7	1.3	0.3	0.9	12.0
Justin Verlander, DET	2009	240.0	1.8	1.8	1.7	2.1	0.3	0.2	11.6
Jeremy Bonderman, DET	2006	214.0	1.7	2.1	0.7	1.3	1.0	0.6	11.5
CC Sabathia, ---	2008	253.0	1.9	3.0	1.4	1.4	0.1	0.0	11.5
Max Scherzer, WAS	2015	228.2	1.7	3.0	2.7	1.2	0.0	0.0	11.4
Tim Lincecum, SF	2008	223.0	1.9	2.1	0.5	1.6	0.8	0.0	11.3
Michael Pineda, SEA	2011	171.0	1.1	2.3	1.3	1.6	1.3	0.6	11.2
Cole Hamels, PHI	2007	183.1	1.8	2.8	2.1	0.4	1.0	0.0	11.1
Zack Greinke, MIL	2011	171.2	2.3	1.6	0.3	0.8	0.1	1.0	11.1
CC Sabathia, CLE	2006	192.2	1.6	2.0	2.2	1.5	0.6	0.0	11.1

Before discussing the names atop this particular list, allow me to restate: The numbers here are figured relative to each pitcher's seasonal contemporaries and not to all pitchers from 2006 to '15. That's relevant because of all the numbers one finds in the *next* table.

MLB Strikeout Rate, 2006-2015			
Season	K%	Season	K%
2006	15.9%	2011	17.7%
2007	16.1%	2012	18.7%
2008	16.6%	2013	18.9%
2009	17.1%	2014	19.4%
2010	17.6%	2015	19.5%

Those are the average strikeout rates among all starting pitchers from the years 2006 to '15. The trend, one finds, is distinctly upward. The average starter in 2006 struck out fewer than 16 percent of opposing batters; the average one in 2015, approaching 20 percent. Were the pitcher NERD scores calculated all together, with all the seasons mixed, the leaderboard would be occupied almost entirely by starters from the last three years. That's not how it's calculated, though. Rather, pitchers are evaluated according to their success in each metric *relative to their seasonal peers.*

That's what renders the top of the qualified pitcher leaderboard even more notable, owing to how it's occupied by two player-seasons from 2015, those belonging to Chris Sale and Clayton Kershaw. In a year when pitcher dominance was, by some definitions, at an all-time high, Sale and Kershaw were the most dominant relative to their seasonal peers.

Of the 830 qualified pitcher seasons since 2006, Sale and Kershaw's 2015 seasons are responsible for producing the fourth-best and actual best-best park-adjusted xFIPs during that interval. They each also recorded top-10 league-relative swinging-strike rates among those 830 pitchers seasons. Nor are there really any weaknesses elsewhere in their watchability profiles. Both throw strikes, both throw hard, and both are young.

One might be compelled to suggest there "aren't enough superlatives" to relate adequately the success of Sale and Kershaw relative to their peers. In fact, this probably represents an instance of hyperbole. A rough estimate by the editors of the *Oxford English Dictionary* suggests the English language possesses over 60,000 adjectives, from each of which one is able (presumably) to construct a superlative form. Certainly, that's an adequate supply to relate the accomplishments of anyone.

Instead of dwelling on Kershaw's and Sale's excellence, however—and to what extent one is capable of rendering it into English—what I'd like to do with the remainder of this section is to call attention to what represents an actual *impediment* to enjoying both pitchers.

At the core, what we're discussing here is the watchability or aesthetic pleasure of pitchers. NERD scores account for those aspects of watchability that lie within the control of those pitchers. There's at least one variable that pitchers can't control, however, but which *does* influence an observer's ability to fully *appreciate* them. It's not accounted for by the NERD algorithm, but that doesn't render it immaterial, either. The issue is center-field broadcast cameras.

Of the 30 most commonly used center-field cameras in major-league ballparks, seven of them feature straight-on shots, while the remaining 23 skew in varying degrees towards the direction of the left-field foul pole—that is, over pitchers' right shoulders. While these offset shots document somewhat faithfully the deliveries of right-handers and the flight paths of their respective pitches, they produce distortive effects for left-handers—effects that render it difficult to entirely appreciate the work of those same left-handed pitchers.

Consider, by way of example, the following pair of images—one documenting Sale's release point, another the batter (Brian Dozier's) point of contact—from the first inning of Sale's start on Sept. 1, 2015 at Minnesota.

Here is the release point:

To point of contact.

The center-field camera at Target Field is among the seven in the league that offer a straight-on shot—and, as such, depicts left-handed and right-handed pitchers in equal fashion. Because of Sale's nearly side-arm delivery, this angle doesn't fully document the ball's true path out of his hand. That said, it's also not that bad.

To get a sense of the difference between that sort of camera and the offset sort, consider the next pair of images—in this case, from the first inning of Sale's start on Aug. 21, 2015, at Seattle. As above, the shots document (first) Sale's release point and (then) the ball just as it's crossing the plate (because Ketel Marte swings but also misses).

From release point:

To the point at which Marte *would* have made contact:

If we mark the left-most edge of these images as zero and the right-most edge as 100, Sale's release point occurs about 25 here. The point at which the ball crosses the plate? About 65, maybe. Despite the fact that this pitch and the one above are both

(a) fastballs and (b) cross the plate at roughly the same horizontal point, the latter "travels" a much longer distance across the screen, thus rendering it more difficult for a viewer to fully appreciate its actual flight path.

In an attempt to illustrate the discrepancy more clearly, I've combined each pair of video stills above into single frames, making it possible to measure the distance each pitch has traveled across the respective image.

Here's the first case, in Minnesota:

Connecting the points from the middle of the ball at release to the middle of the ball at the plate produces a line that is 120 pixels long on my home computer.

How does that compare to the Seattle shot?

The same, very crude methodology produces a line of 394 pixels between release and the plate in Seattle—or, more than *three times* the length of the Minnesota camera. What that means for viewers is that, with little variation, all of Sale's pitches are marked by considerable glove-side movement. And while, of course, the brain is able to adjust partially for the parallactic distortion, much of the information regarding the actual movement of the baseball is obscured—to the point where the difference between changeups and breaking pitches, despite featuring quite distinct flight paths, is basically impossible to detect. The left-hander's repertoire is flattened more or less to a question of faster or slower, higher or lower, while horizontal movement is obscured.

Is the distortion of left-handers' pitches the greatest current threat to our happiness and/or democracy? No. Is it worthy of passing consideration in a lengthy annual publication dedicated entirely to baseball? This seems reasonable.

Team NERD

Next we move to team NERD scores—and begin, again, with a review of the components that inform that metric.

Note that, just as Pace figures—which appear in the daily NERD scores at FanGraphs—were omitted from the pitcher scores above, so has the Luck element, which normally is included in team NERD scores, been omitted from the version of team NERD that appears below. Again, a lack of data—or, at least, the ease which it could be integrated into the historical NERD scores, is to blame. Even so, the Luck variable is capped at two points—and even then only a handful teams benefit from that bonus. As such the omission of luck from the team NERD formula is unlikely to greatly influence the final results.

That said, here are the components of *this* edition of team NERD:

1. Park-adjusted batting runs (Bat)
2. Park-adjusted home-run rate (HR%)
3. Baserunning Runs (BsR)
4. Bullpen xFIP- (Bull)
5. Defensive Runs (Def)
6. Opening Day Payroll (Pay)
7. Average Batter Age (Age)

To calculate this edition of team NERD, I found each pitcher's z-score (standard deviations from the mean) for categories one through five. I divided both the bullpen and defense scores by two. Payroll and Age are notable insofar as they are included only if they contribute a *positive* value—which is to say, a team won't be penalized for having a payroll higher than league average or for having reached an age older than league average. Those are only bonuses. (Also, as one might assume, Bull and Pay and Age are calculated such that numbers *lower* than the league-average figure receive a positive z-score.)

Adding a constant (around 3.4 for most years) gives all teams a score (roughly) situated between zero and 10, with an average among the population of exactly 5.0.

The final equation looks like this:

$$\text{BATz} + \text{HRz} + \text{BSRz} + (\text{BULLz} / 2) + (\text{DEFz} / 2) + \text{PAYz} + \text{AGEz} + \text{C}$$

As with the pitcher scores, the results of the algorithm are then capped at 10 (on the high side) and zero (on the low), although even more of the team scores fit comfortably within that range.

Below is a collection of the top 20 team NERD produced between 2006 and 2015. Below *that* is an assortment of unkempt thoughts regarding some of the names on that list. rNERD denotes "raw NERD"—which is to say, the score before being rounded down to 10 (or up to zero).

Top 20 Team rNERD Scores, 2006-2015									
Team	Year	BATz	HRz	BSRz	BULLz	DEFz	PAYz	AGEz	rNERD
Astros	2015	0.6	2.1	0.7	1.6	-0.6	1.3	1.6	11.4
Marlins	2006	-0.5	0.6	1.3	-1.0	0.5	2.0	3.2	10.9
Marlins	2007	0.1	1.6	0.4	0.1	-0.1	1.5	2.0	10.0
Rays	2009	1.1	1.2	1.8	-0.7	0.7	0.7	0.4	9.8
Blue Jays	2015	2.3	1.7	1.0	0.7	-0.3	0.0	0.0	9.8
Rays	2010	0.7	0.3	2.7	0.6	0.2	0.5	0.4	9.6
Mets	2006	-0.1	1.4	2.1	1.6	1.6	0.0	0.0	9.6
Brewers	2007	0.0	2.5	0.7	1.1	1.0	0.3	0.4	9.5
Phillies	2008	-0.3	1.3	2.1	1.4	2.2	0.0	0.0	9.4
Rays	2008	0.6	0.7	0.5	0.1	1.1	1.2	1.3	9.4
Athletics	2012	-0.3	1.7	2.0	0.3	-0.1	1.0	0.3	9.3
Angels	2012	1.7	1.2	1.3	-1.0	1.2	0.0	0.3	9.2
Athletics	2013	0.9	1.7	0.8	0.8	-0.3	0.7	0.1	9.0
Yankees	2009	2.2	2.2	0.0	0.4	-0.6	0.0	0.0	8.9
Yankees	2011	1.4	1.6	0.6	1.3	0.2	0.0	0.0	8.9
Yankees	2012	1.7	2.1	0.2	1.2	-0.6	0.0	0.0	8.8
Rangers	2011	1.3	1.3	2.0	-1.0	0.4	0.0	0.0	8.8
Phillies	2009	0.4	1.4	1.6	0.0	1.5	0.0	0.0	8.7
Reds	2010	0.7	0.5	0.9	0.3	1.9	0.4	0.4	8.7
Marlins	2008	-0.5	1.8	0.5	-0.4	0.7	1.8	0.4	8.7

I'll remind the reader, to begin, the scores here don't account for a club's starting pitchers—so, in those cases in which a team has assembled a compelling group of hitters and defenders and relievers but *not* starters, that team will receive a higher NERD score than might seem appropriate given one's impression of it.

Atop the leaderboard here, the 2015 edition of the Houston Astros featured not only a compelling group of hitters and defenders and relievers, but also of starters. Or, at least one very notable starter in Dallas Keuchel plus a pair of above-average ones (Lance McCullers and Collin McHugh) and other useful pieces.

Even in the absence of the rotation, however, the Astros offered an appealing profile. Despite recording the lowest average batter age among all major-league clubs (at 26.6 years), Houston also produced the highest park-adjusted home-run rate in the majors (3.6 percent, over two standard deviations above league average). They were young and powerful—a combination that, in tandem with the strong rotation, conspired to produce a playoff team one or two years earlier than one otherwise might have expected.

Less obviously compelling, but almost a dynasty by the methodology used here, are the 2006 and 2007 editions of the Florida Marlins. The reader is excused for not remembering this iteration of the club as a juggernaut: Over the two relevant seasons, the Marlins recorded a combined record of 149-175, finishing no better than fourth place in either one.

Much of that mediocrity was a product of the club's pitching, however. Between '06 and '07, Marlins starters produced the fifth-lowest collective WAR among all major-league rotations. Marlins batters, meanwhile, recorded the seventh-best park-adjusted batting line over that same interval.

Most impressive, however, is the production of those hitters relative to their collective age. The '06 and '07 Marlins each possessed among the league's youngest collection of position players. Consider, by way of illustration, the following table, which features the 10 youngest collective batter ages by team between the 2006 and 2007 seasons (via Baseball-Reference).

Youngest Batter Ages, 2006-2007					
Team	Year	Age	Team	Year	Age
Florida	2006	25.6	Atlanta	2006	27.4
Tampa Bay	2007	26.1	Atlanta	2007	27.6
Arizona	2007	26.6	Cleveland	2006	27.8
Florida	2007	26.7	Pittsburgh	2006	27.8
Pittsburgh	2007	27.2	Milwaukee	2007	27.8
Tampa Bay	2006	27.3			

At the core of those Marlins clubs—and in no small part responsible for their presence near the top of the NERD leaderboard—were two players at the beginning of impressive careers: Miguel Cabrera and Hanley Ramirez. No club during the two-year period in question featured a pair of field players who offered Cabrera and Ramirez's combination of youth and performance.

Consider, by way of example, the following table, which depicts the top 10 pairs of teammates between 2006 and 2007. aAge denotes the average age of the pair over the relevant two-year period; aWAR, their average (combined) annual WAR.

Top Position Player Teammate Duos, 2006-2007				
Team	Teammate 1	Teammate 2	aAge	aWAR
Mets	David Wright	Carlos Beltran	27.0	13.0
Phillies	Chase Utley	Jimmy Rollins	28.0	12.8
Cardinals	Albert Pujols	Scott Rolen	29.0	11.8
Yankees	Alex Rodriguez	Jorge Posada	32.0	11.7
Indians	Grady Sizmore	Travis Hafner	27.0	11.3
Tigers	Curtis Granderson	Magglio Ordonez	29.0	10.6
Marlins	Miguel Cabrera	Hanley Ramirez	23.0	10.4
Braves	Chipper Jones	Andruw Jones	32.0	10.1
Mariners	Ichiro Suzuki	Adrian Beltre	30.0	9.7
Red Sox	David Ortiz	Mike Lowell	31.0	9.3

Nine of the 10 best twosomes between '06 and '07 featured an average age somewhere in the 27-32 range. Cabrera and Ramirez, meanwhile, recorded an average combined age of just 23 years old in that same interval. On average, they produced four seasons of roughly 5.0 WAR at 23 years of age. To understand the extent of that accomplishment, consider that in 2015 only four *total* position players aged 24 or under even reached the five-win threshold: Bryce Harper, Mike Trout, Manny Machado, and Kris Bryant.

Conclusion

After I submitted to him the text above, editor Paul Swydan responded by saying that, while the piece was mostly fit for publishing, that he was "sad when [it] ended" and asked if I could "add some sort of fancy conclusion." Those who recall the *Misery*-like scene I invoked at the beginning of this monstrosity will recognize the threatening subtext to Swydan's comments. "You'll be free of this burden soon," he's saying, "but only when I say you're free." So now here we all are together.

For basically five straight months of the year, I publish the NERD scores every day—and basically every time I do that I'm compelled to wonder what I've just done. Those colleagues of my wife's who have a vague notion of my job will sometimes ask on what articles I've been working recently. To reply that I've "once again provided a nearly objective assessment of the aesthetic pleasure likely to be supplied by the day's games" would be mostly accurate. It's also the sort of comment that, upon its utterance, reveals to those present that the speaker isn't actually a human at all, but rather an android-like creature—potentially one with wicked intentions. So mostly I say, "I actually have no idea what I've been doing," because that's also true and paints me less as evil and more as clueless.

What I've *endeavored* to do, I think, by means of the NERD scores is rather simple. At the most basic level, I watch baseball to find my pleasure. The game is an end in itself. It doesn't help one find a better job or live longer. Or, if it does do those things, that's not *why* it exists. Baseball, like all spectator sports, is meant to be enjoyed—either as a vehicle for tribal allegiance or as an allegory for all forms of struggle or as a stage for expressions of human potential. The idea of NERD has always been to identify objectively which of the day's games best lend themselves to enjoyment. If they fail sometimes to match the reader's own predilections, it's because they (the NERD scores) are woefully incomplete. There's a lot for which one is unable to account when it comes to *predicting* joy. They're also not entirely without merit, however. As such, they'll continue to appear at the site for the tens and tens of people who read them daily.

References & Resources

- Rob Neyer, ESPN.com, "Thursday Throneberries," *espn.go.com/blog/sweetspot/post/_/id/3751/thursday-throneberries-9*
- *Oxford Dictionaries*, "How many words are there in the English language?," *oxford-dictionaries.com/us/words/how-many-words-are-there-in-the-english-language*

Analysis

Command Is a Moving Target

by Eno Sarris

"Hey, raise your hand if you're a catcher," Dave Hudgens remembers asking his newly assembled team in the spring. "How often do you hold your mitt out there and the pitcher sticks it?" His question was greeted with laughter.

Hudgens, currently serving as the hitting coach for the Houston Astros, was trying to make a point about how hitters should treat plate discipline, but this realization should be a sobering one for any fan of the game. Pitchers don't do a great job of putting the ball right where they want it. Sportvision and Major League Baseball Advanced Media (MLBAM) created a COMMANDf/x metric that tracked the catcher's glove from target to catch and found pitchers missed the glove by an average of 13 inches. They miss by almost the width of the plate...on average!

You might just throw your hands up and give up on command, instead focusing on finding pitchers with great stuff. Some of the pitchers I've talked to agreed with this idea. Colin McHugh talked of focus and execution when I talked about command: "An aggressive pitch executed poorly is better than a non-aggressive pitch executed well," the Astros' righty said.

But there's still a spread when it comes to command, and there are a few ways we might improve our understanding of this undeniable, yet difficult-to-measure skill, especially if we ask the pitchers to help us understand it better.

After talking to two Bay area catchers, it was immediately clear context was the most important thing to any measure of command. The 13-inch finding didn't sit well with the Athletics' Stephen Vogt, for one. "Seems way too high," he said. "The plate is only 17 inches wide!" He went on to point out that if there are runners on base, the target changes—"we're moving late because the other team likes to relay location."

On the other side of town, Buster Posey thought the numbers were reasonable, even if he did "show the glove differently with runners on base." Maybe it was years of Tim Lincecum peppering his thighs with splitters and breaking balls, but he thought showing great command is very difficult. "Everything's moving," he pointed out. Athletics pitcher Kendall Graveman agreed. "Not too surprising, because of the movement today," he said of the finding. The Giants' Tim Hudson went even further, with his ever-present smile: "That's it? Seems low."

Unfortunately, Sportvision was not able to correct for runners on base, so that may have an effect on the numbers. Vogt wondered if big misses skewed the data, and that's certainly possible. One standard deviation in the data was 8.4 inches, and the movement of the glove from target to completion did not follow a normal distribution.

Graveman wondered if these data included breaking balls. "If you're missing by 13 inches with your four-seamer, you're in trouble," he said. And yet, Sportvision confirmed these numbers were based on fastballs. Today's fastballs do move a little more than yesterday's, so maybe Graveman's other statement still holds. But that's still an unsettling finding.

Movement is the ticket to trying to analyze command better. You really have to split out the pitches by movement so you're not lumping in big 12-to-6 curveballs with your four-seam fastballs.

So I asked Brandon McCarthy how I might best judge his fastball command. "You really have to break the plate into halves or thirds," he said. "If you're still on the outer half or third of the plate on a 3-0 count, that's very good command."

That seems reasonable. So let's look at fastball command in 3-0 counts when the aim is obvious and the movement usually is straighter. Here are the 10 best and worst starters at hitting the outside half of the strike zone on 3-0 counts with their fastball since 2013.

Outside Half Zone Percentages In 3-0 Counts, Fastballs Only, 2013-2015			
Best		Worst	
Player	3-0 Outside Zone%	Player	3-0 Outside Zone%
Eric Stults	61.7%	Trevor Bauer	14.5%
Dan Haren	59.5%	Allen Webster	20.9%
Patrick Corbin	59.5%	Jhoulys Chacin	21.7%
Ervin Santana	55.0%	Dan Straily	22.2%
R.A. Dickey	54.8%	Phil Hughes	22.6%
Erik Bedard	54.3%	Matt Harvey	23.7%
Hyun-Jin Ryu	53.7%	David Hale	24.2%
Jason Vargas	52.4%	Jose Quintana	24.5%
Matt Shoemaker	51.5%	Yordano Ventura	25.5%
Dallas Keuchel	50.0%	Tyler Matzek	25.6%

n= 230 starters with minimum 30 3-0 counts

For the most part, this list passes the sniff test. Dan Haren walked merely five percent of the batters he saw in his now-concluded 13-year career. Eric Stults, Jason Vargas and Matt Shoemaker have the kind of borderline stuff that must come with decent command, or how else could they be major leaguers? There are many who think David Hale's shortcomings have to do with the inability to put the fastball where he wants it, and Allen Webster may have the worst command in the big leagues when judged strictly by the eye test.

There is at least one name on this list that makes you reconsider the entire enterprise. Phil Hughes has the fourth-worst outside part of the plate percentage in 3-0 counts since 2013? That can't be right, can it?

Guess where Hughes likes to throw his 3-0 fastballs—high and tight. If you divide the plate in thirds instead of halves, over half of the fastballs he's thrown have come on the inside two-thirds of the plate.

That lines up well with something Javier Lopez said about command. "Command is, at least personally, relative," the Giants lefty told me. "My command is down in the zone, not so much corners. I need to be there to be effective. I can generalize spots. I don't think I could paint the inside corner consistently." So Hughes' best command probably is high and tight, which is great for him considering he throws a rising fastball and gets infield fly balls 50 percent more often than league average.

Let's re-do the 3-0 leaderboard with straight zone percentage in case we have other high-and-tighters who are messing up our math.

Zone Percentages In 3-0 Counts, Fastballs Only, 2013-2015			
Best		Worst	
Player	3-0 In Zone%	Player	3-0 In Zone%
Dan Haren	85.7%	Allen Webster	42.2%
Erik Bedard	82.9%	Jarred Cosart	50.0%
Eric Stults	80.0%	Yu Darvish	50.8%
John Lackey	80.0%	Jose Quintana	50.9%
R.A. Dickey	79.5%	Francisco Liriano	51.0%
Patrick Corbin	78.4%	Chris Heston	51.2%
Jimmy Nelson	77.8%	Michael Lorenzen	51.5%
Jake Peavy	77.8%	J.A. Happ	52.3%
Matt Garza	76.6%	Nate Karns	53.1%
Tanner Roark	76.5%	Martin Perez	53.3%

n= 230 starters with minimum 30 3-0 counts

Now our list is mostly rid of head-scratchers. And yet, the strike zone is a big place. Is it really great command if a pitcher can generally find the zone when he needs to? What if we re-visit the COMMANDf/x finding and look at glove movement, but limit it now to 3-0 counts? Let's see how the best pitchers do when they are expected to nail the catcher's mitt and the batter is not expected to swing.

Sportvision and MLBAM were kind enough to create a top-10 leaderboard for glove movement on 3-0 counts, and you may be surprised by how much pitchers still miss. Dallas Keuchel has excellent command, but he misses the glove by nine inches in 3-0 counts.

Least Glove Movement, 3-0 Counts, 2015	
Pitcher	Avg_Command (in)
Dallas Keuchel	8.9
Joe Kelly	9.1
Michael Pineda	9.3
Tommy Milone	9.7
Kendall Graveman	9.9
Masahiro Tanaka	10.0
Ubaldo Jimenez	10.2
Jerome Williams	10.2
Taijuan Walker	10.2
Jon Lester	10.3

Avg_Command: Inches glove moved from target to catch.

You may notice Joe Kelly and Jimmy Nelson on the list of good command guys above. Both of those pitchers can get into trouble in that department, though, and maybe they seem out of place on a list of guys with good command. Perhaps it has something to do with their command of breaking pitches, which is a completely different can of worms.

Listen to Hunter Strickland about commanding the fastball. "I'm a big hunter," the hard-throwing Giants reliever said with a smile. "You have a direct target, and you can't pull off, and you want to throw it through that target."

Now listen to Corey Kluber about commanding his big breaking ball. "To get it to end up where you want to, you have to start it one spot," the Indians ace told me. "If you think about a golfer trying to play a draw, you have to start it one spot to get it to draw. Then you learn through throwing and muscle memory where that starting point is for going away and going inside so that you're not just starting it generally outside or inside. My focal point is where I want to start it at."

Sliders are used all sorts of different ways, and break all sorts of different ways, so in order to test this, let's focus a bit more on the (slightly) more predictable curveballs. Its clear movement and location are huge here, so the glove maybe is no longer useful. "The glove is fairly arbitrary other than for the four-seamer," said McCarthy, which echoes what Kluber said about how a breaking ball is thrown.

It's still not completely clear which situations are best for curveball analysis. The typical first-pitch curveball thrown to get a called strike may not look anything like a curve thrown with the intention of generating whiffs. For one, it has to be thrown in the zone. And curves thrown in the zone often are called hanging curveballs. Maybe it's for this reason curves have the biggest discrepancy between in- and out-of-zone whiff rates among all the pitch types in baseball.

Before we look at two-strike curveballs to look for "buried" curves vs "hanging" curves, McCarthy had a thought. "Throwing it with two strikes is a little different—the successful breaking ball is in a count where the hitter wants to swing," he said. The hitter may not want to swing in a two-strike count because any hint that the pitch is a ball will put him back into defensive mode.

"The well-commanded breaking ball comes out in the 2-1 count, makes the hitter think fastball, and then the bottom drops out," McCarthy said. There has to be an element of fear that the pitch is a fastball in the zone to get a batter ready to swing. Furthermore, pitchers want that less defensive and more aggressive mindset that comes more often in one-strike counts than two-strike counts.

Let's first look at movement in those one-strike counts, with the idea that a hanger somehow looks different from a crisp breaking ball. If we study the standard deviation of a pitcher's curveball movement in these one-strike counts, we'll find the guys who have a large variety of curveballs when they're really trying to throw a curve for a swinging strike. The theory is that those pitchers have a hard time commanding their curve.

Curveball Movement in One-Strike Counts, 2013-2015					
Worst			Best		
Player	stdev	avg(pfx_z)	Player	stdev	avg(pfx_z)
Roenis Elias	4.38	-6.18	Jeremy Affeldt	1.21	-8.08
James Shields	3.85	-6.17	Evan Scribner	1.37	-11.53
Bronson Arroyo	3.69	-0.32	Nathan Eovaldi	1.37	-7.07
Danny Farquhar	3.63	-5.92	Chad Bettis	1.43	-2.95
Chris Heston	3.60	-2.64	Chase Anderson	1.47	-7.05
John Danks	3.36	-1.25	Jeff Francis	1.49	-4.96
David Price	3.30	-2.98	Will Harris	1.50	-9.39
Daisuke Matsuzaka	3.29	-5.89	Paul Maholm	1.51	-6.47
Rich Hill	3.27	-7.08	Jake Arrieta	1.51	-8.92
Joe Saunders	3.26	-5.22	Adam Wainwright	1.52	-9.37
John Lackey	3.20	-4.61	Jason Hammel	1.54	-7.55
Jose Veras	3.13	-5.98	Brandon McCarthy	1.56	-4.50
Eric Stults	3.07	-6.19	Scott Diamond	1.63	1.05
Esmil Rogers	3.03	-4.12	Marco Estrada	1.67	-6.87
Scott Feldman	3.00	-5.33	Mike Fiers	1.67	-11.51

stdev = standard deviation on curve movement, inches; avg(Pfx_z) = average vertical drop on the curve, inches; n=155 pitchers with at least 50 one-strike curveballs thrown

This list is amazing. Roenis Elias throws a curve that drops about half as much Evan Scribner's curveball, and yet the movement on Elias' curves is spread out almost four times as wide as Scribner's. After watching Jake Arrieta dominate this season by manipulating his many breaking balls, you have to wonder if this list isn't a decent way to get at breaking-ball command.

Except that the difference between the leaders and laggards in outcomes doesn't seem to match. The top 10 percent in this curve command metric had a swinging strike rate of 12.7 percent on their curve, while the bottom 10 percent showed an 11.8 percent rate. That's a small difference, especially when put up against the fact that a guy like Elias has a better swinging-strike rate on his poorly commanded smaller curve than Mike Fiers with his well-commanded huge curve.

Some feel location is a better way to judge hangers. Especially when they aren't thrown to get a called strike, curves are supposed to be thrown to the bottom part of the plate. A hanger is a high curve. Easy enough to judge. Let's now look at the leaders and laggards by curve location, in the same one-strike counts.

Curveball Average Vertical Location in One-Strike Counts, 2013-2015						
Best				Worst		
NAME	STDDEV(pz)	avg(Pz)		NAME	STDDEV(pz)	avg(Pz)
Zach Duke	0.61	1.55		Rich Hill	0.73	2.53
Will Harris	1.12	1.62		Barry Zito	0.88	2.51
Wei-Yin Chen	1.02	1.63		A.J. Griffin	0.96	2.39
Tommy Milone	0.81	1.64		Michael Wacha	1.10	2.39
Tanner Roark	0.76	1.66		Jhoulys Chacin	0.82	2.39
Jake Arrieta	1.06	1.68		Anibal Sanchez	0.83	2.38
Jeff Francis	0.80	1.68		John Danks	0.97	2.34
Wade Miley	0.86	1.69		Joel Peralta	0.97	2.34
Yovani Gallardo	1.04	1.69		Manny Parra	0.94	2.33
Chase Anderson	0.81	1.69		Bronson Arroyo	0.69	2.33
J.A. Happ	0.93	1.70		Kevin Correia	0.94	2.33
James Shields	1.01	1.73		Mike Bolsinger	0.99	2.30
Jon Niese	0.95	1.73		Matt Cain	0.77	2.30
Lance Lynn	0.79	1.74		Nathan Eovaldi	1.06	2.30
Edwin Jackson	1.20	1.74		Clayton Kershaw	1.35	2.29
David Hale	0.72	1.75		Zach McAllister	0.97	2.27
Odrisamer Despaigne	0.73	1.76		Tommy Hunter	0.72	2.27
Jacob deGrom	0.73	1.77		Erik Bedard	0.87	2.27
Charlie Morton	0.69	1.79		Brad Hand	1.12	2.27
C.J. Wilson	1.01	1.80		J.J. Hoover	0.87	2.26

stdev = standard deviation on curve location, inches; avg(Pz) = average vertical location on the curve, inches; n=155 pitchers with at least 50 one-strike curveballs thrown

Zach Duke has both the lowest average location as well as the smallest standard deviation, meaning he can bury the curve either way you look at it. Once again, though, there are great curveballs on both sides of this list. Clayton Kershaw was a guy who came up as having amazing fastball command. Does that command completely leave him as he goes to the curve?

Now it's time to test these measures to see if we have anything here. And this is the hardest part, because how do we test these possible command measures against any outcomes when we've decided there aren't any great outcome measures for command? It's a dilemma.

But let's say you have great fastball or curve command. You would figure to get some results from that in some way or another. So let's test the fastball command list against walk and homer rates—can they avoid the walk and the homer with their command? And for curves, let's check those rates, as well. But you'd also think you would get more swinging strikes with good command, so let's add in fastball and curve swinging strike rate.

R^2 Relationship Between Command Metrics and Outcomes			
Measure	BB/9	HR/9	Pitch swSTR%
3-0 Fastball Zone%	0.12	n/a	n/a
One-Strike Curve Location	n/a	n/a	0.12
One-Strike Curve Movement	n/a	n/a	n/a

R-squared shown for all situations where p value less than .0001

We did…poorly. A lot of the above are listed as n/a. That's because those were the situations where the P value—which helps you determine the significance of your results—was insignificant. It's sort of amazing that a pitcher who can replicate his curveball movement well doesn't necessarily get more whiffs from that curveball, and that he doesn't have a lower walk rate or give up fewer homers.

The only relationships we did find were no-duhs. Oh, a guy who can find the zone on 3-0 counts can suppress his walk totals a bit? Yeah, because if he misses the zone on that 3-0 pitch, it's a walk. And a curve below the zone is better for whiffs than one higher up in the zone? Yup.

And so we come full circle—command is hard to put your finger on. We might be circling around an answer, but it's doubtful it'll ever be *the* answer. That might be because a pitcher's delivery itself is very difficult to replicate, and you have different stuff every day. How can you repeat the exact same motion when your velocity is different and your body is moving differently every day?

The Indians' Trevor Bauer decried the difficulty when I talked to him this season. I asked him what he can do when he's not commanding a pitch well, where can he look to improve it? "Maybe my shoulder isn't getting that full rotation, or something about how the ball is coming out and the spin axis on the pitch that goes away," Bauer said with a sigh. "Maybe it's because I'm throwing harder now than I was in spring training. From the beginning of the year to August, about a mile and a half more. If you throw the two-seam at 90 mph and it has four seconds to move, and you throw it at 95, it has 3.8 seconds to move."

But there's more to why a measure of command is so difficult to pin down. There's too much thinking going behind each pitch to really nail down the pitcher's intent in any given situation. Some of those one-strike curveballs, for instance, were thrown in the zone on purpose because the pitcher figured the batter wouldn't swing despite the count.

Listen to Zack Greinke talk about his evolving relationship with command and the strike zone, and you really get a sense of how command is a moving target.

"Early in my career, I thought, I'll just try to throw strikes with every pitch," Greinke told me. "And that's why I got hit, because early in my career my stuff wasn't that great, and I was throwing strikes with every pitch. When I got behind in the count, I would just throw a strike. Now, when I get to 2-0, about half the time I throw a ball. Maybe that's an exaggeration. I'm just trying to figure out what the hitter wants to do."

This sounds a lot like what McHugh was saying. Your command doesn't always have to be great if your pitches are aggressive and calculated. Hitters pop it up in batting practice and miss pitches down the middle all the time. Good command might actually be good stuff, thrown in the right count, in the right order.

And that's even harder to measure than the ability to hit a target or replicate movement. Good luck to us.

References and Resources

- Thanks to Dave Hudgens, Colin McHugh, Steven Vogt, Buster Posey, Kendall Graveman, Tim Hudson, Brandon McCarthy, Javier Lopez, Hunter Strickland, Corey Kluber and Zack Greinke for their time and insight.
- Thanks to Sportvision and Major League Baseball Advanced Media for the data.
- PITCHf/x

Revisiting the Hot Hand

by Mitchel Lichtman

In the sabermetric community, it is conventional wisdom that hot and cold hands in baseball have little predictive value. At the same time, it's obvious to almost everyone who does not worship at the shrine of Bill James that the hot hand is very much a real thing in sports. The analyst would say when a player has been torrid over the last X number of games, he is likely to perform in his next few opportunities at a fixed level defined by a forecaster's best estimate of his true talent, after taking the streak into consideration as the most recent sample of performance. The more conventional and insider point of view is that the hot or cold player will perform above or below his established level of performance until the former cools off or the latter fixes whatever ails him.

There have been dozens of studies looking at the hot hand in sports ever since the pioneering study of NBA players by Gilovich et al. in 1985. For major league baseball, however, the research is limited. Seymour Siwoff of *Elias Baseball Annual* fame concluded in 1988 that batting averages were just as likely to be high after a five-game cold period as after a similar hot period. Albert and Albright in 1993 concluded the *streakiness* exhibited by hitters was similar to what would be expected by chance alone. In 1995, Stern criticized Albert's and Albright's results, claiming their methods lacked the statistical power to detect true hot and cold streaks at the individual player level. He found evidence of streaks at the group level. In 2006, myself, along with Tom Tango and Andrew Dolphin, published *The Book: Playing the Percentages in Baseball*, in which we presented research suggesting being hot or cold had some predictive value beyond what a projection model would imply but not enough to have much practical import. In 2010, Russell Carleton, a popular Baseball Prospectus author and sabermetric researcher, did a similar study to ours and concluded a hot or cold streak for batters had no predictive value whatsoever.

In this chapter, we will discuss two of the most recent studies on the hot hand in baseball: one, "The Hot-Hand Fallacy: Cognitive Mistakes or Equilibrium Adjustments? Evidence from Major League Baseball," by Brett Green and Jeffrey Zwiebel; hereinafter referred to as "Green-Zwiebel," and two, new research from myself.

First some background on the Green-Zwiebel study. In February of last year, my colleague and co-author of *The Book*, Tom Tango, and I read a draft of Green-Zwiebel's study and were surprised at the results. Here is an excerpt from that working paper:

Strikingly, we find recent performance is highly significant in predicting performance in all ten statistical categories that we examine. In all cases, being "hot" in a statistic makes one more likely to perform well in the same statistic. A recent history on the order of about 25 at-bats, which equals about five games or close to one week for the average hitter, has the most predictive power over the next at-bat. Furthermore, these effects are of a significant magnitude: for instance, a 30 percent increase in the number of times a batter has gotten on base in the last 25 at-bats predicts a five percent increase in the likelihood of getting on base in the next at-bat, after controlling for all other explanatory variables.

That implies that a .300 OBP hitter who has an OBP of .390 (.300 times 1.30) during a hot streak (not so hot really) will have an OBP of .315 (.300 times 1.05) after the streak. So a 90-point increase begets a 15-point increase. That's a lot.

He writes, "For example, column (1) in Table A.7 indicates that a .100 difference in a batter's recent on-base percentage translates to a .00628 increase in the probability of getting on base in the next PA."

That is the result of an OLS (ordinary least squares) regression in which they controlled for opposing pitcher, park, home/road, and platoon. According to these numbers, a 30 percent increase in OBP for a .300 hitter over a 25-plate appearance span would result in a 5.6 point increase in OBP in the next PA—not 15 points as they first wrote. In their logistic regression alternative, they got a slightly larger effect. Still, almost six points per 100 points of "streakiness" is a lot of predictive value. A typical hot batter might have an OBP of .500 over his last 25 PA, 200 points higher than his normal OBP. That would correspond to an 11-point "hot hand effect" right after the streak. That is quite a bit larger than what we found in *The Book*, although we looked at wOBA and not OBP.

In *The Book* we report an increase of four wOBA points in the game following a five-game hot streak or in the three games following a seven-game hot streak. For cold players, we find a six to eight point drop in wOBA. Our hot players averaged around 220 points higher than their normal wOBA during the streak. If these were OBP points, Green-Zwiebel's regression would have expected a 14-point increase. *Their result is more than three times greater than ours.* A .185 point drop in OBP during a cold streak would mean a 12-point drop in the next PA for Green-Zwiebel, which is twice the effect we found.

Green-Zwiebel used the Retrosheet play-by-play database from 2000 to 2011. Using 12 years of "panel data," as they call it, enables them to get a large enough sample of hot and cold streaks and subsequent plate appearances such that even small effects were likely to be statistically significant. In *The Book*, we used only four years of data, reducing the statistical power of our study, thus increasing the likelihood that we might make a Type I or II error.

Green-Zwiebel looked at all consecutive 25-PA performances within a certain time period and classified them as hot, cold or neither, according to various criteria. Their OLS regressions used a continuous independent variable, and their logistic regressions used various dummy criteria for classifying a streak as either hot or cold. The dependent variable in the regressions was the PA immediately following the 25-PA streak. For hitters, they used five statistical outcomes: OBP, BA, homers, walks and strikeouts per at-bat. This variable, the result of the 26th PA, was presented relative to each player's ability. *In other words, they were trying to find out whether the performance in the PA immediately following a hot or cold streak was less than or greater than the player's overall ability. That is the essence of all these studies on hot and cold streaks in baseball, including those in* The Book.

The null hypothesis is that the 26th PA is just like any other PA, relative to the player's true talent. The alternative hypothesis is that after a hot streak, players, in the aggregate, will perform better than their overall ability and that after a cold streak they will underperform their ability—at least immediately subsequent to the streak and presumably for some time afterward until the effect of the streak is gone and the player's performance stabilizes. As you will see, "the player's normal ability," "true talent," or whatever you want to call it—the baseline performance to which the post-streak period is compared—is not so easily defined.

Not only is ability not easily defined, it is also difficult to estimate. Why do we need to do that? Why can't we just compare the 26th PA of the hot group with that of the cold group? Because the hot group is composed of much better players than the cold group, assuming hot and cold are defined absolutely, not relative to a player's ability. In *The Book* study, the hot group had an aggregate wOBA ability of .365. For the cold group it was .336. In Green-Zwiebel's study, hot players were also a more talented group than cold players, when they used their primary, *absolute* method for defining a hot or cold streak.

How do we estimate player ability to establish our baselines? Green-Zwiebel used several methods. Their primary one was to use that season's total performance, excluding not only the 25 PA that comprise the streak, but also a "window" around it, namely 50 PA before and 50 PA after. The reason for the "window" was that those 100 PA are also likely to be a little hot or cold, biasing the baseline for each player either up (hot) or down (cold)—assuming the alternative hypothesis is true, of course. Their method seems reasonable; however, excluding a total of 125 PA per season reduces the sample size of each player's baseline performance. It may also tend to skew the data toward the beginning and end of the season, when offensive performance tends to be at its lowest due to colder weather conditions.

There is one bigger problem with this methodology that Green-Zwiebel fails to address, as far as I can tell. As you will see, their definition of the hot hand includes a "learning" effect—the degree to which a normal estimate of true talent would change from *before* to *after* the streak in question. Given that, they would want to compare the result of the PA immediately subsequent to the streak with a baseline of ability computed before the streak. Including data after the streak in the estimate of ability necessarily includes the learning component. Their baseline is essentially half pre-learning and half-post learning, yet they suggest that the difference between the baseline ability and the performance in the 26th PA represents *streakiness plus learning*. That would only be the case if the baseline were pre-learning only. Interestingly, that should result in a *smaller* hot hand effect than would be found using the proper methodology for establishing the baseline ability of the players.

I mentioned earlier that Green-Zwiebel controlled for park, opponent pitcher, platoon and home/road. They did not control for other relevant factors like weather and umpires. The reason it is critical to control for as many contextual variables as possible is this: When you use their method, which is to continuously sample consecutive 25 PA for each batter, the outcome variable, the 26th PA, often has the same pitcher, park, weather, umpire, score, etc., as the tail end of the streak. If you don't control for each of these variables, the 26th PA will tend to have an upward or downward bias in the same direction as the streak.

There are several ways around this problem: one, define streaks by game and then look at an entire game or games following the streak, as we did in *The Book*, or two, look at the outcome a few PA after a 25 PA streak rather than just the very next PA. Even under the alternative hypothesis—that hot and cold streaks have significant predictive power—we would not expect to see such an effect dissipated after only a few PA.

The method by which the authors of *The Book* estimated ability was to use the prior and subsequent years as well as the current year, including the streak period. Carleton, in his Baseball Prospectus study, used the current season, *also including the streak period*, as a measure of ability. As Green-Zwiebel points out in their paper, this is a mistake. By including the streak period, the estimate of ability will be biased upward for the hot players and downward for the cold players. When a player has a hot streak in a season, he tends to have had a lucky season regardless of his ability, and vice versa for a player with a cold streak. Therefore, the conclusions in *The Book*, and certainly those in Carleton's study, need to be revised to include an unbiased estimate of ability. Green-Zwiebel did well to point out this error.

Green-Zwiebel discusses another interesting and somewhat philosophical point. I've already touched on this several times. they say the notion of a hot or cold streak having predictive value includes two components. One is what they call the learning component, which is to say that after a hot or cold streak our estimate of a player's ability changes. The second is what we generally think of as the effect of being hot or cold, over and above a player's true ability.

Our finding, that recent past performance strongly predicts future outcomes, after controlling for player ability (excluding recent performance), can be attributed to streakiness or to learning new information about a player's long-term ability through this short-term performance. In line with the literature, we refer to a "hot hand" as the ability to predict future outcomes from recent past performances, without making the distinction between streakiness and learning. Indeed, this is the strategically relevant definition; how should one expect performance to change conditioning on the recent past. This distinction, however, is interesting, and we undertake several tests in Section 4.2.1 to provide a decomposition of the hot hand into these two components. Our results vary across the different statistics, but in general we find streakiness accounts for just over 50 percent of the hot-hand effect, with learning attributable to a bit less than 50 percent of the effect.

When an analyst or forecaster estimates a player's current ability with respect to some metric like wOBA, he or she naturally assumes that ability is constantly changing due to aging, learning, physiological and psychological changes, etc. That is why a typical algorithm for a player projection includes a "recency weighting." In other words, performance that occurred most recently is weighted more heavily than performance that occurred prior to that. After a hot or cold streak—even over 25 PA—a player's projection, notwithstanding the alternative hypothesis of a hot (or cold) player remaining hot (or cold), our normal estimate of true talent can change significantly.

So when Green-Zwiebel says a certain 25-PA hot streak causes a 25-point bump in expected OBP in the 26th PA, their definition of "expected" is the player's true talent before the streak started (although, as I pointed out earlier, their baseline includes post-streak performance). The analyst, on the other hand, already has included the hot streak in their "expected performance." To find that a streak has any effect on the next PA, there must be evidence of performance *over and above the revised estimate of talent.* Comparing apples to oranges, Green-Zwiebel's 25-point bump is really 25 points minus the increase in our talent estimate after the streak has occurred. In fact, Green-Zwiebel finds "the effect of a streak" actually consists of about half learning and half streakiness. So their 25-point bump is what an analyst would consider a 12- or 13-point bump after accounting for a revised estimate of talent. Actually, 25 points is what they found to be the difference between a hot and cold player, so really that's 12 or 13 points for a hot player and the same for a cold player. Then we have to cut those in half to separate learning from streakiness. *This is an important and fundamental difference between Green-Zwiebel's work and that of other researchers, including myself.* Given that, Green-Zwiebel's results are not too different from what we found in *The Book*, and are not as large and shocking as they appear to be at first glance.

Even though Green-Zwiebel clearly explains the difference between learning and streakiness and gives us an estimate of the proportion of each for each of the five statistics, I can't help but think that calling a combination of these two components the "hot hand" is misleading. They say, "*In line with the literature* (emphasis added), we refer to a 'hot hand' as the ability to predict future outcomes from recent past performances, without making the distinction between streakiness and learning." It depends upon what literature they are referring to, but certainly studies such as that in *The Book*, as well as Carleton's (and others, I'm sure) either explicitly and implicitly define "the hot hand" as *residual and temporary* hot and cold performance over and above that expected by a credible forecast at the time of the post-streak PA or game in question.

Imagine that we have no data on a player, so we project him to hit at the league-average rate. He starts off the season on fire and hits .400 for the first month. Clearly we estimate him to be an above-average hitter now—maybe 20 points above league average or so. If he continues to hit 20 points better than the average hitter, exactly as we expected, would anyone other than Green-Zwiebel call that evidence of "the hot hand?" I don't think so. An analyst would look for him to hit +25 or +30 as evidence of a hot hand (five or 10 points better than our new estimate of his true talent). In addition, the hot hand is implicitly assumed to be a temporary state. Green-Zwiebel is combining streakiness, a transient state by definition, with learning, a permanent state by definition, and calling the sum the hot hand effect. I don't think that is a reasonable perspective.

Analyzing The Results

Let's look at more of Green-Zwiebel's results. I've already explained their methodology. For batters, using one of their reduced OLS regressions, they found that a .100 point OBP difference between a batter's recent 25 PA performance and an estimate of his ability yields a 6.28 point difference in the 26th PA. That would correspond to a 25-point difference between a cold (.100 OBP during the streak) and hot (.500 OBP) hitter.

In their logistic regressions where the hot and cold variables were categorical rather than continuous, one interpretation, according to Green-Zwiebel, was, "the difference between a hot and cold hitter as defined in these two specifications…is about 28 OBP points for both specifications." Again, according to Green-Zwiebel, about half of that 12 to 14-point bump for the hot player and corresponding decrease for the cold player reflects a revised estimate of each player's true talent. The other half is due to what they call streakiness and what most analysts call the hot hand.

Green-Zwiebel also looked at batting average and HR rate. They found a more muted effect with BA. I will explain a little later why I find that telling. Their OLS coefficient for BA was less than half that of OBP. A .400 point difference in BA between a very hot and cold player corresponded to a 12-point hot and cold hand effect, compared to 25 points for OBP. In addition, Green-Zwiebel estimates 74 percent of that is due to learning—or a revised estimate of ability. **That leaves a**

1.5 point streakiness effect for hot hitters and presumably the same for cold hitters (they assume linearity in their regressions).

Green-Zwiebel finds that the streakiness portion of OBP is four times that of BA. One reason for that, according to Green-Zwiebel, is how the defense—the pitcher in this case—reacts to a batter exhibiting a hot or cold hand. They hypothesize pitchers might "pitch around" batters right after (or "during," I guess) a hot streak. What they did was compare the normal walk rates for above-average power hitters to the walk rates of batters who were hot in power for the last 25, and then again, five PA. They found that pitchers walked the 25-PA hot hitters at the same rate as normal high-power batters. However, batters who were hot for only five PA were walked disproportionately too often. In other words, opposing pitchers react rationally to longer hot streaks but over-react to shorter ones. Green-Zwiebel did in fact find evidence that pitchers overreacted to the 25-PA hot streaks; however, the result did not reach a threshold of statistical significance.

If it is true batters who are hot and cold BA-wise see a very small (around 1.5 points) streakiness effect, and a moderate (around six points) effect in OBP, *and* most of that OBP effect is in their walk rate, I think we can conclude one and/or two things. Either the hot and cold effect is mostly in a batter's walk rate, or pitchers are causing—or at least contributing to—a hot and cold OBP effect by *irrationally* pitching around hot hitters and challenging cold hitters. The latter seems more plausible to me.

Green-Zwiebel's OLS coefficients for home runs per AB suggest that a 10 percent increase in HR rate over the last 25 AB, or 2.5 additional HR, yields a 0.75 percent increase in the 26th AB. The logistic regressions showed a 0.79 percent difference between hot and cold batters. Again, those numbers includes learning and streakiness. In their "disentanglement analysis" they found that for home run rate, around 57 percent of the increase following a streak was due to learning; thus a little less than half was due to streakiness, or what an analyst would consider the "predictive effect of being hot or cold." That implies a hot home run hitter (say 12 percent above normal) who typically would hit a home run in four percent of his at-bats (after revising our forecast to include data from the streak) would have a HR rate of around 4.4 percent following the streak—a .4 percent true hot hand effect. That is like turning a 20-home run player into a 22-homer player. It sounds like a lot if you combine learning with streakiness and couch it this way: "After a hot streak during which a hitter hits 12 percent more home runs than expected (before the streak), they hit 25 percent more home runs than we originally thought, due to the effect of the hot hand."

While that sentence is technically correct, it still represents a two-HR increase per 500 AB if we use only the streakiness portion. Even if we define the hot hand as streakiness plus learning, a 25 percent increase in HR rate represents a five-homer increase for a 20-HR player—hardly enough to turn a good home run hitter into

Barry Bonds. That's a classic example of a small increase in a small number looking like a large increase when it is expressed in percentage terms.

New Research

Now let's take a look at my new study and compare it to Green-Zwiebel's. I did not use any regression formulas, and I looked only at OBP, wOBA, BA and HR per AB—no walk or strikeout rates. I used Retrosheet data from 2000 to 2014. My basic methodology was to look at all 25-PA runs occurring within a 10-day period, starting with Day 1 of each season and ending with Sept. 20. Like Green-Zwiebel, I created two buckets for those runs—a hot bucket and a cold bucket—using various thresholds for defining a hot or cold streak. For example, with wOBA, I defined a hot streak as a wOBA greater than 200 points better than the league-average wOBA for that season. A cold streak was less than 150 points worse than that season's league-average wOBA.

For each player-specific hot or cold steak identified, I looked at the results one plate appearance after the streak *and six PA after the streak*. Green-Zwiebel only used the former as their outcome variable. The problem with that is that even though they controlled for several variables in the regressions—namely park, opposing pitcher, platoon, and home/road—there are other factors they didn't control for that would tend to create a correlation between the end of the steak and the dependent variable, such as the umpire, weather, and score of the game.

One way to eliminate most of these effects, other than trying to control for them in the regressions, is to look at the outcome in the sixth PA after the streak rather than the first PA after the streak. That way, there will be very few contextual factors shared between the end of the streak and the outcome variable. In doing so, the assumption is that under the alternative hypothesis of "streaks having predictive value," the effect of the streak is still prevalent six PA after the streak.

For estimating player talent, or ability, Green-Zwiebel primarily used the season in which the streak occurred, minus the streak and a 100-PA window around the streak. I have already articulated why I am not crazy about that mehodology. I used a *standard* forecasting algorithm using data going back three years prior to the streak season, as well as the streak itself. My model weights performance by recency, age adjusts, and regresses to that season's league average or mean. This forecast includes what Green-Zwiebel calls the *learning component*, since it includes performance during the streak and gives that the most weight. Any difference between the expected performance and the actual performance right after the streak is attributable to what they call *streakiness* and I call the *hot hand* (they call the hot hand *streakiness plus learning*). Remember, Green-Zwiebel found a streakiness effect on the order of six or seven points in OBP for a hot or cold hitter, only 1.5 points for batting average, and around 0.4 percent for HR rate.

Here are the results of my study with respect to OBP. For the OBP formula, I excluded intentional walks and sacrifice hits, and sacrifice flies were counted in the denominator. We'll look at hot and cold hitters, as well as hitters that fell into neither category as a control.

OBP, Difference Between Forecast and Actual Performance, By Streak Type						
	Hot Hitters (n=36,842)		Cold Hitters (n=54,017)		Neutral Hitters (n=1,052,630)	
Breakdown	OBP	Diff	OBP	Diff	BA	Diff
Average OBP during streak	.5737		.1430		.3429	
Expected OBP using forecast	.3498		.3260		.3365	
Actual OBP 1 PA after streak	.3588	.0090	.3175	.0085	.3367	.0002
OBP 6 PA after streak	.3545	.0047	.3195	.0065	.3366	.0001
Average OBP all batters	.3290		.3290		.3290	

Using my post-streak forecast as the baseline, I get a hot hand effect of between 4.7 and 9.0 points of OBP and a cold hand effect of 6.5 to 8.5 points, depending upon whether I use the PA immediately following the streak or the one five PA hence. I prefer to use the latter since I did not control for park, weather, umpire, home/road, platoon, score, and opposing pitchers. In fact, I find the PA following a hot streak occurred in warmer weather, more hitter-friendly parks, more at home, and against worse pitchers than the PA following a cold streak. So it *is* necessary to control for these factors *or* to use the sixth PA after the streak rather than the first. The control players who were neither hot nor cold had a 26th and 31st PA performance almost exactly equal to the forecast, as expected.

Comparing my results to Green-Zwiebel's, we get:

Streakiness/Hot-Cold Hand Effects		
Gr-Zw hot/cold streakiness effect	Lichtman hot hand effect	Lichtman cold hand effect
6-7 points	4.7 points	6.5 points

Although there is clearly a substantial *two sigma* (95 percent) confidence interval surrounding these values (one standard deviation is likely on the order of two or three points of OBP), I am not surprised the cold hand effect would be greater than the hot hand effect. It's far more likely that the players in the cold bucket were injured than the players in the neutral or hot buckets.

I also computed a pre-streak forecast, using the same projection algorithm, in order to estimate the magnitude of what Green-Zwiebel calls the learning portion of the hot hand effect. For the hot hitters, their forecast was .3452 prior to the streak, so the learning was 4.6 points, 49 percent of the total of learning plus streakiness. For the cold hitters, their pre-streak projection was .3301, 4.1 points greater than the post-streak projection, or 39 percent of the total. These numbers are similar to Green-Zwiebel's estimate that 47 percent of their total OBP effect comes from learning.

If I had defined my baseline the entire season in which the hot or cold streak occurred, as Carleton did in their study, there would be no evidence of any streakiness. In fact, it would look like there was "reverse" streakiness, or the "due" gambler's fallacy. For example, the true .350 hot hitters hit .364 in any season in which they had a hot streak, 14 points higher than their true ability. Using three or more seasons including the season in question, as we did in *The Book*, would mitigate this mistake, but it still would over-estimate the talent of the hot-streak hitters and underestimate that of the cold-streak batters.

Here are my results for batting average. Remember that Green-Zwiebel found a very small streakiness effect of 1.5 points for hot or cold hitters.

BA, Difference Between Forecast and Actual Performance, By Streak Type						
	Hot Hitters (n=50,054)		Cold Hitters (n=64,408)		Neutral Hitters (n=1,078,838)	
Breakdown	BA	Diff	BA	Diff	BA	Diff
Average BA during streak	.4466		.0867		.2492	
Expected BA using forecast	.2777		.2651		.2706	
Actual BA 1 PA after streak	.2818	.0041	.2666	-.0015	.2717	.0011
BA 6 PA after streak	.2818	.0041	.2642	.0009	.2715	.0009
Average BA all batters	.2656		.2656		.2656	

For BA, I am getting a streakiness effect of 4.1 points for a hot hitter and 0.9 points for the cold batters. The average effect is 2.5 points. Unlike with OBP, we don't see a greater effect after a cold streak. Again, keep in mind that my numbers (and theirs) are subject to a fairly wide confidence interval. The true cold or hot hand BA effect could quite easily be anywhere from one to five points.

Earlier, I suggested the OBP hot hand effect may be at least partially a result of an endogenous (and irrational) response by the opposing pitcher. Green-Zwiebel found pitchers overreacted to five- and 25-PA hot streaks in power, although the latter was not statistically significant at the five percent level.

From my data, here is a look at the walk rates in the post-OBP streak periods:

On-Base Percentage, Hot Hitters			
Time Period	OBP	BB+HBP per PA	Normal Walk Rate for that OBP
1 PA after streak	.3588	11.53%	10.26%
6 PA after streak	.3545	10.79%	9.94%

Looking at the final column, we see that the hot batters are being walked one percent more often than their OBP suggests. If opposing pitchers are overreacting to hot batters, that alone will elevate their OBP, and their perception becomes a self-fulfilling prophecy. So perhaps the effect of a hot streak, without help from the pitcher, is less than it appears on the surface. It is possible, of course, that being hot means your ability to draw walks is enhanced.

On-Base Percentage, Cold Hitters			
Time Period	OBP	BB+HBP per PA	Normal Walk Rate for that OBP
1 PA after streak	.3175	7.52%	8.20%
6 PA after streak	.3195	7.83%	8.47%

We see a similar effect in that opposing pitchers walk cold batters *less* often than what would be expected given their OBP, but the magnitude is smaller than with the hot hitters. It's also possible cold hitters have a difficult time with plate discipline.

wOBA

We can look at another measure of offensive performance in which walk rate does not play such a significant role, such as wOBA, a metric that reflects the context-neutral run value of a PA or a player's entire body of PAs. In OBP, a walk carries the same weight as any other on-base event. In wOBA, a walk is worth around 72 percent of an average on-base event. In addition, any time we talk about offense in general, especially at the player level, it is prudent to use a comprehensive metric like wOBA.

For wOBA, I used exactly the same methodology as I did with OBP.

wOBA, Difference Between Forecast and Actual Performance, By Streak Type						
	Hot Hitters (n=60,220)		Cold Hitters (n=64,408)		Neutral Hitters (n=1,078,838)	
Breakdown	wOBA	Diff	HR/AB	Diff	HR/AB	Diff
Average wOBA during streak	.5834		.1451		.3420	
Expected wOBA using forecast	.3545		.3292		.3385	
Actual wOBA 1 PA after streak	.3573	.0028	.3233	.0059	.3378	.0007
wOBA 6 PA after streak	.3582	.0037	.3238	.0054	.3374	.0011
Average wOBA all batters	.3295		.3295		.3295	

With wOBA, we get a moderate hot hand effect of 3.7 points and a larger cold hand effect of 5.4 points. Compare this to what we found when using OBP as our metric of choice—a 4.7 point bump for hot hitters and a 6.5 decrease for cold hitters. Each of these is around one point less in effect for wOBA than for OBP. The extra one-point effect we see in OBP *may be* due to the aforementioned sub-optimal response by the opposing pitcher (or it may just be sample error).

HR per AB

Remember Green-Zwiebel reports that a 10 percent increase in home run rate during a hot streak results in around a 0.75 percent increase post-streak. Here are my results using my basic methodology. Hot hitters had at least three homers in their last 25 PA, and cold hitters had zero.

HR/AB, Difference Between Forecast and Actual Performance, By Streak Type						
	Hot Hitters (n=66,003)		Cold Hitters (n=599,980)		Neutral Hitters (n=537,299)	
Breakdown	HR/AB	Diff	HR/AB	Diff	HR/AB	Diff
Average HR during streak	.1322		0		.0515	
Expected HR using forecast	.0439		.0287		.0359	
Actual HR 1 PA after streak	.0508	.0069	.0259	.0028	.0376	.0017
HR 6 PA after streak	.0498	.0059	.0259	.0028	.0375	.0016
Average HR all batters	.0304		.0304		.0304	

Here we have a large hot hand effect and a much smaller cold hand effect by a factor of almost three. The reason is that the lowest we can go in defining a cold home run hitter is zero home runs in 25 PA, which represents only around a three percent decrease in home run rate from their normal levels. The hot hitters hit home runs during their streaks at a rate that was around nine percent higher than their normal rates. The difference between my pre- and post-streak forecast suggests the learning component is around 0.2 percent for the hot hitters, or only 25 percent (0.2 percent divided by the sum of 0.2 percent and 0.59 percent) of the "learning plus streakiness" effect. I may not be using an aggressive enough recency weighting for HR (I used the same forecast algorithm as I did for other metrics), in which case I may be overstating the streakiness effect. If I increase the weighting scheme, the streakiness effect reduces to 0.51 percent (from .59), and the proportion of learning increases to 35 percent.

Interestingly, the difference between expected and actual HR rate after a hot streak suggests an increase in wOBA of almost 12 points, assuming every other offensive event remains the same. However, if we look at the wOBA of the same hitters in the above chart who were hot and cold with respect to HR rate, we find a much more muted effect:

wOBA, Hot HR Hitters	
Breakdown	wOBA
During streak	.5819
Forecast right after streak	.3548
In 26th PA (1 PA after streak)	.3615
In 31st PA (6 PA after streak)	.3599

Using the 31st PA (sixth PA after the streak) for the post-streak outcome, we find only a 5.1-point wOBA streakiness effect, even though there is a 5.9-point HR rate effect for these same batters, which would correspond to an 11.5-point increase in wOBA. So while hitters who have been on a home run tear are continuing to hit homers at a rate that is around 0.6 percent higher than expected, the other components of wOBA aside from walks are depressed. This suggests that part of being hot, HR-wise, is swinging for the fences while sacrificing hits overall.

Summary

The new study by Green-Zwiebel makes some interesting and eyebrow-raising claims about the magnitude of the hot hand effect in baseball. They appear at first glance to contradict several prior studies, including one we published in *The Book*. For example, Green-Zwiebel's results indicate, "the difference between a recent on-base percentage of .100 and .500 (representing a recent cold run and hot run, respectively) translates to an increased probability of getting on base of...25 OBP points. **This magnitude is quite significant from a strategic perspective** (emphasis added)."

Twenty-five points of OBP sounds like a lot. That is the difference between a poor hitter and an average one or an average hitter and a very good one. But if you read that sentence carefully, Green-Zwiebel is not saying that a hot hitter picks up 25 points in OBP or a cold hitter loses that amount. They are saying a hot hitter will gain about half that and a cold hitter will lose about half that. It's sort of the old "double counting trick," or the "swing" as gamblers might say—the difference between losing and winning. I'm not suggesting that Green-Zwiebel is *deliberately* trying to deceive anyone or misrepresent their work. In fact, they are very clear and thorough in explaining their methodology and results.

The second reason that number is deceiving is it represents what Green-Zwiebel call *learning plus streakiness*. In fact, they go to great lengths to explain why the hot hand *should* include both of these components and not just the streakiness part. Learning is the difference between our estimate of the player's true talent before the streak and after it. There is no magical "hot hand effect" in the learning part. Learning is permanent, and streakiness is transient.

When we look more closely at that "25-point OBP," it turns out the actual hot hand effect, *as I and most other analysts define it*, is not so large, and is similar to the effect described in *The Book* (despite the error in that study) as well as my more recent research. While Green-Zwiebel makes a valiant case for defining the hot hand effect as including a revised estimate of talent after the streak, I am not convinced. Not only that but if they want to compare their research to that in *The Book* and other sabermetric research, they need to compare apples to apples. Few baseball analysts are going to include the learning aspect of a streak in the definition of a hot hand. The "hot hand" is generally considered to be the *short-term* effect of recent hot or cold performance *over and above an estimate of a player's true talent*. Using a pre-streak estimate makes little sense to me, other than to exaggerate the hot hand effect.

According to Green-Zwiebel, the learning part of an OBP hot hand effect is around half, so not only is the 25 points down to 12 for the hot hand and 13 for the cold hand, but we have to cut those numbers in half again. Which sounds more impressive, "The difference between a hot and cold player of the same ability is 25 points," or, "A batter after a cold or hot streak hits six or seven points better or worse than his revised talent estimate?" The first is ambiguous because "ability" can mean before or after the streak, but the second is precise.

On-base percentage also appears to be the metric most affected by hot and cold streaks. That may be due to a suboptimal response by the opposing pitcher, who will pitch around the hot hitter and go "right at" the cold one. Surprisingly, being hot or cold in batting average—which is what casual fans, and thus pundits and commentators typically focus on—has almost *no* predictive value. Green-Zwiebel found around a six-point effect, with 75 percent of that from learning, leaving only around 1.5 BA points for streakiness. That is further evidence that at least some of the OBP hot hand effect may be due to an irrational response from opposing pitchers.

Both Green-Zwiebel and I found a modest home run hot hand effect. A 10-12 percent increase in HR per AB yields around a 0.5 percent increase after the streak. That corresponds to around two or three extra home runs per season. That doesn't turn an ordinary home run hitter into a great one. There is also evidence that part of the HR hot hand effect may be a conscious approach by the batter to swing for the fences, which serves to deflate his other hitting stats, so that the net result of a hot HR streak is modest at best, around five points in wOBA.

It is unfortunate that Green-Zwiebel did not include in their five basic metrics a comprehensive one, like OPS or wOBA. After all, we really want to know whether being hot or cold makes a hitter a better or worse hitter overall, not necessarily whether a hot home run hitter keeps hitting homers (but suffers in his other stats), or a hot hitter walks more (but *hits* the same or worse).

In my study, I included wOBA, a comprehensive *all-around* offensive statistic, and found a modest 3.7 point hot hand effect (streakiness only—including learning would double that) and a larger 5.4 cold hand effect. I have always hypothesized the cold hand effect would be larger because the pool of players who have had a cold streak probably includes a disproportionate number of hitters who are not 100 percent healthy.

I don't think that Green-Zwiebel's study or my new research has changed the ultimate verdict: There appears to be a modest "unexplained" hot and cold hand effect among hitters in baseball. It's not enough for the manager of either team to significantly alter their strategies, but enough perhaps to break a tie, so to speak. I think we also learned there is a good chance that opposing pitchers change their strategy, perhaps sub-optimally, in response to a hot or cold streak. Finally, there is some evidence hitters may change *their* approach when perceiving themselves as hot or cold, such as swinging for the fences after hitting lots of home runs in a short period of time.

One thing should now be clear. If you are going to talk about the hot hand in any sport, or you are going to compare one bit of research to another, you need to define *exactly* what you mean by the hot or cold hand.

References & Resources

- Brett S. Green, Jeffrey Zweibel, Social Science Research Network, "The Hot-Hand Fallacy: Cognitive Mistakes or Equilibrium Adjustments? Evidence from Major League Baseball," *papers.ssrn.com/sol3/papers.cfm?abstract_id=2358747*
- T. Gilovich, R. Vallone, & A. Tversky, *Cognitive Psychology*, "The hot hand in basketball: On the misperception of random sequences," 17, 295-314, 1985
- S. Siwoff, S. Hirdt, & P. Hirdt, *The 1988 Elias Baseball Analyst*, New York, Collier
- J. Albert, & S.C. Albright, *Journal of the American Statistical Association*, "A statistical analysis of hitting streaks in baseball: Comment," 88, 1175-1188, 1993
- H.S. Stern, American Statistical Association, "Who's hot and who's not: Runs of success and failure in sports," in 1995 Proceedings of the section on statistics in sports, pp. 26–35
- Tom Tango, Mitchel Lichtman, and Andrew Dolphin, *The Book: Playing the Statistical Percentages in Baseball*, Potomac Books, 2007
- Russell Carleton, Baseball Prospectus, "Going Streaking," *baseballprospectus.com/article.php?articleid=27524*

The Physics of the Longest Possible Homer

by David Kagan

How far can a major leaguer actually hit a ball? According to Baseball Almanac, there have been many claims to the throne.

Baseball Almanac's List of the Longest Homers			
Date	Batter	Stadium	Distance
April 17, 1953	Mickey Mantle	Griffith Stadium, Washington	565 ft
May 6, 1964	Dave Nicholson	Comiskey Park, Chicago	573 ft
June 8, 1926	Babe Ruth	Navin Field, Detroit	600 ft
Sept. 10, 1960	Mickey Mantle	Briggs Stadium, Detroit	600 ft
May 22, 1963	Mickey Mantle	Yankee Stadium, New York	620 ft
April 14, 1976	Dave Kingman	Wrigley Field, Chicago	630 ft

Since 2006, ESPN Home Run Tracker has scientifically calculated the distance for every homer. At the end of the 2015 season, it has data for a bit in excess of 48,000 round-trippers. There have only been about 275,000 homers hit since 1900. Remarkably, ESPN Home Run Tracker has data for more than 17 percent of all homers ever launched.

The longest in ESPN Home Run Tracker's database? A blast by Adam Dunn in Chase Field in Arizona on Sept. 27, 2008 with the roof closed totaling 504 feet. This is the only homer in excess of 500 feet in the entire collection. The second longest was 498 feet by Matt Holliday in the rarified air of Coors Field. There have been only about 50 long balls of 475 feet or more since 2006.

Simple(?) Statistics

We can make an estimate of the number of homers ever hit that were longer than 500 feet by saying this happens roughly one in 48,000 times. Since 1901 there have been about 275,000 home runs, so there may have been six homers hit in excess of 500 feet.

We can go a little deeper with the statistics before we delve into the physics. If you toss a fair coin, the chance of heads is 50/50. If you toss two of them, there is a 25 percent chance you'll get no heads, a 50 percent chance you'll get one head, and a 25 percent chance you get two heads. You can continue doing this with more and more coins. If you want to know how to calculate the odds each time, run a Google search for "Binomial Distribution."

The chart below shows the results of tossing 10 coins at a time and repeating the task 5,000 times. As you would guess, the mostly like situation—the tallest bar—is at five heads. Four heads or six heads are equally likely but less likely than five. It is so unlikely that all 10 coins come up heads that you can't even see it on the graph. This will probably happen about five times out of the 5,000 tosses.

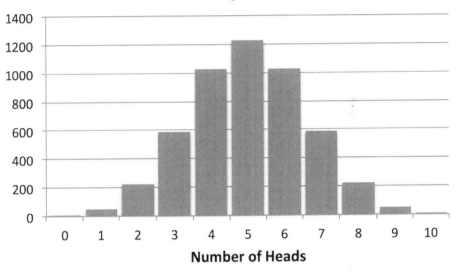

Number of Times by Number of Heads

Number of Heads

The results for tossing 10 coins 5,000 times listed by the number of heads in each toss.

What does this have to do with home runs? Well, below is a chart tabulating the nearly 5,000 homers listed on ESPN Home Run Tracker in the year of Dunn's blast, 2008. This chart looks remarkably similar to the coin toss chart above. Some of the similarity is because of a bit of trickery on my part. However, it illustrates a point I'm trying to make.

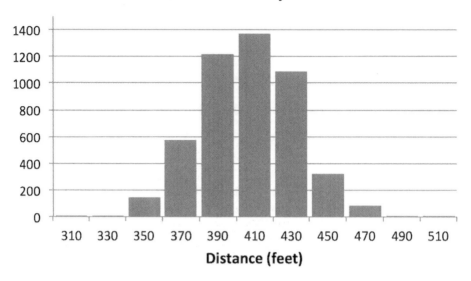

Number of Homers by Distance

The 5,000 home runs from the 2008 seasons, separated by 20-feet intervals.

The shape of the coin toss chart has several names: "Normal Distribution" or "Normal Curve" or simply "The Curve"—as in "Do you grade on the curve?" So, your teacher was grading based upon the statistical rules for coin tossing as opposed to the quality of your work—very reassuring! Anyhow, there is a very well-known method for estimating the probability of an event from the normal distribution.

For the Dunn dinger, the chance estimated by the distribution is only 0.0013 percent. That's pretty darn small. Another way of thinking about it is that it is equivalent to one 504-foot bomb out of every 79,000 home runs. At this rate you would expect only about three shots of this length out of all the homers ever hit.

For Mickey's 565-footer, the chances are only 0.000000002 percent, or one in 50 billion homers. Those odds are even longer than the probability of hitting the Mega Millions jackpot!

Statistics are fun as far as they go, but there are subtle differences between the coin toss and the homer charts. The coin toss chart is completely symmetric. It is just as hard to toss only three heads as it is to get seven. However, 370-foot homers are far more likely than 450-foot blasts. In fact, longer homers are always harder to hit than shorter ones.

Some of the discrepancy is due to the fact that a 370-footer is not always a homer, but no park can contain a 450-footer. However, more 370-foot fly balls counted as homers would result in an even more skewed chart. There must be something deeper going on. The asymmetry of the curve hints at some physical explanation. Let's explore.

Simple(?) Physics

Newton's Laws tell us the ball will do what it does because of the forces that act on it. The figure at right shows these forces as solid straight arrows. The dashed arrow represents the velocity of the ball, while the circular arrow indicates the backspin on the ball.

Two things exert forces on a long fly ball; Earth pulls it down, and the air pushes it around. Gravity is relatively straightforward, but the force air exerts on the ball is complex and subtle. That's part of the reason the force exerted by the air is usually considered as two distinct forces, the drag (or air resistance) and the lift (or Magnus force).

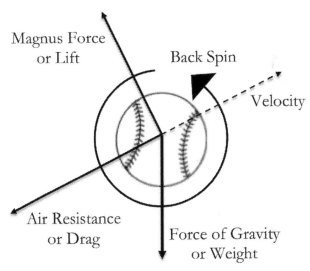

The forces on a ball in flight with backspin are
lift, drag, and weight.

The gravitational force, or weight, always pulls the ball downward. Baseball Rule 1.09 requires the weight of the ball to be "not less than five nor more than 5 1/4 ounces." In other words, the weight of the ball is between 0.31 and 0.33 pounds. The batter has no control over the force of gravity on the ball.

Air resistance, or drag, always acts opposite the velocity of the ball. Drag, as the name implies, slows the ball down. It is caused by the ball having to move the air in front of it out of the way. You have experienced air drag every time you stuck your hand out the window of a moving vehicle. The force the air exerts on your hand can be quite strong at highway speeds, which incidentally are around the average speed of a homer in flight. A batter has no control over the drag. The harder they hit it, the more drag there will be.

The other force exerted by the air is the Magnus force, or lift. It is always perpendicular to the velocity and is in the direction of the spinning motion of the front of the ball as it moves through the air. Due to the spin, the front of the ball in the sketch is moving mostly up the page and slightly to the left, matching the direction of the lift.

The backspin on a well-hit fly ball will result in an upward Magnus force or lift. This lift will keep the ball from falling as fast as gravity demands. So a fly ball can, under the right circumstances, travel further at the same speed if it has more backspin. The Magnus force is the one force the batter has some control over by creating more backspin.

In summary, the drag will tend to slow the speed and lower the distance of a fly ball. On the other hand, backspin on the ball will result in an upward Magnus force helping the ball stay in the air longer and, under the right conditions, go further.

The distance a ball will travel before hitting the ground depends upon the speed it leaves the bat (launch speed), the angle it leaves the bat (launch angle), and the amount of backspin on the ball.

To create backspin, the ball must collide with the top half of the bat as shown in Figure 4. The frictional force between the bat and ball will cause the ball to develop backspin, while the perpendicular (often called "normal") force will cause the ball to head off toward the outfield.

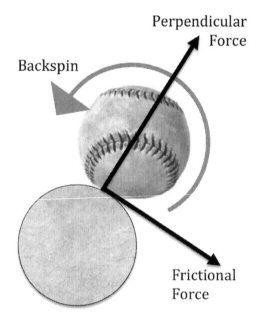

The ball moving to the left collides with the top half of the bat moving to the right.

If the center of the ball collides with the center of the bat, there will be little frictional force. The result will be a line drive with almost no backspin. On the other extreme, when the bottom of the ball collides near the top of the bat, the result will be a ball headed toward the backstop with lots of backspin. The point is, there must be some connection between the launch angle of the ball and the resulting backspin.

In addition, the outgoing speed of the ball depends upon where it strikes the bat. If the center of the ball collides with the center of the bat, the ball will head off with the largest speed, but it will have too low a launch angle for a homer. On the other hand, if the ball strikes higher up on the bat, the ball will have a higher launch angle but less speed.

The point is that not all high-speed launches will be homers. Below is a table of Statcast data from the 2015 season through early August showing all balls hit with speeds over 115 mph. Only three of the 23 are long balls.

The Fastest Balls Off the Bat, Statcast, 2015					
Velocity (mph)	Batter	Result	Velocity (mph)	Batter	Result
120.3	Giancarlo Stanton	1B	116.5	Alex Rodriguez	HR
119.7	Giancarlo Stanton	2B	116.5	Mark Trumbo	1B
119.2	Giancarlo Stanton	HR	116.5	Hanley Ramirez	1B
119.0	Nelson Cruz	1B	116.4	Giancarlo Stanton	Out
118.5	Giancarlo Stanton	HR	116.3	Giancarlo Stanton	Out
118.5	Giancarlo Stanton	1B	116.3	Giancarlo Stanton	1B
117.7	Mike Trout	1B	116.3	Jose Bautista	Out
117.3	Giancarlo Stanton	1B	116.2	Jorge Soler	2B
117.3	Giancarlo Stanton	2B	116.1	Giancarlo Stanton	2B
117.1	Giancarlo Stanton	1B	116.1	Giancarlo Stanton	1B
117.1	Carlos Gonzalez	Out	116.1	Avisail Garcia	2B
117.0	Giancarlo Stanton	1B	116.1	David Peralta	Out
116.7	Carlos Gonzalez	1B	116.0	Carlos Peguero	1B
116.6	Hanley Ramirez	Out	116.0	Bryce Harper	2B
116.6	Chris Davis	2B			

So, it takes a very special combination of launch speed, launch angle, and backspin to clear the fences. All three of these parameters depend upon where the bat collides with the ball.

Alan Nathan and others have conducted experiments to work out the details of the collision. Applying their findings to a fastball coming in at 100 mph with a 2,000 rpm backspin colliding with a bat moving horizontally at 75 mph gives the results in the table below.

Effects of Bat-Fastball Collision, By Center-to-Center Height				
Center-to-center height (in)	Launch Speed (mph)	Launch Angle (deg)	Backspin (rpm)	Landing Distance (ft)
0.0	123.9	-2.5	-398	48.8
0.2	123.5	3.2	817	227.2
0.4	122.5	8.9	2,031	458.9
0.6	120.9	14.7	3,245	516.7
0.8	118.6	20.6	4,459	513.2
1.0	115.7	26.7	5,673	484.0
1.2	112.1	33.2	6,887	438.3
1.4	107.7	39.9	8,102	381.1
1.6	102.4	47.3	9,316	311.8

Note: Pitch traveling 100 mph with 2,000 rpm of backspin; bat moving horizontally at 75 mph.

The first column is the vertical distance between the center of the ball and the center of the bat. So for the case of the bat striking the ball dead center, it has the highest launch speed, the launch angle is negative due to the backspin from the pitch, and the ball develops topspin causing it to land in the infield.

As the center-to-center height increases, the launch speed drops slowly as the launch angle and backspin rise. The distance the ball goes at first increases to a bit over 500 feet. Then it decreases because it is hit with too high a launch angle.

You might notice the calculated backspin just keeps getting bigger and bigger. Most physicists, even the ones who made the measurements to build this theory of the ball-bat collision, believe these spins to be too large. Also, most measurements indicate a batter can't get the bat quite up to 75 mph, and fastballs rarely exceed 100 mph. So, if anything, these home run distances are overestimates.

The table below is for a curveball thrown at 85 mph thrown with 2,000 rpm of topspin and the bat moving horizontally at 75 mph. The results are very similar, and again we see the maximum distance is a bit over 500 feet.

Effects of Bat-Curveball Collision, By Center-to-Center Height				
Center-to-center height (in)	Launch Speed (mph)	Launch Angle (deg)	Backspin (rpm)	Landing Distance (ft)
0.0	119.8	2.6	398	156.6
0.2	119.6	8.0	1,508	395.7
0.4	118.8	13.4	2,618	489.1
0.6	117.4	19.0	3,728	505.3
0.8	115.4	24.6	4,838	489.5
1.0	112.7	30.5	5,948	455.3
1.2	109.4	36.7	7,058	408.6
1.4	105.2	43.3	8,168	350.4
1.6	100.2	50.4	9,278	282.7

Note: Pitch traveling 85 mph with 2,000 rpm of topspin; bat moving horizontally at 75 mph.

The top five launch velocities for 48,000 homers at ESPN Home Run Tracker are listed in the table below. It is interesting to note that Dunn's homer is not even on the list.

The Five Highest Launch Speeds from ESPN Home Run Tracker				
Date	Batter	Dist. (ft)	Launch Speed (mph)	Launch Angle (deg)
4/19/2006	Reggie Abercrombie	485	122.1	28.3
4/20/2010	Mark Reynolds	481	122.3	27.4
7/19/2008	Jeremy Hermida	441	122.3	21.7
10/2/2009	Wladimir Balentien	495	122.3	27.5
5/21/2012	Giancarlo Stanton	462	122.4	25.3

The launch angles for these blasts are all much higher than the calculated values from the theory. This is another indication the backspin from the theory is an overestimate.

One could argue The Mick simply hit the ball harder than anyone before or after. If so, how much harder would have had to hit it to go, say, 600 feet? Using the mean values of around 4,000 rpm and 21.2°, the speed off the bat would have to have been 137 mph. It seems pretty unlikely Ol' Number Seven could have hit the ball 12 percent faster than anyone has in the last 43,000 homers.

The prediction of the physics, despite the issue of overestimated backspin, is remarkably consistent with the results from ESPN Home Run Tracker, at least as far as the maximum possible homer. It seems that the limit is somewhere a bit above 500 feet.

So, it seems 600-footers are out of the question. But there's one factor we haven't taken into account—a stiff outgoing wind. Let's examine that issue.

Simple(?) Weather

If you read about wind for a while, you'll stumble across the Beaufort Scale developed in 1805 by Sir Francis Beaufort of the U.K. Royal Navy. Turns out, meteorologists are as crazy about numbers as baseball nuts. (Right, Mike Trout?) This fellow categorized winds as indicated in the chart below.

Wind Categories, by speed (mph)			
Scale Value	Speed	Name	Conditions
0	< 1	Calm	Smoke rises vertically.
1	1-3	Light air	Smoke drifts and leaves rustle.
2	4-6	Light breeze	Wind felt on face.
3	7-10	Gentle breeze	Flags extended, leaves move.
4	11-16	Moderate breeze	Dust and small branches move.
5	17-21	Fresh breeze	Small trees begin to sway.
6	22-27	Strong breeze	Large branches move, wires whistle, umbrellas are difficult to control.
7	28-33	Near gale	Whole trees in motion, inconvenience in walking.
8	34-40	Gale	Difficult to walk against wind. Twigs and small branches blown off trees.
9	41-47	Strong gale	Minor structural damage may occur (shingles blown off roofs).
10	48-55	Storm	Trees uprooted, structural damage likely.
11	56-63	Violent storm	Widespread damage to structures.
12	64+	Hurricane	Severe structural damage to buildings, wide spread devastation.

It stands to reason that a tailwind would propel a ball further. Here's the physics. Both the drag and the Magnus force depend upon the speed of the ball with respect to the air. As a result, both forces are smaller with a tailwind. So, the ball feels less lift, tending to shorten the flight, but it also feels less drag, so the ball moves faster.

Which effect is more dominant? Here's the key idea. The drag force depends upon the square of the speed, while the lift depends only on the speed to the first power. So, the drag gets smaller faster than the lift gets smaller. Thus, the ball will go further with a tailwind.

With that in mind, below is a plot of the distance traveled by a homer with a launch speed of 122 mph, launch angle of 27°, and a 3,000 rpm backspin. You can see the distance increases by a bit over four feet for every mph of wind.

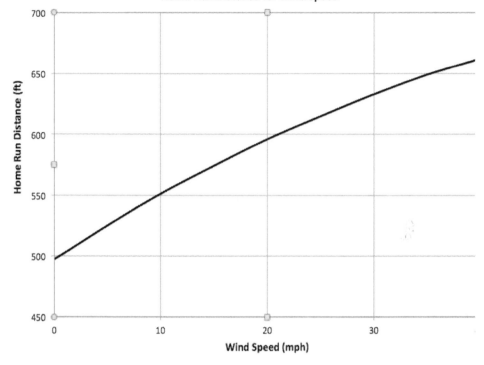

Home Run Distance vs. Wind Speed

Home run distance versus wind speed for a launch speed 122mph, launch angle 27°, and 3,000 rpm backspin.

To manage a 600-foot shot, Mickey would have had to hit the ball just right with a Beaufort Scale "strong breeze" blowing at 22 mph directly behind the ball. Believe it or not, you can look up the wind speed for Detroit on Sept. 10, 1960. The maximum speed was only 10 mph NNE, which was in from center field, although the ball was hit to right. At best, the ball went 550 feet.

Let's look at Dave Nicholson's 573-foot bomb on May 6, 1964 in Comiskey Park, Chicago. The average wind that day was 18 mph SSW, a "fresh breeze" according to Beaufort. The wind was indeed blowing toward left field where the ball cleared the roof. There were gusts up to 32 mph. Looking at the graph, a ball could actually go about 630 feet if it caught a 30 mph tailwind. So, I guess that one could have happened.

What of the famous 502-foot "red seat" homer by Ted Williams? David Ortiz, a prodigious power-hitter and an amateur physicist (who knew?) was recently asked about it, "The red seat, cough—bull****—cough. I don't think anyone has ever hit one there. I went up there and sat there one time. That's far, brother."

"Maybe the wind helped, but it had to be a hurricane behind it," Ortiz claimed correctly. Well, it wasn't a hurricane at 64-plus mph. Instead there was a tailwind of about 20 mph that day, more than enough to get it there.

Simple(!) Summary

Statistical evidence, as well as the underlying physics limit the longest home run to a bit over 500 feet in still air. A well-struck ball can gain an additional four feet or so for every mile per hour of wind speed, assuming the ball was hit in a direction to provide a tailwind.

Why don't we see those long homers anymore? The most likely answer Is that ballparks are taller and more enclosed. The outfield seats in most parks were once very much lower than the grandstand and open to the elements. In modern parks there are huge video boards, gigantic ads, and even restaurants that block the wind.

If the actual configuration of the ballparks isn't enough to reduce the wind, the average height of buildings around the parks has grown over time, thus acting as additional windbreaks. If this explanation is correct, the era of homers over 500 feet may have ended.

References & Resources

- Alan Nathan has a nice discussion of the Mantle homer at Griffith Stadium on his web site: *baseball.physics.illinois.edu/mantle565.html*
- ESPN Home Run Tracker, *hittrackeronline.com*
- Alan M. Nathan et al., *Procedia Engineering 34*, "Spin of a batted baseball," 2012, 182-187, *baseball.physics.illinois.edu/ProcediaEngineering34Spin.pdf*
- Greg Rybarczyk, ESPN Home Run Tracker, "Ted Williams, Fenway Park, June 9, 1946," *hittrackeronline.com/historic.php?id=1946_2*
- Alex Speier, *Boston Globe*, "Ted Williams's blast remains Fenway Park benchmark," July 13, 2015, *bostonglobe.com/sports/2015/07/13/why-aren-there-more-foot-home-runs/RYL4nuQcFltbTsf0lwABiK/story.html?#*

Is There Really a Well?

by Owen Watson

Unlike every other article I wrote for FanGraphs during the past year, the piece that formed the primordial substrate from which this study grew was directly inspired by something Curt Schilling said. Schilling has been in the news a lot during the past year, and not for baseball reasons, and reasons that are best kept outside of this particular Hardball Times undertaking. However, one thing is for sure: Schilling knew how to pitch, and when he talks about the specifics of life on the mound, I tend to listen.

Back in 2014, Schilling mentioned on a broadcast an idea of a pitcher "going to the well," i.e. dipping down into a reservoir of extra energy to produce a pitch that needed to be, well, better than his usual pitches—faster, nastier, and more unhittable. A pitcher could go to the well only a certain number of times, Schilling postulated, before tiring to the point of ineffectiveness. If he had to dip too many times, the well would run dry. It figured that these "anomalous" pitches would occur mostly during periods of high leverage: times when the game was on the line, when win expectancy was most in flux, and when that little something extra on a pitch might just end a scoring threat and preserve the game as it stood at the time.

In late February of 2015, I did a preliminary study—a foray into the subject, if you will—that addressed this question of leverage and velocity. Did a pitcher's velocity actually increase during high-leverage situations? Looking specifically at a three-game sample of starts from Oakland A's pitcher Sonny Gray, the answer seemed to be *yes*. As game situations transitioned from average leverage (for example, with runners on first and second base with the pitcher's team up three runs in the sixth inning) to high leverage (i.e. the previous situation except only up by *one* run), Gray's average velocity did increase. Just take a look at the graph from the original piece to get an idea of the way it worked for Gray.

Sonny Gray Velocity Changes with Leverage

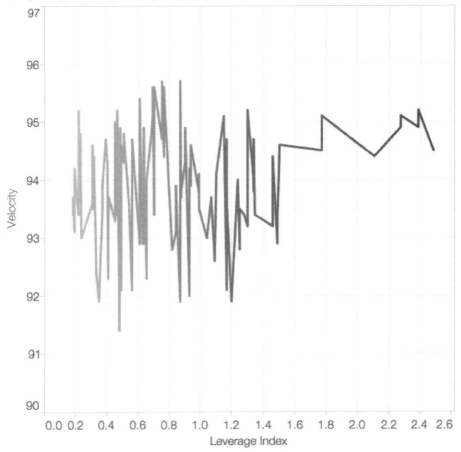

There were obvious limitations to the study, however, with the biggest being that it was only focused specifically on one pitcher. There was a larger sample of pitchers I used to establish factors like velocity decline as the game wore on, but those pitchers weren't included in the study of velocity and leverage.

We're going to change that by looking at all the starting pitchers for the entire 2015 season, forming broad and far-reaching conclusions about the impact game pressure (i.e. leverage) has on pitching velocity. Then, in addition, we're going to see if added pressure has any bearing on factors like the amount of spin on breaking pitches.

The fundamental question is this: When the game is on the line, does a pitcher throw harder fastballs and breaking pitches with different amounts of spin?

To begin with, it's a good idea to have a basic understanding of the concept of leverage index and win probability. Tom Tango laid the groundwork for the concept of Leverage Index we're using here all the way back in 2002. Leverage, as Tango describes it, is the measurement of the possible change in win probability at a certain time of the game. The closer and later a game finds itself, the higher impact an event will have on the outcome of the contest, and thus the higher the leverage rating for those game situations.

For this study, we're going to be using the standard rankings of Leverage Index situations:

- Low leverage: <0.85
- Average leverage: 1
- High leverage: >1.5
- Very high leverage: >3

Here's a handy guide for the prevalence of each level of leverage: only 10 percent of all real game situations have a Leverage Index greater than 2, while 60 percent have a Leverage Index less than 1. When we enter high-leverage times in a game (and especially very high leverage situations), we are dealing with more uncommon moments, but moments that certainly do happen over the course of a normal game.

To give some perspective to these index numbers, know that a LI of 1 is average, 2 is high leverage and 3.6 is very high. While very high leverage situations can happen in most innings (a Leverage Index of 3.0 is first possible in a one-run, two-out, bases-loaded situation in the second inning), they occur far more frequently later in the game, when possible events have a greater impact on win probability. We'll get into the specifics of this later, but for now it's something to keep in the back of your mind.

As far as the sample of data we're looking at, I've pulled game data from all of 2015. It's a lot of pitches—over 500,000, in fact. From there, I've whittled the data down to only starting pitchers who started every game they appeared in, and every pitch they threw along with the Leverage Index rating for the situation before the pitch was thrown. That gets us down to 246,695 pitches: this is the sample we'll draw all of the following conclusions from.

For the sample as a whole, I've calculated the average decline in velocity as the game has gone on, which will help us understand one of the forces at play in this study: fatigue.

First, let's establish the average velocity decline on hard pitches (for four-seam and two-seam fastballs) for our sample as a game advances. The following chart will give us a baseline idea of how velocity depreciates over time. Take a look:

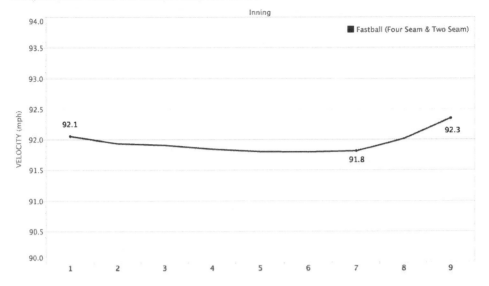

The change isn't a huge one. However, starting pitchers do lose velocity, on average, to the tune of almost 0.5 mph from the beginning of the game to the seventh inning. In the eighth and ninth inning, however, velocity rebounds in our sample.

Why is this?

Because most starters don't get all the way through nine innings. Those who do most often are elite starters, and elite starters tend to throw harder than other pitchers. As we get into the later innings, our sample size grows smaller, and that sample size is now populated by starting pitchers who throw harder fastballs.

If we were to look only at nine-inning starts and complete games this year, we get a velocity curve that isn't quite as skewed by the sample size issues as our previous graph, just like if we only looked at the first six or seven innings of this sample.

Velocity decline is something we should always be aware of with this study, as it assumes an important counterforce in relation to leverage, which naturally has a chance of increasing as the game unfolds.

We can also see the same velocity phenomenon with breaking and offspeed pitches. As the innings go by, their velocity diminishes along the same lines as hard pitches. That's not too surprising; the same arms are throwing all different types of pitches, and as those arms get tired, all types of pitches trend downward in velocity. Take a look at sliders and changeups.

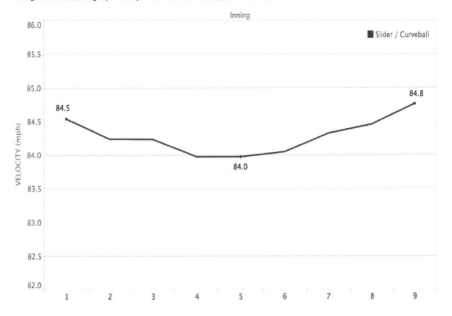

We see about the same velocity dip over the first seven innings with our big sample, then the same increase in the last two innings due to our complete-game, elite tier of pitchers that remain. The same trend also shows up with curveballs.

Now that we've established these baseline readings for how velocity changes over the course of a game, let's move onto the main aspects of the study. We'll look at an overall example of the impact pressure (leverage) has on velocity and then bring in spin rate to round everything out.

Let's get straight to the main event, answering our main question of velocity and leverage. I've taken all the pitchers in our sample and averaged the velocities of the fastballs they've thrown at each Leverage Index interval, selecting intervals of 0.10 so we can get more of a specific picture. Because the lowest leverage we regularly measure is around 0.20 on the index, we'll start the scale there and end it at 3.50 (past that point, the number of pitches per leverage point falls precipitously, effectively skewing the data). Here are the results.

Change in Changeup/Slider Velocity Due to Increased Leverage, 2015 Starters

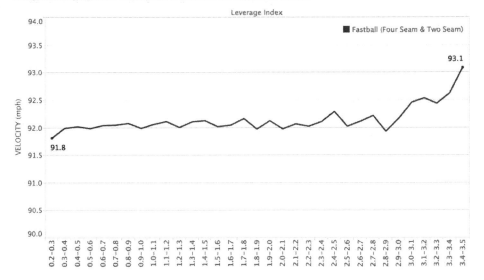

This answers our preliminary question: How does increased leverage affect average fastball velocity? We saw earlier how increased pressure impacted Gray's velocity; here we can see the same trend holds up over a much large sample size of starting pitchers.

As our Leverage Index increases, we see a steady rise in velocity of hard pitches, with a peak of just over a full mph difference for very high leverage situations compared to the lowest leverage ones. It's interesting to note that velocity truly only starts to trend significantly upward past the 2.00 Leverage Index mark (the point at which the Index refers to leverage as "high") and really jumps past 3.00 (which the Index refers to as "very high").

What about sliders and change-ups? Do they share a similar velocity trend to fastballs as leverage increases? Let's see.

Change in Changeup/Slider Velocity Due to Increased Leverage, 2015 Starters

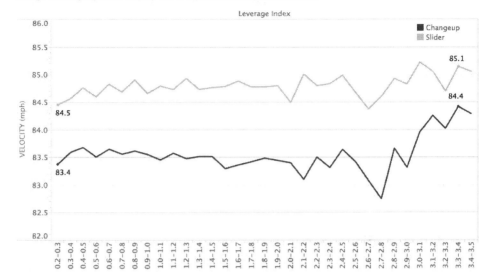

Again, we see almost the same Leverage Index points serving as a catalyst for increased velocity. Past 2.0 we see a bump, and 3.0 again serves as the start of the largest increases. As mentioned before, this confirms what we saw before: The same arms are throwing fastballs, change-ups, and sliders, and just as those arms get tired over the course of the game (leading to velocity decline), added leverage affects all types of pitches by increasing their velocity. Curveballs show the same trend.

Change in Curveball Velocity Due to Increased Leverage, 2015 Starters

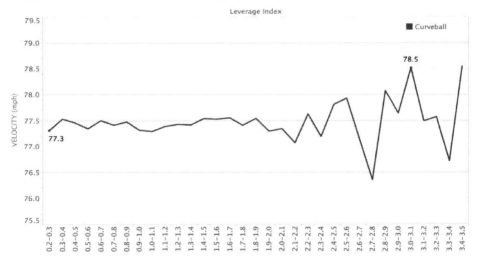

What makes this study really compelling is when we bring the two elements of fatigue and leverage together. We've seen that pitchers fatigue as the game goes on, leading to velocity decline. We also know that the higher the leverage is (which naturally tends to be later in the game), the more velocity increases. Reconciling these two opposing forces, we can see that not only do pitchers compensate for their natural velocity decline when they're under added pressure, they in fact rally to perform above their non-fatigued starting velocity.

This is *the well*, a reservoir of energy that seems to exist separately from the standard fatigue curve.

To further explain this relationship of late-inning fatigue and high-leverage velocity increase, let's look into when these high-leverage situations actually can occur. We'll use Tango's Leverage Index chart to calculate the possibilities of high-leverage situations happening during each inning of a standard nine-inning game by using base/out situations (such as runner on second, no out, home team up by three, etc.).

The following chart does not give the *probability* of high-leverage situations occurring, simply the percentage of situations classified as having high or very high marks on the Leverage Index during the past season.

Percent of High-Leverage (Leverage Index >1.5) Plays per Inning

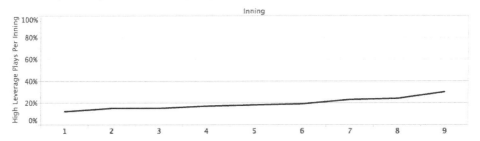

This, along with our velocity depreciation chart, shows us the relationship between fatigue and leverage in a different way. As the game unfolds (and as a pitcher tires), the possibility of a high-leverage situation increases, and the chances a pitcher has to throw a pitch that is higher than average velocity does as well. In effect, this tells us that velocity gains in crucial situations are probably slightly more impressive than they appear to be on the surface, as they are far more likely to occur in situations in which fatigue has already set in.

Now that we've established the impact of leverage on velocity, let's look at the spin rates of breaking pitches. Does increased leverage make pitchers throw tighter curveballs and sliders with more spin?

Here's where the study starts to get a little more intriguing. Unlike velocity, the spin rate on breaking pitches stays pretty steady as the innings of a game go by; however, the same can't be said of leverage's effect on spin. First, we'll look at curveballs and change-ups, as they're in the same general RPM range. Here is the spin rate change for those pitches, plotted along the same Leverage Index points as our previous graphs.

Change in Curveball/Changeup Spin Rate Due to Increased Leverage, 2015 Starters

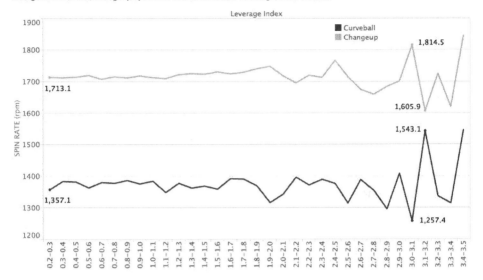

As we can see, the spin rates of these pitches differ at low/medium/high leverage points: curveballs decrease in spin rate with added leverage, while changeups actually increase as we move up the Leverage Index. At very high leverage points, we see wild variation (this could be partially attributed to some small sample size concerns at the highest leverage points, though grouping into large leverage buckets to overcome this shows much of the same variation). Sliders are all over the map.

Change in Slider Spin Rate Due to Increased Leverage, 2015 Starters

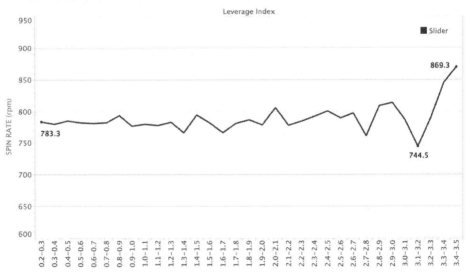

As it turns out, the trends for low/medium/high Leverage Index points isn't unexpected. Research by Jonah Pemstein this year at FanGraphs showed that increased velocity decreases spin on curveballs and increases spin on change-ups. Sliders are harder to pin down, as they don't show a linear relationship between spin rate and velocity (which causes our graph above to make more sense). The truly interesting aspect of this is how the correlation between spin and velocity could impact both batter and pitcher performance in these high-leverage situations.

Among many other findings, Pemstein discovered that increased spin leads to a slight decrease in contact rate on change-ups, telling us that an increase in Leverage Index could potentially make change-ups "nastier" than their low leverage counterparts. The same is true for the spin rate on curveballs, except with a different result: contact rate goes down as spin rate increases (following the opposite trend we see when leverage increases) making them theoretically easier to hit.

Whether these spin rate changes are an extension of increased velocity or increased leverage is hard to discern; as with almost everything in baseball, it is difficult to completely isolate the cause of each effect. The truth, as it often is, most likely lies along a spectrum, with both velocity and high pressure situations linked to spin rate changes. Do pitchers spin pitches at different rates when the pressure is high because they're trying to, or is it simply a result of the increased velocity that accompanies those situations? We might never know the exact answer, but it's most likely a little of both.

One final wrinkle remains in regard to spin and leverage. A batter's *swing rate* also falls with the spin rate changes that correspond to increased leverage for these offspeed pitches. Change-ups, sliders, and curveballs with more spin aren't offered at by batters as often as those with less spin. This means hitters might be less prone to making contact with pitches in high-leverage situations, but they also may be less liable to swing in the first place. This would make sense, as pitcher walk rate increases dramatically during high-leverage situations. Take a look at walk rates for low-, medium-, and high-leverage situations for starters in 2015.

Walk Rate By Leverage, 2015	
Situation	BB%
Low Leverage	7.4%
Medium Leverage	7.6%
High Leverage	8.9%

That's a big spike in walk rate for high leverage, and it supports the data we're seeing here. While it might be assumed the increased pressure alone would lead to pitchers being "wild" in high-leverage situations (due simply to the psychological impact that crucial situations have on players), a factor in this decreased control could be the physical way the pitches move, as well as the way hitters react to that change in average spin and velocity.

To assess the actual hitting production against these pitches in different leverage ranges, I've also pulled the average wOBA for hitters against each pitch type. This helps to answer the simple question: is "going to the well" actually worth it for the pitcher? I've plotted the different pitch types together, drawing a trendline to assess the relationship between increased leverage and hitting production by wOBA. Take a look:

Hitter wOBA vs. Increased Leverage, All Pitch Types

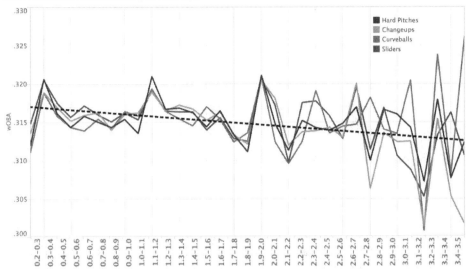

While there is a lot of variability in the data (the R-squared of the regression analysis was 12%, telling us that there isn't much predictive value in this relationship), the p-value of <.0001 tells us there is a connection between hitter wOBA and different types of pitches thrown with increasing leverage. There *is* a benefit in going to the well for a pitcher, and we can see its direct impact on hitting production in the chart above. The impact might not be huge—on average, about .10 points of wOBA from the lowest leverage points to the highest—but that is enough to take a hitter from an "average" classification on the FanGraphs rating system to a "below average" classification. Imagining a high leverage game situation, that possible difference could be all-important in how a crucial section of an inning unfolds.

Different types of pitches also show different levels of effectiveness as the leverage index increases, supporting the data we see in regard to velocity and spin rate: curveballs show the smallest increase in effectiveness at high leverage points compared to low ones (~-.04wOBA), hard pitches show the next smallest increase (~-.07 wOBA), and sliders and change-ups show the most (~-.18 wOBA). This matches the findings earlier in this study, supporting the hypothesis that sliders and change-ups actually do get "nastier" when pitchers go to the well.

After putting all of the many parts of this study together, we find Schilling was right about one thing: There *is* a "well" that pitchers can dip into, and it's fairly well-defined—especially with respect to our velocity data. When situations transition from medium to high leverage, there's a noticeable spike in velocity, just as there is when we move to the most important times of a game, with very high leverage moments.

The same goes for spin rate, but in a slightly different manner: Pitches respond individually to increases in either velocity, leverage, or both, impacting the performance of both pitcher and batter. That influence on performance, though not tremendous (especially for hard pitches and curveballs), is large enough to register as significant on the scale we use to evaluate hitters.

Starting pitchers get themselves into situations when they need something extra on their pitches, something faster, nastier, and more deceptive. We might have gotten a feeling this was occurring by watching our favorite starters perform during this situation. Now we know: They're just going to the well.

References & Resources

- Special thanks to Adam Sax, Jeff Zimmerman and David Appelman for MySQL help and support.
- Tom Tango, The Hardball Times, "Crucial Situations," *hardballtimes.com/crucial-situations*
- Jonah Pemstein, FanGraphs, "On Rotation, Part 1: The Effects of Spin on the Flight of a Pitch," *fangraphs.com/blogs/the-effects-of-spin-on-the-flight-of-a-pitch*
- Jonah Pemstein, FanGraphs, "On Rotation, Part 2: The Effects of Spin on Pitch Outcomes," *fangraphs.com/blogs/on-rotation-part-2-the-effects-of-spin-on-pitch-outcomes*

Creating Values for Trading Prospects

by Jeff Zimmerman

Back in 2006 when Dayton Moore was hired as the Royals general manager, he said, "Pitching is the currency of the game." Before the 2015 non-waiver trade deadline, he put his words into action when he traded off five pitching prospects—Aaron Brooks, Sean Manaea, Brandon Finnegan, Cody Reed and John Lamb—to acquire stars Johnny Cueto and Ben Zobrist for a World Series push.

Historically, trading prospects to help the major league team make—and win in—the playoffs has been a no-brainer: Win now and worry about tomorrow later. But in the last decade or so, prospects have been valued more and more by teams; they prefer players with small controlled salaries to the point where prospects may be overvalued. The following is an attempt to put a future WAR grade on prospects via different valuing methods, especially the 20-80 scouting scale.

For this study, I will look at several ways to value prospects. I will start with putting a value on prospects using their draft position, as well as their ranking in *Baseball America's* (*BA's*) top 100 prospects list. This is not the first attempt at valuing prospects with these two methods. Victor Wang in the *By the Numbers* newsletter, Scott McKinney at Royals Review and Neil Paine at FiveThirtyEight have looked at the difference in prospect values, including the difference between how pitchers and hitters are evaluated. Andrew Ball also wrote on valuing draft picks at Beyond the Box Score in 2013. I recreated quite a bit of their work for this research to help find additional information.

The key for me was to incorporate the 20-80 scouting grades into the prospects' values. The top 100 list is static for a very short time period, and then players get hurt or traded. Unknown players emerge. A draft could have more or less talent than a normal year, which could make average prospect rankings inconsistent. To help with the ever-changing prospect world, it can be easier at times to use the 20-80 forecasting scale, as those values shouldn't change as frequently or drastically as prospect rankings. A grade of 20 is a non-prospect; an 80 grade is a potential league MVP. Here is how the scale is divided up according to the *2015 Baseball America Prospect Handbook*:

Baseball America Grading Scale		
Grade	Hitter Role	Pitcher Role
75-80	Franchise Player	No.1 starter
65-70	Perennial All-Star	No. 2 starter
55-60	First-Division Regular	No. 3 starter, Elite closer
50	Solid-Average Regular	No. 4 starter, Elite set-up reliever
45	Second-Division Regular, Utilityman	No. 5 starter, Set-up reliever
40	Reserve	Swingman, Relief specialist

Unless I note otherwise, the player grades I use are *Baseball America (BA)* prospect grades and refer to this grading scale.

An issue I encountered with the *BA* grades is the lack of data. For only the past four years has every player in their annual *Handbook* been given a grade, so the data set is relatively small. FanGraphs has compiled grades for just one season, and while MLB.com has done so for a few years, their grades are rolling, and as such their data can not be directly compared to others.

As more prospect grades become available in the future, the results can continue to be refined. Also, I combined data from one time frame (Wins Above Replacement or WAR production) with these grades at another time frame. This work process is not ideal, but it is all that can be done with publicly available data.

Finally, the one difference I wanted to stick to was to use just a WAR value and not dollar amounts. As the cost of WAR increases in the future, the surplus amounts can just be changed without reverse engineering the previous study's dollar values to current ones. I will use some dollar amounts to help with calculations, but I will always finish with a WAR value. Additionally, for all the WAR calculations, I used FanGraphs WAR values.

I started with the two easiest data sets to work with, draft pick and prospect rankings. I will then move onto international signings, the Rule 5 draft, and finally, trades.

Draft Pick Value

For the draft and the prospect rankings, I will be looking at how much value the average prospect generated in his first seven years in the league. If a rookie starts on a team at the beginning of the season, the team has six years of player control before the player becomes a free agent. If a team waits a couple of weeks to bring up a player, the team get another season of player control. I will assume teams are at least this smart and will look at the seven-year value.

The seven controlled years and the time the player spends in the minors push back which drafts I could use to find players' future value. Additionally, I wanted the data to be as recent as possible. I ended up using draft data from 1995 to 2002 so I could get the amount of surplus WAR. I limited the scope of information to the first 100 picks mainly because players much further down in the draft didn't get a prospect grade from *Baseball America*. Also, the first 100 picks incorporate the two competitive balance picks that are at the end of the first and second rounds. These picks currently are the only ones that can be traded. Basically, the prospect values are being set for the first three rounds of the draft where most of the prime talent is picked.

Here is a graph of the average total WAR generated by the players over their first seven years in the big leagues.

Average Career WAR by Draft Pick, First 7 MLB Seasons

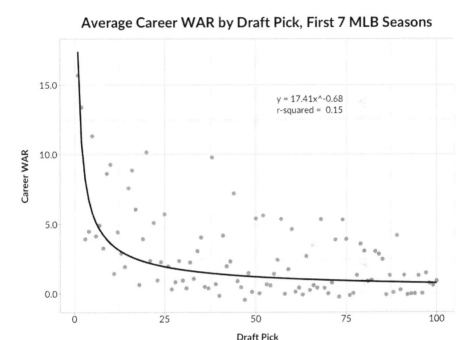

$$y = 17.41x^{-0.68}$$
$$r\text{-squared} = 0.15$$

I used the best-fit line from this graph to determine the total WAR values for each pick. From those values, I needed to find out how much of the WAR is surplus compared to similar players on the free-agent market.

Here are the assumptions I made with the 2015 WAR values.

- The cost for one WAR in free agency is $8 million.
- The league minimum salary used for the first four years was $500,000.
- For arbitration, I assumed players were going to get 40 percent, 60 percent, and 80 percent of their free-agent value in their three arbitration years. These arbitration values are under dispute, but the values are close enough so as to not make a huge difference in the output.

For example, here is the process for figuring out the No. 1 pick's excess WAR.

- Total WAR: 20.7 WAR

- Dollar value for the WAR: 20.7 WAR * $8 million/WAR = $165.4 million.
- Pre-arbitration salary removed: $165.4 million − (4 years * $500,000/year) = $163.4 million.
- Arbitration salary removed: $163.4 million−((0.4 +0.6 + 0.8) * (3.0 WAR/year*$8 million/WAR)) = $120.4 million.
- Excess salary converted to excess WAR: $120.4 million / $8 million/WAR = 15.0 WAR

Once I got all the excess values, I found the average BA grade for each draft position. For the data, I used the player's prospect grade for the year right after he was drafted. Here are the data plotted out.

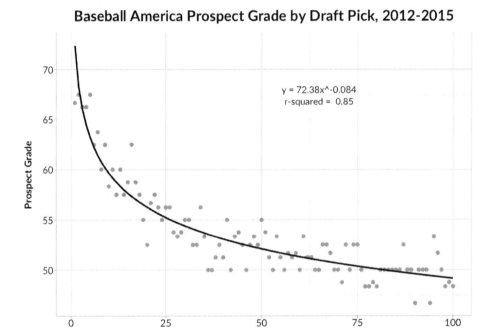

And here is it all in table form:

Average Pre-Free Agency WAR and Prospect Grade For Top 100 Draft Slots, 1995-2002

Pick	Total WAR	Surplus WAR	Avg Prospect Grade	Pick	Total WAR	Surplus WAR	Avg Prospect Grade
1	20.7	15.0	71.5	51	1.6	0.9	52.2
2	13.2	9.5	67.6	52	1.6	0.9	52.1
3	10.1	7.2	65.4	53	1.6	0.9	52.0
4	8.4	5.9	64.0	54	1.5	0.8	51.9
5	7.3	5.1	62.8	55	1.5	0.8	51.9
6	6.5	4.5	61.9	56	1.5	0.8	51.8
7	5.8	4.0	61.2	57	1.5	0.8	51.7
8	5.4	3.7	60.5	58	1.5	0.8	51.6
9	5.0	3.4	59.9	59	1.5	0.8	51.6
10	4.6	3.1	59.4	60	1.4	0.8	51.5
11	4.4	2.9	59.0	61	1.4	0.7	51.4
12	4.1	2.7	58.6	62	1.4	0.7	51.4
13	3.9	2.6	58.2	63	1.4	0.7	51.3
14	3.7	2.5	57.9	64	1.4	0.7	51.2
15	3.6	2.3	57.5	65	1.4	0.7	51.2
16	3.4	2.2	57.2	66	1.4	0.7	51.1
17	3.3	2.1	57.0	67	1.3	0.7	51.0
18	3.2	2.0	56.7	68	1.3	0.7	51.0
19	3.1	2.0	56.5	69	1.3	0.7	50.9
20	3.0	1.9	56.2	70	1.3	0.7	50.9
21	2.9	1.8	56.0	71	1.3	0.6	50.8
22	2.8	1.7	55.8	72	1.3	0.6	50.8
23	2.7	1.7	55.6	73	1.3	0.6	50.7
24	2.6	1.6	55.4	74	1.3	0.6	50.6
25	2.6	1.6	55.2	75	1.2	0.6	50.6
26	2.5	1.5	55.1	76	1.2	0.6	50.5
27	2.4	1.5	54.9	77	1.2	0.6	50.5
28	2.4	1.4	54.7	78	1.2	0.6	50.4
29	2.3	1.4	54.6	79	1.2	0.6	50.4
30	2.3	1.4	54.4	80	1.2	0.6	50.3
31	2.2	1.3	54.3	81	1.2	0.6	50.3
32	2.2	1.3	54.2	82	1.2	0.6	50.2
33	2.1	1.3	54.0	83	1.2	0.6	50.2
34	2.1	1.2	53.9	84	1.2	0.5	50.1
35	2.1	1.2	53.8	85	1.2	0.5	50.1
36	2.0	1.2	53.7	86	1.1	0.5	50.0
37	2.0	1.2	53.5	87	1.1	0.5	50.0
38	1.9	1.1	53.4	88	1.1	0.5	49.9
39	1.9	1.1	53.3	89	1.1	0.5	49.9
40	1.9	1.1	53.2	90	1.1	0.5	49.9
41	1.9	1.1	53.1	91	1.1	0.5	49.8
42	1.8	1.0	53.0	92	1.1	0.5	49.8
43	1.8	1.0	52.9	93	1.1	0.5	49.7
44	1.8	1.0	52.8	94	1.1	0.5	49.7
45	1.7	1.0	52.7	95	1.1	0.5	49.6
46	1.7	1.0	52.6	96	1.1	0.5	49.6
47	1.7	0.9	52.5	97	1.1	0.5	49.6
48	1.7	0.9	52.4	98	1.1	0.5	49.5
49	1.6	0.9	52.3	99	1.0	0.5	49.5
50	1.6	0.9	52.3	100	1.0	0.5	49.4

This information can become extremely handy since teams are now able to trade competitive balance picks. In three instances, a pick became a major trade piece. Let's take a look. (Draft picks have been traded at other times, but in those instances it was a smaller part of a bigger trade, so its value was more difficult to ascertain.)

Trade 1: April 6, 2015. Atlanta Trades Victor Reyes (BA grade, 50) to Arizona for the 75th Overall Pick

Using our comprehensive table, we can see this trade fits perfectly into the data I formulated, as the 75th overall pick has a 50.6 grade.

Trade 2: July 1, 2014. Pittsburgh Traded Bryan Morris to Miami for the 39th Overall Pick

The 39th pick has a total WAR value of 1.9, or an **excess WAR value of 1.0** ($8 million). Morris has pitched 103.2 innings of 0.6 WAR baseball for the Marlins since being traded. Now, Morris is one of the few pitchers who has an extreme groundball rate (59.4 percent in the majors). Extreme flyball and groundball pitchers historically have a better ERA than FIP, and FanGraphs use FIP for its WAR calculation. Morris is just such a player, and Morris' 2.3 Run Allowed WAR with the Marlins makes him already look like a good deal. He has three more seasons until he is a free agent, so he still can generate additional excess value.

Another way to look at the trade is to compare Morris to other 39th picks:

39th Overall Draft Pick, 2001-2010					
Player	Year	Career WAR	Player	Year	Career WAR
Wyatt Allen	2001	--	David Huff	2006	1.3
Mark Teahen	2002	2.2	James Adkins	2007	--
Tony Gwynn Jr.	2003	4.7	Lance Lynn	2008	13.5
Jay Rainville	2004	--	Kentrail Davis	2009	--
Hank Sanchez	2005	--	Anthony Ranaudo	2010	-0.7

A team can get the known 4.5 seasons of Bryan Morris or a one-in-10 chance of Lance Lynn. While the Marlins' end of the deal initially was panned, it looks like it could end up being a good move for them.

Trade 3: April 13, 2015. Dodgers Paid $2.75 million for Baltimore's 74th Overall Pick

While draft picks can't directly be bought, the Dodgers did so indirectly. I will let Craig Calcaterra explain how the Dodgers pulled off the trade:

> On Thursday the Dodgers acquired reliever Ryan Webb from the Orioles along with a minor league catcher and competitive balance draft pick. In exchange, the Dodgers sent righty Ben Rowen and minor league catcher Chris

O'Brien to Baltimore and agreed to pick up Webb's entire $2.75 million salary for 2015.

Over the weekend, they outrighted Webb to Oklahoma City. Today they just released him. Which means that, minor league spare parts aside, the Dodgers basically just decided to pay $2.75 million for a competitive balance draft pick, the 74th overall pick in this year's draft. They will also get over $800K in draft pool money since they have that extra pick.

Looking at the 74th overall pick, a team can expect 0.6 surplus WAR from the draft pick. With a free-agent win costing $8 million, the Dodgers got at least $4.8 million in future value by paying $2.75 million now.

Time to move on to prospect rankings.

Prospect Ranking Value

Using *Baseball America's* top 100 prospect list was a huge advantage—it has been around since 1990. While the ranking process has improved over the years, the lists give us a great look back at which prospects were getting valued the highest and how they ended up performing. Again, I acknowledge quite a bit of work already has been done on prospect rankings previously, but I want to concentrate on WAR values and prospect grades.

I used the same draft pick procedure (i.e., overall seven-year WAR, surplus value, etc.) to value prospects. For the WAR values, I used the top 100 prospects from 1997 to 2004. Here is a graph of the average WAR generated by each ranking over the timeframe, along with the best-fit line I will use to estimate the WAR value.

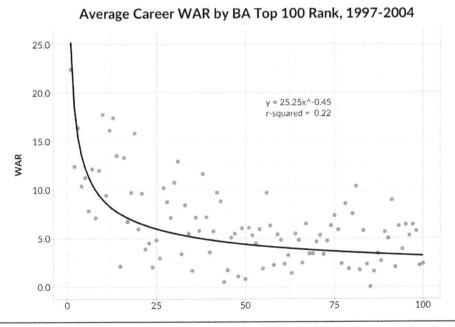

Average Career WAR by BA Top 100 Rank, 1997-2004

$y = 25.25x^{-0.45}$
r-squared = 0.22

Next, I averaged the *BA* 20-80 grades over the past four years that corresponded with the players' top 100 rank and created this best-fit line.

BA Prospect Grade by BA Top 100 Rank, 2012-2015

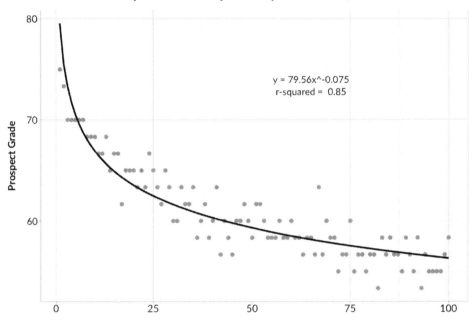

With the above prospect rank information, the overall BA rank, total WAR, surplus WAR, and projected BA grade were calculated easily.

Rank	Total WAR	Surplus WAR	Avg Prospect Grade	Rank	Total WAR	Surplus WAR	Avg Prospect Grade
			Average Pre-Free Agency WAR and Prospect Grade For *BA* Top 100, 1995-2002				
1	25.3	18.5	79.5	51	3.9	2.4	59.2
2	18.2	13.0	75.5	52	3.8	2.3	59.1
3	15.0	10.6	73.2	53	3.8	2.3	59.0
4	13.0	9.2	71.6	54	3.8	2.3	58.9
5	11.7	8.2	70.5	55	3.7	2.3	58.9
6	10.7	7.5	69.5	56	3.7	2.2	58.8
7	10.0	6.9	68.7	57	3.7	2.2	58.7
8	9.4	6.5	68.0	58	3.6	2.2	58.6
9	8.9	6.1	67.4	59	3.6	2.2	58.6
10	8.4	5.8	66.9	60	3.6	2.2	58.5
11	8.0	5.5	66.4	61	3.5	2.1	58.4
12	7.7	5.2	66.0	62	3.5	2.1	58.3
13	7.4	5.0	65.6	63	3.5	2.1	58.3
14	7.2	4.8	65.2	64	3.5	2.1	58.2
15	6.9	4.7	64.9	65	3.4	2.1	58.1
16	6.7	4.5	64.6	66	3.4	2.0	58.1
17	6.5	4.4	64.3	67	3.4	2.0	58.0
18	6.4	4.2	64.0	68	3.4	2.0	57.9
19	6.2	4.1	63.7	69	3.3	2.0	57.9
20	6.0	4.0	63.5	70	3.3	2.0	57.8
21	5.9	3.9	63.3	71	3.3	1.9	57.7
22	5.8	3.8	63.1	72	3.3	1.9	57.7
23	5.7	3.7	62.8	73	3.3	1.9	57.6
24	5.5	3.6	62.6	74	3.2	1.9	57.6
25	5.4	3.5	62.4	75	3.2	1.9	57.5
26	5.3	3.5	62.3	76	3.2	1.9	57.5
27	5.2	3.4	62.1	77	3.2	1.9	57.4
28	5.1	3.3	61.9	78	3.2	1.8	57.3
29	5.1	3.3	61.8	79	3.1	1.8	57.3
30	5.0	3.2	61.6	80	3.1	1.8	57.2
31	4.9	3.1	61.4	81	3.1	1.8	57.2
32	4.8	3.1	61.3	82	3.1	1.8	57.1
33	4.8	3.0	61.2	83	3.1	1.8	57.1
34	4.7	3.0	61.0	84	3.0	1.8	57.0
35	4.6	2.9	60.9	85	3.0	1.7	57.0
36	4.6	2.9	60.8	86	3.0	1.7	56.9
37	4.5	2.8	60.6	87	3.0	1.7	56.9
38	4.4	2.8	60.5	88	3.0	1.7	56.8
39	4.4	2.8	60.4	89	3.0	1.7	56.8
40	4.3	2.7	60.3	90	2.9	1.7	56.7
41	4.3	2.7	60.2	91	2.9	1.7	56.7
42	4.2	2.6	60.1	92	2.9	1.7	56.6
43	4.2	2.6	60.0	93	2.9	1.7	56.6
44	4.1	2.6	59.9	94	2.9	1.6	56.5
45	4.1	2.5	59.8	95	2.9	1.6	56.5
46	4.1	2.5	59.7	96	2.9	1.6	56.5
47	4.0	2.5	59.6	97	2.8	1.6	56.4
48	4.0	2.5	59.5	98	2.8	1.6	56.4
49	3.9	2.4	59.4	99	2.8	1.6	56.3
50	3.9	2.4	59.3	100	2.8	1.6	56.3

Now, I matched up the prospect grades and surplus values to get the equivalent top 100 ranking for a specific draft pick. Here are the two tables.

Grade-Matched Table					
Draft Pick	Top 100 Rank	Prospect Grade	Draft Pick	Top 100 Rank	Prospect Grade
1	4	71.5	11	53	59.0
2	9	67.6	12	58	58.6
3	14	65.4	13	64	58.2
4	18	64.0	14	69	57.9
5	23	62.8	15	75	57.5
6	28	61.9	16	80	57.2
7	33	61.2	17	84	57.0
8	38	60.5	18	90	56.7
9	44	59.9	19	94	56.5
10	49	59.4			

So, what we're saying here is the number one draft pick will end up with an average grade of 71.5, and he'll end up on average being ranked fourth overall. Now, let's look at it by surplus value:

Surplus Value-Matched Table					
Draft Pick	Top 100 Rank	Surplus WAR	Draft Pick	Top 100 Rank	Surplus WAR
1	2	15.0	12	40	2.7
2	4	9.5	13	42	2.6
3	7	7.2	14	45	2.5
4	10	5.9	15	52	2.3
5	12	5.1	16	56	2.2
6	16	4.5	17	61	2.1
7	20	4.0	18	66	2.0
8	23	3.7	20	71	1.9
9	27	3.4	21	78	1.8
10	31	3.1	22	85	1.7
11	35	2.9	24	94	1.6

The first item that sticks out is that, when using prospect grades, only 19 draft picks line up with the top 100 list. Historically, 14.2 draft picks make the top 100 list the next season, so recently drafted players seem to be getting the short straw. When looking at surplus values, we find 24 values line up, but again, recently drafted players seem to be lacking in recognition.

There are two reasons these values aren't aligned. First, there is not much information on recently drafted players, especially on how they will perform against more talented players, so a conservative stance is taken on their grades. Second—and this goes along with the first idea—a top-100 list is too arbitrary and/or static. At the bottom end, is there really much difference between the 100th and 101st ranked player, or the 100th and 110th for that matter?

Former FanGraphs lead prospect analyst Kiley McDaniel's 2015 prospect list ran 200 players deep, and he grouped his rankings by grades. His 80th- to 142nd-ranked prospects all had a 50 grade. He gave 63 players that same 50 grade, but if he just used the normal 100-player cutoff, 42 prospects would have been removed. When ranking by an arbitrary number, like 100, instead of by talent, some similarly talented players will get cut off. In this case, those left off seem to be players with the least amount of pro experience.

While the prospects' grades and future values don't line up perfectly, they are close. I have taken the step of averaging them together to get an overall and surplus WAR values for each player grades.

One issue I found with the top 100 draft picks and prospect grades is that the lowest possible grade is a 50. Not every prospect is going to end up as an every-day regular. The four prospect handbooks have a smattering of 45 grades on recent picks—in all, I was able to find 94 players who were given a 45 grade the year after they were drafted. The median draft pick for these players was 160. These players ended up have effectively no major league value. They averaged 0.37 WAR for their first seven major league seasons and actually provided a small negative return when salary was taken into account. Since teams probably would move on from these players, I will just put their future value at zero. Let's take a look:

Prospect Grade to WAR Conversion		
Grade	Total WAR	Surplus WAR
80	25.0	18.5
75	18.0	13.0
70	11.0	9.0
65	8.5	6.0
60	4.7	3.0
55	2.5	1.5
50	1.1	0.5
45	0.4	0.0

Notice the average increase in both WAR values from one level to the next almost doubles (85 percent average increase).

This table can be extremely important in that it provides a way to value a group of prospects on a team, league or trade. For example, here are McDaniel's grade 50 to 70 prospects grouped by team, with the total amount of surplus value. It's 50 to 70, because he didn't grade anyone out at 75 or 80, because those kinds of players almost never come around.

Kiley's Prospect Grades						
Team	70	65	60	55	50	Total Surplus Value
CHC	1	1	2	1	3	22.0
MIN	1		2	3	1	18.9
LAD		2	1		1	12.4
TEX			2	3	5	11.4
HOU		1	1	1	3	10.0
BOS			2	3	1	9.4
NYM			1	4	3	9.2
ATL				5	3	8.0
COL			1	3	3	7.9
WSH		1		1	3	7.5
CHW		1		1	3	7.5
CIN			1	2	4	7.1
TOR			1	2	3	6.6
PIT			1	2	2	6.1
NYY			1	1	4	5.8
KC				3	3	5.4
BAL			1	2		5.1
PHI			1	2		5.1
ARZ				3	2	4.9
SEA			1	1		3.8
CLE			1		2	3.5
STL				1	4	3.3
SD				2	1	3.1
TB				1	3	2.8
LAA				2		2.6
SF					3	1.5
OAK				1		1.3
MIA				1		1.3
MIL					2	1.0
DET					1	0.5

Some teams, like the Cubs, had a large number of good prospects, so having the most surplus value is not a surprise. The Dodgers show that quality can make up for quantity, as while they only had four rated prospects, they had two of the six 65s and another 60. Twelve teams didn't have a single player rate over a 55. While we could dig in and decipher the specific team data all day, the main takeaway is that measuring a team's current prospect value just got a whole lot easier.

International Free Agents

I considered not writing this section because of the recent changes in the international signing guidelines and how teams are just blowing past the spending limits. An entire annual article or five could be written about how the player acquisition system is broken in Central America. If you want to understand some of the issues, read some of Kiley's work, both here in this book and in his piece at FanGraphs entitled "Signing July 2nd Players Has Gotten Even More Complicated."

Despite these issues, I decided to forge ahead. Take the following analysis with a grain a salt as I know there are multiple issues that could change the results and make them useless, such as an international draft. But I would like to start creating some framework for future research, if nothing else.

First, I am looking only at the young players signed from Central America, not the older free agents from Cuba or Japan. One convention I am going to use, for good or bad, is to examine players with the 20 highest bonuses. Possibly, the best deals are for players with smaller contracts, but I don't have a complete database of international signings, so I need to work off the top. I know these 20 are not going to be the all the top players, but it represents one way to place a value on more than a handful of players. To start, I will look at the total outlay to the top 20 signees from 2010 to 2015.

Top 20 Bonus Totals, 2010-2015	
Year	Bonus Totals
2010	$27 million
2011	$33 million
2012*	$26 million
2014	$33 million
2015	$44 million

*New CBA implemented in 2012

It can be seen how the CBA and slotted bonus pool kept the top bonuses suppressed for a while, but they have escalated quickly.

With only four years' worth of *BA Handbooks* with grades, a group of players far from the majors, and huge changes in how the bonus are given out, finding some future values was daunting, but I gave it a try while making some assumptions. I am going to look at the 2010 to 2015 signings. One issue I had to deal with regarding these signings was the players' ages. Most of these players can and will be signed by their 16th birthday. They are not even close to being big-league ready. I will start with 2010 and 2011 signings, because I have grades for them three years later when their prospect value is better understood.

Looking back at 2010, teams spent $27.4 million on the top 20 bonuses. With *BA's* 2014 values, the top 20 signings contain two 60s, two 55s and two 50s. Going back to the prospect grade to WAR conversion table from before, this works out to a total of 16.8 WAR, or an excess of 8.6 WAR. In 2011, the total was $33.5 million for the top 20 players, with the range in bonuses from $759,000 to $4.95 million. In the next (2012) *Handbook*, only six players got grades—three 55s and three 50s (10.8 total WAR and 6.0 surplus WAR). Three years later, the players got grades of one 65, one 60, two 55s and five 50s, for 23.7 total WAR and 14.5 excess WAR. The 2011 class is the only one I looked at with initial and three-year values.

Looking at just this 2011 season, a possible pattern appears that is similar to *Baseball America's* conservative ranking of the draft prospects. If money is any indicator, teams are getting more information on the top-paid players, as seen by the same players having doubled their value just a few years later.

Moving on to 2012 and 2014 (I could not find a list of the top salaries from 2013), here are the total bonuses spent, prospect rankings, and total WAR values for the top 20 bonuses.

2012, 2014 Bonus Pool Info		
Category	2012	2014
Top 20 bonuses	$26 million	$33 million
60 grades	1	1
55 grades	6	1
50 grades	2	4
Total WAR	21.9	11.6
Surplus WAR	13	6.5
$/Total WAR	$1.2 million	$2.8 million
$/Surplus WAR	$2.0 million	$5.1 million

Now, here is a comparison of the slotted draft bonuses for each of those two years and the grades (min. 50) that were given to the top 20 signed players.

2012, 2014 Bonus Pool Info 2		
Category	2012	2014
Top 20 bonuses	$62 million	$63.5 million
70 grades	4	0
65 grades	1	4
60 grades	8	9
55 grades	6	4
50 grades	1	1
Total WAR	106.2	104.4
Surplus WAR	75.5	69.5
$/Total WAR	$600,000	$600,000
$/Surplus WAR	$800,000	$900,000

The total amount spent on international bonuses is quite a bit more than the draft bonus total given the amount of talent acquired. However, we do find that three years after the players signed, they have generated surplus value—right around $3 million for the players signed in 2010 and 2011.

While all the future values are compared to the $8 million free agent WAR value, international signees are getting several times more money per level of talent compared to recently drafted domestic players; with them fairly strict penalties are in place if teams spend too much. The international signing pools was supposed to limit the amount of this disparity, but the consequences of going over the limit are not strong enough. So teams will spend their abundance of cash in this one arena and still get a decent return on their investment.

With international prospect values, spending slots can be traded as a way to increase the amount of money available to teams. Teams that are certain to go over the cap can trade away these slots, as they no longer matter to these teams. In 2015, five players were traded for slot money:

- Braves traded pitcher Garrett Fulenchek (grade: 55) to the Rays for $495,000.
- Braves traded pitcher Cody Martin (grade: 40, 238th overall draft pick) to the Athletics for $388,000.
- Braves traded pitcher Aaron Kurcz (310th overall draft pick) to the Athletics for $167,000.
- Rangers traded pitcher Jason Hoppe (816th overall pick) to the Angels for $879,500.
- Mets traded pitcher Gaither Bumgardner (686th overall pick) to the Angels for $239,400.

The Angels and Braves were on two extreme ends of valuing slot bonuses. The Braves gave up Fulenchek and Martin, both among their preseason top 30 prospects, for $883,000 in bonuses. On the other hand, the Angels got Jason Hoppe, who was a 27th-round pick with a 5.04 ERA in A-ball, for almost the same amount of cap space ($880,000). With so few slots being traded one-for-one, no values can really be put on them yet, especially with teams so far apart in their valuations. As more of these slots get traded, a better understanding of their values will be known.

Rule 5 Draft

The Rule 5 draft is normally uneventful, with all but a handful of players returned to their original team...until this past season. In 2015 season, only three players were returned in the major league phase. It seems teams did their homework for the draft and found some usable talent. Here are the 2011 to 2014 selections:

Year	Player	Kept?	Pos	Team	Grade
Rule 5 Draft Picks, 2011-2014					
2014	Oscar Hernandez	Yes	C	ARI	
2104	Mark Canha	Yes	IF	COL	45
2014	Delino DeShields Jr.	Yes	OF	TEX	50
2014	Jason Garcia	Yes	RHP	HOU	50
2104	J.R. Graham	Yes	RHP	MIN	50
2014	Jandel Gustave		RHP	BOS	50
2014	Taylor Featherston	Yes	SS	CHC	45
2014	David Herrera	Yes	IF	PHI	
2014	Andrew McKirahan	Yes	LHP	MIA	45
2014	Sean Gilmartin	Yes	LHP	NYM	45
2014	Daniel Winkler	Yes	RHP	ATL	50
2014	David Rollins	Yes	LHP	SEA	
2014	Logan Verrett		RHP	BAL	40
2014	Andrew Oliver		LHP	PHI	
2013	Patrick Schuster		LHP	HOU	
2013	Adrian Nieto	Yes	C	CHW	45
2013	Kevin Munson		RHP	PHI	
2013	Thomas Kahnle	Yes	RHP	COL	
2013	Brian Moran		LHP	TOR	
2013	Seth Rosin		RHP	NYM	
2013	Wei-Chung Wang	Yes	LHP	MIL	50
2013	Marcos Mateo		RHP	ARI	
2013	Michael Almanzar		3B	BAL	
2012	Josh Fields	Yes	RHP	HOU	45
2012	Hector Rondon	Yes	RHP	CHC	
2012	Daniel Rosenbaum		LHP	COL	45
2012	Ryan Pressly	Yes	RHP	MIN	
2012	Chris McGuiness		1B	CLE	45
2012	Alfredo Silverio	Yes	OF	MIA	55
2012	Jeff Kobernus		2B	BOS	45
2012	Kyle Lobstein		LHP	NYM	45
2012	Starling Peralta		RHP	ARI	50
2012	Ender Inciarte		OF	PHI	
2012	Angel Sanchez	Yes	INF	CWS	50
2012	T.J. McFarland	Yes	LHP	BAL	40
2012	Coty Woods		RHP	TEX	
2012	Nate Freiman		1B	HOU	
2012	Braulio Lara		LHP	MIA	
2011	Rhiner Cruz	Yes	RHP	HOU	45
2011	Terry Doyle		RHP	MIN	40
2011	Lucas Luetge	Yes	LHP	SEA	
2011	Ryan Flaherty	Yes	2B	BAL	50
2011	Cesar Cabral		LHP	KC	
2011	Lendy Castillo	Yes	RHP	CHC	
2011	Gustavo Nunez		SS	PIT	
2011	Robert Fish	Yes	LHP	ATL	
2011	Erik Komatsu		OF	STL	
2011	Marwin Gonzalez	Yes	SS	BOS	45
2011	Brett Lorin		RHP	ARI	45
2011	Brad Meyers	Yes	RHP	NYY	

In all, 50 players were drafted over the four seasons, and 28 stuck with their new team (without being traded for later). Of the 28 who stuck, 17 made the top 30 players for their new team in the *BA Handbook*. One had a 55 grade, seven 50s, eight 45s and a 40 grade. Of the 22 who were sent back, nine had grades (two 50s, five 45s and two 40s). Not a ton of conclusions can be drawn here, but it does seem like players with a 45 or higher grade are targeted as potential keepers in the Rule 5 draft.

Trading prospects

Prospects are always getting traded in the offseason or at the trade deadline. Figuring out their trade value can be difficult, since prospects often are part of larger trades. I am going to attempt to show how prospects are valued in trades by looking at the few instances when a single graded prospect was traded straight up for another player. I will split this up a bit further by looking at offseason trades and those at the non-waiver trade deadline. Since I was looking at four years of salaries, I assumed an average $6.8 million WAR value (which is based on way-too-complex math that I think would be more confusing described than without the description).

Let's start start off with the complete list of trades.

Trade Deadline Prospect Trades								
Team 1			Team 2	Remaining				Surplus WAR
Player (Pos)	Gr		Player (Pos)	Yrs	Salary ($M)	WAR/ Year	Sur- plus $	Non- Pros.	Pros- pect
R. Kaminsky, LHP, STL	55		B. Moss, OF, CLE	1.3	9.6	2.0	$8.7	1.3	1.5
C. Culberson, 2B, SF	50		M. Scutaro, 2B, COL	0.3	2.0	2.0	$2.6	0.4	0.5
F.D.L. Santos, RHP, OAK	50		G. Kottaras, C, MIL	3.3	3.4	0.4	$5.7	0.8	0.5
L. Garcia, 2B, TEX	50		A. Rios, RF, CHW	1.3	16.6	1.5	-$2.9	-0.4	0.5
K. Smith, RHP, KC	50		J. Maxwell, CF, HOU	1.3	1.2	1.0	$8.0	1.2	0.5
E. Lopez, RHP, LAA	50		D. DeJesus, OF, TB	0.3	1.7	1.0	$0.6	0.1	0.5
Z. Davies, RHP, BAL	45		G. Parra, OF, MIL	0.3	2.1	1.5	$1.3	0.2	0
T. Bortnick, 2B, TB	45		R. Roberts, 2B, ARI	1.3	3.6	1.0	$5.5	0.8	0
G. Green, 2B, OAK	45		A. Callaspo, IF, LAA	1.3	6.3	2.0	$12.0	1.8	0
X. Avery, LF, BAL	45		M. Morse, LF, SEA	0.3	6.3	0.8	-$4.6	-0.7	0
C. McHugh, RHP, NYM	45		E. Young, LF, COL	1.3	2.0	0.5	$2.6	0.4	0
I. Pineyro, RHP, WAS	45		S. Hairston, LF, CHC	1.3	3.3	1.0	$5.8	0.8	0
E. Staments, SS, LAA	40		D. Murphy, OF, CLE	0.3	2.0	1.0	$0.3	0.0	0
Z. Cox, 3B, STL	55		E. Mujica, RHP, MIA	0.3	0.5	1.0	$1.7	0.3	1.5
E. Rodriguez, LHP, BAL	55		A. Miller, LHP, BOS	0.3	0.6	1.5	$2.8	0.4	1.5
C. Meisner, RHP, NYM	50		T. Clippard, RP, OAK	0.3	2.7	1.5	$0.7	0.1	0.5
J. Jones, SS, PIT	50		J. Soria, RHP, DET	0.3	2.3	1.0	-$0.0	0.0	0.5
N. Delmonico, 3B, BAL	50		F. Rodriguez, RHP, MIL	0.3	0.7	1.5	$2.7	0.4	0.5
B. Jacobs, LF, BOS	50		M. Thornton, LHP, CHW	0.3	1.8	1.5	$1.6	0.2	0.5
M. Clevinger, RHP, LAA	45		Vi. Pestano, RHP, CLE	3.3	3.3	0.5	$8.1	1.2	0
J. Ramsey, OF, STL	50		J. Masterson, RHP, CLE	0.3	3.2	1.5	$0.2	0.0	0.5
A. Sampson, RHP, PIT	45		JA Happ, P, SEA	0.3	2.2	1.0	$0.1	0.0	0
P. Frazier, RHP, COL	40		A. Galarraga, RHP, CIN	4.3	2.2	0.1	$0.8	0.1	0
					Position Players			6.6	4.0
					Relief Pitchers			2.6	5.0
					Starting Pitchers			0.2	0.5

Offseason Prospect Trades								
Team 1			Team 2	Remaining				Surplus WAR
Player (Pos)	Gr		Player (Pos)	Yrs	Salary ($M)	WAR/ Year	Sur- plus $	Non- Pros.	Pros- pect
A. Meyer, RHP, WAS	60		D. Span, CF, MIN	3.0	$20.3	3.0	$41.7	6.1	4.7
A. Heaney, LHP, LAD	55		H. Kendrick, 2B, LAA	1.0	$9.5	2.5	$7.7	1.1	1.5
D. Travis, 2B, DET	50		A. Gose, CF, TOR	5.0	$5.0	0.5	$12.2	1.8	0.5
J. Diaz, RHP, LAA	50		J. Rutledge, 2B, COL	4.0	$2.0	0.0	-$2.0	-0.3	0.5
D. Dietrich, 2B, TB	50		Y. Escobar, SS, MIA	2.0	$10.0	2.0	$17.5	2.5	0.5
J. Soptic, RHP, CHW	50		C. Gillaspie, 3B, SF	6.0	$7.5	0.5	$13.1	1.9	0.5
J. Wendle, 2B, CLE	45		B. Moss, 1B, OAK	2.0	$13.0	2.0	$14.5	2.1	0
S. Gilmartin, LHP, ATL	45		R. Doumit, LF, MIN	1.0	$3.5	0.8	$1.7	0.2	0
M. Reynolds, LHP, COL	45		R. Wheeler, 3B, ARI	5.0	$1.5	0.0	-$1.5	-0.2	0
J. Alvarez, LHP, DET	40		A. Romine, SS, LAA	5.0	$3.0	0.2	$3.9	0.6	0
M. Davidson, 3B, ARI	55		A. Reed, RHP, CHW	4.0	$15.5	0.5	-$1.7	-0.3	1.5
N. Molina, RHP, TOR	50		S. Santos, RHP, CHW	3.0	$8.2	1.0	$12.4	1.8	0.5
A. Ranaudo, RHP, BOS	45		R. Ross, LHP, TEX	4.0	$6.0	1.0	$21.5	3.1	0
J. Barbato, RHP, SD	45		S. Kelley, RHP, NYY	1.0	$2.8	0.5	$0.6	0.1	0
B. Burns, LF, WAS	45		J. Blevins, LHP, OAK	2.0	$3.3	0.8	$7.0	1.0	0
R. Rasmussen, LHP, HOU	45		J. Ely, RHP, LAD	6.0	$2.0	0.0	-$2.0	-0.3	0
S. Geltz, RHP, LAA	40		D.D.L. Rosa, RHP, TB	2.0	$2.0	0.5	$4.9	0.7	0
Z. Putnam, RHP, CLE	45		K. Slowey, RHP, COL	1.0	$2.8	1.0	$4.1	0.6	0
						Position Players		15.8	8.2
						Relief Pitchers		6.2	2.0
						Starting Pitchers		0.6	0

First, the one way the tables can be used can be used is to find comparable trades. With the A's wanting to move Tyler Clippard at this past trade deadline, they could expect to get a 50 to 55 graded prospect from another team. A light-hitting fourth outfielder could return a 45-50 graded prospect.

Teams can expect to get a little more value at the trade deadline compared to the offseason. Here is a look at how the trade values compare between the offseason and regular season. There is not enough info to evaluate starting pitchers this way.

Relief Pitchers			
Trading period	Total prospect surplus WAR	Total MLB player surplus WAR	Prospect/MLB player ratio
Offseason	2.0	6.2	0.32
Trade deadline	5.0	2.6	1.92

Position Players			
Trading period	Total prospect surplus WAR	Total MLB player surplus WAR	Prospect/MLB player ratio
Offseason	8.2	15.8	0.52
Trade deadline	4.0	6.6	0.61

The best time to trade relief pitchers, especially top closers, is at the trade deadline. I don't see this trade deadline-overpaying trend changing, because teams will be looking for comparable returns. The only comps that exist are these overpayments. Some additional value can be extracted from position players at the deadline, but not nearly as much as relievers.

With the all the above information, it is now easier to evaluate more complex trades to find the "winners" and "losers." The trade evaluation process always will have some other factors at work besides surplus value, but I will start with it.

Let's take the example we started with, the Royals' Ben Zobrist and Johnny Cueto trades. For the prospect values, I will use the *2015 BA Handbook* values, but the prospects values could/probably did change during the season. I will use the dated values with the understanding they may be off a grade.

Zobrist was probably around a 4.5 WAR player coming into the 2015 season, but because of injuries and offensive struggles, he had produced only 0.7 WAR for the A's before the trade with KC. After the trade, Zobrist was worth 1.5 WAR in his one-third of the season, which is in line with his projections. Additionally, KC needed to pay one third of Zobrist's $7.5 million salary, or $2.5 million. That works out to 1.2 surplus WAR. For Zobrist, the Royals gave up Sean Manaea (Grade: 55) and Aaron Brooks (no grade). Only Manaea has surplus value—1.5 WAR, which is almost what the Royals got from Zobrist. While the Royals had to overpay, it was not by much.

For Cueto, the Reds got Brandon Finnegan, Cody Reed and John Lamb. Cueto has also been about a 4.5 WAR player over each of the last few seasons. The Royals could be expected to get 1.2 WAR from him, while paying one-third of his $10 million contract, or $3.3 million. His projected surplus WAR at the time of the trade works out to ~1.1 WAR. Of the three pitchers who were traded, only Finnegan had a grade, but it was a nice, shiny 60, which on average produces 3.0 surplus WAR. The excess paid compared to Zobrist is not a surprise, even though there is not much historical data showing individual starting pitchers costing more for prospects in one-for-one trades. Teams pay a premium for relief pitchers at the trade deadline, so it is no surprise they would pay a premium for starters also. Of course, this is just regular season value, and the Royals were banking on some postseason value as well.

Wrapping Up

I hope I was able to answer a few questions about prospect values, especially with the work on the 20-80 scale. I feel good about the future WAR values for draft picks and players on the *BA* Top 100 prospect lists. If only one item is to be taken from this article, it is the table on page 261, which I created using the draft and prospect list data. While it may be the smallest table in the entire article, it provides the conversion from prospect grade to the value seen on the field. With only four years' worth of data, I could see the 20-80 information change over time.

I gave an initial stab at player values in the international player market and the Rule 5 draft, though the future values are murky at this point. Finally, I looked at trades in which prospects were involved and provided some initial understanding of how much teams are willing to overpay at the trade deadline compared to the offseason.

There can always be more work done on this subject. One item I have not seen fully researched is the ability of teams, with the draft, and publications, with top 100 lists, to better evaluate prospects over time. We have years' worth of draft and prospect rankings, so have there been any changes?

On international signings, I have barely scratched the surface by looking at only the top 20. The biggest improvement on this front could be from creating a database of all signings to help with research. More websites could give more prospects a 20-80 grade. More information can lead only to better analysis. Finally, I can see the information being used to help evaluate major trades where several major league players and a half dozen prospects are involved. Instead of guessing at the projected value, we would have a basis for it.

Some people feel baseball analytics has hit a wall, with no new theories to be found. I disagree. I think valuable information can be found if people are willing to collect data. The prospect grades didn't just jump off the pages of the prospect annuals into a spreadsheet. Once data are collected, so much work can be done with them, like getting better ideas of players' future values. Some of those values are estimates, but as in any bit of research, so much more can be done.

References & Resources

- Craig Calcaterra, Hardball Talk, "The Dodgers Essentially Paid $2.75 Million for a Competitive Balance Draft Pick," *hardballtalk.nbcsports.com/2015/04/13/ the-dodgers-essentially-paid-2-75-million-for-a-competitive-balance-draft-pick*
- Victor Wang, *SABR By The Numbers Newsletter*, "How Much is a Top Prospect Worth?," *philbirnbaum.com/btn2007-08.pdf*
- Scott McKinney, Royals Review, "Success and Failure Rates of Top MLB Prospects," *royalsreview.com/2011/2/14/1992424/success-and-failure-rates-of-top-mlb-prospects*
- Neil Paine, FiveThirtyEight, "What to Expect From Baseball America's Top 100 Prospects," *fivethirtyeight.com/datalab/what-to-expect-from-baseball-americas-top-100-prospects*
- Andrew Ball, Beyond The Box Score, "2013 MLB Draft: How valuable are draft picks?," *beyondtheboxscore.com/2013/6/25/4457048/2013-mlb-draft-how-valuable-are-draft-picks*
- *The Baseball America Prospect Handbook*, 2012 through 2015 editions
- Robert Falkoff, MLB.com, "Notes: Duckworth Acquired," *mlb.mlb.com/content/ printer_friendly/mlb/y2006/m06/d11/c1500302.jsp*
- Kiley McDaniel, FanGraphs, "Signing July 2nd Players Has Gotten Even More Complicated," *fangraphs.com/blogs/signing-july-2nd-players-has-gotten-even-more-complicated*
- Kiley McDaniel, FanGraphs, "The FanGraphs Top 200 Prospect List," *fangraphs. com/blogs/the-fangraphs-top-200-prospect-list*

Combining Technologies to Measure Swing Development

by Bryan Cole & Dan Kopitzke

Across sports, consistent mechanics are the hallmark of the expert athlete. Basketball players spend hours in the gym to develop a consistent jump shooting form. Golfers hit buckets of balls to drive the ball the same way off the tee every time. And baseball scouts drool over prospects with "repeatable" deliveries and swings.

As hitters develop, their mechanics evolve over time into a swing that both shares many commonalities with other players and is unique to their own game. But tracking a player's progress on that journey to a consistent swing has always been tricky. Scouting and video analysis can give players a sense of how repeatable their mechanics are, but these are expensive, time-consuming, and limited to players at the highest level, whom we would expect to already have the most consistent mechanics.

Enter technology. Technological developments, including inertial bat sensors and camera-based ball tracking systems, should make it possible to develop a quantitative measure of consistency readily available to a wider range of players, with a wider range of abilities. This will allow young hitters to better measure their progress while also giving scouts and coaches a tool to judge prospective players.

In this article, we look for a way to quantify that relationship between consistency and hitter quality. We measured over 1,500 individual swings from 25 hitters, ranging in age from Little Leaguers to NCAA Division 1 players. We also collected different kinds of swings from each hitter, having each player hit off a tee and a pitching machine, with the goal of hitting first for power and later for contact.

The New Technologies

Two new technologies have made it easier to dig into the swing, immediately quantifying things coaches previously could only describe using video. Bat sensors are inertial measurement unit (IMU)-based systems that are attached to the knob of the bat using a flexible strap. For this study, we chose the SwingTracker system from Diamond Kinetics, which is based in Pittsburgh. The SwingTracker sensor contains an accelerometer—which is used to identify the bat-ball impact and track the direction of the swing—and a gyroscope to track the rotational velocity. Combined, these sensors are used to construct a three-dimensional model of the swing, describing the bat's speed and orientation from trigger to follow-through. The raw data are sent via

Bluetooth to a smartphone app, which reports 11 metrics that describe the swing, as listed in the table below.

Metrics Reported by Diamond Kinetics SwingTracker			
Speed Metrics	Power Metrics	Quickness Metrics	Control Metrics
Max barrel speed	Applied power	Trigger to impact	Approach angle
Speed efficiency	Impact momentum		Hand cast distance
Max hand speed	Maximum acceleration		Distance in zone
Forward bat speed			

These are combined into an overall swing score normalized based on the user's age and ability level. But a single sensor on the bat can only describe the bat path. To describe the path of the ball, we must use a different system. Major league teams use SportVision's HITf/x system (a camera-based system) and Trackman (a radar-based system) to track the direction and velocity of the batted ball.

We don't have access to those tools, unfortunately. So for this experiment, we used HitTrax—developed by InMotion Systems, based in Northborough, Mass.--a camera-based data collection and simulation system. Designed for use in indoor batting cages, the HitTrax system uses three near-infrared cameras to track both the incoming pitch and the batted ball, simulating the complete path of the batted ball based on its initial trajectory. The table below describes the pitch and batted ball metrics reported by HitTrax.

Metrics Reported by InMotion Systems HitTrax	
Batting Metrics	Pitching Metrics
Exit ball velocity	Pitch velocity
Hit distance	Pitch location
Horizontal launch angle	Late horizontal and vertical movement
Vertical launch angle	Percent strikes
Hit quality	Batted ball distribution
Batting average/slugging/OPS	Spray charts
Hard hit average	Batting average against
Batted ball distribution	
Spray charts	

By combining these technologies, we can characterize the swing in more detail than previously done. We then can begin to answer questions about how the swing evolves into something that is more or less universal, yet unique to each hitter's game. In this article, we will try to identify when a player starts to settle on one consistent swing rather than between wildly varying versions. We will also try to measure the similarity between different players' swings and when (if ever) they begin to converge.

Procedure

We measured the swings of 25 right-handed hitters, with ages ranging from 11 to 21, using both the SwingTracker and HitTrax systems. Details about each age group are provided in the table below. Within each age group, hitters used a common bat size and faced pitches of a common speed. All data collection was performed at the K-Zone Academy in Apex, N.C.

		Players In Study, By Age Group			
Age	Players	Swings	Bat Length	Bat Weight	Ending Pitch Speed
12U	10	597	31"	21 oz.	52 mph
14U	4	236	31"	28 oz.	54 mph
16U	4	225	32"	29 oz.	56 mph
18U	4	277	33"	30 oz.	58 mph
College	3	216	33"	30 oz.	60 mph

Note that 12U players used "big barrel" bats, which are 2.75" in diameter, as opposed to the standard 2.25".

Each batter took a total of 60 swings, equally divided between hitting off a tee and hitting off a pitching machine set up 45 feet from home plate. These two sets of swings were then further divided between hitting for power (i.e., trying to hit a home run to the pull field) and hitting for contact (i.e., trying to hit a line drive to center field). To control for the effects of fatigue, we randomly selected the order of the four groups of swings, so that some hitters hit for power off a tee first, while others hit for contact off a pitching machine. The pitching machine was adjusted to aim for the middle of the strike zone, as measured by the HitTrax system that tracked the incoming pitches.

In all, a total of 1,551 swings were recorded. Note that only those swings captured by both SwingTracker *and* HitTrax were included. If, for example, a player swung and missed at a pitch, HitTrax data were generated but SwingTracker did not record the swing. On the other hand, if a player fouled off a pitch so that it did not pass in front of the HitTrax optical cameras, SwingTracker data would be generated without the corresponding HitTrax data. Data were compiled with assistance from Diamond Kinetics and InMotion Systems, who sent me all metrics recorded for each player in a single, machine-readable file, and were aligned using the timestamps provided in the respective files.

Results

We will focus on max barrel speed (MBS), which is the highest velocity reported by the sensor during the swing. We note, however, that all reported metrics exhibit the same relationship. To start, let's look at the distribution of MBS by age when hitting line drives off a pitching machine, presented as a boxplot in Figure 1 below. Naturally, MBS tends to increase with age: the median (represented by the solid horizontal line in the middle of the boxplot) steadily increases from the youngest to the oldest group, as does the 99th percentile whisker on top of each box.

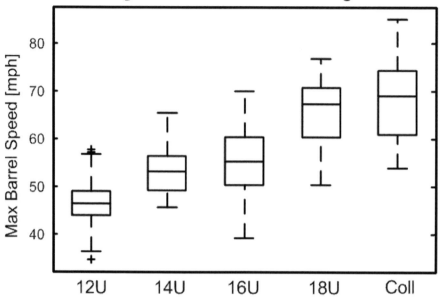

Figure 1: Distribution of max barrel speeds (MBS) observed while attempting to hit line drives off a pitching machine, broken down by age group.

What this graph does not show is any obvious relationship between age and consistency. In this context, we would expect more consistent swings to be grouped more closely together. But none of the distribution measures presented in this boxplot suggest any correlation with age. The solid boxes that represent the interquartile range all get wider, suggesting a broader (i.e., less consistent) distribution; the whiskers that represent the first to 99th percentile range also grow further apart as the subjects get older.

Figure 2 below gives a more detailed picture for the four hitters in our 14U group and the three hitters in the college age group. Here again, we see an increased spread in MBS values—that is, less consistency—as the average MBS increases. The effect only gets more dramatic if we compare the two age groups: By this measure, at least, the college hitters tend to be less consistent than even the hardest swinging 14-year-olds.

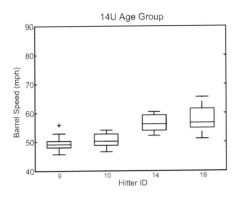
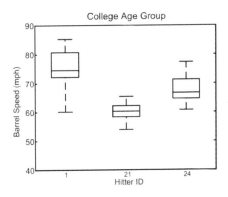

Figure 2: Comparison of max barrel speed (MBS) distributions observed while attempting to hit line drives off a pitching machine, broken down by hitter for the 14U and college age groups.

We noticed during data collection that the IMU sensor attached to the end of the bat tended to shift, especially during harder swings, which could affect the accuracy of those readings. Compare also Hitter 21 (the middle hitter in the college age group) and Hitters 14 and 16 (the rightmost hitters in the 14U age group). Although the median values for all three hitters are approximately equal (around 60 mph), the college hitter has a smaller interquartile range than the other two. So what if we looked only at those hitters with similar average MBS?

Figure 3 below shows the MBS distribution across all swing types for those hitters with median speeds around 60 mph. The boxplot colors correspond to the hitters' age group, so college hitters have gold boxes, 18U hitters have black, 16U blue, and 14U red. Again, there is no relationship between age and consistency: the 14U hitter (Hitter 16, second from the left) has one of the smallest ranges despite being the youngest (and presumably the least advanced) of the hitters.

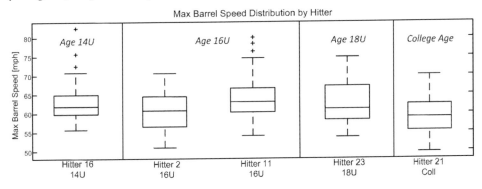

Figure 3: Distribution of max barrel speeds (MBS) observed across all swing sets, for those hitters whose average MBS was approximately closest to 60 mph.

The relationship holds at lower speeds as well. Figure 4 below presents the MBS distribution across all swing types for those hitters with median speeds around 50 mph. Most of the hitters in this group are 12U (represented by blue boxes), but the few 14U (red) and 16U (black) are indistinguishable by distribution alone. In fact, the 16U hitter (Hitter 12) has the widest spread of the whole group!

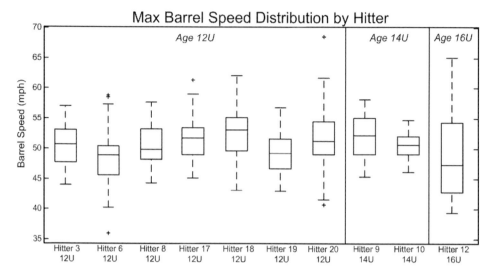

Figure 4: Distribution of max barrel speeds (MBS) observed across all swing sets, for those hitters whose average MBS was approximately closest to 50 mph.

Although the results of this qualitative investigation were not promising, we also tried a more rigorous approach. Trevor Stocking has done similar research in his role as baseball product manager for Zepp, which makes a competing bat sensor. In a recent interview, he said he had found the hypothesized relationship by counting the number of swings within 10 percent of the average MBS. This relationship may not show up on the graphs presented so far, since they dealt only with the spread of values and not necessarily with the distribution of values within a certain range.

But, as Figure 5 below shows, this normalization did not improve our outcomes. These graphs show the percentage of swings within five percent (on the left) and ten percent (on the right) of the average MBS across all swing types. Once again, we see the exact opposite of the expected relationship: as hitters mature, the percentage of swings within a given percentage of the mean value decreases.

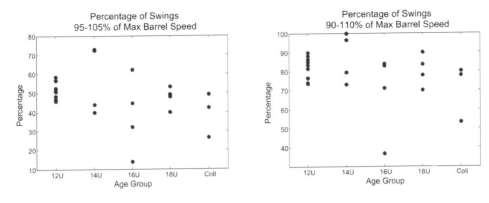

Figure 5: Scatter plot showing percentage of swings within five (left) and ten (right) percent of average MBS for each hitter, with hitters grouped by age.

Discussion and Future Work

Although it seems obvious hitters' swings become more advanced as they age, we found no evidence to support this hypothesis in our data set. Hitters in fact seemed to become less consistent with age, at least according to the collected data. More than anything else, this suggests issues with our methodology. We have already mentioned the tendency of the bat sensor to shift on the bat knob, especially during more violent swings. This will result in the axes inside the IMU becoming misaligned with the axes of the bat, and thus a misrepresentation in the energy experienced by the bat during the swing. Diamond Kinetics has created a thicker, less flexible strap that they recommend for older hitters, which may have led to more reliable results.

Beyond the physical limitations, one could also raise concerns about our sample size. It's difficult to draw sweeping conclusions about how hitters evolve based on 25 subjects, with only one data collection session for each. In addition to the (comparatively) small number of hitters tested, we had no truly objective measure of talent by which to measure our hitters.

We have used age throughout this article as a proxy for ability, under the assumption the older hitters in our study were better hitters than the younger ones. And while this may be true on aggregate over a larger sample of hitters, it is not necessarily the case that every 12U hitter is worse than every 14U hitter, and so on. One might have more success with a longitudinal study, testing the same hitters after a few months, to more directly compare players' growth.

Future studies might also focus on the swing path more directly, rather than metrics derived from it. The Diamond Kinetics software can produce a three-dimensional representation of the swing, tracking the position of the bat in space throughout the swing. Researchers at Stanford recently showed that the use of IMUs to track large impacts was prone to large artifacts. Their specific area of interest was the use of head-mounted accelerometers to identify the high-G impacts thought to cause concussions. However, these types of artifacts are analogous to the sensor shifting we saw during harder swings and thus may have adversely affected several of the metrics measured at or near impact (including MBS). Focusing on multi-dimensional correlations derived from the swing path can reduce the role of these artifacts, which only appear in the few samples around the bat-ball impact.

Despite these disappointing results, the combination of SwingTracker with HitTrax offers unique opportunities to explore the relationship between swing and batted-ball trajectory. Those familiar with the physics of baseball may recall the relationship between batted-ball exit velocity, incoming pitch speed, and swing speed discussed by Dr. Alan Nathan in last year's *THT Annual*:

$$v_{bb} = qv_p + (1+q)\, v_s$$

Here, v_{bb} is exit velocity, v_p is the pitch speed at impact, and v_s is swing speed at impact. The remaining term, q, is a constant referred to as the "collision efficiency," a measure of the percentage of energy transferred from the bat to the ball. As one might expect, this constant is dependent on where on the bat contact is made, with a maximum of 0.2 at the sweet spot.

By combining the swing speed reported by SwingTracker with the exit velocity and incoming pitch velocity reported by HitTrax, we can get a sense of the quality of contact a hitter is making. In other words, how often is the hitter squaring up the ball and hitting it with the sweet spot of the bat? In golf, the "smash factor" is the ratio of exit velocity to club speed; to create an analogous metric for baseball, we rewrite the above equation to account for the effect of pitch speed:

$$SF = v_{bb} + v_p / v_s + v_p$$

Note that SF, the smash factor, is equivalent to $1+q$ in the first equation. Like q, SF depends on where contact was made. For a wood bat (or a metal bat that meets the BBCOR standards), SF varies from a maximum value of around 1.2 at the sweet spot (six inches from the end of the bat) to a minimum value of 0.6 near the handle. The equations above suggest a linear relationship between exit velocity vbb and smash factor, which naturally translates to a similar relationship between batted ball distance and smash factor. Figure 6 below demonstrates that relationship for a constant pitch speed of 60 mph and constant swing speed of 75 mph, derived using the trajectory calculator available on Alan Nathan's website.

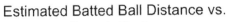

Estimated Batted Ball Distance vs. Smash Factor

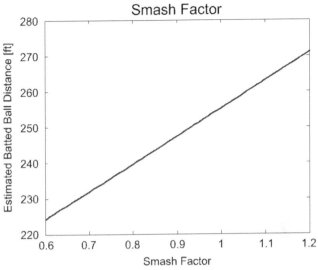

Figure 6: Relationship of exit velocity (v_{bb}) on smash factor (SF) for a given pitch speed (v_p, 60 mph) and swing speed (v, 75 mph).

This smash factor calculation could be used to infer where contact was made on the bat. One could imagine a "spray chart" report, allowing a hitter to track how many balls he or she hit with the sweet spot of the bat. Figure 7 below provides an example of one such report generated from one of the hitters in our database. The bat is divided into segments with similar smash factor; the segments are colored and labeled according to the percentage of balls hit with that smash factor. The data below comes from a hitter who plays for a Division I college program. An advanced hitter, this subject made good contact during our session, hitting over 80 percent of all balls at or very close to the sweet spot of the bat. One could imagine adding this type of metric to existing SwingTracker and HitTrax reports, providing insight beyond what either system offers on its own.

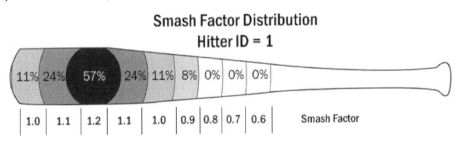

Figure 7: Illustration of smash factor (SF) report from one of the hitters in our database. Each colored strip represents the SF associated with that section of the bat, and the percentages represent the percentage of all batted balls that produced this SF.

References & Resources

- We would like to thank the many people who made this article possible: C.J. Handron, Jeff Schuldt, and Dr. Buddy Clark at Diamond Kinetics; Mike Donfrancesco and Tom Stepsis at HitTrax; Dr. Alan Nathan for his feedback; Ashley MacLure for designing the smash factor graphic; and everyone who took part in our study.

- Bryan Cole, Beyond the Box Score, "Diamond Kinetics' SwingTracker Released," *beyondtheboxscore.com/2014/12/9/7357287/diamond-kinetics-swingtracker-released*

- Sportvision, "HITf/x," *sportvision.com/baseball/hitfx%C2%AE*

- Rob Ristagno, SABR40, "An Introduction to TrackMan Baseball," *baseball.physics. illinois.edu/trackman/Rob%20Ristagno.pdf*

- Bryan Cole, TechGraphs, "HitTrax System Makes Batting Practice Perfect," *techgraphs.com/hittrax-system-makes-batting-practice-perfect*

- Bryan Cole, TechGraphs, "How David Ortiz Keeps Hitting Homers," *techgraphs. com/how-david-ortiz-keeps-hitting-homers*

- Lyndia Wu, Vaibhav Nangia et al, *Annals of Biomedical Engineering [e-pub]*, "In Vivo Evaluation of Wearable Head Injury Sensors," *researchgate.net/ publication/281284623_In_Vivo_Evaluation_of_Wearable_Head_Impact_Sensors*

- Alan M. Nathan, *The Hardball Times Baseball Annual 2015*, "Regulating the Performance of Baseball Bats," 2015.

- TrackMan, "What Is Smash Factor?" *blog.trackmangolf.com/smash-factor*

- Alan M. Nathan, The Physics of Baseball, "Trajectory Calculator," *baseball.physics. illinois.edu/trajectory-calculator.html*

Analyzing Catcher Pop Time

by Neil Weinberg

Stopwatches are ubiquitous in baseball. The idiosyncrasies of baseball men and women likely result in a subculture of stopwatch elitism. The location of the buttons. The weight. The material of which it's made. The quality and feel of the stopwatch matter because the stopwatch is tasked with measuring the fractions of seconds between success and failure.

The stopwatch generally has three primary functions in baseball: to measure a player's time from home to first, to record the time between the pitcher's first move and the pop of the catcher's glove, and to record the time it takes that catcher to get that ball down to second base. It is the third of those measurements that will be the focus of this article.

The time it takes a catcher to remove the ball from his glove and throw it so it reaches the glove of one of his middle infielders is commonly called "pop time," after the sound the ball makes when it collides with leather.

Measuring and judging catchers by their pop times has been part of the game for decades, as it is one of the cleanest ways to evaluate a catcher's ability to limit the running game. While there is certainly plenty of attention paid to statistics that measure a catcher's caught stealing rate, intuitively we know the pitcher plays a role in the overall success or failure of that effort, meaning caught stealing rate and its relatives are not really statistics solely designed to measure catchers.

This explains why we time pitchers to the plate, and it lines up with recent research from Max Weinstein and the stat team at Baseball Prospectus that suggests pitchers play a significant role in limiting the running game. Weinstein's work suggests the pitcher is the key actor, and Baseball Prospectus' work suggests the catcher is the key actor, but while they disagree on the exact amount of credit each deserves, both lines of research strongly imply you cannot simply use a catcher's caught stealing rate as a measure of his ability to prevent stolen bases.

The pitcher plays an important role, so the catcher can only do so much to catch would-be base stealers. The base runner travels a certain distance before the ball gets to the catcher, and that initial distance is the responsibility of the pitcher. If the runner is 50 percent of the way to second when the catcher gets the ball, the catcher has a better chance to throw him out than if the runner is 60 percent of the way there.

This makes pop time an attractive statistic for measuring catchers. The actual time it takes to get the ball from home to second is almost entirely independent of all other actors. It is an individual statistic. Certainly the batter could interfere, the middle infielders could receive the ball poorly, or the pitch could put the catcher in a bad throwing position, but in general, pop time is exclusively a measurement of the catcher and is independent of the outcome of the play.

The speed with which the catcher delivers the ball is a true measurement of the catcher's performance. It doesn't cover every aspect of catcher defense, but it is an important aspect, and it doesn't require a great deal of complicated analysis to understand. One aspect it misses is the accuracy of the throw, as an ankle-high throw can come in a bit slower than a head-high throw to the same overall effect. But in general, we can agree pop time is superior to caught stealing rate or even some type of statistic that measures caught stealing rate while controlling for the pitcher and other contextual factors.

Pop time gives you a precise measurement of how long it took the catcher to get the ball to second. If a catcher fires off an elite throw, we want to be able to credit him even if the pitcher took forever on that specific pitch. Even pitchers with good times to the plate occasionally will take their time, and we want to be able to credit catchers for how well they performed regardless of the circumstances of any one situation. Catchers who throw well help their teams to some degree, and statistics that shine light on good throwing catchers would be useful for understanding catcher defense, which remains a trickier business to measure than the other positions. Weinstein's work indicates we should care more about pitchers' times to the plate than catcher pop time if we care about stolen bases, but pop time remains an important way to evaluate the catcher's role in stolen base prevention.

While teams very likely track this data for their own players and upcoming opponents, we previously haven't had public, comprehensive data on catcher pop time. You can watch games with a stopwatch in hand, but you can't watch every game with a stopwatch in hand. However, thanks to MLB Advanced Media's Statcast system, which debuted in all 30 parks for 2015, we now have a comprehensive way to measure this essential aspect of the sport's most important defender.

To conduct the following analysis, MLBAM provided me with every recorded pop time from 2015. As with any new system, Statcast was not perfect in its rookie season, meaning this is not a complete list of every throw to second that took place in 2015. The data set has 1,784 throws to second base, which is short of the full number of throws. There were 3,085 attempted steals of second base in 2015, although some percentage of them did not draw a throw, meaning we have data for more than half of all throws. The Statcast team believes it is a representative sample from which we can draw meaningful conclusions.

I cannot guarantee the system tracked every throw perfectly and there are no errors or biases in the data. With a data set of this size, there are bound to be imperfections, but the MLBAM team felt confident in the sample, and I did not discover anything alarming while conducting the analysis.

The 1,784 pop times in the data set represent 94 different catchers, with the overall average pop time coming in at 1.975 seconds. The best single throw belonged to

Christian Bethancourt, who delivered the ball to second in 1.688 seconds during a Matt Kemp stolen base. The throw came in slightly to the left of second base, but even with an elite pop time and decent accuracy, Kemp was safe easily thanks to a good jump and slow time to the plate from Julio Teheran.

The worst throw in the data set took 2.635 seconds, courtesy of Nick Hundley. If you go back and watch it, the story checks out. Hundley scoops it out of the dirt moving to his right and winds up throwing from behind the left-handed batter. The throw sails directly into the back of Paul Goldschmidt as he slides in safely at second base.

The system doesn't register a pop time if the catcher fails to get the ball to second base for one reason or another, so really terrible throws and bobbles by the catcher create some bias here when talking about true talent. All this means is that we're talking about pop times for completed throws. If a catcher is known for dropping the ball on the transfer, we're not going to catch it with this evaluation method, but I can confirm the system will record pop times if the middle infielder doesn't glove it cleanly.

Here's a peek at the best and worst throws of 2015:

Best Individual Pop Times, 2015			
Rank	Catcher	Team	Pop Time
1	Christian Bethancourt	Braves	1.688
2	Salvador Perez	Royals	1.693
3	Matt Wieters	Orioles	1.702
4	J.T. Realmuto	Marlins	1.719
5	J.T. Realmuto	Marlins	1.727

Worst Individual Pop Times, 2015			
Rank	Catcher	Team	Pop Time
1,780	Stephen Vogt	Athletics	2.547
1,781	Hank Conger	Astros	2.553
1,782	Stephen Vogt	Athletics	2.600
1,783	Martin Maldonado	Brewers	2.632
1,784	Nick Hundley	Rockies	2.635

And here's a look at the best and worst average pop times of 2015, minimum 10 recorded pop times:

Best Average Pop Times, 2015				
Rank	Catcher	Team	Avg. Pop Time	# Throws
1	J.T. Realmuto	Marlins	1.867	29
2	Chris Stewart	Pirates	1.876	27
3	Christian Bethancourt	Braves	1.890	16
4	Austin Hedges	Padres	1.896	28
5	Martin Maldonado	Brewers	1.903	30

Worst Average Pop Times, 2015				
Rank	Catcher	Team	Avg. Pop Time	# Throws
54	Tyler Flowers	White Sox	2.066	29
55	Stephen Vogt	Athletics	2.072	22
56	Carlos Ruiz	Phillies	2.080	37
57	Brayan Pena	Reds	2.105	37
58	Hank Conger	Astros	2.141	24

The number of throws may seem a bit small, but keep in mind that the overall average number of throws was 19, and just three catchers made over 45 throws. Additionally, the distribution of all pop times is illuminating. While 1.975 is the average pop time, the right tail of the distribution is much longer than the left tail. This makes intuitive sense. There's some type of lower limit on how quickly a human being can throw to second, but the only thing creating an upper bound is that at some point the base runner is too close to the base to warrant a throw. You won't see any 4.500 pop times in the data set because the catcher would hold onto the ball at that point and not make a throw, but you would expect to see more especially slow pop times than especially fast ones for this reason.

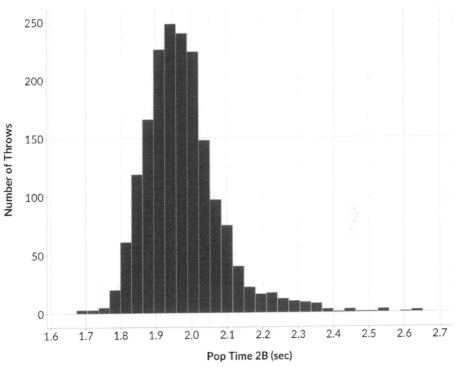

Catcher Pop Times Recorded by Statcast, 2015

Now that we have some sense of the overall nature of pop times, a particularly interesting question is how much each catcher's pop times vary. We know catchers are capable of 1.7 second and 2.6 second times, but are the good catchers routinely offering good times or is their performance distributed much like the entire league's? Let's start by looking at distribution of pop time standard deviations for catchers with at least ten pop times in the data set.

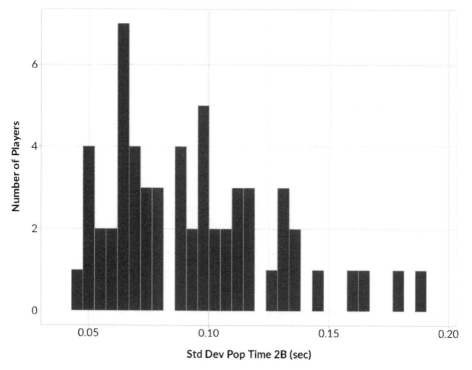

Catcher Pop Time Standard Deviations, 2015

You can see in the plot that most catchers have standard deviations between .05 and .15 seconds with the overall standard deviation sitting at .112. However, this distribution is much wider than the one for pop times themselves and is not normally distributed. Those differences may seem like small numbers, but the overall range between the best and worst throw is less than one second, so 0.1 seconds is relatively meaningful.

Another way to look at this is to plot the catchers' standard deviations against their averages. The previous graph is not terribly intuitive except that it allows you to get a sense of the overall potential range of deviations. But do those ranges mean anything? Are certain catchers more consistent? For example, would you prefer a cacher who averages 2.00 seconds with a very low variance or would you prefer a catcher with a 1.95 average with a wider variance?

The following is a graph that plots each catcher's (min. 10 pop times) average pop time and pop time standard deviation.

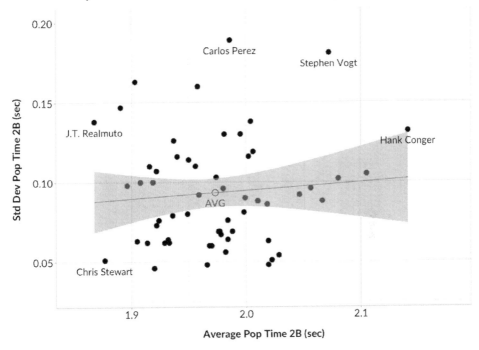

Pop Time Standard Deviation vs. Average Pop Time, 2015

Std Dev Pop Time 2B (sec)

Average Pop Time 2B (sec)

You can see from that plot there isn't a meaningful relationship between average pop time and pop time standard deviation. This doesn't mean there isn't an inherent skill in pop time consistency, simply that it isn't directly related to a catcher's overall average pop time. Catchers with good average pop times seems no more likely to be consistent throwers than catchers with bad average pop times.

Now that we have a sense of the average times and how much they vary within a season, we can turn our attention to the idea of a stabilization point. In general, how many throws do you need to see from a catcher in order to have a good sense of his ability?

To do this, we turn to split-half reliability, popularized in baseball research by Russell Carleton. The basic methodology is to divide a catcher's pop times in half and run correlations between the two samples. The "target" correlation coefficient is 0.7 because that is equivalent to an r-squared of 0.49, or a model that explains at least half of the variance. It is important to remember the idea of a stabilization point is a little misleading, as stabilization is a curve rather than a single point, but given this is an exploratory study with a limited sample, we will keep it relatively simple.

In order to create the samples, I used a random number generator to divide each catcher's observations in half and then took the average of each catcher's two samples and ran simple correlations. If we set the minimum number of pop times at 10 for inclusion in the sample, we are left with 58 catchers and achieve a correlation coefficient of 0.723. In other words, setting the minimum number of pop times per catcher at 10 is sufficient for this statistic to "stabilize." I also increased the cutoff point to 20 pop times and found a correlation coefficient of 0.845 with a sample size of 40.

It is important to recognize that most analyses of this kind rely on larger data sets and multiple seasons. A portion of one season might not be sufficient enough to give us a definitive answer to this question, but it does indicate that you only need a small number of pop times to get a sense of a catcher's true talent level. The "true" number might be higher or lower than 10, but it certainly appears as if average pop time is a statistic that becomes reliable very quickly. In general, it is more like fastball velocity or swing rate in terms of stabilization than BABIP or HR/FB%.

The public only got a small glimpse of Statcast during its inaugural season in 2015. Since the system was announced in 2014, baseball fans have salivated over the potential to measure a host of things we've never been able to track in a comprehensive way. It appeared Statcast would offer the most value in the realm of defense, providing much more accurate data than (video) scouts were previously able to offer. Additionally, batted-ball exit velocity was the most available bit of data in 2015 and became the number most associated with Statcast during its first year.

Yet from the very first moment I heard about MLBAM's plans for Statcast, catcher pop time was the data that most interested me. This is partly because I happen to find catcher defense very compelling, but it was also because pop time is something we have been anecdotally tracking for a very long time. Coaches and scouts carry stopwatches for a few reasons, but tracking how long it takes the pitcher to get the ball to the plate and the catcher to get the ball to second is a huge part of evaluating players and preparing for an opponent.

Pop time is also especially visible to the average fan. If you showed a half dozen throws to second to reasonably well-versed fans, they could separate the good from the bad. They might not be able to pin a number to each record, but they could identify the good times.

In other words, pop time is a widely accepted and understood way to measure catchers, but until this year we didn't really know a lot about it other than the anecdotal pieces of information that would come up on broadcasts or if you happened to have a scout's phone number.

Throwing to second and, more broadly, preventing stolen bases is just one part of a catcher's job on defense. Receiving and game-calling have a larger impact on the game, but preventing the other team from moving up on the bases is valuable. Previously, we've only been able to measure catchers by their results. Their raw caught stealing rate, or number of runners caught stealing, is tremendously unsatisfying because untangling the catcher's role in that event is very difficult.

Baseball Prospectus has built statistics relying on mixed models that control primarily for the pitcher and runner, but their approach is about the overall quality of the other parties rather than those parties' actual performance on that given play. If a pitcher who is normally 1.05 to the plate (a good time) takes 1.50 seconds on a particular delivery and a slow runner happens to get a great jump, would you consider that a tough assignment for the catcher or an easy one? Using the mixed-model approach, it would be an easy assignment, but in reality it would be quite difficult to nab the runner. Using pop time is beneficial because it allows us to measure what the catcher did on each play rather than relying on a modeling strategy to infer the share of the credit that is his. Weinstein's work might suggest catcher's are limited in how much they can influence the results, but even if that's true, pop times offer us a better tool for determining that impact.

Pop time is a very old stat, but it wasn't a stat most baseball fans could utilize prior to Statcast. As the system matures and the data become widely available, understanding catcher defense will get a little easier. There is a lot of ground left to cover, but the first year of Statcast pop time data provided us with a good set of baselines off which to work.

The average pop time is around 1.975 seconds with the very best throws coming in just under 1.7 seconds. We have a sense that consistency and average time are not related, and you don't need a large sample of pop times for a catcher to get a good handle on his ability. While we have to be cautious because we're only looking at the first slice of comprehensive pop time data, none of the results here push too hard on our expectations. It's always exciting to discover something totally new, but bringing evidence to the table that supports what we think we know is also important.

Pop time is a great example of a simple statistic that can provide a lot of information to teams, fans, and analysts alike. It can be measured from youth leagues all the way through the majors. While projecting major league success from minor league numbers is difficult for many reasons, pop time fits into a category of stats like pitch velocity in that it doesn't rely on the interaction of other players. We certainly don't have data on how pop time ages or translates from one level to another, but it's not unreasonable to think we could have that data in a few years and it will be useful once we do.

There's something very compelling about an old, simple stat that we can now harness because of a new, fancy technological infrastructure. As baseball decision making becomes more data driven, an important thing to remember is that the data we're collecting isn't any different from the data baseball men and women have been collecting for years. The difference between scouting reports from the 1980s and Statcast in 2015 is Statcast tracks raw information in a way that allows multiple people to observe and interpret it at any time. It removes the filter.

Scouts have been tracking pop times for years, but until recently they would track a small sample of pop times they were present to see, and their report would be all their team would be able to use to infer something about a catcher. Statcast isn't tracking different data, it's doing a better job tracking and logging the raw information, freeing the human analysts to focus more on determining what the information means.

Three decades ago, it would have been easy for a scout to spend time watching Christian Bethancourt make a few throws to second base. The scout likely would determine Bethancourt has an elite arm and would report back to his club he's not someone on which you'd like to run. In fact, it may have been such an assessment that got Bethancourt signed in the first place. The data tracked by Statcast will likely lead you to the same conclusion about Bethancourt, but there are many catchers for which it might be a bit more difficult to determine their abilities. Rather than relying on the slice of information the scout was able to see, Statcast provides you with everything.

The everything Statcast provides might not change the way we think about baseball conceptually, but it will afford us better data to make individual decisions, such as which catchers you can run on and which you can't.

References and Resources

- Special thanks to Matthew Gould and MLB Advanced Media for providing the data for this analysis.
- Russell Carleton, FanGraphs, "525,600 minutes: How do you measure a player in a year?," *fangraphs.com/blogs/525600-minutes-how-do-you-measure-a-player-in-a-year*
- Jonathan Judge, Harry Pavlidis, and Dan Turkenkopf, Baseball Prospectus, "Introducing Deserved Run Average (DRA)—And All Its Friends," *baseballprospectus.com/article.php?articleid=26195*
- Max Weinstein, Beyond The Box Score, "Who Deserves Credit For Throwing Out Base-Runners?," *beyondtheboxscore.com/2013/7/18/4522508/who-deserves-credit-for-throwing-out-base-runners*
- Max Weinstein, FanGraphs, "Exploring The Battery Effect," *fangraphs.com/blogs/exploring-the-battery-effect*
- Max Weinstein, FanGraphs, "2013's Top Batteries At Preventing The Running Game," *fangraphs.com/blogs/2013s-top-batteries-at-preventing-the-running-game*
- Max Weinstein, FanGraphs, "A Prelude To A Study: Caught Stealing Variables and Assigning Responsibility," *fangraphs.com/blogs/a-prelude-to-a-study-caught-stealing-variables-and-assigning-responsibility*
- Max Weinstein, FanGraphs, "The Overrated Value of Catchers' Throwing Arms," *fangraphs.com/blogs/the-overrated-value-of-catchers-throwing-arms*
- Max Weinstein, The Hardball Times, "How Do We Assign Credit for Catching Base-Stealers?," *hardballtimes.com/how-do-we-assign-credit-for-catching-base-stealers*

Is Bigger Better? Player Performance Examined by Height

by Shane Tourtellotte

Baseball is a big man's game. At least that's the collective assumption fans, commentators, and baseball people themselves share.

When 5-foot-6 Jose Altuve comes to bat, the collective reaction borders on amusement. How droll that he's playing the game. How scrappy of him to carve out a niche for himself on the Astros. How witty that we measure distances in Altuves in his honor.

When 6-foot-6 Giancarlo Stanton comes to bat, nobody's making jokes about the weather up there or proposing he should be playing in the NBA instead. That's because the prevalent mood is fear: fear from the spectators in the last row of the bleachers that they're about to get brained by his latest home run. This, naturally, has a lot to do with the divergent attitudes.

How accurately do these attitudes reflect reality? Does the chase for the heaviest slugging and the hottest fastballs tilt the playing field toward the tallest ballplayers? I looked at players' performances broken down by height to find some answers.

One caveat is necessary. This exercise depends entirely upon the height listings issued by the teams. There's no practical way to get these measurements independently. Teams sometimes fudge the numbers, though probably less often with height than with weight, to make their players appear more physically impressive. We can only accept that this practice happens, and conclusions drawn from the figures will not be as precise as we would like.

I can state my conviction about added inches so categorically because I have good evidence within the data that it is being done often in one particular set of cases. That, however, will come later.

The Position Players

The differences between a baseball player in the field and one on the mound are clear, and so is the necessity to consider them separately. I will begin with the position players.

I gathered statistics for everyone who collected at least one plate appearance between the 2010 and 2014 seasons. Heights ranged from 66 inches (5-foot-6) to 80 inches (6-foot-8), with the most common heights being between 72 and 74 inches (note: I will generally render measurements in inches rather than feet-and-inches in the rest of this piece). The following table shows the number of player seasons and plate appearances accumulated by players at each height.

Player Seasons & PAs by Height, 2010-2014					
Ht. (In.)	Player-Yrs.	PA	Ht. (In.)	Player-Yrs.	IP
80	2	301	72	540	139,239
79	1	8	71	359	97,624
78	30	9,748	70	295	82,533
77	86	37,125	69	169	37,561
76	212	63,584	68	43	8,857
75	333	109,065	67	8	3,179
74	533	164,273	66	9	3,952
73	557	143,526			

The top two heights plainly have samples too small to be of use. The lowest two heights have limited reliability also, the majority of their data produced by one player apiece. (Jose Altuve at 66 inches and Jimmy Rollins at 67 inches.) I will exclude the top two heights henceforth and will offer conclusions regarding the bottom two with grains of salt.

A common stereotype about player size is that big players will slug their way to good offensive numbers, but their bulk will hinder them defensively and when running the bases. Contrarily, little players will struggle at the plate but be terrors on the basepaths and death to batted balls on defense.

The numbers back up those impressions. I looked at FanGraphs' values for offensive, defensive, and baserunning runs against average for the range of heights, prorated to 600 plate appearances.

Off/Def/Baserunning Runs by Height, 2010-14

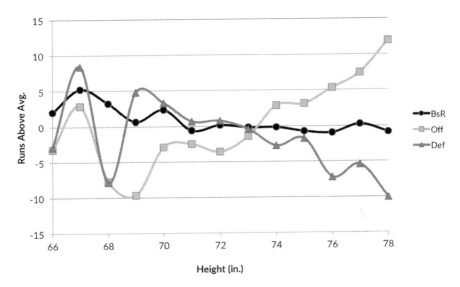

The trends do not track perfectly, but they are clear in all cases. The most notable blips happen at the far ends of the height bell curve: baserunning at 77 inches, offense at 67 inches, and defense at 68 inches.

It's also generally true, though not as often, that the magnitude of separation from zero is greater for offense than for the other two components, even put together. In short, that means offense dominates the overall production, which means we can expect the taller players to do better.

To answer that question, we'll switch to FanGraphs' Wins Above Replacement (WAR) statistic. There are two useful ways to measure performance above replacement, and the first is pro-rated to plate appearances. I'll use 600 as the number again, approximating a fairly full season of play.

The second is to count WAR per player season, no matter how long or short. This favors heights at which players more often play the full year due to being starters and/or avoiding injuries. This generally means favoring the greater heights: taller players, especially past six feet, get more PA per year. From 206 plate appearances per year at 68 inches, the rate reaches a peak of 432 at 77 inches. (There is another peak at 66-67 inches, comparable to that at 77 inches, but I must note again the sample size.)

I had a difficult time deciding which is a better measure of performance. Getting more playing time reflects confidence in your ability to produce, and avoiding injury is, if not wholly a skill, certainly an important part of what you bring to the team. However, if there is a prejudice, unconscious or otherwise, about how big a "real" ballplayer is that helps determine playing time, this makes for a self-fulfilling prophecy in the data.

With trepidation, I have chosen to risk information overload and use both. If you have a strong preference, you can read that set of data and disregard the other.

Either method shows the overall trend is upward, peaking at 77 or 78 inches—with one notable but problematic exception.

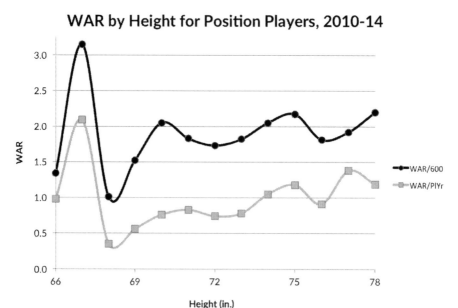

Defying the trend is that great spike at 67 inches. However, that's not a group of players, but one. Five of the eight player seasons and all but 180 of the 3,179 plate appearances at 67 inches belong to Rollins. His fine performance in the decline phase of his career overwhelms minimal contributions by Caleb Gindl and Terrance Gore to beat all other heights single-handedly. (Had the study included 2015, when Rollins's play fell off a cliff, matters would be different.)

Discounting Rollins' solo efforts, the peak is at 78 inches by plate appearances and 77 inches by seasons. Here we may question the influence of another single player: Giancarlo Stanton. Did his spotty injury record raise the per-PA rate at 78 inches while depressing the per-year rate?

Yes and no. He has nearly 30 percent of the PAs at 78 inches but with just one-sixth of the player seasons. The combined PA advantage and season disadvantage for 78-inch position players comes to 0.47 WAR. Without Stanton, the margin drops to 0.09 WAR. This is not nearly a rigorous measure, comparing apples and oranges as it does. Still, it suggests Stanton may be responsible for most of the separation, but not all.

(Going by raw numbers rather than the margin between 78 and 77 inches, of course Stanton raised both marks for 78-inch players, substantially. Claiming, though, that 78-inchers aren't as good when you remove their best player is pure tautology.)

There is also an argument for 75 inches being the ideal height. This group almost matches 78 inches in both WAR rates, and a sample size over 11 times larger makes its values more reliable. There are also historical reasons for leaning toward this value, which I will show later.

Even beyond this, saying the best position players are 77 to 78 inches tall is incomplete, because there are different types of position players. A right fielder, shortstop, and catcher have different physical requirements for their positions, with perhaps different physiologies being best suited to them. The right fielder may well be the most productive player, but you still need a shortstop and a catcher.

I broke down the numbers for catchers, and for infielders minus first basemen, since those are akin to outfielders in the offensive and defensive expectations laid upon them. Playing 40 percent of one's games at catcher, or 50 percent of one's games at second base, third base, and shortstop combined, was necessary for inclusion in these subsets.

Catchers have a fairly narrow band of heights in our survey years, from 70 to 77 inches, plus one low-PA year at 69. Their WAR numbers show no decisive pattern, except for a spike at 77 inches that seems to confirm taller is universally better. This high point comes from a mere two players: Matt Wieters and Joe Mauer. I won't commit myself on what is a marginal sample size (nine seasons and 4,403 PA) without something stronger. I will show how much stronger later on.

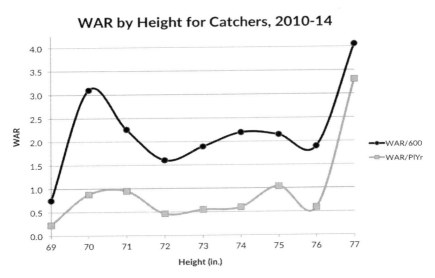

WAR by Height for Catchers, 2010-14

Infielders ranged from 66 to 76 inches, with a lone low-PA year at 77. The WAR trend here is much clearer: the taller the better, excluding an odd hiccup at 73 inches.

We see the Rollins spike at 67 inches, and the neighboring high mark at 66 inches is from a sample just over a tenth the size of the one for the peak at 75 inches.

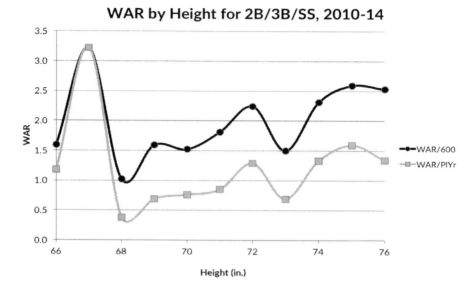

So while catchers and infielders have height ceilings short of their outfield and first base teammates, this does not mean they are best at modest heights. Definitely for infielders and perhaps for catchers, the best height is at or near the top height.

But surely there's one thing shorter players can do better, right? (Apart from the defense and baserunning, as mentioned before.) With a smaller strike zone due to their smaller stature, they ought to be better at drawing walks, oughtn't they?

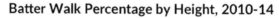
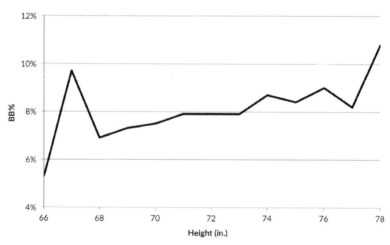

It turns out they aren't. Apart from Rollins, the rise in walk rate with height is rather steady. The reason is clear: home run rates rise very strongly with height, and pitchers will work around power hitters. The power component overwhelms the shrinking-zone component, and walks rise with height. With strikeouts, power and strike zone work in tandem, and K rates soar as players get taller.

The Pitchers

I used the same timeframe, 2010 to 2014, for pitchers, counting everyone who faced at least one batter during those seasons. Their heights ranged higher than the position players', from 66 to 83 inches, with the peak between 74 and 76 inches.

Pitcher Seasons and IP by Height, 2010-2014					
Ht. (In.)	Pitcher-Yrs.	IP	Ht. (In.)	Pitcher-Yrs.	IP
83	4	184.0	74	560	33,088.1
82	5	326.1	73	397	24,769.1
81	8	453.1	72	393	24,460.1
80	27	2,097.2	71	157	8,313.2
79	78	7,799.0	70	76	4,227.0
78	152	12,479.0	69	14	447.0
77	314	22,777.0	68	5	141.0
76	505	32,783.2	67	5	255.2
75	628	42,820.0	66	2	32.2

Again, extreme heights have low sample sizes, so I'm excluding the top two and bottom three from analysis. The next most extreme heights, 69 and 81 inches, are borderline cases, so we should treat any conclusions from them with strong caution.

A common stereotype is that bigger pitchers are faster pitchers, and thus likelier to pile up huge strikeout totals. The data tell a different story. Very tall pitchers have some of the lowest K/9 IP rates, and the best numbers come between 69 and 71 inches.

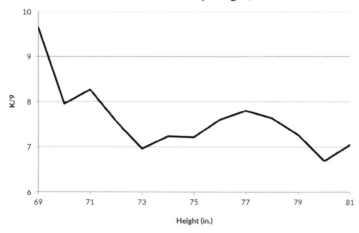

Pitcher K/9 Rate by Height, 2010-14

I also examined walk and home run rates, which had somewhat similar patterns. They showed signs of improvements as height rose, notably in the 78-80 inch range, but the overall trends were not as clear.

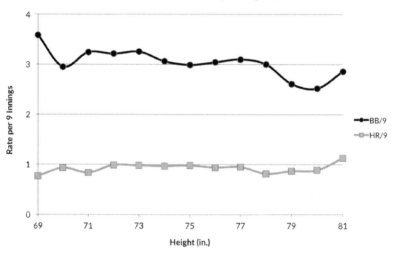

Pitcher BB & HR Rates by Height, 2010-14

For measuring overall performance, again there are two viable methods. One is WAR, pro-rated to a 180-inning season. The other is an ERA-scaled measure, preferably FIP or xFIP. The former is better at capturing in-season value, while the latter is better for projection. I will work with both of them, along with the WAR metric.

Using WAR, we get a decidedly Bactrian shape. The first hump tops out at 71 inches, drops to a nadir at 73 inches, then rises to a taller hump at 78 and especially 79 inches before fading again.

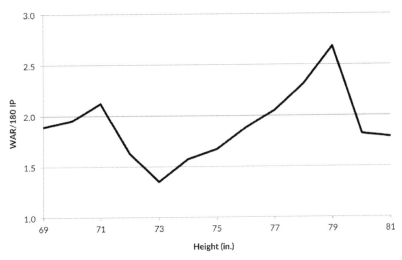

Pitcher WAR/180 IP by Height, 2010-14

The sight of that peak below six feet may gladden the shorter among us, but there is a slightly disappointing explanation. Innings pitched per season follows a pretty steady upward line, from 32 innings a year at 69 inches up to 100 IP/yr at 79 inches. The early peak is mainly for relievers, while the later and taller peak covers the, in absolute terms, more valuable starters.

The FIP family of metrics produces a dromedary shape. Using an average of FIP and xFIP, the graph produces high (bad) numbers in the middle with valleys (good) at both ends. This time, the excellence at 78-79 inches is matched at 70-71 inches, and exceeded in the small sample of 69-inchers.

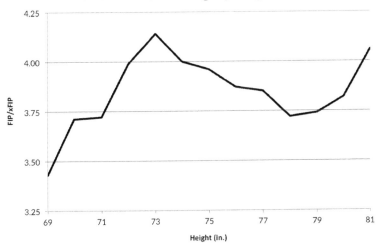

Pitcher FIP/xFIP Avg. by Height, 2010-14

Overall, the best height for a pitcher is 78 or 79 inches, presuming you're looking for a starter who by nature can produce more value per season. For relievers, there is a secondary or even an equal island of primacy an inch or two below six feet.

This is for all pitchers, of course. Breaking down the set between lefties and righties could reveal further shadings, so I divided the data into those buckets. (Here I am thankful I stopped gathering stats at 2014, before switch-pitcher Pat Venditte made his debut in the majors. I am glad he finally made it, but he's going to be a pain in the neck to conscientious sabermetricians.)

Right-handed pitchers are the taller group, going 68 to 83 inches while the lefties range from 66 to 81. Despite this, lefties are more successful, producing 1.89 WAR per 180 innings against 1.73 for the righties. This shows up prominently with the upper peak of 78 and 79 inches. Lefties beat righties by 3.28 to 2.06 WAR at 78 inches, and 3.46 to 2.51 WAR at 79 inches.

There is another big difference between the lefties and righties, which I will defer momentarily so I raise it in the context of another unusual effect emerging from the data: the spike in height-faking.

The Rollover Effect

As I observed earlier, teams have an incentive to portray their players as taller than they are, to give a greater impression of physical might and presumably playing ability. Indeed, the players themselves probably participate in the fudging, or even initiate it, to appear better specimens to scouts, fans, and teams that might be calling them up to the bigs. This game-playing would originate early in players' careers, even as early as high school.

This practice happens even more often at a particular threshold. We all know the phenomenon of retail pricing where an item is listed at, say, $3.99 rather than $4. We react to the difference as though it were much greater than one cent, and our higher likeliness to buy easily offsets the lost per-item revenue.

A similar thing happens in baseball at the border between 5-foot-11 and 6-foot. There are more players listed at 72 inches, and fewer at 71 inches, than we would expect from a smooth distribution of heights. The difference is great enough, for position players but especially for pitchers, that we can dismiss chance unevenness as the cause.

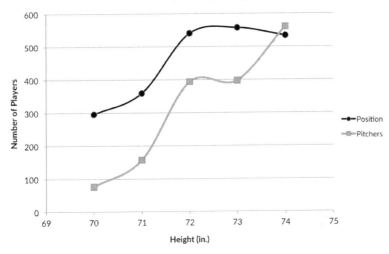

Number of Players by Height, 2010-14

The gain of rolling over into 6-foot territory is so much greater than that of the other one-inch increments that players and teams (it's tough to say who's more responsible) are much more likely to fudge that last inch. The margin over regular fudging, by eyeball test, amounts to about eight position players each year and around a dozen pitchers.

Those little lies don't do the players boosted by them any on-field favors. Players listed at 71 inches outperform those listed at 72 inches. The margin is 1.83 to 1.73 WAR/600 PA for position players, and a wide 2.12 to 1.63 WAR/180 IP for pitchers.

An explanatory hypothesis suggests itself: less proficient 71-inchers are more likely to fake that extra inch to look better, while stronger players are more content to do without such artificial confidence. However, the overall upward WAR trend is not strong or constant enough to require an explanation other than chance. However much I like my neat little theory, it remains unverified and may not be verifiable.

There is irony to pitchers who add that 72nd inch, at least some of them. It has long been a truism in scouting circles that short pitchers can succeed if they are left-handers, far more so than if they are right-handed. "Little lefties" can thus get away with being 5-foot-something, though the splits show, if anything, a stronger tendency for lefties than righties to bump themselves from 71 inches to 72.

The greater irony, though, is that the assumption is fallacious. Comparing lefty/righty values from 69 inches (the first height where both have pitchers) up to 72 inches shows the righties outperforming the lefties in WAR, ERA, FIP, and xFIP. The samples are admittedly small at lower heights, but they rise to over 10,000 innings apiece at 72 inches.

L/R Splits for Little Pitchers, 2010-2014							
Lefties				Righties			
Ht. (In.)	WAR/180	FIP	xFIP	Ht. (In.)	WAR/180	FIP	xFIP
69	-0.70	4.30	4.07	69	2.23	3.24	3.42
70	1.71	3.91	3.90	70	2.06	3.65	3.60
71	1.39	3.92	3.94	71	2.13	3.53	3.64
72	1.48	4.16	4.14	72	1.73	3.89	3.87

This disparity happens despite lefties' superior overall WAR. Neither can this be attributed to little lefties being consigned more to the bullpen as presumed inferiors. From 68 to 72 inches, 23.8 percent of lefties' games were starts against 19.4 percent for righties.

The scouting stereotype is backwards. It is the little righties who have been a secret source of pitching ability. Indeed, at every height from 72 inches downward, they perform at or better than the total average WAR for all right-handed pitchers, while the little lefties all have underperformed.

There could be a selection bias underlying this, with more marginal short lefties getting through the sieve due to the stereotype while short righties have to be even better to be given a chance. This just recasts, rather than changing, the conclusion that baseball people ought to re-evaluate their thinking about little righties.

Years Gone By

The range of heights in baseball isn't what it used to be. Due to improved health and nutrition, among other causes, average adult heights in America (and many other countries) have been rising for several generations. This carries over into the pool of ballplayers.

I was curious to see not only how the height range has changed but how optimum heights for ballplayers have changed. I therefore surveyed two ranges of years in the past. One was 1962 to 1964, half a century before the "current" one, and the other was 1937 to 1939, 75 years before. Again, I analyzed position players and pitchers separately, though I didn't drill down to lefty/righty pitcher splits.

To provide a feel for the changes, I will list not only mean heights in each era but ranges also. I found heights for the 10th, 50th, and 90th percentiles of players in each category.

Heights by Era, Average and Range		
Group	Mean Ht. (in.)	90/50/10 Pctile.
2010-2014 Pos.	72.75	76/73/70
1962-1964 Pos.	72.23	75/72/70
1937-1939 Pos.	71.06	73/71/69
2010-2014 Pit.	74.53	78/75/72
1962-1964 Pit.	73.34	76/73/71
1937-1939 Pit.	72.63	75/73/71

Mean height has risen close to two inches for both categories since the 1930s, though with different patterns. Position players made most of their gains in the first quarter-century, while pitchers rose at a steadier pace. The percentile ranges show widening spreads, from four inches in the '30s to six inches today. Shorter players are not being abandoned so much as very tall players are entering in rising numbers.

For position players of both past eras, patterns in batting, defense, and baserunning track with those of today. Taller players were more prolific batters but produced less in the field and on the basepaths. Similar to today, the boost in batting more than compensated for the losses in other areas.

In the 1962-64 stretch, there isn't quite a progression upward as height rises. It's more of an uneven plateau for the middle heights, with a drop at the bottom and a rise at the top.

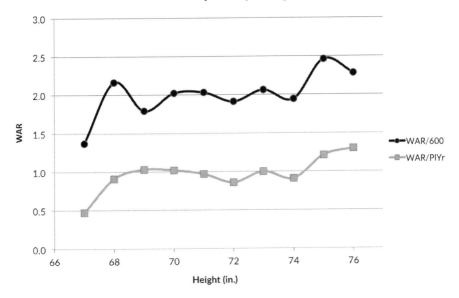

WAR for Pos. Players by Height, 1962-64

The peaks in the 75-76 inch range are bettered by extremes not included in the chart, at 65 and 79 inches. These are small samples of roughly 2,000 PA, though, smaller than the already thin ones at 67 and 68 inches, and around a tenth the size of that for 76 inches. Also, there is not one dominant player like Rollins creating the by-PA spike at 68 inches, though good seasons by half-time catcher Smoky Burgess help.

The 1937-39 era follows a similar pattern. There are spikes at lower heights, then a plateau, then the true quality arrives near the top. And does it ever.

WAR for Pos. Players by Height, 1937-39

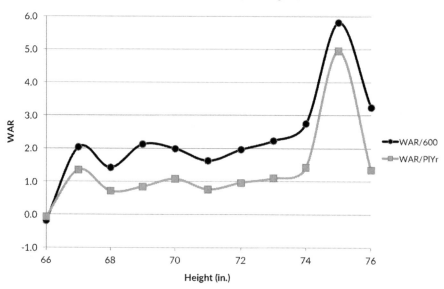

There are just eight player seasons and 4,090 PA at 75 inches, but those tremendous numbers are no fluke. One of the four players in that category you have never heard of: Len Gabrielson of the Phillies. The other seven seasons and 4,070 PA were produced by more familiar names: Hank Greenberg, Ernie Lombardi, and Ted Williams.

Adapting an observation by the title character of Ian Fleming's *Goldfinger*: once (Rollins) is chance, twice (Wieters/Mauer) is coincidence, three times is a pattern. Given those three players' historic excellence, plus the strength of the numbers just above and below 75 inches, I consider the peak to be genuine, if perhaps a bit exaggerated in sheer magnitude.

That pattern helps fill in the larger pattern. It's strange given the rise in heights over the generations, but a valid argument can be made that the ideal height for a baseball player in the field has remained 75 inches for the last three-quarters of a century. Cases can be made for 76 inches in the '60s and 77 or 78 inches today,

---

but the crown has not yet decisively been taken from the likes of Schnozz and the Splinter.

Things are more fluid with peaks at the other end. While 67 inches saw good numbers in the '30s and 68 inches did in the '60s, today the likely height for a good short player is 70 inches (unless it's Rollins). There remains a place for the short player on the field, but the value of "short" is changing, and the place itself is shrinking.

Results for old-time pitchers are clearer in favor of tall players. In 1962-64, FIP hovers in the 3.60 to 3.80 range from 70 to 75 inches, then takes a clear downward turn until it's 3.20 for 78 inches. WAR measures are kinder to the shorter pitchers, notably at 70 inches, but the peak again is at 78.

WAR for Pitchers by Height, 1962-64

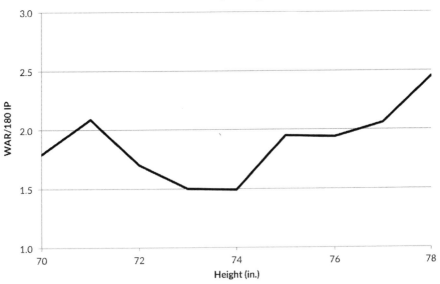

Note: There were higher peaks both above the maximum and as low as 66 inches, but with unreliably small IP samples.

For 1937 to 1939, with 69 to 77 inches the range of trustworthy samples, the matter almost needs no analysis. The only heights with a FIP below 4.00 or a WAR/180 above 2.0 are 75 and 77 inches, with 77 clearly best by both measures. (The sample size at 77 is a little marginal at 1,082 IP.) Also, pitchers at 75 and 77 inches were starters in a higher percentage of their games than any other height, at 71 and 69 percent compared to 61 percent. This in an age when the bullpen was almost entirely for the second-rate arms.

In all three eras, pitchers have been better as they've gotten taller, though in the two later times there has been a secondary peak at 71 inches. There is some indication of the trend breaking down with extremely tall pitchers of today, but since my survey missed the entire career of 6-foot-10 Randy Johnson, this could be illusory.

Wrapping Up

Taller baseball players are, on average and with just a mild tendency toward diminishing returns, better baseball players, and they have been for generations. This is clearest for position players and largely independent of their place on the diamond. The offensive boost that comes with a taller frame outweighs the attendant defensive and baserunning liabilities.

The case is more complicated for pitchers, with handedness and starting or relieving playing substantial roles. From the sweet spots in evidence over the last five years, the ideal setup would be having big lefties as starters and little righties in the bullpen.

This can, naturally, be taken too far. While Rollins may be an outlier, he is also a caution. It is treacherous to judge individuals by collective tendencies. Dismissing a prospect for his non-optimal stature is quicker and easier than actually scouting him, but that doesn't make it better.

However, in a business combing through thousands of candidates to fill hundreds of minor-league roster spots each year, there will be economies of scale. Scouts and GMs will cast nets for the big fish. So we should probably appreciate guys like Jose Altuve and Jimmy Rollins, who bucked some long odds to reach the majors and prosper.

Fewer jokes wouldn't hurt, either.

Reference and Resources

- Baseball-Reference provided the sortable height data; FanGraphs provided the performance statistics. Both were indispensable.
- I credit my knowledge of the "little lefty" phenomenon to Kevin Kerrane's *Dollar Sign on the Muscle*, partly for the actual information and largely because the reprint of this excellent book deserves a plug.

The Effectiveness of Full vs. Partial Shifts

by Joe Rosales & Scott Spratt

The escalation of the use of defensive shifts throughout baseball has garnered a lot of attention over the last few years. For every team in the majors, it is no longer a question of *if* they shift, but *how much*. And by "how much," we are really asking two things: How often do they shift, and how extremely do they shift? While there sometimes can be a tendency to discuss defensive shifts in terms of "The Shift," as if it were a singularly defined alignment, in practice, defensive shifting involves a wide spectrum of infield alignments.

The defensive shift was first popularized for its use against Ted Williams. He was not the first player against whom opposing managers ever decided to stack one side of the field with infielders, but prior to the explosion of shifts of the last few years, he was the most famous historical example of a player who elicited such a strategy on a regular basis. Most of the time we associate a traditional shift as one where three infielders are positioned to the right field side of second base against a left-handed hitter. However, as you can see from the image below, there actually were instances even back in 1946 when opposing teams were even more unorthodox than that. In this instance, with Ted Williams in the midst of the last season in which a hitter batted over .400, the Cleveland Indians put all four of their infielders on the right field side of second base in an attempt to slow Williams down any way they could.

Because Williams was so inextricably associated with defensive shifts when we began collecting data on them at Baseball Info Solutions (BIS), we classify shifts according to two primary groupings: Full Ted Williams Shifts and Partial Ted Williams Shifts.

Full shifts represent instances when a team deploys three infielders or more to one side of second base. An example of the Baltimore Orioles using this alignment against David Ortiz is shown below.

Partial shifts are instances when a team still positions two infielders to either side of second base, but at least two of those infielders are playing at a significant distance away from what would be considered the typical starting spot for their position. A common example of this is when a shortstop will play almost all the way up the middle with the third baseman moving over into the hole between second and third against a left-handed hitter, as can be seen in this image of the Oakland Athletics aligning themselves against Prince Fielder.

Generally speaking, we have found both of these forms of shifts help teams save runs defensively. However, when we take a closer look at each type of shift, we find full shifts are significantly more effective at saving runs than partial shifts.

Full vs. Partial Shifts: Frequency of Use

BIS has been tracking shift usage since 2010. The table below shows the breakdown of full shifts and partial shifts on all balls in play through the 2015 season.

Shift Usage on All Balls In Play by Season, 2010-2015				
Season	Total Shifts	Full Shifts	Partial Shifts	Full Shift Pct
2010	2,464	1,502	962	61%
2011	2,357	1,389	968	59%
2012	4,577	3,170	1,407	69%
2013	8,180	3,254	4,926	40%
2014	13,298	8,354	4,944	63%
2015	17,738	11,524	6,214	65%

As shift usage has grown, some interesting trends have developed. In 2010 and 2011, teams were in a pretty established groove of shifting against certain left-handed, pull-heavy power-hitters, using about a 60/40 split between full and partial shifts. Beginning in the 2012 season, shift totals just about doubled, with the increase in full shift usage outpacing the increase in partial shift usage. In 2013, shifts almost doubled again, but this time partial shift usage tripled while full shift usage held steady, reversing the split between full and partial shifts to be 40/60 in favor of partials. However, in 2014, the proportions switched back, with full shifts again becoming the more popular choice, and that trend has held constant through 2015.

There are various factors that could have contributed to the unusual spike in partial shifts in 2013 that are beyond the scope of this particular study. One of those factors might be the expansion of shift usage to include right-handed hitters and non-power lefties. Another factor almost certainly would have to be the changing philosophies on shifting within certain organizations. For example, in 2013, 27 of the 30 major league teams increased their use of the shift from what they had done in 2012. Of those 27 teams, 11 of them actually *decreased* the number of full shifts they used compared to the year prior.

One other possible factor for that spike in partial shifts in 2013—particularly as it relates to full shifts becoming the predominant tactic again in 2014—may be that some teams began to realize how much more effective full shifts are than partial shifts. This is the specific point we want to examine a little more deeply here.

Full vs. Partial Shifts: Batting Average on Ground Balls and Short Line Drives

We all have seen how effective shifts can be. A ball gets hit into the hole that would normally be a hit but ends up being easily corralled by an infielder. A screaming line drive is hit to right field, but it ends up being caught by the second baseman positioned well into the outfield grass. It can be infuriating for a hitter that makes solid contact to see hits taken away from him that other batters would not.

Of course, shifts also can work against a defensive team. By shifting its infielders toward the pull side of the infield, teams leave themselves larger holes on the opposite field side where they are susceptible to giving up a hit. That is the calculated risk inherent in shifting. However, not every team calculates that risk in the same way. That is why we see teams deploy such a wide variety of defensive alignments. Some teams favor full shifts while others favor partial shifts. Different hitters have different pull tendencies, which can dictate how extremely teams decide to shift them, but there are even certain hitters who get different treatments from different teams in terms of the use of full and partial shifts against them.

One way to look at how effective the different types of shifts are is to look at the Batting Average on Ground Balls and Short Line Drives (BAGSL)—we like to pronounce this acronym like the word "bagels"—that batters achieve against them. Because infield shifts primarily impact ground balls and short line drives, those are the ball-in-play types we are going to focus on.

The table below shows the league-wide BAGSL allowed for each of the last six seasons on full shifts, partial shifts, and situations when the defense was not aligned in a shift.

League-wide BAGSL, 2010-2015			
Season	Full Shifts	Partial Shifts	No Shift
2010	.203	.239	.252
2011	.202	.212	.259
2012	.199	.287	.254
2013	.189	.260	.262
2014	.210	.270	.266
2015	.208	.267	.263
Total	.205	.263	.259

However, the hitters that are heavily shifted are a different group of players from the ones that never get shifted. A disproportionate number of full shifts are going to be used against the most pull-heavy hitters, meaning that there is a selection bias that could be clouding the comparison of the numbers in the table above.

In order to address this issue, our approach was to calculate a weighted average. We started by looking at all hitters that have seen each of the three types of alignments: full shifts, partial shifts, and no shifts. We then prorated each player's performance against each of the three alignments to a common number of at-bats. In this case, we chose to use the minimum number of at-bats that a player had in any one alignment as that common number.

Here's an example. Let's say that Player X has 70 at-bats and 10 hits in full shifts, 20 at-bats and six hits in partial shifts, and 10 at-bats and four hits with no shift. The minimum number of at-bats that he has seen in any one alignment is 10, so we would prorate his results in each alignment to that number of at-bats. That means his numbers would become 10 at-bats and 1.42 hits in full shifts, 10 at-bats and three hits in partial shifts, and 10 at-bats and four hits with no shift.

By taking this approach, we ensure that the performance by players who see an extreme number of one alignment or another doesn't overly influence the overall results. Once we do this for every hitter, we total everything up across all hitters:

Weighted BAGSL, 2010-2015			
Season	Full Shifts	Partial Shifts	No Shift
2010	.187	.273	.225
2011	.210	.230	.254
2012	.203	.286	.246
2013	.189	.251	.271
2014	.233	.268	.260
2015	.211	.267	.258
Total	.212	.265	.258

These numbers fluctuate a bit from year to year, as all batting average-type statistics do, because of the variance involved with balls in play. However, the trend is pretty definitive. Across the majors, full shifts resulted in a lower BAGSL than partial shifts and no shifts in every season. Furthermore, more often than not, partial shifts actually resulted in a *higher* BAGSL than when teams did not use a shift at all.

We can also look at how much more effective full shifts have been than partial shifts among individual teams by comparing the BAGSL allowed on shifts by the teams that use the highest percentage of full shifts (as a frequency of all the shifts they deploy) to the teams that use the lowest percentage of full shifts. For instance, the table below lists the five teams that used the highest percentage of full shifts in 2015 and their BAGSL against on all shifted grounders and short liners (full and partial).

BAGSL Allowed on Shifts, Top 5 Full Shifting Teams, 2015		
Team	Full Shift Pct	BAGSL on Shifts
Astros	87%	.210
Rays	84%	.238
Orioles	82%	.205
Padres	79%	.170
Diamondbacks	76%	.216

Now compare that to the five teams that used the lowest percentage of full shifts in 2015.

BAGSL Allowed on Shifts, Bottom 5 Full Shifting Teams, 2015		
Team	Full Shift Pct	BAGSL on Shifts
Cardinals	26%	.282
Marlins	32%	.307
Nationals	36%	.257
Cubs	36%	.215
Mets	37%	.243

There is not a perfect linear trend between the percentage of full shifts used and the BAGSL allowed on shifts because in a single season sample there is a high degree of variance on the outcome of balls in play. However, this example still serves to illustrate that teams that use more full shifts than partial shifts generally prevent more hits than teams that use more partial shifts than full shifts.

As to the point made earlier that partial shifts actually result in a higher BAGSL allowed than when teams do not shift at all, that is not to say those partial shifts have not been effective. Generally speaking, teams are saving runs with their partial shifts. However, as we will see next, those partial shifts are not saving very many runs, and they certainly are not saving anywhere near the number of runs as full shifts are.

Full vs. Partial Shifts: Run Saving Effectiveness

Another way to compare the effectiveness of full shifts versus partial shifts is to look at how many runs teams save through the use of each. Since 2003, BIS has been calculating data on Defensive Runs Saved (DRS) for all major league players. DRS uses the likelihood of a given play being made based on its trajectory and how hard it was hit to determine how much positive or negative credit a player should receive for making or not making that play. These positive and negative play values are then converted into run values.

Using a similar system, we also calculate Shift Runs Saved. For Shift Runs Saved, we treat the entire infield as a single unit, and we compare how many plays a team does and does not make on ground balls and short line drives while in a shifted alignment to how many plays it would have been expected to make overall, shift or no shift. Then we convert those values to runs.

The following table shows the yearly breakdown of full shifts versus partial shifts—the proportions of full shifts versus partial shifts on grounders and short liners generally mirrors those proportions on all balls in play—as well as the total estimated runs saved by those shifts and the runs saved per 100 shifts.

Full & Partial Shift Runs Saved on Ground Balls & Short Line Drives, 2010-2015							
		Full Shifts			Partial Shifts		
Season	Shifts	Total Runs Saved	Runs Saved/100	Shifts	Total Runs Saved	Runs Saved/100
2010	684	31	4.6	343	5	1.5
2011	669	25	3.7	371	17	4.6
2012	1,523	74	4.9	747	1	0.1
2013	1,536	94	6.1	2,383	41	1.7
2014	3,958	189	4.8	2,655	7	0.3
2015	5,621	259	4.6	3,348	8	0.2
Total	13,991	672	4.8	9,847	79	0.8

The difference in run saving effectiveness between full and partial shifts is very striking. Besides a brief spike in 2011, the partial shift has not been nearly as effective as the full shift. Even in 2013, when there were 55 percent more partial shifts than full shifts used on grounders and short liners, full shifts still saved more runs than partial shifts by a ratio of greater than two-to-one overall. Across the last five seasons, the full shift has averaged 4.8 runs saved per 100 shifts, whereas the partial shift has only averaged 0.8 runs saved.

Full vs. Partial Shifts: Right-Handed Batters

As was alluded to earlier, the fluctuation in full shift and partial shift usage from year to year is somewhat related to the approach that teams have taken to shifting against right-handed hitters. Because the first baseman does not have the same freedom to move away from the line as a third baseman does when facing a lefty, there are times when certain teams have been reluctant to commit three infielders to the left side of the infield against righties.

First, here is the breakdown of full and partial shifts against right-handed batters on all balls in play over the last six years.

Shift Usage Against RHB on All Balls In Play by Season, 2010-2015				
Season	Total Shifts	Full Shifts	Partial Shifts	Full Shift Pct
2010	40	9	31	23%
2011	84	29	55	35%
2012	787	528	259	67%
2013	1,731	591	1,140	34%
2014	3,671	2,157	1,514	59%
2015	4,142	2,664	1,478	64%

Starting in 2012, the trends in shift usage against right-handed hitters have followed the same general trends in shift usage against all hitters, albeit with a slightly lower percentage of full shifts used. However, the difference in effectiveness of those shifts has been even more stark against righties than the offensive population as a whole.

Full and Partial Shift Runs Saved on Ground Balls and Short Line Drives Against Right-Handed Batters, 2010-2015				
Season	Shifts	Total Runs Saved	Shifts	Total Runs Saved
2010	4	1	18	-3
2011	22	3	39	-1
2012	275	16	150	-2
2013	279	20	568	11
2014	1,024	34	842	-11
2015	1,334	31	787	2

Overall, partial shifts have actually *cost* teams runs against right-handed hitters. The one year partial shifts actually had a somewhat substantial positive impact, 2013, was the year the use of partial shifts outpaced the use of full shifts. With proportionally fewer of the more effective full shifts included in the baseline of plays for that year, even that positive may be a bit misleading.

Conclusion

With partial shifts, the shortstop for left-handed hitters or the second baseman for right-handed hitters is often positioned up the middle, but to the non-pull side of the second base bag. This can be an inefficient place to position that infielder for two reasons.

First, when batters hit the ball up the middle, they still hit it to the pull side of second base more often than they hit it to the opposite field side of second base. Of all ground balls and short line drives hit to within five degrees of the second base bag by all hitters that have been shifted at least 200 times in the last six years, those players hit the ball to the pull side of the bag about 57 percent of the time. Therefore, if a team is going to play an infielder in the middle of the field, it would generally make sense to at least position him on the pull side of second base.

Second, balls hit up the middle can potentially be fielded by the pitcher, meaning that when they are aligned in a partial shift, the defense is providing somewhat overlapping coverage of one region of the infield, while leaving other areas exposed. Depending on the specific tendencies of the hitter involved, this could suggest a team should either have that infielder play closer to his typical starting location or move him completely over to the pull side of the infield. Given that the team deems it necessary to shift against that hitter in the first place, more often than not it probably makes more sense to do the latter.

A team's infield alignment always will depend to some degree on the game situation—which runners are on which bases, how many outs there are, what the count is, etc.—and different hitters have different tendencies. Therefore, partial shifts always will have a role to play in defensive tactics. However, while more study needs to be done on the particular ways in which the partial shift is being beaten in order to better understand why its value is so limited, the overall takeaway here is that teams should commit to using full shifts as much as possible to maximize the value they get out of their defensive shifting.

You Can't Identify DIPS Beaters

by Jonah Pemstein

This past August, I gave a presentation at Saber Seminar, an annual baseball conference in Boston, regarding "DIPS Beaters." DIPS Beaters, of course, are pitchers who can *beat their DIPS*—their defense-independent pitching statistics, metrics such as strikeout and walk rates—and consistently perform better than those DIPS would suggest.

My question: Do those guys exist? Are there actually pitchers out there who have the ability to outperform their DIPS, or is every pitcher who appears to be doing so just getting lucky? After all, in a sample of pitchers as large as all the ones pitching in the majors, we're bound to have some outliers, guys with extremely low batting averages on balls in play (BABIP) just due to chance.

My exact methodology in answering that question will be explained a bit more later, but essentially, it involved finding the number of outliers and determining whether that was more or less than would be expected. As it turns out, there are *many* more outliers than one would expect from a truly random distribution, indicating that some of those outliers really do have the ability to suppress hits on balls in play and beat their DIPS. Further proving that point was the fact that the outliers I found, by and large, maintained their excellent defense-dependent numbers in the next season.

So, DIPS Beaters exist. That much is almost certain, and probably shouldn't be surprising. But now the question becomes this: How do we identify these guys? How do we tell which are getting lucky and which are actually talented in this regard? Can we predict which pitchers who are currently not beating their DIPS will begin to do so in the near future? How do we find out *what allows these pitchers to beat their DIPS*? Do they throw harder, have better command, have "heavier" groundball-inducing pitches, throw breaking balls with more break?

It's not easy, that's for sure. There's a reason this piece is titled as it is. Take, for example, the matter of "late break." In talking with people at Saber Seminar after I gave the talk, I heard many people suggest some sort of measurement of late break be tested as a proxy for DIPS beating. That, intuitively, makes a lot sense. When a pitch breaks later rather than sooner, the batter has less time to react to the change in flight pattern and often can react only after he has committed to swinging. This would lead to more weak contact, since the batter is either swinging when he doesn't want to or misjudges where the pitch is going to cross the plate.

I tried to find a way to quantify late break because that made a lot of sense to me. I didn't know how to do that, because deriving the flight pattern of a pitch from limited points of PITCHf/x data is very hard, so I looked online for some help. Instead of a way that might help me, I found, rather, an article by Alan Nathan declaring late break to be more or less a myth. Essentially, the proportion of break that has already occurred just depends on the amount of time the ball has been in the air and how much total break there will be. The bulk of the movement for *every* pitch occurs once the pitch is most of the way to the plate. So a pitch that doesn't break a lot will not have much discernable movement until the batter has committed to swinging or not, whereas a pitch that does break a lot will have plenty of discernable movement from very shortly after it's released.

That means the simple magnitude of break from the PITCHf/x data should be enough to tell us if the pitch breaks late. Magnitude of break, however, has almost no relation with DIPS beating. The difference in average break for every pitch that PITCHf/x classifies is no different for the DIPS beaters than it is for the non-DIPS beaters. So the theory of late break, what seems like one of the most intuitive hypotheses for why some pitchers can beat their DIPS, is likely misleading.

And take the idea of command. Command seems like it's probably a good proxy for DIPS beating as well. If a pitcher can paint the corners well and keep the ball away from the places where hitters can do damage, he will more likely induce weak contact. But not only is command nearly impossible to quantify, the limited methods we *do* have to quantify it publicly don't correlate to DIPS beating at all. I wrote an article several months ago called, "Batted Balls: It's All About Location, Location, Location," in which I tried to come up with an expected wOBABIP (weighted on-base average on balls in play, including home runs) for pitchers based on where they threw their pitches. Expected wOBABIP, however, had effectively zero relation to either current or future wOBABIP. And as you'll see later, there are no differences at all in the general areas where DIPS beaters and non-DIPS beaters throw their pitches.

There really aren't many departments where we can conclusively say the DIPS beaters and non-DIPS beaters perform differently. There's also nothing that's a red alert, a proverbial flashing sign signaling "THIS PERSON IS A DIPS BEATER." So we'll try, and we'll come to some helpful conclusions, but don't expect a great revelation at the end.

Methodology

Before we get to the meat of this research, it's important to cover the methodology. I took every pitcher-season from 2009 to 2015 with a minimum of 30 balls in play (a sample size of 3,879) and used their overall wOBABIP, the standard deviation of all their wOBABIP values, and the number of balls in play they allowed. Using these numbers, I calculated a p-value. P-values, generally speaking, represent the probability a statistic is as different from the sample average as it is just due to chance; in our situation, they represent the probability a player's wOBABIP is as low as it is just due to chance. So a pitcher with an extremely low wOBABIP will have an extremely low p-value, since the more extreme the statistic the less likely it was caused by random variation. This method of finding p-values is known as hypothesis testing.

Why use wOBABIP instead of BABIP? BABIP is a useful stat, but it doesn't tell the whole story. It shares batting average's problem of treating all hits equally, which they are obviously not—a single is different from a double, which is different from a triple. It also doesn't include home runs. By using wOBABIP, however, we have a much better idea of how much damage the pitcher's balls in play did, and we can streamline our stats more by not having to use both BABIP and HR/FB percentage. (Some notes on wOBABIP: the year-to-year correlation for pitchers is no higher or lower than that of BABIP, and the league average typically hovers between .355 and .365. It was .366 in 2015.)

The sample of pitchers was split into two categories, "DIPS Beater" and "Non-DIPS Beater." DIPS Beaters were defined as pitchers with a p-value under 0.01, meaning that the probability their wOBABIP was so low due to chance was under one percent. Obviously, the DIPS Beater ("DB") category was much smaller than the Non-DIPS Beater ("NDB") category; only 5.31 percent of pitchers fell into the DB group. However, that is still far more than we would expect in a normal distribution. If the distribution of wOBABIP was truly normal, one percent of pitchers would have a p-value under 0.01. So while it's likely that some of the pitchers in the DIPS Beater group really did have low wOBABIPs because of luck, the sheer (relative) quantity of pitchers in that group indicates that there have to be some who are actually talented at keeping their wOBABIPs low.

After splitting up the pitchers, I looked for differences between the two groups. This, I hoped, would highlight differences inherent in the pitchers themselves (righty/lefty, starter/reliever, etc.), differences in their results (grounders/fly balls, low/high contact, etc.), and differences in their pitches (lots/little spin, more/less velocity, etc.), all of which should give us clues as to what makes DIPS beaters unique.

But before going over those differences, we need to take a look at the year-to-year ability of DIPS beaters to maintain good defense-dependent stats. This is crucial. If the DIPS beaters show little or no ability to keep their wOBABIP low the year after they beat their DIPS, we can throw this whole analysis out the window since it would seem likely this is really just luck. On the other hand, if the DIPS beaters display a continued tendency to post low wOBABIPs, that is an extremely strong piece of evidence in favor of DIPS beaters actually existing.

So let's take a look at a boxplot of the DIPS Beaters' wOBABIP compared to the Non-DIPS Beaters' wOBABIP in the year of the DIPS Beaters beating their DIPS to establish the baseline difference.

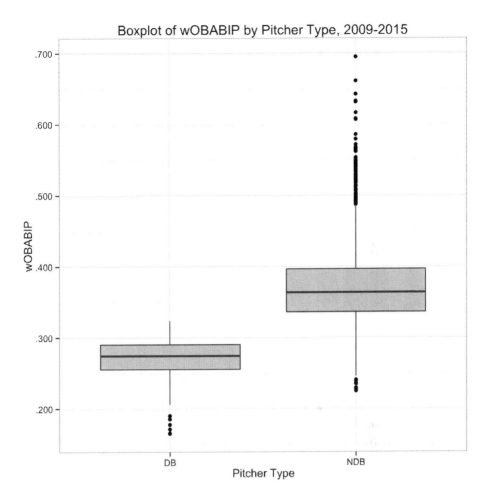

Boxplot of wOBABIP by Pitcher Type, 2009-2015

There's a pretty substantial difference here, which is obviously to be expected. Not every single DIPS Beater has a lower wOBABIP than every Non-DIPS Beater, since the cutoff includes the number of balls in play allowed, and there are some pitchers who didn't have enough balls in play to declare them DIPS Beaters despite a very low wOBABIP.

So then what does this difference look like the next year? Do the pitchers who were DIPS Beaters continue to have a low wOBABIP, and those who weren't continue to have a normal or high one?

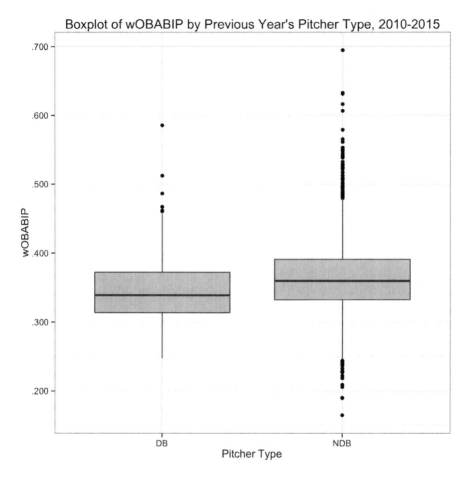

Uh oh. Not entirely convincing. This is obviously a much smaller difference, although the DIPS Beaters from the previous year still do come out on top. (Or bottom, depending on which way you look at it; either way, their wOBABIPs are generally lower.)

But once again, hypothesis tests come to the rescue. When we perform a test for a difference between two means, we get a p-value of 0.000007, meaning that there is roughly a 0.0007 percent chance this difference is random chance, and a 99.9993 percent chance there is a real difference between these two groups. I think that's enough evidence to say this is a repeatable skill pitchers can control.

Now that we've done this check, let's move on to what separates the two groups.

What Makes DIPS Beaters Unique?

Don't forget, just because DIPS Beaters display a tendency to do something more or less often than Non-DIPS Beaters doesn't mean all DIPS Beaters are that way. For example, you'll see DIPS Beaters tend to have higher strikeout rates, but Chris Young has had a BABIP under .240 each of the past two years while having a strikeout rate under 16.5 percent in each of those years as well. The tendency is exactly that, a tendency. It's never a hard and fast rule.

Part 1: Inherent Differences

As I mentioned earlier, we're looking for differences inherent in the pitchers themselves, differences in their results, and differences in their pitches. First, we'll cover the inherent differences part, since that is the simplest.

				Inherent Differences			
Type	Pitchers	Righty	Age	Height (in.)	Weight (lb.)	American%	Starter
DB	206	76.2%	28.08	74.56	213.2	59.7%	30.6%
NDB	3,673	71.7%	28.09	74.60	214.0	59.5%	39.5%

Note: Starters are pitchers with more innings as a starter than as a reliever; American = born in the U.S.

I've bolded what are really the only notable differences: righties vs. lefties and starters vs. relievers. While 76.2 percent of the DIPS Beaters are righties, only 71.7 percent of the Non-DIPS Beaters are. This is a little deceiving, though. When we perform a hypothesis test on the difference between these two proportions, we get a p-value of 0.161, which means there is a 16 percent chance this difference is just due to random variation in the data. That is nobody's definition of a significant difference. While I do suspect it's likely being righty has *some* effect on DIPS beating, I don't think this is enough to say it's a major factor.

On the other hand, the starter-reliever difference is much more significant, with a p-value of 0.010. It appears, then, that being a reliever makes it more likely to be a DIPS Beater. This is probably because these pitchers usually face each batter only once a game, so the hitters can't adjust to them as well and make good contact the next time up. This is the concept of the times-through-the-order penalty: Pitchers perform worse after already having facing a batter in a game. And, to support this, relievers overall tend to have slightly lower wOBABIPs than starters do (in 2015, it was a nine-point difference—.360 for relievers to .369 for starters).

Nothing else in that table really matters. Average age is almost exactly the same between the two groups, as are height and weight. I even checked if DIPS Beaters tended to be American more or less often than Non-DIPS Beaters. These results all indicate that age, size, and country of birth (which *could* influence development, although I'll concede that was a reach) have zero correlation to DIPS beating.

Our conclusion from this evaluation: Relievers, and maybe righties, are more likely to be DIPS Beaters.

Part 2: Differences in Results

Now on to the differences in the pitcher's results. We'll split this up into two tables, because there are lots of things to cover here. The first is batted-ball distribution:

				Differences in Batted-Ball Distribution				
Type	GB%	FB%	LD%	IFFB%	PU%	BIA%	LD/BIA%	BIP%
DB	**48.40%**	33.50%	18.10%	10.30%	3.70%	51.60%	36.40%	69.10%
NDB	**43.70%**	36.20%	20.10%	9.50%	3.60%	56.30%	36.40%	71.20%

Note: BIA% = FB%+LD%; IFFB% = infield fly balls per fly ball; PU% = pop ups
per batted ball = IFFB%*FB%; BIP% = balls in play per batter faced

The biggest difference that jumps out here is that DIPS Beaters tend to keep balls on the ground a lot more than Non-DIPS Beaters. This is evidenced by a groundball rate 4.7 percentage points higher on average (a difference that comes with a p-value of—ready?—0.0000000011, indicating there is an effectively zero chance this difference is random). So obviously, the DIPS Beaters have a much lower proportion of their balls in play hit into the air, which means both a lower flyball rate and a lower line-drive rate. The line-drive rate by itself, however, is only lower for DIPS Beaters because they allow so many fewer balls in the air—the LD/BIA percentage is the same for both groups. So DIPS Beaters don't appear to have any special ability to limit line drives.

The DIPS Beaters only barely have a higher PU percentage than the Non-DIPS Beaters, but since they allow fewer balls in the air their IFFB percentage is a good deal higher, with a p-value of 0.016. However, no pitcher has ever demonstrated an ability to keep their IFFB percentage high—when a pitcher gets lucky with their IFFB percentage, they just get lucky with their wOBABIP as well. IFFB percentage is not a factor to look at to predict or gauge true DIPS Beating. The DIPS Beaters also keep the ball out of play more than the Non-DIPS Beaters, as evidenced by the lower ball in play (BIP) percentage, but the difference there is minimal as well.

Our conclusion from batted balls: More grounders means more DIPS Beating.

On to strikeouts, walks, and plate discipline stats:

			Differences in Strikeouts, Walks, and Plate Discipline Stats			
Type	K%	BB%	Contact%	Swing%	SwStr%	Zone%
DB	**21.60%**	8.40%	**76.40%**	46.40%	**10.30%**	48.90%
NDB	**19.10%**	8.80%	**78.40%**	45.90%	**9.30%**	49.30%

Note: SwStr% = swinging strikes per pitch = swing%*(1-contact%); Zone% = percentage of pitches in the strike zone

The biggest difference here comes from strikeout rate. The DIPS Beaters strike out many more guys than the Non-DIPS Beaters do; the p-value there is 0.000000034, so, again, essentially zero. Contact rate, which is closely related to K rate, also has a relatively big difference, and by extension so does swinging-strike rate.

Walk rate is lower for the DIPS Beaters, but the difference, while not negligible, is not particularly significant: the p-value is 0.08, which is low but not low enough. As with Righty percentage in the first table, I think there is really a difference here, but a) we can't be sure and b) the difference is probably small if it does exist.

Zone rate is obviously closely related to walks, just as contact rate is with strike-outs, and we see more or less the same thing here: some difference, but not enough to make any conclusions. I also did look at more refined metrics such as O-Swing percentage (swings at pitches outside the zone divided by pitches outside the zone) and Z-Contact percentage (number of pitches on which contact was made on pitches inside the zone divided by swings on pitches inside the zone) but found nothing that wasn't captured with these stats. Lastly, swing rate isn't much different between the two groups.

Our conclusion here: Less contact and more strikeouts (which are fairly similar things) correlate with DIPS beating.

Part 3: Differences in How they Pitch

The final way in which DIPS Beaters and Non-DIPS Beaters might differ is in how they throw their pitches. This, too, we'll split up into a few subsections, and we'll look first at *where* they throw their pitches.

Differences in Where Pitches are Thrown						
Type	MM%	High%	Low%	Inside%	Outside%	Edge%
DB	6.00%	27.10%	43.40%	29.00%	50.90%	9.60%
NDB	6.20%	27.50%	42.80%	29.00%	50.70%	9.60%

Note: MM = middle-middle, pitches dead in the middle of the strike zone; edge = pitches on the edge of the strike zone; all others include both pitches inside and outside the strike zone.

I'm not going to spend too much time on this because the *only* stat here with a p-value even remotely significant is middle-middle rate, which, interestingly, has a p-value of 0.009 despite the seemingly tiny difference between the two groups. But even if the DIPS Beaters absolutely and certainly have a lower middle-middle rate than Non-DIPS Beaters, the gap isn't big enough to warrant worrying about.

Differences in Pitches Thrown							
Type	Fastballs	Change-ups	Curveballs	Sliders	Sinkers	Cutters	Splitters
DB	99.50%	52.40%	49.50%	75.20%	52.90%	21.80%	6.30%
NDB	99.90%	63.70%	52.60%	75.30%	50.70%	20.20%	5.70%

Note: To qualify here, pitchers had to throw their fastballs and sinkers at least 10 percent of the time, and their change-ups, curveballs, sliders, cutters and splitters five percent of the time, as classified by PITCHf/x.

I know, the percentages here don't add up to 100. Don't read it that way. Read it like this—"99.5 percent of DIPS Beaters throw a fastball at least 10 percent of the time." For the most part, the two groups are similar again. The one exception is change-ups: DIPS Beaters are *much* less likely to have a change-up in their arsenal, with a p-value of 0.001. That's especially interesting because of this table:

Average wOBABIP by Pitch Type, 2015		
Pitch type	wOBABIP	BABIP
Fastball	0.374	0.299
Sinker	0.357	0.310
Slider	0.350	0.289
Curveball	0.352	0.290
Cutter	0.343	0.282
Change-up	0.342	0.279
Splitter	0.341	0.276

Change-ups have one of the lowest wOBABIPs and one of the lowest BABIPs out of any pitch, second only to splitters in both cases. There must be something sequencing-related there, and if not I have no explanation for why fewer DIPS Beaters throw change-ups. But fact is fact: DIPS Beaters throw change-ups less often than Non-DIPS Beaters.

There's also spin, break, velocity, and all manner of things related to the pitches themselves and how they come out of the pitcher's hand. I'm not going to bore you with all those details, because none of them are different between DIPS Beaters and Non-DIPS Beaters...except for curveball spin. I don't know what it is about curveball spin, but among pitchers who do throw curveballs, the average DIPS Beater had a curveball with a mean RPM of 1,358.5, whereas the average Non-DIPS Beater had a curveball with a mean RPM of 1,231.4. The p-value is 0.0004. (For context, the average curveball thrown in 2015 had a spin rate of 1,305 RPM.)

To summarize all the differences we found, DIPS Beaters:

- More often are right-handed
- More often are relievers
- Have a higher ground ball percentage
- Have a higher strikeout percentage
- Have a higher swinging strike percentage
- Have more curveball spin
- Have a lower contact percentage
- Throw change-ups less often

And to summarize them in table format:

Summary of Important Differences								
Type	Righty	Starter	GB%	K%	SwStr%	CB rpm	Contact%	Change-up
DB	76.2%	30.6%	48.4%	21.6%	10.3%	1,358.5	76.40%	52.40%
NDB	71.7%	39.5%	43.7%	19.1%	9.3%	1,231.4	78.40%	63.70%

Note: CB rpm = Curveball spin (rpm), change-up = throws change-up

The Final Step: Identifying the DIPS Beaters From their Other Stats

Great! We've established there are certain things DIPS Beaters tend to do differently from Non-DIPS Beaters, which is an exciting step. But it doesn't take us very far. We need a quantitative way to set the two groups apart using their other stats, the ones we just went over.

The first method that jumps to mind is generalized linear models. Broadly speaking, GLMs are regression methods intended for models where the response variable (the dependent variable) has a distribution other than a normal distribution. This includes a binary distribution, as in our case. Our response variable, DIPS Beater/ Non-DIPS Beater, is a binary, yes-no variable. The final output is the probability, between zero and one, the pitcher is a DIPS Beater. In this scenario, GLMs are a much better option than ordinary least squares regression, as OLS regression doesn't account for scenarios where the response variable is binary.

Running a generalized linear model using the eight stats in the table above, however, yields very weak results. There's no r-squared (r^2) for GLMs, but there are several ways to calculate a pseudo-r^2, a rough indicator of how well the model fits the data. One such pseudo-r^2 is called Tjur's r^2. The way it works in our situation is this: Take all the DIPS Beaters and find the average likelihood they're a DIPS Beater according the model, then take all the Non-DIPS Beaters and find the average likelihood they're a DIPS Beater according to the model, then find the difference between those values. The average likelihood for the DIPS Beaters was 0.09—already not very good. The average likelihood for the Non-DIPS Beaters was 0.051, which is barely any lower. Tjur's r^2 comes out to 0.039, and while the scale isn't quite the same as it is for traditional r^2 (Tjur's r^2 is typically much lower), that is still extremely low. So while the model does work somewhat, it is extremely ineffective in identifying DIPS Beaters.

GLMs clearly aren't the answer here. Then what is? Normal regression certainly isn't, because that wouldn't be any better than GLMs in this situation. Perhaps the best way to do this is to have qualifiers for pitchers based on the stats in the table above. For example, find every pitcher with a strikeout percentage over 20, a curveball spin over 1,300 rpm, and so on, then see how many of them are actually DIPS Beaters.

I wanted to do that in a non-arbitrary way, so I iterated through over 100,000 combinations of those stats and found which combinations of qualifiers identified the most DIPS Beaters. The best combination was this:

- At least a 40 percent groundball rate
- At least a 19 percent strikeout rate
- Right-handed
- A starter
- At least a nine percent swinging strike rate

- Throws a curveball with at least 1,260 rpm
- At most a 78 percent contact rate
- Throws a change-up

There were 69 such pitchers in my dataset, and 14 were DIPS Beaters. In other words, the best combination only found 14 DIPS Beaters, and it found 55 Non-DIPS Beaters. Not exactly a good success rate. Maybe, I thought, my groups are too tight. There aren't enough people in each group to get a large proportion of the DIPS Beaters.

So I looked only at ground ball and strikeout percentage, two of the stats with the biggest differences. Initially, the results were encouraging: one group composed of pitchers with at least a 40 percent groundball percentage and a 19 percent strikeout percentage (the same criteria from earlier) found 101 DIPS Beaters...but it also found 1,035 Non-DIPS Beaters. Fewer than 10 percent of the pitchers it found were actually DIPS Beaters, and it didn't even find half the DIPS Beaters! So that method clearly wasn't working at all.

When I think about it now, that really shouldn't have been surprising. I hadn't thought about it much at the time, but there's obviously huge variability in the DIPS Beaters' individual statistics. So I looked for pitchers who met at least a few of the criteria instead of all. This, combined with eliminating some of the categories to expand the sizes of the groups, worked only a little bit better, if at all. Pitchers who met three of at least a 44 percent groundball rate, a 19 percent K rate, a 10 percent swinging strike rate, and at most a 77 percent contact percentage included 108 out of 206 DIPS Beaters and 1,174 out of 3,673 Non-DIPS Beaters.

It's like the classic statistics problem about finding rare diseases. A test is administered for a disease that exists in 0.01 percent of patients. When the patient actually has the disease, the test finds it 99 percent of the time. When the patient doesn't have the disease, the test mistakenly thinks it's there 0.1 percent of the time. It seems like a pretty good test. But in actuality, a positive test result is actually a false positive over 90 percent of the time due to how few true positive cases there actually are.

The situation here is a little less extreme, but it's similar. Over half the DIPS Beaters can be found by selecting all pitchers who meet the criteria just outlined. But the likelihood that somebody selected using those criteria is actually a DIPS Beater is under 10 percent. It's not a very effective way to identify DIPS Beaters, just as the above medical test wasn't a very effective way to identify the disease.

Maybe, though, pitchers who did meet three out of those four criteria are "truer" DIPS Beaters. Maybe the ones who *don't* meet the criteria are actually outliers, and the ones who do are the real DIPS Beaters. Maybe the real DIPS Beaters can be identified in some way because they're unique, while the lucky ones are muddying up our models and can't be identified in any way because they're not actually unique.

To test this theory, I found the next-season wOBABIP of every player who had met the criteria and been a DIPS Beater the year before; 87 out of the 108 pitched again the next season (some of the ones who didn't pitch the next year really just haven't yet, since their DIPS Beating season was 2015). Out of those 87, 15 were DIPS Beaters again, and 29 had a wOBABIP higher than league average.

Compare this to the next-season stats of DIPS Beaters who didn't meet the criteria. There were 98 of those guys; 79 pitched the next season. That's nearly the exact same percentage as the other group (both 80.6 percent). Nine of the 79 repeated as DIPS Beaters. Here the second group is a little behind, as the qualifiers had a 17.2 percent repetition rate compared to 11.4 percent for the non-qualifiers (but the p-value for the difference between those proportions is quite large at 0.28, so the difference isn't big enough to be significant). And 25 out of 79 (31.6 percent) non-qualifiers had a wOBABIP the next season higher than league average. That's actually lower than the qualifiers, who were at 33.3 percent.

If there is a difference there, it's infinitesimally small and easily can be ignored. The qualifiers were no different from the non-qualifiers, except possibly in that they repeated slightly more often as DIPS Beaters, and that's not a certainty at all.

This whole section has essentially been a long way to say, "I can't do this." I don't think there really is a way to divide DIPS Beaters and Non-DIPS Beaters into distinct groups without getting far too many false positives and false negatives.

None of this is to say this research has been useless. We still have found out some useful things. High groundball rate and low contact rate, among others, correlate to DIPS beating (though we can't prove causation). DIPS Beaters can beat their DIPS in all sorts of ways, as not all are high-strikeout or high-groundball pitchers. And, most importantly, there is no real way, with our data, to predict DIPS beating or measure which instances of past DIPS beating are most likely to be repeated, which is an important thing to know. And, of course, that's in addition to the fact that we have established DIPS Beaters exist, which is also important.

Perhaps this is where statistics meet their limit. The eye test might be all we need and all we can use to identify DIPS Beaters. I want to believe, but until or unless we can quantify pitch sequencing, command, and quality of contact more effectively, we simply don't have any good way to differentiate DIPS Beaters from Non-DIPS Beaters.

References and Resources
- Pitch data came from PITCHf/x
- Play-by-play data came from Baseball Info Solutions
- Alan Nathan, Baseball Prospectus, "Is 'Late Break' Real?," *baseballprospectus.com/article.php?articleid=19994*

Supplementing Minor League Statistics with Background Data

by Chris Mitchell

The acclaimed British novelist C.S. Lewis once said, "Don't judge a man by where he is, because you don't know how far he has come." You might be wondering why I'm bringing up a 20th-century novelist in an essay that's supposed to be about minor league statistics. But Lewis' quote gets at the point I'm trying to make. When applied to prospect evaluation, this means a prospect's current talent level relative to his age tells only part of the story when evaluating his potential. It also helps to know a bit more about his pre-professional background.

Minor league baseball players come from a wide array of backgrounds. Members of any short-season team may have been in wildly different environments as recently as a couple of years earlier. Some are Dominican-born teenagers who have been playing professionally since they were 16. Others are a year or two removed from high school, where they played only semi-regularly against a low level of competition, often not even year-round. And then there are the draftees who are already 21 or 22 but are just now embarking on their pro careers after spending three or four years in college.

Since these players come from drastically different backgrounds, one might also assume they develop a bit differently. For example, a 21-year-old Dominican-born hitter likely signed at 16 and has played professionally for perhaps five years already. While he's far from a finished product, his age-21 season certainly isn't his first rodeo. He has five years of experience against professional pitching and by now has adjusted to the minor league lifestyle. A 21-year-old college draftee, however, is fresh off campus. He's likely never faced such a high level of competition, at least not regularly, and isn't used to being on the road as often as minor league ballplayers are. Heck, depending on his living situation in college, this might even be the first time in his life he's lived away from his parents. Furthermore, on the field, he's tasked with transitioning from metal bats to wooden bats. A 21-year-old U.S.-born high school draftee would fall somewhere in between.

These hypothetical developmental differences show up in the data. The graphics below demonstrate how the average hitter transitions from advanced Rookie ball to Low-A by way of four statistics: walk rate, strikeout rate, isolated power and batting average on balls in play. I split these data into three categories: college draftees, high school draftees and Caribbean-born players, which includes the Dominican Republic, Venezuela and Puerto Rico. Due to sample size concerns, I did not consider hitters who were born outside of those places, nor did I consider hitters born in the Caribbean who went to college. Each statistic was regressed for sample size and normalized to league average. If the last sentence or two made your eyes glaze over, don't worry. Even if you're a little fuzzy on the technical details, I'm confident you'll get the gist. Let's take it one metric at a time, starting with walk rate.

All three groups of hitters saw their average walk rate tumble. This isn't overly surprising considering the jump from Rookie ball to Low-A is pretty sizable in terms of competition level. But it's interesting the decline isn't uniform across the board. For college hitters, the drop is almost non-existent, while it's noticeably larger for high-school draftees and Caribbean-born players.

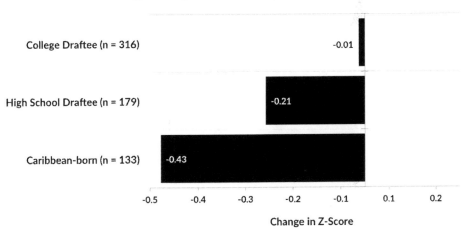

Average Change in Walk Rate, Rookie Ball to Low-A

Although the differences aren't as pronounced, college hitters also have the smoothest transition in terms of strikeout rate. Their strikeout rate drops by 0.18 standard deviations, on average, which is on par with their Caribbean counterparts. High school draftees, on the other hand, tend to see their strikeout rates increase.

Average Change in Strikeout Rate, Rookie Ball to Low-A

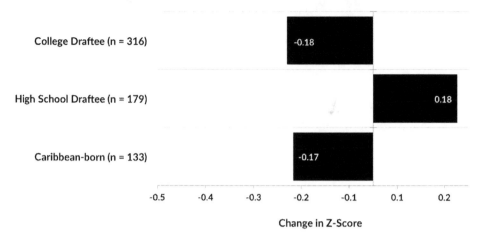

Just as they do with walk rate, Caribbean-born hitters have the toughest time carrying their power output over into full-season ball. High school hitters and college hitters lose only a tick of ISO in the transition from Rookie ball to A-Ball, but Caribbean hitters often see their power output take a dive.

Average Change in Isolated Power, Rookie Ball to Low-A

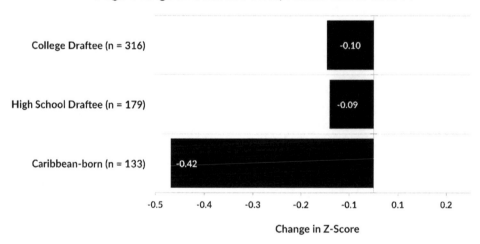

For BABIP, there isn't as much of a discernible trend. All three groups fared roughly the same in Low-A as they did at the Rookie level. This makes sense given how much that metric can bounce around in one-season samples.

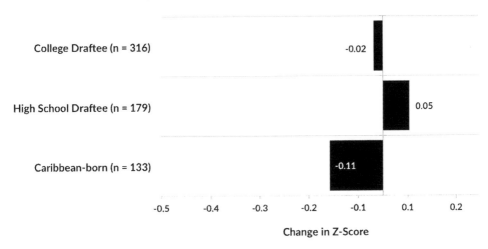

Average Change in BABIP, Rookie Ball to Low-A

Here's a look at some density plots for isolated power and walk rate, the metrics with sizable differences. There's clearly some overlap between these distributions, but it's also obvious college hitters and Caribbean-born hitters aren't quite cut from the same cloth.

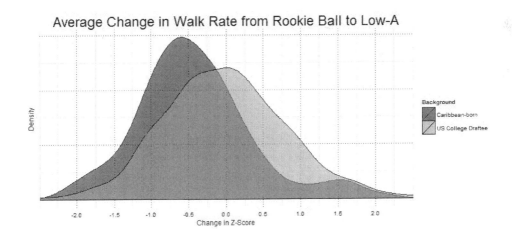

Average Change in Walk Rate from Rookie Ball to Low-A

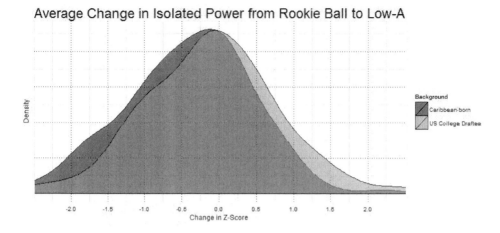

Average Change in Isolated Power from Rookie Ball to Low-A

I should note that I repeated this exercise for hitters transitioning from short-season A-Ball to Low-A to see if the same trend existed there. I'll save you from a second parade of graphs: To sum things up, the results were similar. College hitters had the smoothest transitions in terms of walk rates and power output, while Caribbean hitters fared the worst. The trends were largely the same, although the differences between the groups were less stark.

These findings seem to suggest hitters with fewer years of professional experience are more apt to improve as they climb the minor-league ladder. But before jumping to this conclusion, I'd be remiss if I didn't first make sure the data are saying what I think they are. Comparing the progress of foreign-born hitters to college hitters isn't exactly apples-to-apples due to these players' age differences. The average age in a short-season league falls between 19 and 21. Almost all college hitters aren't drafted until at least their age-21 seasons. As a result, the college hitters making this transition tend to be older than everyone else. Meanwhile, the youngest players at any given minor league level tend to be Caribbean-born teenagers, who signed at age 16. Who's to say the trends outlined above aren't a matter of old players vs. young players rather than college players vs. Caribbean players?

To answer this question, I took things a step further and created some multivariable regression models to predict each of the four statistics in Low-A. I included three variables in my model: the hitter's statistics in Rookie ball, his background (high school, college or Caribbean), and his age. Unsurprisingly, the hitter's statistics in Rookie ball had the most predictive power. In other words, if a hitter hit for a lot of power in Rookie ball, he was likely to do the same in Low-A. More interestingly, though, a hitter's background added some predictive value in three of the four categories, while age came up insignificant across the board. This shows that it's these hitters' backgrounds, rather than their ages, that differentiate how they progress.

Statistical Significance in Predicting Low-A Performance			
Metric	Rookie-Ball Performance	Background	Age
BB%	Yes	Yes	No
K%	Yes	Yes	No
ISO	Yes	Yes	No
BABIP	Yes	No	No

As with any analysis that doesn't take place in a controlled environment, there are some potential flaws and biases with this study that I should mention. In a perfect world, I would require all players to play a full season in Rookie ball followed by a full season in Low-A. Alas, we don't live in a perfect world, and I don't have that type of power. Not yet, at least! Instead, we live in a world where teams promote players when they're ready, which makes things a tad murky.

For example, a hitter who was promoted to High-A after 200 Low-A plate appearances wouldn't make it into my sample. Nor would a hitter who was promoted from Rookie ball after 100 trips to the plate. And since players out of college tend to be older than most viable prospects in the low minors, they're probably promoted more frequently than their non-college counterparts. This might be grounds for sampling bias, but I feel these sampling biases mostly come out in the wash. Yes, college players in short-season ball are more likely to be promoted if they're doing well, but the same goes for college players in Low-A. I feel these effects cancel each other out enough, and happen rarely enough, not to skew my results too badly.

Of course, as is the case with most classifications, pigeonholing the entire universe of players into just a few categories overlooks the individual differences among them. Simply labeling a hitter as "high school," "college," or "Caribbean" doesn't even come close to fully explaining his pre-professional background. Not only do backgrounds vary between these groups, but they also vary within them.

In particular, I'm thinking of what takes place during the high school years of an American-born player's career. Some kids are bred to be baseball players. They specialize in baseball early on, at the expense of other sports, and start playing baseball year-round when they're freshmen in high school, if not sooner. Others, however, enter pro ball with little baseball experience. Some were multi-sport athletes who never gave their undivided attention to baseball, while others grew up in cold parts of the country, where playing baseball year-round simply wasn't feasible.

Players from the latter group are often referred to as "cold-weather kids" by the scouting community and are widely thought to be further behind in their developments than their counterparts from warmer areas. As a result, they often receive something of a pass if their performances lag behind their tools. This premise sounds reasonable in the abstract. The thinking goes that these players often have steeper development curves than their warm-weather counterparts.

However, while it passes the smell test, the cold-weather trope is backed entirely by theory and anecdotal evidence. Surely, there have been cases of toolsy, cold-weather prospects who were late bloomers. But anecdotes don't make for good science. And who's to say these players' struggles were the result of their cold-weather background, rather than any of the countless other factors that influence performance?

From the standpoint of scouting stat lines, the cold-weather-kids question ultimately boils down to this: Given the same statistical performance, does a player coming from a cold climate have any more upside than one who comes from a warm climate? Or, put differently, should we give a pass to cold-weather kids who struggle in the low minors?

For obvious reasons, we can't know exactly how often each hitter played baseball before he went pro. That type of data simply isn't available. But it's probably fair to conclude that players hailing from warm regions got more reps in high school than players from colder ones, on average. So, let's see how high school and college draftees from different climates transition between Rookie ball and Low-A.

I grouped each player as either "warm weather" or "cold weather" depending on the average temperature in two ways—by his birth state and the state in which he attended high school. States with average temperatures of 70 degrees or higher were "warm weather," while states with average temperatures below 70 degrees were "cold weather." Due to the state's myriad climates, I split California into Southern California and Northern California, which were classified as "warm weather" and "cold weather," respectively. Next, I divided the data set into high school and college draftees to examine each group separately.

When it finally came time to look at the data, I didn't find a heck of a lot. Even the largest differences between warm and cold were less than two-tenths of a standard deviation, which is essentially a rounding error. Once again, I built a regression model to predict a hitter's Low-A stats using his Rookie Ball numbers. This time, I tried to include a variable for both high school and birthplace temperature, and I came up empty handed. Whether I treated a hitter's high school or birthplace temperature as a continuous variable (using the actual temperature) or as a dummy variable (simply distinguishing cold versus warm), I could not find any predictive value. This was also true for hitters transitioning from short-season A-ball to Low-A.

So, what does this tell us? Well, that's a little hard to say. I don't think it tells us the stereotype of the slow-developing cold-weather hitter is completely myth.

For one, the lack of signal in my data may not be entirely due to the players observed but might also have something to do with the study itself. Simply looking at the temperature of the state where a player was born or went to high school is a crude way to measure his pre-professional baseball experience. A better-constructed study would assign a temperature to each individual player's birth or high school city, rather than his birth or high school state. This would be more precise, as climates can vary across some of the nation's larger states.

Furthermore, this study relies on the assumption that a warm-weather birthplace equals ample baseball experience in high school, which isn't always true. There have been plenty of players from warm parts of the country who picked up baseball late or didn't specialize until after they went pro, yet my study does not account for this. In sum, this study isn't perfect, largely because it would be impractical to pinpoint the pre-professional experience of every minor league player in recent memory.

However, flaws and all, I also think it's telling that there was absolutely no signal in my data. Caveats or no, if inexperienced, cold-weather prospects developed differently from everyone else, I'd expect to at least see something. But there's nothing there. The evidence does not suggest that cold-weather players have some sort of hidden potential beyond their stat lines. Or at least not in a way that's pronounced or common enough to think twice about.

One explanation might be that most of the "catching up" done by cold-weather hitters happens before they go pro. I discussed the cold-weather-kid phenomenon with Kiley McDaniel, who until recently was FanGraphs' lead prospect analyst. He noted that many high school draftees don't go pro unless they're taken in the first few rounds. And teams generally don't draft hitters that high unless they've proven their merit by taking a lot of reps. As a result, most uber-raw cold-weather guys choose to go to college rather than sign for a bonus of $100,000 or so. Examples provided by McDaniel of cold-weather hitters who got significantly better with more reps include George Springer, Nick Ahmed, Derek Fisher and Joe Panik. But, aside from Rocco Baldelli, it's a lot harder coming up with high school hitters from this mold.

This isn't to say there's no such thing as a late-blooming cold-weather minor league hitter. Baldelli happened, after all. He was a multi-sport athlete from a Rhode Island high school who spent his first two years hitting .237/.288/.364 in the low minors. He quickly learned how to hit good pitching, however, and was a league-average hitter in the big leagues by age 21. Brandon Drury, who reached the big leagues this past September, also seems to fit the mold. After growing up in Oregon, Drury hit .198/.248/.292 over 52 games in his first crack at Rookie ball but got progressively better as he gained experience.

However, examples like this appear to be few and far between. In most cases, knowing where a U.S.-born minor leaguer grew up isn't an important piece of information in forecasting his future and tells you very little you couldn't have gleaned by looking at his stat line.

Summary and Conclusion

- College hitters tend to have the smoothest transition from short-season ball to full-season ball, while Caribbean-born hitters have the toughest transition. High school draftees fall in between. This suggests that, at least in the low minors, hitters from different pre-professional backgrounds move along different development curves. While a hitter's age certainly matters, one should also consider the extent of his professional experience.

- American hitters who grew up in cold climates do not transition to full-season ball any better or worse than hitters from warmer parts of the country. This suggests minor leaguers from cold areas—where baseball isn't frequently played year-round—do not develop any differently from their warm-weather counterparts. Put differently, cold-weather kids who are playing professionally rarely have any hidden upside beyond their stat lines.

All my analysis for this essay looked at hitters' transitions from short-season ball to full-season ball. Of course, in and of itself, a baseball player's transition to A-Ball isn't terribly interesting. What we really care about is how he'll perform in the major leagues, which I ignored here. I had a method to my madness, though. While it answers a less interesting question, zeroing in on the one-year jump between two levels allows for a much cleaner study, data-wise. The several-year transition from the low minors to a hitter's peak is a lot messier. Not only is there a lot else going on over those years, but the sample size is decimated since the majority of minor leaguers never log a single big league at-bat. I felt focusing on a one-year jump was the ideal scenario for testing whether these phenomena are real.

Although I've yet to examine the data, I'd bet the differences between Caribbean-born hitters vis-à-vis high school and college hitters are most pronounced in the low minors. I'd bet the effect sizes dwindle—if not disappear completely—at the higher levels, as hitters move further away from their diverse backgrounds. For players at the Double-A level, for example, it's my guess that knowing a hitter's pre-professional background isn't useful in most cases. But at the very least, it makes sense to mentally handicap hitters at the lowest levels based on what they did before they went pro.

At this point, my prospect projection system—KATOH (named after Yankees prospect Gosuke Katoh)—doesn't do this. KATOH will come down pretty hard on a 21-year-old in the low minors if he's not putting up Bryce Harper-type numbers. It doesn't account for the fact that this hitter might be a recent college draftee who's still adjusting to playing professionally while many of his peers have already done so. For example, although they were both well-regarded prospects, KATOH would have hated Kyle Seager and A.J. Pollock after their unspectacular pro debuts. However, now that I'm aware of this blind spot, I will take into account players' pre-professional backgrounds when building the next iteration of KATOH.

That may not be easy, of course. While I've pretty convincingly proven players from different backgrounds aren't all on equal footing, the effect sizes from my study weren't huge, even when observing year-to-year changes for hitters in the dawns of their careers. As I mentioned earlier, the several-year transition from the low minors to a hitter's peak is a lot messier. The data might be too noisy for my models to pick up on something as nuanced as this. Nevertheless, incorporating it will be on my to-do list.

There's more to judging a player's future potential than his age and current talent level. Some of this is nearly impossible to quantify, such as a player's makeup or physical tools. But some of it can be gleaned by looking at where he came from before he joined his organization's minor leagues.

Stats are great, but it's always important to complement them with qualitative information. The numbers can sometimes deceive us if taken without context. Knowing whether a 21-year-old signed out of the Dominican or was recently drafted out of college is a prime example. At the same time, though, it's also important to know which of these qualitative factors are meaningful. And sometimes, the ones that are promoted by conventional wisdom—such as the climate where a hitter grew up—aren't very meaningful in reality.

References & Resources

- Thanks to Kiley McDaniel for his input.
- Temperature data from Current Results: *currentresults.com/Weather/US/average-annual-state-temperatures.php*
- Birthplace, high school and draft data purchased from The Baseball Cube
- Minor league statistics from Baseball-Reference

Who Watches the Watchers? Introducing Umpire Consistency Score

by Peter Bonney

In August, Tom Tango published a blog post with a proposed umpire evaluation metric. In this article I will describe an implementation of that metric, present some of its results, and discuss areas for further research.

Tango's metric is defined as $(2p-1)*(c-p)$, where p is the called strike probability of a pitch in that exact location, and c is the actual call: 1 for strikes and 0 for balls. Mitchel Lichtman compared this to "UZR for umpires," but one noteworthy difference is that for fielders an out is always good and a non-out is always bad; in contrast, with umpires a ball or a strike can be either "good" or "bad" depending on the pitch location.

When moving from definition to implementation, a number of questions arise. The most important is, "How do you estimate p?" I have chosen to use a neural network model to generate a continuous probability estimate at every point of the strike zone. An alternative approach might be to divide the zone into bins, calculate actual strike frequencies within each bin, and then apply some kind of smoothing to eliminate discontinuities.

For those unfamiliar with neural networks, here is a basic primer. A "neural network," or more formally an "artificial neural network," is a mathematical model that mimics a biological neural network and can approximate unknown and complex functions, such as the probability that a pitch in a given location will be called a strike. There are nodes (akin to neurons) that are activated by some function based on their inputs and connected by weights to other nodes that are likewise activated by some function based on their inputs, and so on, leading to an output node (or nodes).

A neural network is typically visualized like this (from Wikipedia):

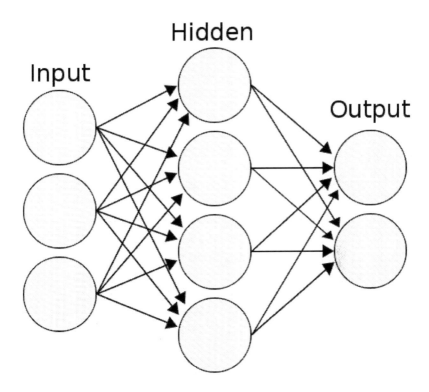

Stylized Neural Network Diagram

In the case of modeling binary variables, training a neural network is very much akin to performing logistic regression, only with the capacity for producing much more complex models. Note that there is no closed-form expression for determining the neural network weights; an iterative process is used instead. For this analysis, I have used the tools in R's "neuralnet" package.

There are a few downsides to neural networks. One is that they are opaque. You can't look at a trained neural network and easily come up with a "plain English" explanation of its calculation. That is a real weakness, and in general I strongly prefer not using "black box" models like neural networks. But this is exactly the sort of analysis in which they tend to perform very well, and ultimately I decided performance outweighs opacity for this purpose.

Another problem is they are prone to overfitting if not thoughtfully constructed. The issue arises when the hidden layer contains too many nodes relative to the size of the training data (the size of the input and output layers are determined by the number of input and output variables—in our case the input variables are horizontal and vertical location, and the output variable is the probability of a strike call). Sizing the hidden layer of a neural network is a topic unto itself, but for this analysis I sized it by trial and error with a few representative strike zones. Two hidden nodes are insufficient to model a strike zone at all, so we need a minimum of three. I opted to (somewhat arbitrarily) use four hidden nodes: on smaller data sets, three-node models frequently produced oddly-shaped zones, while five-node models showed clear signs of overfitting. But in general, more hidden nodes lead to more discriminating power, and an alternative approach might be to increase the number of hidden nodes while also adding ball/strike calls from a sample of umpires to prevent overfitting (sort of akin to regressing the strike zone to the mean).

Now that we've discussed neural networks and some of their considerations, we can move on to other important methodological choices. One is how to define pitch location. Yes, I know that sounds silly. And in terms of horizontal location, it is a little silly: the horizontal dimensions of the strike zone theoretically should be the same for all hitters. But that is not the case for the vertical dimensions of the strike zone—"letter high" is not the same for Jose Altuve and Kris Bryant!

To address this issue, I have calculated the difference between the top and bottom of the average strike zone for each hitter/season and scaled vertical location to this distance. I modeled each hitter's strike zone for a full season the same way I modeled umpire zones: with a neural network model with four hidden nodes. Where there were insufficient data to establish a strike zone model (I drew the line at 200 called pitches, which is about 100 plate appearances on average), I used an average strike zone based on 2,500 called pitches from each season.

With each individual strike zone modeled, I found the highest and lowest points where a pitch had at least a 50 percent chance of being called a strike. The vertical dimensions of each of these two points define the top and bottom, respectively, of the strike zone for every hitter. Finally, I scaled the vertical location of every pitch such that middle height is 0, the top of the zone is +1, and the bottom of the zone is -1. The choice of scale is irrelevant to the analysis; choosing a range from -1 to +1 just creates some uniformity between the horizontal and vertical dimensions of the zone since a typical strike zone ranges to about one foot on either side from the center of the plate (this makes the strike zone visualizations a little nicer, in my opinion, but it is completely arbitrary).

Another methodological choice is what data set(s) we should use to develop the model(s) for p. Should umpires be measured against the average or against themselves? Do we care more about consistency across all umpires or an umpire's personal consistency from game to game? And what time period should we use to establish the strike-zone model? We know the strike zone has evolved in the PITCHf/x era; what balance should we strike between (a) having a long window and thus more data, and (b) have a shorter window and therefore a more "current" view?

For the purposes of this analysis, I have chosen to consider each umpire's personal strike zone, updated monthly, modeled over the lesser of 2,500 called pitches or a full calendar year. So, for example, to evaluate a given umpire on Sept. 15, 2015, I am using his strike zone as modeled with the most recent 2,500 called pitches from 9/1/14 to 8/31/15. Whenever there are fewer than 600 training pitches available (which happens anytime an umpire has called fewer than four games in the previous year, more or less), I use a model based on 2,500 arbitrary pitches from other umpires in that same month. The reason I have used personal strike zones rather than league averages (other than cases where individual data is lacking) is I believe pitchers and catchers are well adapted to varying their approach based on umpire tendencies. If so, they probably would prefer an umpire who calls his strike zone as consistently as possible from game to game over one who is inconsistent but closer to the "average" zone. I can see an argument for either approach, and I think each one answers important (but different) questions. Personally, I am more interested in the question of how umpire strike zones vary from game to game, but anyone reading this article should feel free to take this methodology and apply it differently!

(As an aside, on average an umpire has to make a call on about 53 percent of pitches. The average game from 2007-15 had about 292 pitches between both teams, so an umpire calls about 150 pitches per game. On average, 2,500 pitches therefore covers about 16 games.)

The reason for monthly updates, as opposed to daily or pitch-by-pitch, is that the neural network training is computationally intensive, typically taking at least a few seconds to train each model with the pitch limits above. More training data take even longer. I settled on monthly updates as a reasonable compromise between keeping the strike zone models current and making this undertaking feasible. A typical umpire calls four or five games per month, so with monthly updates each umpire's strike zone should only be about two or three games stale, on average.

Finally, and probably least controversially, I have computed separate strike zone models for left-handed and right-handed hitters for all umpires. Additional extensions might be to break up the strike zone by pitch type, by pitcher hand and by other criteria, but for this analysis LHH/RHH is the only additional factor used.

To give a flavor for what all of this looks like in practice, let's look at recent example in more detail: Dana DeMuth's strike zones for both hands in September of 2015.

Here is the visual representation of the model of DeMuth's strike zone for right-handed hitters:

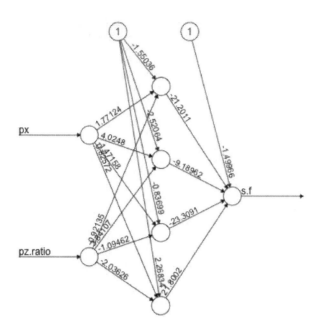

Neural Network Model of DeMuth's 9/2015 Strike Zone For RHH

It's a confusing jumble of arrows, nodes and arbitrary numbers. But it leads to this probabilistic strike zone:

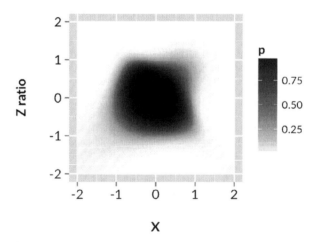

Visualization of DeMuth's 9/2015 Strike Zone Model for RHH

Note that the vertical ("Z ratio") axis is the vertical pitch location ("pz" in pitchF/X terminology) scaled to the batter's personal strike zone (+1 is the top of the zone, -1 is the bottom of the zone). The horizontal ("X") axis is the horizontal pitch location ("px") in feet from the center of the plate, viewed from the catcher's perspective. The color gradient ("p") is the probability a pitch in that location will be called a strike, according to the model. Darker indicates a pitch is more likely to be called a strike, lighter indicates less likely.

Is this visualization an accurate picture of how likely DeMuth was to call a strike against right-handed hitters at the beginning of September of this year? Who knows? But it doesn't look obviously wrong.

Here is the model for left-handers in the same period:

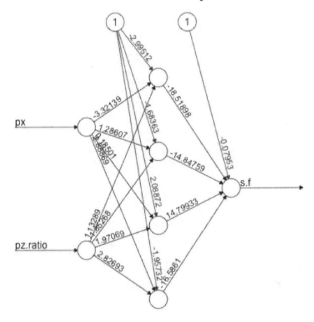

Neural Network Model of DeMuth's 9/2015 Strike Zone For LHH

Again, there is no obvious way to interpret these numbers, and comparing it to the right-handed model is a pointless exercise—everything is different. But once again, it leads to something resembling a plausible strike zone:

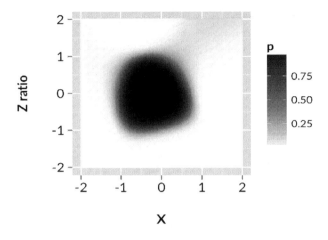

Visualization of DeMuth's 9/2015 Strike Zone Model for LHH

Note that the lefty zone is visibly different from the righty zone. The difference in strike calls between lefties and righties is well-documented, and in this example it is obvious: the lefty zone extends well beyond the righty zone on the left side and ends well short of the righty zone on the right side.

Does that mean a neural network is a perfect model of an umpire's strike zone? No, it doesn't. Later in this article I'll show some fairly bad strike zone models arising from this approach. But every modeling approach likely will lead to difficult edge cases, and this seems like a fairly reasonable starting point.

Now that the preliminaries are out of the way, let's go back to the real purpose of this analysis: umpire consistency.

For the rest of this article, I'm going to refer to Tango's metric as "umpire consistency score" or "UCS." There is no "Z" or "R" in there to avoid confusion with the various *ZR fielding metrics. I will use "raw UCS" to refer to the cumulative score over any number of observations, from a single pitch to a whole career. While I'm at it, let's define a couple additional metrics:

- UCS: raw UCS re-normalized to an average of zero
- UCS150: UCS (re-normalized) per 150 pitches (i.e. UCS per typical game)

Let's look at some extreme outcomes to sanity-check the framework and to see if there is anything interesting to learn. Since the strike zone models are updated monthly, we'll look at the best and worst months as measured by UCS150 from 2008 to 2015. (Data from 2007 are used for training subsequent models but not for evaluating umpires, since, e.g., in April, 2007 there is no prior data to develop a model against).

Here are the five worst monthly performances according to this framework:

Five Worst Monthly UCS150 Performances, 2008-2015				
Umpire	Month	Called pitches	UCS150	Full Shift Pct
Mike Winters	Oct-09	139	-10.7	61%
Doug Eddings	Oct-10	126	-10.1	59%
John Hirschbeck	May-09	1,202	-10.0	69%
Damien Beal	Aug-09	438	-9.9	40%
Marcus Pattillo	Jul-15	158	-9.9	63%

Most of these bad months are just single games, and of course it's easier to have an extreme result when the sample size is smaller. But just to see if there is anything aberrational about these strike zones, let's look at Mike Winters' modeled strike zone coming into October 2009:

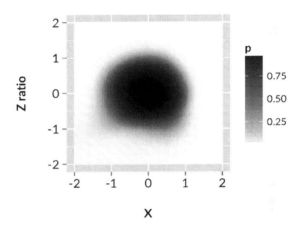

Visualization of Mike Winters' 10/2009 Strike Zone Model for RHH

It doesn't look great, but it's not obviously a bad model. How about the lefty zone?

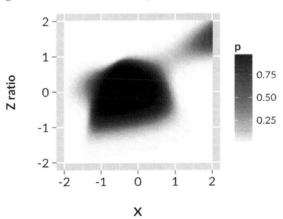

Visualization of Mike Winters' 10/2009 Strike Zone Model for LHH

The dark spot on the top right is obviously a little concerning. If he is getting penalized for a "bad" ball call there, then there is a problem. But, as it turns out, there were no pitches thrown anywhere near that region during Winters' single game in October, 2009 (ball or strike), so it had no impact on his UCS. And, in fact, there were no called strikes around that region in the training data either. This is an example of model artifacts you'll occasionally see with neural networks when there are sparse training data.

It might be more instructive to look at John Hirschbeck's strike zones for May 2009, since he called a whopping 1,202 pitches that month:

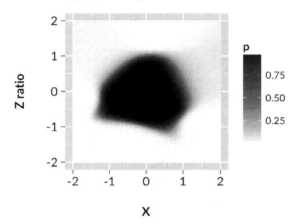

Visualization of John Hirschbeck's 5/2009 Strike Zone Model for RHH

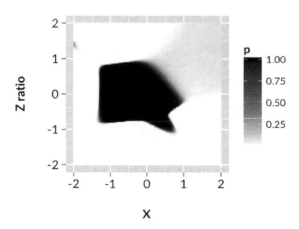

Visualization of John Hirschbeck's 5/2009 Strike Zone Model for LHH

These are a little more troubling. Both zones are quite oddly shaped and almost certainly *don't* reflect the zone Hirschbeck was calling on any given day. A quick look at the data suggests a potential problem with my training approach: Hirschbeck took 2008 off for back surgery, called 618 pitches in April 2009 (*just* over my 600 pitch training threshold), and then was judged on 1,200 pitches in May 2009 against a model based on just those 600 April pitches. In contrast, his April 2009 performance, judged against a league average strike zone, grades out with a UCS slightly above zero. This is a fairly strong argument for using a regressed strike zone in a future implementation.

For the other side of the coin, let's look at the five best UCS performances:

Five Best Monthly UCS150 Performances, 2008-2015			
Umpire	Month	Called pitches	UCS150
Lance Barrett	Apr-13	147	5.6
Mike Everitt	Apr-08	590	5.0
Scott Barry	Apr-08	298	4.8
Larry Vanover	May-08	1,009	4.5
Larry Vanover	Apr-08	593	4.4

One thing that jumps out is the preponderance of performances from early 2008. A quick comparison of the aggregate UCS for each year shows that 2008 was, in fact, the most consistent season for umpires in the data set:

Aggregate UCS for All Umpires, 2008-2015	
Season	Aggregate UCS
2008	676
2009	-549
2010	150
2011	-96
2012	114
2013	236
2014	-294
2015	-237

There might be a logical explanation, or there might be an issue with the 2008 data, or it might just be random variation. One of the seasons has to be the best, and there is nothing insanely outlier-ish about the 2008 value (standard deviation of the series is 378).

A more interesting, and possibly troubling, takeaway from the "five best" table is related to Vanover's strong performance at the start of 2008. Over the first two months measured, he posted a cumulative UCS of +47.8, but he then posted a cumulative UCS of -5.9 over the next seven-plus seasons. Was he just an average umpire who happened to have a great two months? Is there a problem with the strike-zone models? Is this measure of umpire consistency just completely random?

Let's start with a look at Vanover's April 2008 strike zone models:

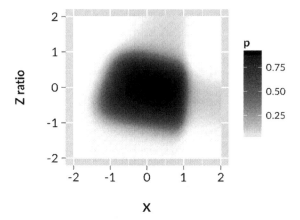

Visualization of Vanover's 4/2008 Strike Zone Model for RHH

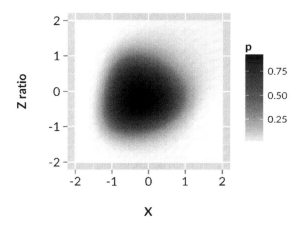

Visualization of Vanover's 4/2008 Strike Zone Model for LHH

Neither zone is what you might call "textbook," but neither is either visibly egregious (the lefty zone won't please strike zone purists, but it's not terribly different from DeMuth's lefty zone).

This leaves the possibility that this measure of UCS is completely random. To try to determine how much skill is actually involved in UCS, I measured split-half reliability at different sample sizes. That is, I split the data up into odd/even pitches for each umpire, grouped all the pitches into consecutive samples of a certain size, and then computed the correlation between the odd and even samples. I repeated this process for samples of 100 pitches, 200, 300, etc., until I found the smallest sample size that yielded a correlation of 0.5 between the odd and even samples. That value is about 940 pitches. Conveniently, this quantity also tells us how many pitches we would add for regressing UCS toward the mean. In addition, it tells us that UCS is *not* completely random, even with the potential methodology problems I have identified. After about six games' worth of called pitches, an average umpire's measured strike-zone consistency is equal parts luck and skill.

Returning to the curious case of Vanover, what are we to conclude? Well, the safest thing is probably to conclude nothing at all. This is a new methodology, not yet subjected to rigorous review and likely to change appreciably before it's ready for real-world use. But if you *must* conclude something from it, conclude either Vanover had a lucky couple of months (remember 940 pitches is the point at which we estimate performance is *half* due to skill—in a sample of over 300 umpires we should see some exceptionally good and bad performances over 1,500+ pitches just from random variation) or his skill level changed (always a possibility when humans are involved).

Now that we've established that UCS has at least *some* element of skill to it, we can meaningfully consider the career performances of MLB's umpires. Over longer periods, the quirks of bad individual strike-zone models should wash out, particularly for the more seasoned umpires who have a good amount of data for model training. Here is the full career ranking (by UCS150) of all umpires with a minimum of 10,000 called pitches from 2008 through 2015:

Career UCS150 Performances, 2008-2015 (Min. 10,000 Called Pitches)					
Name	Called Pitches	UCS150	Name	Called Pitches	UCS150
Mike Reilly	16,013	0.47	Ed Hickox	32,663	0.01
Jerry Layne	33,410	0.39	Brian Knight	39,841	0.01
Jim Joyce	33,956	0.35	Mark Carlson	35,792	0.01
Mark Wegner	37,701	0.31	Fieldin Culbreth	40,704	0.01
CB Bucknor	39,737	0.30	Rob Drake	40,421	0.01
Clint Fagan	12,929	0.29	Todd Tichenor	37,053	0.00
Chuck Meriwether	10,564	0.27	Mike Winters	39,060	0.00
Andy Fletcher	39,567	0.26	Bill Welke	39,246	0.00
Alfonso Marquez	34,653	0.22	Dan Bellino	29,404	0.00
Jeff Nelson	41,157	0.22	Ron Kulpa	39,181	-0.01
James Hoye	42,090	0.21	Chris Conroy	21,085	-0.03
Paul Nauert	37,665	0.21	Joe West	42,154	-0.04
Derryl Cousins	25,824	0.21	Marty Foster	38,158	-0.04
Bill Miller	40,759	0.18	Angel Hernandez	41,378	-0.04
Gary Cederstrom	39,034	0.18	Jim Reynolds	39,853	-0.05
John Tumpane	14,726	0.17	Ed Rapuano	23,404	-0.08
Adam Hamari	11,370	0.17	Gerry Davis	39,032	-0.08
Jim Wolf	36,710	0.17	Tom Hallion	39,368	-0.08
Eric Cooper	39,072	0.16	Ted Barrett	41,128	-0.09
Jeff Kellogg	38,965	0.16	Jordan Baker	16,632	-0.09
Larry Vanover	39,171	0.16	Lance Barrett	15,973	-0.09
Dale Scott	39,912	0.16	Will Little	10,088	-0.10
Cory Blaser	22,519	0.15	Tim McClelland	32,297	-0.10
Hunter Wendelstedt	37,019	0.15	Mike DiMuro	34,797	-0.12
Chad Fairchild	37,431	0.15	Vic Carapazza	25,977	-0.14
Kerwin Danley	32,150	0.13	Sam Holbrook	34,611	-0.15
Paul Schrieber	37,103	0.12	Mike Muchlinski	26,515	-0.16
Tim Tschida	23,395	0.11	Tony Randazzo	32,868	-0.17
Tim Timmons	41,290	0.11	Jerry Meals	41,056	-0.18
Chris Guccione	40,001	0.11	Doug Eddings	39,574	-0.19
Dana DeMuth	37,354	0.10	Bruce Dreckman	27,663	-0.22
Scott Barry	37,347	0.10	D.J. Reyburn	23,221	-0.24
Phil Cuzzi	40,264	0.10	Brian O'Nora	37,019	-0.27
Paul Emmel	39,399	0.10	Angel Campos	20,068	-0.27
Bill Hohn	12,882	0.09	Brian Runge	21,339	-0.32
Adrian Johnson	40,481	0.09	Alan Porter	25,791	-0.33
Mike Everitt	40,239	0.08	Marvin Hudson	41,201	-0.34
Lance Barksdale	38,597	0.07	Mike Estabrook	32,833	-0.34
Dan Iassogna	40,053	0.06	Manny Gonzalez	19,681	-0.42
Bob Davidson	42,257	0.06	Mark Ripperger	11,740	-0.43
Brian Gorman	35,004	0.06	Quinn Wolcott	10,772	-0.52
Greg Gibson	39,322	0.06	David Rackley	13,334	-0.53
Gary Darling	30,747	0.05	Jerry Crawford	11,393	-0.90
Tim Welke	39,126	0.03	John Hirschbeck	22,033	-0.94
Wally Bell	32,006	0.02	Tripp Gibson	10,714	-1.23
Laz Diaz	40,956	0.02			

The most remarkable thing about this list is how close to zero the career UCS150 scores are across the board compared to the wide range of values we saw on a monthly basis. But it's not obvious whether this tells us something about the real-word distribution of umpire talent or if it points to an issue with the approach. Either way, it's another area for further investigation. Another interesting observation is that UCS150 is positively correlated with the number of called pitches an umpire has made in his career: the correlation is 0.32 for all umpires and 0.40 for the umpires on this list. I can't yet say whether this is because (a) more experienced umpires are more consistent, (b) less consistent umpires get fewer opportunities, or (c) the modeling approach is kinder to umpires with more training data, but it should be possible to test (a) and (b) within this framework.

What I have presented here is a first stab at modeling and evaluating umpire strike zones. Future work will focus on:

- Developing an appropriate method for building partially regressed strike-zone models to address possible issues with models built on limited training data.
- Comparing umpires' performance against a league-average strike zone vs. their personal strike zone, to see which is a better predictor of an umpire's future ball and strike calls.
- Analyzing the fairly tight spread in career UCS150 values for evidence of a problem with this methodology.
- Examining the correlation between experience and UCS150 to help validate or invalidate the modeling approach.
- When (if) this approach is validated and stable, investigating the impact of catchers on umpire consistency. Does a "good" pitch receiver make an umpire appear less consistent, more consistent, or neither?

Tom Tango presented an interesting concept for umpire evaluation, and I'm hopeful that with some further refinement the approach described here can eventually turn into a standard methodology.

References and Resources

- Special thanks to Tom Tango for his helpful feedback on the initial drafts of this article.
- Tom Tango, "Evaluating the effectiveness of an umpire… effectively," *tangotiger. com/index.php/site/comments/evaluatiing-the-effectiveness-of-an-umpire-effectively*
- The R "neuralnet" package, *cran.r-project.org/web/packages/neuralnet/index.html*
- Russell Carleton, FanGraphs, "525,600 Minutes: How Do You Measure a Player in a Year?," *fangraphs.com/blogs/525600-minutes-how-do-you-measure-a-player-in-a-year*

Et Cetera

Glossary

BABIP: Batting Average on Balls in Play. This is a measure of the number of batted balls that safely fall in for hits (not including home runs). The exact formula we use is (H-HR)/(AB-K-HR+SF).

Batted ball statistics: When a batter hits a ball, he hits either a ground ball, fly ball or line drive. The resulting ground ball, fly ball and line drive percentages make up a player's mix of statistics, with infield fly balls, or pop-ups, being tracked as a percentage of a player's total number of fly balls.

BB%: Walk rate measures how often a position player walks—or how often a pitcher walks a batter—per plate appearance. It is measured in percentage form.

BB/9: Walks allowed per nine innings

BsR: UBR+wSB. UBR, or Ultimate Base Running, accounts for the value a player adds to his team via baserunning. It is determined using linear weights, with each baserunning event receiving a specific run value. wSB, or Weighted Stolen Base runs, estimates the number of runs a player contributes by stealing bases, as compared to the average player.

ChampAdded: The proportion of a World Series championship contributed by a player or team, based on the impact of a play on a team's winning a game, and the value of that game within the context of winning the World Series. Please refer to "To Err is Human, But Not Royal," for more information.

Defensive Efficiency: The percentage of balls in play converted into outs. It can be approximated by 1-BABIP.

DRS: Defensive Runs Saved. DRS rates players as above or below average based on "runs," with data from Baseball Info Solutions used as an input. It tracks a number of different aspects of defensive play, including stolen bases, double plays, outfield arms, robbing home runs and range.

ERA: A pitcher's total number of earned runs allowed divided by his total number of innings pitched, multiplied by nine.

ERA-: A pitching version of wRC+: 100 represents a league-average ERA, and a smaller ERA- is better.

ERA+: ERA measured against the league average and adjusted for ball-park factors. An ERA+ over 100 is better than average, less than 100 is below average.

FIP: Fielding Independent Pitching, a measure of all things for which a pitcher is specifically responsible. The formula is (HR*13+(BB+HBP)*3-K*2)/IP, plus a league-specific factor (usually around 3.2) to round out the number to an equivalent ERA number. FIP helps you understand how well a pitcher pitched, regardless of how well his fielders fielded.

FIP-: A pitching version of OPS+ and wRC+: 100 represents a league-average FIP, and a smaller FIP- is better.

ISO: Isolated power. This is a measure of a hitter's raw power, or how good they are at hitting for extra bases. Most simply, the formula is SLG-AVG, but you can also calculate it as such: $((2B)+(2*3B)+(3*HR))/AB$.

K%: Strikeout rate measures how often a position player strikes out—or how often a pitcher strikes out a batter—per plate appearance. It is measured in percentage form.

K/9: Strikeouts per nine innings

LI: Leverage Index. LI measures the criticality of a play or plate appearance. It is based on the range of potential WPA outcomes of a play, compared to all other plays. 1.0 is an average Index.

Linear Weights: The historical average runs scored for each event in a baseball game.

OBP: On-base percentage, an essential tool, measures how frequently a batter reaches base safely. The formula is: $(H+BB+HBP)/(AB+BB+HBP+SF)$.

OPS: On Base plus Slugging Percentage, a crude but quick measure of a batter's true contribution to his team's offense. See wOBA for a better approach.

PITCHf/x: Sportvision's pitch tracking system that has been installed in every major league stadium since at least the start of the 2007 season. It tracks several aspects of every pitch thrown in a major league game, including velocity, movement, release point, spin and pitch location.

Pythagorean Formula: A formula for converting a team's run differential into a projected win-loss record. The formula is $RS^2/(RS^2+RA^2)$. Teams' actual win-loss records tend to mirror their Pythagorean records, and variances usually can be attributed to luck.

You can improve the accuracy of the Pythagorean formula by using a different exponent (the 2 in the formula). The best exponent can be calculated this way: $(RS/G+RA/G)^{.285}$, where RS/G is Runs Scored per Game and RA/G is Runs Allowed per Game. This is called the PythagoPat formula.

Slash Line: At times, writers may refer to a batter's "slash line," or "triple-slash line." They mean something like this: .287/.345/.443. The numbers between those slashes are the batter's batting average, on-base percentage and slugging percentage.

Total Zone: The lone defensive stat calculated exclusively from Retrosheet play-by-play data. It is the defensive stat used in both WAR calculations for games played prior to the UZR era (2002-present).

UZR: A fielding system similar to Defensive Runs Saved. Both systems calculate a fielder's range by comparing his plays made in various "vectors" across the baseball diamond to the major league average rate of plays made in those vectors. Both systems also look at other factors such as the effectiveness of outfield throwing, handling bunts and turning double plays.

WAR: Wins Above Replacement. A "win stat" that calculates the number of wins a player contributed to his team above a certain replacement level. WAR is calculated at FanGraphs and Baseball Reference. Though the two implementations vary a bit, they share a common framework that includes a linear weights approach to runs created, advanced fielding metrics, leverage for relievers and replacement levels that vary by position. In addition, beginning in 2013, both versions unified their definition of replacement level, making the two versions more directly comparable.

wOBA: A linear weights offensive rating system that is similar to OPS, except that it's set to the scale of on-base percentage.

WPA: Win Probability Added is a system in which each player is given credit toward helping his team win, based on play-by-play data and the impact each specific play has on the team's probability of winning.

wRC+: Like ERA+, wRC+ is scaled so that 100 is average and a higher number is positive. The "RC" stands for Runs Created, but it's not Bill James' Runs Created. It's a "linear weights" version derived from wOBA.

xFIP: Expected Fielding Independent Pitching. This is an experimental stat that adjusts FIP and "normalizes" the home run component according to the number of fly balls a pitcher allowed.

For more information on these and other statistics, visit: *hardballtimes.com/tools/ glossary* or *fangraphs.com/library*.

Who Was That?

Phil Birnbaum is chair of SABR's Statistical Analysis Committee. He has been writing about sabermetrics since 1988, and was co-editor of the eighth edition of *Total Baseball*. Some of his research can be found at his website, *philbirnbaum.com*, and his blog, *blog.philbirnbaum.com*.

Peter Bonney is a data science consultant, technology entrepreneur and former hedge fund manager whose favorite dataset to play with is Gameday. He has a degree in Applied Mathematics from Harvard College and lives in New York City.

Dave Cameron is the managing editor of FanGraphs. More importantly, he's a leukemia survivor, and will take any opportunity given to shamelessly suggest that you donate both blood and platelets. He's happy to still be writing about trivial things like baseball.

Carson Cistulli lives in New Hampshire with his wife and dog.

Bryan Cole is a featured writer for Beyond the Box Score and a contributing writer for TechGraphs. He received his Ph.D. from Boston University in electrical engineering, where his research focused on wearable sensor signal processing and machine learning. He currently works as a research engineer for Delsys, Inc., developing applications for wearable inertial measurement units and electromyographic sensors.

Joe Distelheim is chief copy editor of The Hardball Times. A retired newspaper editor, he was sports editor of the *Detroit Free Press* in the 1980s. He is a lifelong Cubs fan who believes that the team's resurgence means there's hope for anything, including world peace.

Sean Dolinar develops data visualizations and writes for FanGraphs and The Hardball Times. He also works in television production in Pittsburgh and researches social media data.

Adam Dorhauer grew up a third-generation Cardinals fan in Missouri, and now lives in Ohio. His writing on baseball focuses on the history of the game, as well as statistical concepts as they apply to baseball.

August Fagerstrom is a Cleveland-based sports writer and graduate of Kent State University. He covered the Indians for Ohio.com in 2014 and MLB.com in 2015. He is now a daily contributor to FanGraphs.

Tim Healey is a Boston-based sportswriter who works for Sports on Earth and the *Boston Globe*. A graduate of Boston University, he has also written for MLB.com, WEEI.com and SoxProspects.com.

Frank Jackson was born in Philadelphia in 1950, the year of the Whiz Kids, but by the time he was introduced to Connie Mack Stadium, the Phillies were perennial tail-enders. Subsequently living in Illinois and Maryland, he also followed the White

Sox, Cubs and Orioles, but his longest tenure as a fan has been with the Rangers, as he has lived in Dallas since 1976. In recent years, he has written articles for the Rangers program magazine.

Frank has visited 50 major league ballparks, including all but three of the current parks, and has visited all of the current Texas League parks, as well as some that are no longer in use. Altogether, he has visited 80 minor league parks and 40 college parks. Also, he has visited all the Arizona spring training ballparks and all but one in Florida.

Brad Johnson is a baseball addict and a statistics junkie who currently resides in Atlanta, Ga. He played four seasons of injury-plagued baseball at Macalester College from 2006 through 2009, and has since made the transition to a purely off-the-field existence. You can find his work on The Hardball Times and FanGraphs.

David Kagan earned his Ph.D. in Physics from the University of California, Berkeley. He has been a faculty member at California State University, Chico since 1981. He has served as the Chair of the Department of Physics and as the founding Chair of the Department of Science Education. Dr. Kagan is a regular contributor to *The Physics Teacher* as well as The Hardball Times. All the while, he has remained true to his lifelong obsession with baseball by using the national pastime to enhance the teaching and learning of physics.

Dan Kopitzke has over 40 years of baseball experience. In the 1979 Little League World Series, he became the first left-handed catcher in the event's history. Dan went on to pitch and play outfield at NCAA DI University of Detroit (1985-1989). In 1998, Dan began coaching and has been involved in developing athletes and molding young minds ever since.

Dan founded the K-Zone Academy in 2007 with a focus on developing Superior Baseball Athletes. Training at the K-Zone Academy has always been research and data driven. He is continuously looking for new methods and technologies to help players improve and advance fostering key partnerships is support of this goal. He puts his methods to the test personally, leading his Adult team to several Men's Senior Baseball League (MSBL) Regional and National Championships.

Mitchel Lichtman has been performing sabermetric research for over 25 years. He has consulted for several major league teams, most notably the St. Louis Cardinals in 2004 and 2005. He is a co-author of *The Book: Playing the Percentages in Baseball*, and has written dozens of articles in print and on the Internet. He also hosts his own sabermetric blog, *mglbaseball.com*. He has been featured on MLB Network, and holds degrees from Cornell University and the University of Nevada Boyd School of Law. He lives part time in both upstate N.Y., and Henderson, Nev.

Jason Linden teaches English and creative writing in Kentucky. His debut novel, *When the Sparrow Sings*, is out now. He writes and edits at The Hardball Times and also contributes to the Reds blog Redleg Nation.

Erik Malinowski is a freelance writer who contributes regularly to *Rolling Stone*, Sports on Earth, Uproxx, *Wired*, and other publications. His past baseball writing includes the first-ever profile of youth coach/TV pitchman Tom Emanski, a 72-part series on umpires, the untold story of the first MLB Home Run Derby, and a definitive history of the classic "Homer at the Bat" episode of *The Simpsons*. He lives in San Mateo, Calif., with his wife and 2-year-old son.

Kiley McDaniel is the assistant director of baseball operations for the Atlanta Braves. Prior to that, he was FanGraphs' lead prospect analyst, and he has worked in the scouting departments of the New York Yankees, Baltimore Orioles and Pittsburgh Pirates and has written for ESPN, among other outlets.

Chris Mitchell holds degrees in mathematics and economics from Fordham University. He resides in Manhattan, where he works in economic development and contributes regularly to FanGraphs and The Hardball Times. If you know him for anything, it's probably for the KATOH prospect projection system he created.

Jack Moore is a freelance writer based in Minneapolis writing about sports, history, mythology, and the intersection of the trio. He is still waiting for the Twins to tear down their statue of Calvin Griffith.

Dustin Nosler is a writer at Dodgers Digest, co-host of the Dugout Blues podcast, and wears a number of hats for FanGraphs and The Hardball Times.

A former river guide, ranch hand, farm hand, oyster shucker and, most unlikely of all, editor-in-chief of a magazine, **John Paschal** has written sports and opinion for *The Dallas Morning News*, *The (Memphis) Commercial Appeal*, the *Corpus Christi Caller-Times* and other dead-tree publications. Online, he has contributed to The Hardball Times, NotGraphs, Baseball Prospectus, Deadspin and The Good Men Project.

Jonah Pemstein is a contributor to FanGraphs. He is a high school student in a suburb of Boston, Mass., and a Red Sox fan.

Alex Remington writes for The Hardball Times and manages Braves Journal, and is a product manager at *The Washington Post*.

Joe Rosales is a research analyst for Baseball Info Solutions, where he specializes in developing analytics using BIS' unique inventory of baseball data. He was a co-winner of the 2015 MIT Sloan Sports Analytics Conference Research Competition and is a proud native of New England.

Eno Sarris once asked Daniel Straily to show him all 17 change-up grips the pitcher had used in his career. Since then he's been taking pictures of pitchers' fingers for a living. He writes for FanGraphs, runs BeerGraphs and doesn't think deep dives ruin the fun of either baseball or beer.

Greg Simons has been writing about baseball in various formats since the last millennium. He has been part of The Hardball Times since 2010, serving as both an editor and writer. When he's not thinking about baseball, he's playing it, participating in 1860s-era vintage base ball (yep, it was two words back then) matches around the

Midwest. While he is an avid St. Louis Cardinals fan, he never has claimed to be one of "the best fans in baseball."

Alex Skillin is a writer who grew up in New England and now lives in Brooklyn. He writes regularly for The Hardball Times, Over the Monster and BP Boston, and his work has also appeared at SB Nation, Sports on Earth and The Classical. He looks forward to watching Xander Bogaerts and Mookie Betts in a Red Sox uniform for years to come.

Scott Spratt writes for FanGraphs and ESPN Insider, the latter as a research analyst for Baseball Info Solutions. He is a Sloan Sports Conference Research Paper Competition and FSWA award winner.

Jeff Sullivan inarguably continues to write about baseball, here and in other places. Mostly, those other places comprise FanGraphs and previous editions of this very book. He is still alive in Oregon, hopefully.

Paul Swydan is the managing editor of The Hardball Times, and has been writing about baseball for over a decade, somehow. He spends most of his time with his children, Xander and Jasmine.

Shane Tourtellotte is a refugee from the Northeast living in Asheville, N.C. He's published a few hundred thousand words of science fiction, but this didn't strike people as bizarre enough, so he has branched out into baseball. He has visited 16 major-league ballparks, only three of which have since been torn down, which is a pretty good percentage.

Steve Treder contributed a weekly column to The Hardball Times online from its founding in 2004 through 2011, and has been a co-author of many *Hardball Times Annual* and *Hardball Times Season Preview* books. His work has also been featured in *Nine*, *The National Pastime*, and other publications. He has frequently been a presenter at baseball forums such as the SABR National Convention, the Nine Spring Training Conference, and the Cooperstown Symposium.

In his day job, Steve is senior vice president at Western Management Group, a compensation consulting firm headquartered in Los Gatos, Calif. When Steve grows up, he hopes to play center field for the San Francisco Giants.

Owen Watson writes for FanGraphs and The Hardball Times. A native of the east coast, graduate of Hampshire College, and former Red Sox fan, he moved to the Bay Area in 2011. Always seeking the next great baseball heartbreak, he became a fan of the Oakland A's, who have done nothing but wonderfully disappoint him ever since. One day, perhaps, they'll provide the catharsis he so desperately seeks. One day.

Neil Weinberg is the site educator at FanGraphs, a contributor to The Hardball Times, the managing editor at Beyond The Box Score, and also writes enthusiastically about the Detroit Tigers at New English D. He has played nine fewer positions than Don Kelly at the major league level.

Miles Wray contributes to The Hardball Times from Seattle, but pretty much wanted the Astros to win the AL West. He has contributed sportswriting to McSweeney's Internet Tendency, Ploughshares Literary Journal, Vice, and a host of blogs.

Jeff Zimmerman would like to say to his children, "Yes, Cole and Ruby, your names are in the book again."